THE FIRE THIS TIME

Also by Ramsey Clark

Crime in America

THE FIRE THIS TIME

U.S. War Crimes in the Gulf

Ramsey Clark

THUNDER'S MOUTH PRESS

First trade paperback edition
First printing, 1994

Published by
Thunder's Mouth Press
632 Broadway, 7th Floor
New York, NY 10012

LIBRARY OF CONGRESS CATALOGING IN PUBLICATION DATA
Clark, Ramsey, 1927–
   The fire this time : U.S. war crimes in the Gulf / Ramsey Clark. — 1st ed.
      p.   cm.
   Includes index.
   ISBN 1-56025-071-2 :
   1. Persian Gulf War, 1991 – Destruction and pillage – Iraq.   2. Persian Gulf
War, 1991 – Atrocities.   3. Persian Gulf War, 1991 – United States.   I. Title.
DS79.736.C54   1992
956.704'3 – dc20   92-19724

Designed by Susan Hood
Set in Caledonia
Printed in the United States of America

Distributed by
Publishers Group West
4065 Hollis Street
Emeryville, CA 94608
(800) 788-3123

For the poor throughout history who have suffered violence, death, hunger, sickness, and indignity at the hands of powerful oppressors who would not respect their humanity, and especially for the Iraqi, Arab, and other victims of the fire this time — with a call for action to end the scourge of war, economic exploitation, and poverty.

Acknowledgments

In a very real sense, this book is the result of the efforts of tens of thousands of people—the women and men around the world who did everything they could to prevent, and then to try to stop, the U.S. war against Iraq. They showed there is hope for peace. The hundreds who worked with the Commission of Inquiry for the International War Crimes Tribunal to expose the truth—sometimes at great peril—also contributed.

Specifically, the Commission of Inquiry staff deserves credit for doing much of the work that laid the basis for this book: organizing hearings, taking testimony, and gathering material around the world. They are: Adeeb Abed, Paul Ahuja, Sahu Barron, Brian Becker, Richard Becker, John Catalinotto, Joyce Chediac, Kathy Durkin, Gavrielle Gemma, Teresa Gutierrez, Jelayne Miles, Monica Moorehead, Yuriko Okawara, Joan Sekler, Paul Sheehan, Karen Talbot, Jan van Heurck, Diane Wang, and Phil Wilayto. Sharon Murphy and Dierdre Sinnott did outstanding work on fundraising.

Special thanks go to Shreeram Krishnaswami, Bill Doares, and Carl Glenn, who provided valuable material for chapters 1, 4, and 6, and to Professor Francis Boyle for his extensive material.

I am particularly grateful to Ben Chaney for his skill at word processing and Shelley Ettinger for editorial assistance on the first draft.

The Research Committees included the efforts of Kathy Avakian, Max Becher, Wallace Cheatham, Magie Dominic, Pat Hochmeyer, Pandy Hopkins, Jane Moritz, and Barbara Nell-Perrin in New York City, and Gautaum Biswas, Steve Bush, Rachel Davis, Peter Harlan, Shiu Hung, Francis Kelly, Marie Kelly, Ruth Levine, and Paul

Acknowledgements

Greenburg in San Francisco. Paddy Colligan and Lawrence Schilling provided much-needed assistance with fact-checking. Materials available through the Data Center, a nonprofit research center in Oakland, were an invaluable part of this effort.

Thanks to those who through their support enabled the work of the Commission to continue: Dr. Moniem Fadali, M.D., Casey Kasem, Margot Kidder, Kris Kristofferson, Corliss and Beth Lamont, Dr. Chandra Muzaffar, and Dr. M. A. Samad-Matias.

I would also like to thank Robert Weisser for his tireless editing, and Thunder's Mouth Press, without whom this book would not have been published. Special thanks is also due Frances Goldin, my agent, whose strong anti-war committment helped publish it.

Finally, this book would not have been possible without the work of Sara Flounders, who from the book's inception devoted considerable time and much energy into seeing that it get published; Michelle LeBlanc, who spent many long hours compiling research, gathering information, and transcribing documents in addition to overseeing the New York research staff and files; and Tony Murphy, my assistant on this book, who worked tirelessly, many times all night, doing research, fact-checking, editing, rewrites, and general organization of the project. Their work showed their commitment to the goal of the Commission and this book: ending U.S. intervention and the tragic loss of human life.

Contents

Contents

Foreword

It has been more than a year since the first edition of *The Fire This Time* was printed, and there has been no relief for the Iraqi people or the poor throughout the Middle East. The scourge of war, economic exploitation, and poverty have been their daily fare. Economic sanctions continue to impoverish Iraq and take tens of thousands of lives. Military force is threatened and used against Iraq with impunity. U.S. military domination of the Persian Gulf has spread beyond the Straits of Hormuz to the Horn of Africa, the Red Sea, and the Indian Ocean. The media, which have continued to glorify U.S. military violence and demonize Saddam Hussein and certain other regional leaders, make scarce comment while the UN Charter and the U.S. Constitution are violated by the powerful.

SANCTIONS WASTE A WHOLE NATION

The sanctions placed on Iraq have afflicted an entire population with hunger, malnutrition, sickness, and death. The effect of these sanctions is unprecedented because the destruction that preceded them was unique. Alone, the sanctions would have been terribly damaging to the Iraqis. Following the systematic military destruction of the country's infrastructure, the effects have been catastrophic. Water systems, including storage, pumping, treatment, and distribution facilities; electric power facilities from generator to relay station to transmission towers; oil refineries, storage tanks, and gas stations; sewer systems and sewage disposal and treatment facilities; hospitals and health care units; food production, poultry, sheep, goats, crops, silos and storage buildings, processing plants, warehouses, even public markets; fertilizer plants and warehouses; pesticide production, farm equipment plants; rail and air transportation, highways, bridges, automotive parts plants and stores; TV, radio, telephone, and printing facilities were destroyed, damaged, or impaired. Food reserves, medicine and medical supplies were quickly exhausted. The sanctions effectively cut off importation of the most urgent human needs. The accumulation of these acts has had a devastating effect on the whole population.

This devastation was quantified in a special report in the September 24, 1992 *New England Journal of Medicine* about the effect of the Gulf War on infant and child mortality in Iraq. A group of international researchers, independent of the Iraqi government, conducted a nationwide survey of 16,076 children, 768 of whom died during the study. This group concluded that "the Gulf War and trade sanctions caused a threefold increase in mortality among Iraqi children under five years of age. We estimate that an excess of more than 46,900 children died between January and August 1991." Besides the child mortality, the death rate for the chronically ill and the elderly climbed precipitously because of bad water, malnutrition, and lack of medicine and medical supplies. Malnutrition has eroded the health of the general population, and common diseases have multiplied.

Through 1992, health conditions worsened. By December, Iraqi doctors "used to working in one of the region's best health care systems" reported, "We lack even the simplest things" — drugs, syringes, anesthetics, machine parts. "We're short of everything."

A press release from the UN on February 4, 1993 proudly described UN humanitarian relief for "identified vulnerable groups," including 84 UN convoys totaling more than 2,000 trucks which delivered 25,000 metric tons of food and nearly 7,000 metric tons of wheat to the Kurdish areas in northern Iraq. It stated that the basic food, fuel, drug, medicinal, and water and sanitation needs of these areas "are being met." Only a careful reader would realize that the vast majority of the Iraqis living in the central and southern areas were not included. On the back page the release reported, "In the central and southern governates water supply, sanitation, and basic health needs remain critical. Conditions are likely to continue to deteriorate . . . unless assistance is greatly increased."

Immediately after my return from Iraq in mid-February 1993, I wrote to the U.N. Secretary General and members of the Security Council:

Foreword

The following examples from cases reported to the Health Ministry demonstrate the devastating effect of the sanctions:

Disease	Year	No. of Cases	Year	No. of Cases	Percent Increase
Kwashiorkor	1990	485	1992	13,744	2840
Marasmus	1990	5,193	1992	111,477	2150
Cholera	1989–1990	0	1991–1992	2,100	∞
Measles/German measles	1989	6,229	1992	21,823	350
Typhoid fever	1989	1,812	1992	19,276	1060
Pneumonia	1989	6,612	1992	17,377	260
Amoebic dysentery	1989	19,615	1992	61,939	320
Viral hepatitis	1989	1,816	1992	13,776	760
Brucellosis	1989	2,816	1992	14,546	520
Giardiasis	1989	73,416	1992	596,356	810
Whooping cough	1989	368	1992	1,601	440
Poliomyelitis	1989	10	1992	120	1200

Other protein-, vitamin-, and calorie-related malnutrition cases increased eleven times and involved great numbers of people.

All of the child population is affected. The percentage of births under 2.5 kilograms (5.5 pounds) body weight in 1990 was 4.5. In 1992 it was nearly four times higher, at 17.6 percent. It is climbing and is the basis for Western medical assessments that Iraq will have millions of "stunted" children.

Children over five and adults have suffered enormously. The most vulnerable—those with physical disabilities, serious chronic illnesses, and the elderly—have died at greatly increased rates. These deaths comprise much of the approximately threefold increase in the overall death rate.

Medical laboratory examinations declined by 60 percent from 17,928,604 in 1989 to 7,079,4209 in 1992. Major surgery declined 63 percent from 181,506 in 1989 to 65,733 in 1992.

The statistics do not convey the human suffering involved. Anyone who has visited hospitals in Iraq in 1991, 1992, and 1993, as I have, could never tolerate these sanctions. They are the cruelest form of death for their victims, families, and all who understand. The sanctions are the actual, moral, and legal equivalent of taking hostage the lives and health of infants, the sick, and the elderly for the payment of money or other acts of government. They violate humanitarian law because they are known to deprive a population of essential food and medical care.

If you go to Iraq and visit the hospitals, find the facts, and report them to your government, it will immediately direct you to vote to end the sanctions. Nations and individuals are responsible for the consequences of their acts. Can we expect a nation that does not respect the lives and health of the people of other nations to protect the lives and health of its own people?

Your action is essential now. Hundreds of people are dying every day as a direct result of this continuing violation of humanitarian law and crime against humanity.

I urge you to call on the Security Council to immediately revoke the sanctions and to expedite emergency delivery of food, medicine, equipment, and parts purchased by Iraq and needed to protect the life and health of its people.

On February 16, 1993, I wrote to Secretary of State Warren Christopher, among others in the Clinton administration, providing the information sent to the UN. I urged the immediate end of the sanctions; release of frozen Iraqi funds in the United States for emergency purchase of food, medicine, and equipment to purify and deliver water; abandonment of the no-fly zones policy; termination of U.S. military overflights; and early meetings between U.S. and Iraqi officials. As to the sanctions, I observed:

> The sanctions are the product of Bush administration coercion of the Security Council. At this time, the Bush administration bears the responsibility. Failure to address this problem promptly will burden the Clinton administration with the responsibility for future deaths. I believe unilateral action by the United States will have the greatest benefit in terms of immediate relief, international relations, good will among peoples, particularly Arabs and Americans, and respect for the United States. How can a nation that does not respect the lives and health of other people be expected to act to protect the health of its own people?

Acting Secretary of State Clifton R. Wharton, Jr. responded on February 22, 1993:

> This administration shares your concern about the humanitarian situation in Iraq. As I am sure you are aware, the international community has provided the Baghdad government the tools to manage the problem. The obstacle is Baghdad's persistent refusal either to comply fully with UN resolutions, which would end sanctions, or to implement various UN Security Council proposals which would allow Iraq to export oil and purchase humanitarian supplies under UN monitoring.
>
> We feel compassion and concern for the Iraqi people, but it would be a serious mistake to allow the Baghdad government to exploit suffering which is the result of its own policies.

As detailed in Chapter 4, the only way Iraq could sell oil to obtain cash was by agreeing to pay massive reparations from that income. This is holding the lives of Iraqi children hostage for money. To weigh the lives of tens of thousands of Iraqis as less valuable than some exploitation the "Baghdad government" might make from easing sanctions to provide food, medicine, and equipment essential to life as required by international humanitarian law is to hold Iraqi life very cheap.

Of course, the purpose of the U.S. conduct is to exploit the political advantages of its cruel policy toward Iraq, to warn and coerce others, to further debilitate Iraq, and to justify the enormous U.S. military presence that dominates the region. The Clinton administration now bears responsibility for continuing the policies of its predecessor that have taken tens of thousands of lives.

For the month of August 1993, the Iraqi Ministry of Health reported that among children under five there were 1,960 deaths from diarrhea compared to 159 in August 1989, 684 from pneumonia compared to 53, and 1,915 from malnutrition compared to 90. Total deaths of children under five from these three causes increased from 302 in August 1989 to 4,559 in August 1993, a fifteenfold increase.

Also during August 1993, among persons over 50 there were 227 deaths from hypertension compared to 81 in August 1989, 148 diabetes deaths compared to 81, and 681 deaths from malignant neoplasm compared to 316. Total deaths of persons over 50 from these three causes increased from 478 in August 1989 to 1,056 in August 1993, or a greater than twofold increase.

The International Action Center has continued its efforts to persuade the UN, the United States, and anyone who will listen of the criminality of the continuing sanctions. In addition to information it has generated, it has sent copies of official and private reports which show the tragic conditions in Iraq caused by the sanctions.

In its April 1993 report entitled *Children, War and Sanctions,* UNICEF stated:

> Close to 100,000 additional children (in excess of the expected number of deaths) have died since the beginning of the Gulf War. The postwar death rate was estimated at triple the prewar rate. Many of these child deaths were due to diarrheal disease caused by contaminated water supplies. There has been a resurgence of vaccine-preventable diseases including polio, diphtheria, and measles. Health services are barely functioning due to shortages of supplies and equipment. Medicines including insulin, antibiotics, and

anesthetics are in short supply. In fact, shortages are worse in 1993 than during the previous two years.

During the past year, conditions in all sectors were judged to have deteriorated.

Sanctions, unless applied in a manner which safeguards the civilian population, may threaten the more vulnerable members of society — especially children and women.

Indeed, it may be that one fundamental contradiction remains: that politically motivated sanctions (which are by definition imposed to create hardship) cannot be implemented in a manner which spares the vulnerable.

The UNICEF report quoted *Hunger and Poverty in Iraq*, an October 1991 paper by J. Dreze and H. Gazdar of the London School of Economics:

> Dreze and Gazdar, of the London School of Economics and the International Study Team, end their economic assessment with what must also be the inevitable conclusion of this chapter, by stating that "war and prolonged sanctions have now caused such comprehensive damage to the Iraqi economy that it is now impossible to maintain these sanctions in their present form without perpetuating, and perhaps even accentuating, the state of acute poverty in which a large part of the population is now plunged."

The UN report also cited an unpublished 1992 manuscript by Beth Osborne Daponte:

> . . . life expectancy at birth had been reduced from 68 years (prewar) to 47 years by late 1991. She estimated that 30 times as many civilians died after the war (but due to war-related health effects) than during the military conflict itself. The largest contributor to excess deaths was from poor health conditions after the war, estimated at 111,000 excess deaths (60,000 of these children younger than 5 years of age).

In the section of its report on Maternal Health and Prenatal Care, UNICEF drew the following conclusion:

> It is likely that the current epidemic of micronutrient-deficient mothers, low-birth-weight babies, and malnourished infants will retard the mental and physical development of a great number of Iraqi children. With the current poor state of antenatal and delivery ser-

vices in Iraq, it is future generations of Iraqi children who are now being denied their fair start in life.

On the critical needs for potable water and sewage removal, UNICEF found the following:

> The Government of Iraq has had great difficulty importing spare parts for its water purification and supply system except through United Nations agencies. UNICEF being the lead UN agency concerned with water and sanitation, like other agencies with limited budgets, can only provide a small fraction of what is needed.
>
> Sanctions are inhibiting the importation of spare parts, chemicals, reagents, and the means of transportation required to provide water and sanitation services to the civilian population of Iraq. Huge quantities of resources are required if Iraq is to make any real progress toward reestablishing its prewar capacity for managing water and sewage.

The effect of malnutrition from insufficient food affects the whole Iraqi population. As UNICEF reported:

> The presence of postwar maternal malnutrition has manifested itself in an elevated incidence of low-birth-weight babies (less than 2.5 kilograms). One of the strongest predictors of infant survival, the incidence of low-birth-weight babies has climbed from approximately 4 percent in August 1990 to nearly 17 percent of all newborns in 1992.
>
> What has become increasingly clear is that no significant movement toward food security can be achieved so long as the embargo remains in place. All vital contributors to food availability — agricultural production, importation of foodstuffs, economic stability, and income generation, are dependent on Iraq's ability to purchase and import those items vital to the survival of the civilian population.

Medicine and medical supplies, the availability of which humanitarian law mandates, are denied to Iraq by UN sanctions. Again from the UNICEF report:

> Faced with postwar epidemics of disease and malnutrition, Iraq's health facilities were unable to respond to the growing burden of illness due to shortages of basic medicines, equipment, and laboratory diagnostic materials. By 1993, although structural rehabilitation of most damaged facilities has been completed, hospitals and health

Foreword

centers still barely function due to continuing and, in many cases, worsening shortages of drugs and other medical supplies.

Despite the exemption for "supplies intended strictly for medical purposes" having been made explicit in United Nations Resolution 661, adequate mechanisms were not set up to protect these exemptions. Even before the war had started, supplies of some drugs were becoming depleted, compromising Iraq's capacity to care for its children. The sanctions produced reductions in medicines, vaccines, syringes, anesthetics, and materials used for surgery, radiology, laboratory, and diagnostic tests. In February 1991, medical stocks were at one-sixth of normal levels, with many essential medicines having been completely exhausted.

A general shortage of anesthetic has led to the deferment of all non-emergency surgery. Cesarean sections have been carried out using only local anesthetic. The setting of bones and, in some cases, leg amputations have been performed without anesthesia.

The UNICEF report concludes with this chilling summary:

In early 1993, the shortage of medicines and medical supplies appears to be even greater than during previous postwar years. With little access to funds, the hard currency necessary for drug importation has not been available, the result being shortfalls in every sector of health care.

That the United Nations sanctions are the cause of tens of thousands of deaths, illnesses, and disabilities is beyond doubt. Medicine for Peace, a voluntary organization dedicated to providing medical care to children who are victims of war, reported the following in its April 1993 *Health Status in Iraq:*

The mechanism by which Resolution 661 has caused marked shortages in medicine, hospital supplies, and food is described in the "Chronology of UN Resolutions on Iraq" which follows this report. It is quite clear that the functional embargo of medicine and biologicals (vaccines), hospital and laboratory supplies, and most critically, spare parts for medical equipment has resulted in a complete collapse of the health delivery system. Smaller hospitals and clinics have closed and even the best hospitals in Baghdad have restricted availability of many patient beds and are unable to provide adequate medical care. Specialized hospitals, such as ophthalmological and cardiac hospitals, which were closed during the Gulf War, have not reopened. By July 1993, the UN Food and Agriculture Organization found that Iraq risked "massive starvation."

The International Action Center has directed all its efforts at getting the Security Council to stop this continuing crime against humanity by repealing the sanctions. On September 20, 1993, the Security Council voted to maintain the sanctions though the People's Republic of China, Brazil, Morocco, and Pakistan voiced objections. The International Atomic Energy Agency [IAEA] expressed its confidence "that the major elements of Iraq's nuclear weapons program are understood and have been dismantled." The IAEA had earlier placed seals on buildings allegedly housing missile-testing equipment at two disputed silos until TV monitors could be installed.

What conceivable threat can a rational mind find from a crippled and bleeding Iraq that couldn't defend itself against U.S. technology even when fully armed? Did Iraq dare use gas and chemical weapons it clearly possessed when it was under attack by FAEs, superbombs, antipersonnel fragmentation bombs, and napalm, and when its civilians and civilian facilities were the direct object of attack?

The similar and continued use of sanctions against Vietnam have impoverished the people of that nation below their condition in 1954 at the time of Dien Bien Phu. This does not suggest humanitarian concern by the U.S. government for the well being of other people. And sanctions are currently applied against Cuba, North Korea, Libya, and other countries, showing that the United States intends to use such injurious tactics as instruments of foreign policy.

As a result of the sanctions, Iraq has become statistically the poorest country in the world, its per capita income falling below Mozambique's $70 per year, the lowest in Africa, according to an InterPress Service feature story in February 1993. Using UNICEF analyses, John Roberts, the author of the story, estimated the excess death of 80,000–100,000 Iraqi children under age five in 1993.

IRAQ REMAINS FAIR GAME FOR MILITARY ATTACK

Continued violent assaults on Iraq have demeaned life and law while killing scores of people. The United States, Turkey, and Iran have repeatedly attacked Iraq without significant international protest, and in the case of U.S. air strikes, to intense media coverage and public approval. Turkey and Iran have sent ground forces deep into areas of northern Iraq populated by Kurds, attacking villages, camps, refugees, and military units. Turkey particularly has mounted major military operations on Iraqi soil to pursue and assault Kurdish people. Neither the United States nor world opinion seems concerned. Compare this to the rabid negative reaction to Iraq's military actions against the Kurds, who had been encouraged by the United States to rise up against the Iraqi government in 1991, and how that action was used to justify U.S. military intervention in northern Iraq.

U.S. combat planes have continued their overflights of Iraq since the end of the conflict in February 1991. For the Iraqi people, the warplanes pose a constant threat of violence; for the children, they are a constant reminder of the terror of the fire last time. Various reasons are given by the United States for continuing these flights, the favorite being the search for nuclear weapons development, though no one believes there is a nuclear threat from Iraq or that this would be the best way to prevent one. Both the U.S. Department of State and the UN Atomic Energy Agency have denied the existence of an Iraqi atomic threat.

Another reason given for this intervention is the protection of the Kurds in the north and the Shiites in the south. Baghdad has made no aggressive moves against the Kurds since 1991. In contrast, that the Turks have destroyed whole Kurdish villages, encamped large military units on Iraqi territory, and operated openly and at will against the Kurdish people gets barely a mention by the press. And the American and Kuwaiti concern over possible Iranian infiltration among the Shiites in the south is much greater than the concern about Iraqi violence against its own people. Yet it is the Iraqis who are subjected to arbitrary and random attack.

It was universally recognized after the devastation of Iraq that it would take years to rebuild the country. It was understood by the U.S. government, its principal allies, and all careful observers that the sanctions imposed on Iraq would effectively prevent any significant reconstruction. No serious observer believes that even before 1990 was Iraq within years of developing an atomic weapon or would dare to use one except as an act of utter madness. Typical of Western analysis was a piece by Ed Blanche, AP's Middle East news editor, who observed that Iraq "backed off using chemical weapons in the war, apparently for fear the allies might counter in kind or even respond with tactical nuclear weapons . . . ." He concluded that Iraq would not "[risk] massive retaliation for an attack that, at best, would be little more than a defiant gesture." Before President Bush imposed an extensive no-fly zone in southern Iraq on August 27, 1992, which with the northern no-fly zone covered more than half the country, no one believed Iraq posed any military threat to its own people or anyone else. The United States had over 200 warplanes in the area and could easily sweep the skies of all Iraqi aircraft and attack ground forces and installations. According to *Jane's Defense Weekly*, the United States had hundreds more warplanes on call within hours of the Gulf.

The Bush administration's decision to begin periodic aerial assaults against Iraq had the dual purposes of harassing the Iraqi people and reminding American voters of the President's vigilance during the hotly contested 1992 campaign. The upcoming election ruled out major military action against Iraq as too dangerous politically, since it could have been characterized as a play for votes.

Bush was defeated anyway. Customarily after an election defeat, an administration suspends foreign and domestic initiatives, starts looking for jobs, and prepares for the transition. Soon after losing the election, the Bush administration began a series of threats against Iraq that continued right up until President Clinton's inauguration on January 20, 1993.

On December 27, a U.S. F-16 shot down an Iraqi MIG-25, claiming it had entered the no-fly zone. On December 28, the aircraft carrier USS *Kitty Hawk* was diverted from Somalia to the Gulf. The United States then claimed Iraq deployed surface-to-air missiles in the no-fly zone, endangering U.S. surveillance.

On January 7, 1993 the International Action Center, created in early 1992 as one of the major recommendations of the War Crimes Tribunal, sent an urgent appeal to the Secretary General and Security Council of the UN. It followed extensive earlier communications, including the circulation of UN and related reports on the effects on the population of the assault on Iraq and copies of *The Fire This Time*. It said:

> The Security Council must act immediately to instruct the United States that it cannot apply armed force against Iraq as it has threatened to do by Friday afternoon, January 8, 1993. Such an attack would be an act of aggression and breach of the peace. The Security Council cannot permit the United States to usurp the function delegated to the Security Council by Article 46 of the Charter of the United Nations: "Plans for the application of armed force shall be made by the Security Council with the assistance of the Military Staff Committee."
>
> The U.S. threat is an act of vanity by a defeated U.S. President who wants to end his one term in office as he began it: invading Panama and killing thousands with military violence. The specter of the former colonial and present nuclear powers, the United Kingdom, France, and Russia, supporting this threatened unilateral superpower violence should inform the Security Council and Members

of the General Assembly that the most dangerous military powers on earth support the use of violence for their own ends.

Verbal threats by the United States escalated until January 13, 1993, when more than 100 aircraft struck southern Iraq. Radar and missile installations were supposedly their targets. Iraq reported only 19 casualties, but more were probably killed, as Baghdad has consistently underreported casualties to maintain morale, even at the height of the massive bombing attacks. As during the Gulf War, the media did not report what happened where the bombs fell. Instead, correspondents interviewed "jubilant pilots" who described how they "honed in with deadly accuracy" delivering bombs with "2,000 pounds of American anger." No U.S. planes were hit, no U.S. pilots were wounded, and there is no evidence that U.S. aircraft have been fired upon since the beginning of March 1991.

On January 17, 1993, the second anniversary of the most devastating aerial assault on a nation and 72 hours before leaving office, President Bush ordered a major attack across Iraq. Baghdad was hit with as many as 50 cruise missiles. American officials said that the target for the missiles was a $6 billion military-industrial complex known as Djihad Park. White House Press Secretary Marlin Fitzwater said the assault was to "help in the process of eliminating nuclear weapons." However, others pointed out that the park was not bombed during the war, presumably because it was not considered a worthwhile target. And both U.S. and foreign diplomats conceded that the general purpose machine tool factory in the complex had been "dormant" for years. The IAEA, which was responsible for policing Iraqi compliance, said the building "was absolutely out of action" before the raid. Although the Kuwaiti press claimed there were underground bunkers and storerooms at the site, no official source cited that claim as the basis for launching $50 million in deadly missiles.

On that same date, U.S. and British warplanes harassed Iraqi aircraft, shooting down at least one in the north. On January 18, to dramatize the utter defenselessness of Iraq, U.S. planes attacked in broad daylight. Iraq reported 21 dead from those attacks. On January 19, on the eve of President Clinton's inauguration, President Bush ordered more air strikes against Iraq. On that date, U.S. forces in the Gulf had in acknowledged service 75 planes from the *Kitty Hawk*, 20 F-16s, 20 F-15s, 20 F-15Cs, 20 F-4Gs, 12 F-1 Stealths, 12 A-10s, 6 EF-111s, and assorted reconnaissance and support aircraft.

President Bush tried one more time to kill Saddam Hussein, as he had with superbombs in February 1991. The United States had a wide network of well-placed informers and spies operating in Iraq, as it had during the assault in 1991. We are now told the Amariyah bomb shelter was identified by a high Iraqi official in Baghdad who apparently thought it would be a good thing to destroy the families of many Iraqi leaders.

One of the cruise missiles launched on January 17 hit the Al-Rashid Hotel at the very hour Saddam Hussein had been scheduled to address an international meeting of Muslim leadership there. The United States first denied the hotel was hit. Then Fitzwater speculated "an Iraqi antiaircraft shell might have hit the hotel." Later it was argued by Pentagon spokesman Pete Williams, who proved himself completely untrustworthy during the 1990–1991 crisis, "that if it turns out that it was a U.S. cruise missile . . . it was knocked off course" by Iraqi antiaircraft fire.

Lacking the faith the U.S. media has in official assurances about such matters, the Iraqis had transferred Hussein's meeting with the international visitors to another location earlier in the day.

Three weeks later I saw the crater and damage to the Al-Rashid. The hotel had escaped damage during the six weeks of nearly daily bombing in 1991. This missile hit the most vulnerable spot of the hotel, shattering the lobby, nearly entering the bomb shelter, ripping up one side of the tower to the top floor, and damaging the tower's foundation and support.

As I wrote to Secretary of State Christopher on February 16, 1993:

> I do not know what the Pentagon will tell you, but in my judgment the missile that hit the Al-Rashid was no accident. It struck within several feet of the exterior wall of the main lobby and between two vents adjacent to the building, one for the bomb shelter and one for the first basement. The probability of that missile striking there and detonating by guidance error, or deflection from antiaircraft fire, is not one in a million.

Of course, an investigation could be conducted to determine whether that cruise missile was targeted at the Al-Rashid. But it is not clear that anyone with authority would care if it were.

President Bush's deadly attacks on Iraq brought a storm of protest from Arab nations. Demonstrations resulted across the Muslim world. China expressed its deep regret over the raids. King Hussein of Jordan voiced "deep anger and sorrow." Even Iran, Iraq's mortal enemy, condemned the United States for staining "their hands with the blood of the Iraqi people."

The United Kingdom and other major U.S. allies declared that

Saddam Hussein had gotten what he deserved. No one seemed to care much about the illegality of the U.S. action, though French Foreign Minister Roland Dumas stated the obvious when he observed the attacks went beyond anything authorized by UN resolution.

As he left the presidency on January 20, 1993, Bush urged governments around the world to support efforts to oust Saddam Hussein. In one of his last acts he released a five-page report to Congress detailing his support for Iraqi dissidents trying to topple Iraq's government, stating his continued support for the Iraqi National Congress to develop alternatives to "the Saddam regime" and encouraging "other governments to do the same." The same day Brent Scowcroft, Bush's National Security Adviser, told the *Washington Post* that the Bush administration had backed "coup attempts" against Saddam Hussein and had come "pretty close."

Two days into the Clinton administration, the Pentagon reported a U.S. F-16 fired two missiles at an Iraqi air defense site near Mosul, the second such incident in two days. The claim, denied by Iraq, was that the U.S. plane was being tracked by Iraqi SAM radar. In response, Iraq affirmed its public commitment to a ceasefire.

A number of such incidents occurred during the first six months of the Clinton administration, with lethal consequences for Iraqis. At first, it was difficult to tell if the U.S. military was initiating the incidents to implicate the new administration. Its use of cluster bombs against what it called antiaircraft sites, as occurred on April 9, were twice a violation of international law — first for the alleged attack, and second for the use of a prohibited weapon. After at least one U.S. attack, the Pentagon acknowledged that there had been no "locking on" and the attack was a mistake. Another attack was 11 miles outside the no-fly zone. We do not know whether Iraqi radar ever "locked on" U.S. military aircraft in its airspace, or for what purpose if it did. We do not know whether Iraqis ever fired at U.S. aircraft after the beginning of March 1991. What we know without doubt is that no U.S. plane has ever been hit or damaged and no U.S. military personnel on land, sea, or air have been killed or wounded by Iraqis since the war. However, many Iraqis have died violent deaths by U.S. "defensive retaliation."

In May 1993 Kuwait announced that Iraq had attempted to assassinate Bush during his visit there. The fact that nothing disturbed Bush and his party, that U.S. security had no word of such a plan, and that the evidence Kuwait later produced was incredible did not deter extensive media reports, FBI and other leaks, and finally grave threats by U.S. leaders. Finally on June 26, the United States carried out a savage missile attack on Iraq as punishment for the alleged assassination attempt. It claimed to be exercising the right of self defense preserved by Article 51 of the UN Charter. Twenty-three Tomahawk cruise missiles were launched toward Baghdad. Among the civilian fatalities in the attack were internationally known painter Layla al-Altar, director-general of Iraq's National Center for Arts, and her husband. Her death is a powerful symbol of America's attempt to destroy Iraq's culture and its indifference to the lives of Arabs.

The Russian parliament described the action as a return to the "cult of force in international relations." Mikhail Gorbachev, who had widened relations between the Soviet Union and the United States, condemned the United States for disregarding the UN, "adopting a style and methods reminiscent of the Cold War" and playing the role of investigator, prosecutor, judge, and executioner. Senator Mark Hatfield of Oregon objected that "might does not make right . . . .We are being poisoned by the glorification of violence." The European Parliament condemned the United States, citing its failure to submit the issue to the Security Council and rejecting the plea of self defense as justification for an attack on civilians.

For those who hoped the election defeat of George Bush would end the killing of defenseless Iraqis, the missile attack was a bitter lesson. On his way to church on the Sunday after the attack, President Clinton said, "We sent a message we needed to send." Under the headline "The Missiles' Message," the *New York Times* wrote:

> White House officials said today that their only regret about the missile attack on the Iraqi intelligence headquarters was that there was no CNN crew there to broadcast the event live so it could be watched in the Sudan, Iran, and other countries suspected of involvement in the terrorism.

THE LESSONS REMAIN UNLEARNED

The media has continued to glorify the assault on Iraq, both the means and the ends. A few sources, like *Crusade: The Untold Story of the Persian Gulf War* by Rick Atkinson of the *Washington Post*, published in October 1993, have been sharply critical of General Schwarzkopf's "imperial trappings" and vanities. But even Atkinson concludes that the "crusade" was a "limited triumph" that successfully "neutered a despot" and importantly "reaffirmed war as a means of achieving national objectives." While the book confirms the reports in *The Fire This Time* that the U.S. Navy sank a large

Iraqi oil tanker spilling crude oil into the Persian Gulf, that the
United States dropped both napalm and FAEs directly on Iraqi
troops, and that there was extensive "strategic" bombing of Baghdad
and Iraq, it accepts the Pentagon history of the conflict as Atkinson
accepted Pentagon reports during the crisis. According to Atkinson,
except for Schwarzkopf's fits of violence, his volcanic fury, his comment "I want every Iraqi soldier bleeding from every orifice," and
his motorcade, which was longer than the King of Saudi Arabia's,
the war was fine. Indeed, he assures us that Iraqi casualties were
minimal and there was "no significant error of strategy or tactics."

Overwhelmingly, the media praised the war, General Schwarzkopf, President Bush, the allies, and all who approved. There has
been little mention and no discussion of Iraqi casualties. A continuing Pentagon effort to reduce the numbers of Iraqi dead has been
generally accepted without comment. In his own book, Schwarzkopf completely ignored the slaughter of Iraqi troops and the crippling of the entire country without any comment or even a question
about how many humans were killed and why.

The Schwarzkopf book, which reportedly sold a million copies,
was spread across the country with a huge advertising campaign. In
its wake were scores of books by participants in the Gulf crisis, politicians, generals, reporters, historians, and others. Nearly all of these
were completely and uncritically supportive of the war and its
conduct.

The Fire This Time was virtually the only book to condemn U.S.
conduct and to call its acts war crimes. While most of the 15,000
copies of the first printing were sold, there were few reviews in major
publications. No reviews that were printed provided a serious analysis of the book. A year after publication I still meet old friends and
acquaintances who are unaware the book exists. Outside the United
States, reports, reviews, excerpts, and foreign language editions
have been extensive and favorable.

A common criticism, emotional in several reviews, is the perceived
failure of *The Fire This Time* to deal with war crimes by Saddam
Hussein. Why it is necessary to do so in a book dealing with U.S. war
crimes is not clear, though the criminal acts alleged against Iraq —
including its invasion of Kuwait, the false incubator infant death
story, and the Scud missile attacks on Israel — were squarely addressed. Of the hundreds of reviews of scores of books praising the
war and condemning Iraq, there has been no suggestion that the
authors may have erred in failing to suggest the possibility that the
U.S. military action was unnecessary, excessive, or mainly for geopolitical purposes.

The demonization of Saddam Hussein has continued unabated. The Pentagon partially resurrected the incubator infant death claims in 1993 and few bothered to observe that it never happened. In a typical propaganda piece, the *New York Times Magazine* ran a cover story titled "Iraq Accused" by Judith Miller about alleged atrocities against the Kurds. It had no fewer than eight photographs, including the full-page cover picture of Kurdish graves being exhumed. The story had been told, retold, and mistold many times since the Iran–Iraq War, but it was still useful to inflame hatred for the Iraqis, if not to protect the Kurds.

Surprisingly, the Gulf War did not become an issue in the presidential campaign. While the media seemed fascinated by the possibility of an October surprise — either military action or the overthrow of Hussein — nothing happened. It is possible that private polls informed the Bush campaign that glorifying the Gulf War would not win votes and the Clinton campaign that criticizing the Gulf War would not help either. Whatever the reasons, the war which had raised President Bush's popularity to unprecedented heights in the polls did not carry him to victory in the election.

However, it seems clear that a change in the Iraqi government would earn approval from the great majority of American voters. This political reality creates a continuing pressure for U.S. sanctions, air strikes, threats, and encouragement of attempts to overthrow Hussein's government.

The 1993 agreement between Israel and the PLO, settling old disputes and providing some Palestinian autonomy for an area around Jericho and the Gaza Strip, has been seen by many to be a result of the Gulf War, which proved so disastrous for the Palestinians and most other poor people in the region. While all people of good will hope for real peace in the Middle East, the question remains as stated in Chapter 11, "Is peace possible when parties are coerced to accept conditions that deny justice, when they are forced to submit to the conditions of power?"

General Schwarzkopf expressed a "healthy dose of skepticism" about the peace agreement. He observed that Yasser Arafat "ain't the sort of guy you'd want to buy a used car from," and said the defeat of Iraq was a big reason for the pact, adding that since then "Saddam has become irrelevant in Arab and Palestinian politics. He lost face, he lost the Mother of all Battles and proved he was a liar."

The UN Charter and U.S. Constitution have been shown as little respect since the war as they were during it. UN resolutions and U.S. laws are consistently violated by U.S. attacks on Iraq and by sanctions which deliberately kill Iraq's people. Few vote against these violations, much less protest them. It remains a world in which the powerful do as they will and the weak suffer as they must.

The U.S. military presence in the Persian Gulf region continues to grow, giving the United States complete control over the vast oil resources there for the foreseeable future. U.S. arms sales in the region are greater than ever. The U.S. military budget remains near President Bush's request, and U.S. military spending now exceeds the combined expenditures of its ten closest competitors, nearly all allies. The number of independently targeted nuclear warheads on each missile on an American Trident submarine has been reduced to eight in deference to nonproliferation, but those instruments of destruction can still deliver 192 warheads in a single launch.

Kuwait and Saudi Arabia remain major human rights violators. Neither nation has taken any significant step toward democratization, the rule of law, or social justice. The war crimes of Kuwait are unaddressed. Those of Saudi Arabia are slowly coming to light.

Efforts to create a permanent International Court of Criminal Justice with war crimes jurisdiction have made considerable progress. An international campaign is underway. The UN has created a panel to consider war crimes allegations in the conflict in Bosnia-Herzegovina with some suggestion that a permanent tribunal with general jurisdiction is desirable.

U.S. leadership has called for but not pressed war crimes trials of Iraq. There is an obvious concern that the scope of inquiry might be broadened to include U.S. conduct and the sanctions. Compilation of alleged war crimes by Iraq including a claim of 1,082 deaths, torture, and other offenses during the occupation of Kuwait were sent by the United States to the UN in March 1993. After Secretary of State Christopher spoke on the subject to the Iraqi National Congress in late April, I wrote the following to the Secretary General:

> The United States has announced that it will request the Security Council to create a commission to investigate war crimes committed by Iraq during the Gulf crisis.
>
> The creation of an International Court of Criminal Justice to hear and decide all charges of crimes against peace, war crimes, crimes against humanity, and other international crimes is essential to peace and to justice on which peace rests. Fundamental among the principles of such a court must be the equality of all governments, institutions, and individuals before the law. No nation and no person, rich or poor, powerful or weak, loved or feared, is above the law. And none may be discriminated for or against in the equal application of the law to her case. Nothing is more corrupting of law

than "victor's justice." It is merely the continuation of war by other means, the abuse of judicial power.

The failure of the United States to refer to crimes committed by its forces against Iraq, or by Kuwait in the early spring and summer of 1991 against Iraqis, Palestinians, Jordanians, Bedouins, Somalis, Filipinos, and many others does not negate or justify crimes Iraq may have committed, but it reveals a political motive to corrupt international law for impermissible geopolitical purposes. By any measure U.S. war crimes exceed Hammurabi's reputed measure of an eye for an eye by a thousandfold.

I. *Alleged War Crimes Against Citizens of the United States.* The United States alleges that each of the 21 U.S. military persons captured in Iraq were physically or psychologically abused. All were repatriated between March 3–9, 1991. The United States concedes its POWs were generally provided adequate medical attention and hospital care including prompt first aid and adequate medicines. Food, water, and shelter which sustained the lives of the POWs was better than that available to much of Iraq's military and civilian population and did not cause any deaths in contrast to the thousands of Iraqis who died from polluted water, malnutrition, lack of medicine, and bombed dwellings.

Of the 4,900 U.S. "hostages" the United States alleges Iraq took, nearly all were released before the bombing of Iraq began. If 106 U.S. citizens were used by Iraq as human shields, it was in contrast to scores of U.S. and other foreign citizens who chose to place themselves on the Kuwait border in peace camps as barriers between contending armed forces and who were forcibly removed by Iraq and sent to Jordan. The Security Council will want to know whether the sites allegedly shielded by hostages were among the thousands of civilian facilities destroyed by U.S. bombing.

The United States does not claim any loss of U.S. life as a result of crimes against its citizens by Iraq. It states it has found no evidence of war violation against U.S. personnel by Iraq during its 100-hour ground campaign.

II. *Alleged War Crimes by Iraq Against Persons in Kuwait.* The United States claims 1,082 persons in Kuwait lost their lives as a result of Iraqi torture or executions between August 2, 1990 and March 3, 1991. It heads its list with the claim that 120 premature babies died when they were removed from incubators. This claim, used sensationally to create hatred toward Iraq during the crisis, has been overwhelmingly rejected by independent investigations and Western human rights organizations including Amnesty International, which was misled to defend the original reports. Certainly all these claims should be carefully reviewed by investigators gathering evidence for a UN tribunal.

III. *Alleged War Crimes by Kuwait.* Human rights violations by Kuwait beginning in early March 1991 include allegations of as many as 200 summary executions, torture, deportations, the arbitrary cancellation of residence rights and work permits for hundreds of thousands, rape, property confiscation, and other crimes.

New York Newsday reported on March 29, 1991 that according to Western diplomats, "members of Kuwait's ruling family were involved in the killings of Palestinians and other people suspected of collaborating with the Iraqi occupation." Torture was widely reported by human rights groups, fact-finding missions, and reporters. Torture methods included beatings with canes, rods, electrical cables, and rifle butts, electric shock treatment, and having cigarettes extinguished on parts of the body. Such atrocities, as well as the "trials" of suspected collaborators, violated among other laws the Fourth Geneva Convention and its Protocol I.

IV. *Alleged War Crimes by the United States Against Iraq.* The U.S. war crimes were adjudicated by a nongovernmental tribunal of 22 persons from 18 nations following hearings in 20 countries and more than 30 cities in the United States. You have been fully informed of these proceedings and provided two volumes detailing evidence supporting the convictions of all the accused on 19 separate charges including a copy of *The Fire This Time: U.S. War Crimes in the Gulf.* On March 12, 1992 the Security Council was advised: "The war crimes of which U.S. officials have been convicted have resulted in the deaths of at least 250,000 human beings to date and the crippling of Iraq's civilian society. The United States claims 148 U.S. combat deaths, many from its own weapons. There was no war, only a simple, merciless slaughter of tens of thousands by 110,000 aerial sorties dropping 88,000 tons of explosives, 93 percent free falling on a defenseless country."

As the underlying reports show, scores of premature infants died in incubators and during efforts to save them after U.S.

bombing destroyed virtually all electric power transmission in Iraq during the first hours of U.S. bombing on January 17, 1991. Many thousands of Iraqi soldiers were slaughtered by criminal acts of the United States during its "100-hour ground campaign," including by burial while alive when U.S. tanks bulldozed sand over trenches and bunkers, by fuel air explosives, antipersonnel bombs, and from thousands of depleted uranium-tipped rockets and missiles and conventional gunfire against defenseless Iraqi troops often while fleeing and attempting to surrender. Tens of thousands of Iraqis died as a direct result and foreseeable consequence of the deliberate policy of making civilians and civilian facilities the direct object of aerial bombardment.

V. *The Alleged Continuing Crimes Against Humanity Inflicted by Sanctions.* The most urgent issue, about which the Security Council has been heretofore advised in detail, is the continuing crime against humanity arising from the U.S. insistence on the continuation of UN sanctions against Iraq, which kill several thousand people each week. For these acts, too, there must be accountability before an International Court of Criminal Justice.

In April 1993, Kuwait hosted former President Bush and his entourage in a visit to the little nation he liberated. By late August, Bush's office reported it had spent four months cataloging the gifts he had received. He was accompanied by sons Neil and Marvin. Seymour Hersh in an article in the September 6, 1993 *New Yorker* entitled "The Spoils of the Gulf War" reported "they were there to make money." Former Secretary of State James Baker, who accompanied his old friend, also received many gifts. He had proclaimed the purpose of the war to be "jobs," and now he was looking for a job himself. But he was also looking for greater profits as a consultant to U.S. companies seeking contracts with Kuwait. He stayed in Kuwait after Bush left and held a series of meetings with officials and Sabah family members, including the Prime Minister. Baker has declined to release any information about compensation for his efforts.

Retired General Thomas Kelly, who was director of operations for former Chairman of the Joint Chiefs of Staff Colin Powell during the Persian Gulf War, was also on this trip. Like former Secretary Baker, he went among other capacities as a consultant for Enron, a Houston natural gas pipeline company, the largest in the United States. Hersh reported that Enron's 1993 proxy statement shows

General Kelly is to receive millions of dollars if Enron obtains contracts from Kuwait. General Kelly is the officer who told the world on CNN at the beginning of the ground war in February 1991 that there were not many Iraqi soldiers left alive to fight.

The use of violence and impoverishment against Iraq may become a model for the control of poor countries by the powerful. It can be done without setting foot on their soil.

President Clinton's announcement on September 17, 1993 of increased U.S. military presence in Somalia until "stable" government is established that will not collapse once foreign troops leave shows that the means of foreign domination remain many and are determined primarily by purpose and circumstances.

History suggests that mere force, however lethal, rarely has its way for long, but the consequences in the interim for people in its path are tragic. And those who rely on force in turn become its victim.

November 1993

Preface

Life is a journey into the unknown. Changes in direction are determined by choices we make, happenings beyond our control, and conditions that dictate the road we must take. I had little notion where my trip into Iraq might lead when I traveled there during the heavy U.S. bombardment in February 1991.

The early morning air was chilling as we packed an old American sedan with our little luggage and bulky camera equipment, all placed around six 10-gallon plastic gasoline containers. The five of us — myself; John Alpert, an award-winning documentary filmmaker; Maryann DeLeo, Alpert's assistant and an accomplished professional photographer; Mohammad al-Kaysi, our Iraqi American translator and guide; and a Jordanian who volunteered to drive us — piled into the car and headed east out of Amman toward the Iraq border as the sun rose. Though the bombardment was only two weeks old, the feel of war was everywhere. Angry crowds outside the U.S. Embassy in Amman had replaced the lines of people seeking visas to visit America. The usual early morning bustle was muted by the drastic economic effect on Jordan of the embargo against Iraq, Jordan's largest trading partner, and traffic toward Iraq was reduced to a trickle. The military was everywhere. Jordanian Air Force fighters were continuously taking off and landing at the military airfields along the road. At our several stops for bread, bottled water, food, and a stretch during the eight-hour drive to the border, men talked in low, angry tones about the war. Huge oil tanker trucks coming from Iraq lumbered toward us, and along the way many drivers parked to rest and exchange stories on the condition of the road. Closer to the border scores of oil trucks were parked off the road, out of service until travel was less dangerous.

In the last Jordanian settlement before a series of military checkpoints, we filled the car's tank and all the jerry cans with gasoline, for we had been told it might be impossible to get gasoline in Iraq. As we passed burned out and burning vehicles along the way, I'm sure we all thought about what one piece of hot shrapnel could do to our car.

I had last been in Baghdad in November as the pressure for war mounted. The Iraqi Embassy had invited me to meet with Saddam Hussein, and we had talked for several hours late one evening, primarily about how war might be avoided. Now I was returning at my own request to witness and document what U.S. bombing was doing to civilian life in Iraq.

We were to be met at the border and escorted to Baghdad by Iraq Foreign Ministry personnel. Although there were thousands of people in temporary refugee settlements near the Jordanian checkpoints, we passed through without significant delay, as no one was heading east into Iraq. Thirty miles further on, the large Iraqi immigration and customs station was ominously quiet and comparatively deserted. There was no one from the Foreign Ministry to meet us, nor had the officials any word of our coming. The station, its transmitter and relay station bombed early in the war, had had no radio or telephone communications for two weeks. There was no military presence. Edgy immigration officials seemed uncertain whether to admit us, and daylight was fading fast.

We persuaded the border officers to let us enter Iraq, though they wanted us to wait until morning to begin the drive to Baghdad. There had been numerous air attacks on the highway during the day and they were uncertain about the roadway and the bridges. They warned that driving with lights on at night was foolhardy, as aircraft were attacking around the clock.

We decided to proceed that night even after our driver told us he had not been to Baghdad in 20 years. I mistakenly assured him that if he could get us to Baghdad, I could direct him once we were there. It was to be a night of the blind leading the blind.

Fewer than 15 minutes into Iraq, we saw flames from a burning trailer truck. The truck had been carrying animal feed for Iraq's hungry herds when it was blasted off the road. There was no sign of life.

We pressed forward down the modern concrete highway, keeping our headlights off as much as we could. Within minutes we plowed into a large sandpile in the dark that had been dumped in the middle of the highway to keep vehicles from driving into a bomb crater. When we finally got around the crater and back on the highway, we proceeded more slowly.

In the first 100 miles, we passed scores of damaged and destroyed vehicles whose forms we could discern in the dark. At these places and others, the roadway was damaged by strafing and bombing. Several times traffic was switched from one side of the divided highway to the other, apparently to get around damaged overpasses, bridges, or roadbed. On the entire trip to the capital, we did not see a dozen moving vehicles. Fires were visible from time to time, and from one facility on the Euphrates River flames were leaping into the sky. We tried to investigate, since the site was less than a mile from the highway, but we couldn't find a way to get closer.

Baghdad was completely dark and seemed deserted when we reached the outskirts. A number of fires and many smoke plumes were visible from overpasses. Road signs were difficult to find, but civilian defense volunteers parked at darkened intersections offered some help while warning us to keep our lights off. From time to time, we heard bombing in the distance and saw anti-aircraft fire lace the sky. Finally we found a major bus station where people were milling about. When we drove by several days later, the station had been destroyed. There we found a taxi driver willing to lead us toward the Al-Rashid Hotel, where we hoped to find rooms.

Soon we were in the grand marble lobby of this modern, European-built luxury hotel. A single candle was burning at the registration desk. Once registered, our group was given one candle and directed to the stairway to our rooms — up five flights in the dark. Finally inside my room, I groped my way to the bed and just fell asleep, as there was no water for washing anyway.

When the air raid alarm sounded, I decided to stay in the room rather than risk breaking a leg looking for the basement bomb shelter. In the morning I found we had all done the same thing, a practice we followed throughout the trip. From my window I could see four or five severely damaged major buildings in the immediate vicinity, including the central telephone exchange. Daylight did not reach the interior hallways or stairwells, which I soon learned to navigate in total darkness.

The Foreign Ministry found us early the first morning. We were provided two cars with drivers and one protocol officer to help arrange appointments, not an easy task without phones and with officials and others scattered to new locations because of the bombing. Some of us used the first morning to seek relatives of Iraqi-Americans who had asked us to do so, although we did not have much luck because people had moved to places they hoped would be safer. Our Jordanian driver remained with us for a couple of days before starting back to Amman with more passengers than he brought in. Every morning we were up at dawn and went hard all day until dark, trying to schedule at least one meeting in the evening despite the difficulty of travel.

That first night we met the Minister of Health, a military officer who had set up temporary headquarters in the administrative offices of a major hospital. There was little he could tell us in the near-dark of his crowded quarters, and it almost seemed we had as good a grasp of the situation as he did after one day on the streets, an hour with the Red Crescent (the Red Cross affiliate in Muslim countries), and talking with families and people at bomb sites. The minister's communications and command chain were completely disrupted, and he was relying on couriers to bring in reports. Asked his priorities to save life and protect health, he named three without hesitation: water, water, water. He described contaminated water as a threat to the entire nation, and estimated that at least 3,000 were dead, 25,000 were receiving some medical care, and a quarter of a million were sick from drinking polluted water. We were thankful for all the bottled water we had brought with us, as to be severely nauseated, plagued with diarrhea, dehydrated, desperately thirsty, and have nothing to drink but the water that made you sick is a terrible misery. The minister believed all the municipal water systems of the country had been destroyed. A year later, when I returned to Basra, I found all the drinking water there was being brought in by trucks, and people waited in long lines to fill buckets for their homes.

The minister arranged for us to be taken to one of the wards in the hospital. What greeted us was a scene somewhere between Dante's *Inferno* and *M*A*S*H*. Cold and dark, with two candles for 20 beds, the room was crowded with patients, families, health professionals. Sobbing, murmuring, urgent instructions from doctors, occasional shrieks of pain, and the wail of grieving relatives filled our ears. One middle-aged woman had about 30 shrapnel wounds over her whole back. A 12-year-old girl whose left leg had been amputated near the hip without anesthetics was in delirium. A semiconscious woman who had been seriously injured when her house caved in had not yet been told that she was the sole survivor of her family of seven.

A surgeon who had just performed radical surgery on a young man's arm came over to us. He was exhausted and near despair. Trained in England to be a surgeon, he was now working 18–20 hours a day. He told us there was no anesthesia, so patients were held down by aides during operations. Gauze, bandages, adhesive tape, and antiseptics were exhausted. He held out his bare hands and said, "These are my tools to heal the sick. The few hours I have to sleep I wake up to find myself rubbing my hands. I have no clean water to wash them with, no alcohol to kill germs, our glove supply was exhausted a week ago. I move hour after hour from the open wounds of one person to another, spreading infection. I cannot help my patients."

We left Baghdad for the south, where the heaviest urban bombing had been reported. Coming in to Diwaniya, we saw a damaged hospital with all its windows blasted out and a bomb-demolished school. The governor's building was destroyed, but we found him and he led us to two residential areas that were badly hit. The people were dumbfounded and still dazed. They insisted there were no military targets in the area and no troops had moved through. The center of town had been raked with bombs that demolished three small hotels, the train station, the bus station, offices, shops, restaurants, and the post office with its radio relay station and tower. We saw no evidence of military presence.

Pressing on to Basra, we passed streams of taxis with coffins on top heading for the holy shrine in Karbala. Soldiers' coffins were wrapped with a flag; civilians' were covered by a rug. Along the highway were many more of the hundreds of civilian vehicles we saw destroyed. They included buses, lorries, vans, trucks, and taxis.

Basra had suffered greater damage in less than three weeks of U.S. air and missile assault than during the entire months-long Iranian siege of the city during the Iran–Iraq War, according to the governor, who was in office during both assaults. He did not survive the second assault. Civilian defense officers agreed to take us to places as they learned of new attacks, and we were first on the scene at least once. I never paused for long in Basra.

We were the first Westerners to get to Basra during the bombing, and we were the only guests at the Sheraton Basrah on the beautiful Shatt-al-Arab, through which the waters of the Tigris and the Euphrates flow to the Persian Gulf. The chef, happy to have someone to cook for, made fresh rolls for dinner, which we were enjoying in lonely splendor by candlelight when three deafening crashes shook the building. Plate glass windows only a few feet away shattered. Several of us ran up to the roof in time to see in the twilight a huge column of water rise from the Shatt where a bomb fell harmlessly beyond the darkened Teaching Hospital, which had been closed by an earlier hit. Civil Defense arrived in minutes. Our pickup truck ran over a piece of shrapnel within a few hundred yards and blew a tire. We walked the short remaining distance through thick dust and smoke to find two buildings demolished by the bombs.

The next day while visiting darkened, cold General Hospital, John Alpert asked the chief surgeon how it felt to be trained to heal the sick only to find war killing and maiming time after time. Exhausted, the surgeon answered, "It is our destiny."

It was awful to see a city full of human beings bombed that way. In less than 24 hours, we saw hundreds of buildings, whole blocks in 10 separate residential areas, hospitals, mosques, and churches damaged and destroyed. The center of the city was not completely incinerated, as happened to Dresden and Hiroshima. But every service essential to modern city life was severed.

We soon realized that a whole nation lay helpless beneath an alien military that could attack and destroy with impunity. It was months before we knew how much damage the United States had done. Before the assault was over U.S. planes flew more than 109,000 sorties, raining 88,000 tons of bombs, the equivalent of seven Hiroshimas, and killing indiscriminately across the country.

What was visible was a nation with thousands of civilians dead; without water, hospitals, or health care; with no electricity, communications, or public transportation; without gasoline, road and bridge repair capacity, or parts for essential equipment; and with a growing food crisis. Because of the nature of American weapons, Iraq was being crippled from afar and left to a painful struggle for survival. The bombing, as could be seen from the ground, was hardly surgical, but was clearly designed to break a whole country and its population for a long time to come.

As we made our way out of Iraq around newly bombed bridges and more severely damaged roads, I knew the journey was only beginning. On the flight back home, I wrote a detailed letter of what I had seen, offering videotape and other information to President Bush, UN Secretary-General Perez de Cuellar, and President Hussein. The letter was delivered the day after we arrived. A press conference was held at the UN and the incontestable evidence of war crimes against the civilians of Iraq was described.

Of President Bush, the letter asked, "Most urgent, stop the bombing of cities, civilian population. . . . If there is no ceasefire, bombing must be limited to military targets. . . . "

To Secretary-General Perez de Cuellar, the letter pleaded, "The scourge of war will never end if the United Nations tolerates this assault on life. The United Nations must not be an accessary to war crimes."

The trip to Iraq during the bombing proved to be the shortest part of the journey. Within three weeks of my return the U.S. assault was over and Iraq, cut off from outside help while internal rebellion encouraged by President Bush tore at its entrails, was left to bleed some more. Many in the antiwar movement, which had so quickly erupted to oppose the Gulf War, were overwhelmed by the sheer brutality of the crippling of Iraq.

The journey quickly went worldwide. Along with a wide range of organizations and individuals in the United States — including peace activists, African-American and Latino groups, religious groups and leaders, opponents of nuclear arms, Arab-American organizations, labor unions, student and academic associations, and environmentalists — I helped initiate the Commission of Inquiry for an International War Crimes Tribunal.

The Commission of Inquiry became an international effort to gather evidence about all aspects of the assault on Iraq and determine whether war crimes had been committed by the United States. To this end, I drafted 19 detailed preliminary charges of crimes against peace, war crimes, and crimes against humanity committed by my own government, all based on evidence already available as measured by international laws defining crimes against peace and war crimes. These laws included the Hague and Geneva Conventions and the Nuremberg Charter. With these charges as a standard, hearings and meetings held in more than 30 U.S. cities took evidence from eyewitnesses, scholars, and experts. Hearings were organized under many different sponsorships in more than 20 other countries. I attended as many as possible in Asia, North Africa, the Middle East, Europe, and the Americas.

Tens of thousands of people contributed and participated in the fact-gathering and educational process. This entailed the compilation of documents, clippings, photographs, books, videotapes, and eyewitness testimony over a period of 10 months. A wide variety of cultural, ideological, and religious backgrounds were represented in this globally coordinated effort to hold the United States accountable for its acts under international law. All involved recognized the near-total control of the situation wielded by the U.S. government, but were determined not to allow the victors alone to write the history of this war.

At the final judgment of the Tribunal in New York City, on the anniversary of the end of the bombing, 22 judges from 18 nations found the United States and its principal officers guilty on all 19 charges of war crimes. Although ignored by the U.S. media, the event received major coverage by the international press.

However, the truth will out. In the years ahead, a wealth of material will emerge to confirm the decision of the Tribunal. In fact, this process has already begun. The work of the Commission represents the thousands of people determined not to wait generations for the truth to be revealed. U.S. policy must be understood now because other wars and interventions are the agenda of the new world order. Therefore, Commission hearings concentrated not only on what happened to Iraq, but on why the assault occurred, and most important, on what can be done to prevent such a thing from happening again.

This book is the product of the journey so far and the efforts of all who participated. It brings together a description of the history, planning, and preparation that impelled the United States toward domination of the Gulf region. It describes the slaughter of the defenseless Iraqi military, the bombing of essential civilian facilities and the people, the damage to the environment, and the grim aftermath and rising death toll from the destruction compounded by continuing sanctions, which have deprived the whole Iraqi population of food, medicine, clean water, and the means to repair their crippled economy.

It shows how the U.S. Constitution and the UN Charter were violated, and describes the international laws defining war crimes. It analyzes the American media's failure to adequately inform the American public and world opinion: an essential element in understanding the tragedy and preventing its repetition. This failure made possible the celebration of a slaughter and reveals the helplessness of a world, however democratic, that is ignorant or misinformed, even when its life is at stake.

The last chapter of this book brings together all the ideas and experience encountered along the way into a working paper for peace so that those who care can light a candle rather than curse the darkness. To further this effort, the proceeds of this book will go to the International Action Center, established in New York City to implement the proposals put forth by the Tribunal. These include the continued work of the Commission as well as future struggles against U.S. interventions.

I hope you will join this journey for peace. It will be a rough road. There will be little comfort along the way except what can be found in the continuing struggle. This book itself will not be easy going. It is hardest for those who want to love their country and still love justice. Small effort has been made to smooth the way, in either content or presentation. But this book offers you more than additional information about what happened and why. It offers you the chance to join the quest for peace.

We are told that to know and not to act is not to know. If we act, war need not be our destiny. Surely the book offers a fuller opportunity to understand and discuss the perils of military technology, the new levels of inhumanity layered over the age-old disaster of war, the strengths and weaknesses of the U.S. Constitution and the United Nations in crisis, the full meaning of the failure of the media, and the role international law ought to play in preventing war crimes. And hopefully it will help us find ways and means by which together the people can persevere in the pursuit of peace.

THE FIRE THIS TIME

The above arrows show the path we took in our 2,000-mile, three-day trip through Iraq. The purpose of the trip, begun February 2, 1991 during the height of the U.S. bombing campaign, was to document firsthand the civilian damage inflicted by U.S. bombing and censored in the U.S. media. I was accompanied by Jon Alpert, who filmed the damage; Maryann DeLeo, who photographed it; and Mohammed al-Kaysi, who used his familiarity with and contacts in Iraq to make our trip successful.

Chronology of the Gulf War and Its Aftermath

1921 Sir Percy Cox of the British Colonial Office draws a border that separates Kuwait, originally part of Basra province, from Iraq, prohibiting Iraq's access to the Persian Gulf.

1951 Iran's Mossadegh government nationalizes the holdings of the Anglo-Iranian Oil Company (now British Petroleum). Iran is immediately subjected to sanctions by Western countries.

1953 With Iran weakened by two years of sanctions, the CIA helps overthrow Mossadegh. The U.S. installs Shah Reza Pahlevi. General Norman Schwarzkopf, Sr. assists the Shah in forming SAVAK, Iran's brutal state police.

1958 A popular revolution led by Abdel Karim Kassem overthrows the British-installed monarchy in Iraq. Kassem begins to nationalize Western holdings in Iraq.

1963 A coup aided by the CIA overthrows Kassem.

1968 The Baathist Party comes to power in Iraq.

1972 Iraq announces the nationalization of its oil industry. One day before the announcement, President Nixon and National Security Adviser Kissinger plot with the Shah of Iran to arm Iraqi Kurds to weaken Iraq. Iraq is placed on a list of states that support terrorism.

1975 Iraqi Vice President Saddam Hussein and the Shah reach an agreement in Algiers. Control of the disputed Shatt-al-Arab waterway is ceded to Iran. All aid to the Kurds is abruptly cut off.

1979 The U.S.-backed Shah is overthrown by popular revolution.

1980 Carter announces the "Carter Doctrine," which stipulates that the U.S. will intervene militarily in the Persian Gulf region to protect U.S. access to oil resources. In October, the Rapid Deployment Joint Task Force (RDJTF), designed to implement this doctrine, is formed. Iraq invades Iran with the United States' tacit approval. The United States aids both sides in the ensuing eight-year war.

1982 As the Iran–Iraq War continues, Iraq is removed from the list of countries that support terrorism.

1983 The RDJTF takes on unified command status and becomes U.S. Central Command (CENTCOM).

1984 The United States restores full diplomatic relations with Iraq. President Reagan issues a top-secret intelligence finding authorizing increased intelligence-sharing with Iraq. At the same time, the United States begins to share intelligence with and sell weapons to Iran.

1985 Colonel Oliver North, coordinator of the Iran–Contra scheme, tells Iranian negotiators that the United States will help Iran overthrow Saddam Hussein.

1986 The Iran–Contra scandal breaks in November, yet cooperation between the United States and Iraq continues. When it looks as though Iraq may lose the war, U.S. aid increases.

1987 General Norman Schwarzkopf, Jr. is named head of CENTCOM. The same year, the United States intervenes in the Iran–Iraq War by reflagging Kuwaiti tankers, escorting Kuwaiti ships in the Gulf, and bombing Iranian oil platforms.

1988 Advice, manpower, intelligence, loans, and weapons from the United States, Kuwait, Saudi Arabia, Jordan, Britain, France, and West Germany tip the scales for Iraq. A ceasefire agreement is signed between Iran and Iraq in August. U.S. policy toward Iraq shifts dramatically. The Center for Strategic and International Studies begins a two-year study predicting the outcome of a war between the United States and Iraq.

1989 War Plan 1002, originally conceived in 1981 to counter a supposed Soviet threat to the Persian Gulf, is adjusted to designate Iraq as the threat to the region. The plan is renamed War Plan 1002-90.

January 1990   CENTCOM headquarters stages a computer game entitled Internal Look, which tests War Plan 1002-90.

February 1990   General Schwarzkopf testifies before the Senate of the need for the United States to increase its military presence in the Gulf region. He warns that "Iraq has the capability to militarily coerce its neighbors."

May 1990   At a closed session of an emergency Arab summit in Baghdad, Saddam Hussein accuses Gulf states of waging economic war against Iraq.

July 1990   Saddam Hussein publicly accuses Kuwait of conspiring to destroy Iraq's economy. Iraqi troops begin to mass on the Kuwaiti border.

August 2, 1990   Iraq invades Kuwait. President Bush bans all U.S. sales to Iraq and freezes its assets.

August 3, 1990   The UN Security Council passes Resolution 660, which condemns Iraq for the invasion.

August 6, 1990   The Security Council passes Resolution 661, which levies international sanctions against Iraq and freezes its foreign assets. Seventy percent dependent on food imports and now unable to sell oil, Iraq faces starvation.

August 7, 1990   A U.S. delegation to Saudi Arabia, dispatched on August 5, finally convinces a reluctant King Fahd of Saudi Arabia to accept troop deployments on its soil.

August 8, 1990   The United States announces that, with no congressional authorization, it is dispatching 40,000 soldiers to defend Saudi Arabia, though satellite photos show no Iraqi troops near the Saudi border. Iraq announces that it is annexing Kuwait.

August 12, 1990   Iraq calls for a settlement linking withdrawal from Kuwait to Israeli withdrawal from occupied territories. The United States rejects the offer. A later proposal from Iraq, which does not propose linkage, is rejected by the United States as a "complete nonstarter."

September 2, 1990   Iraq orders rationing of food supplies.

November 8, 1990   With no material change in the crisis, President Bush changes the deployment from defensive to offensive, doubling the number of troops in the Gulf to 400,000.

November 29, 1990   The UN Security Council passes resolution 678, authorizing the use of military force to drive Iraq from Kuwait if it does not voluntarily leave by January 15, 1991.

December 22, 1990   Infant mortality in Iraq is doubled because of lack of medical supplies due to sanctions.

January 9, 1991   Secretary of State James Baker and Foreign Minister Tariq Aziz meet in Geneva. Baker hands Aziz a letter addressed to Saddam Hussein that threatens the destruction of Iraq should it fail to withdraw from Kuwait by January 15, 1991. Asiz refuses to deliver the letter.

January 12, 1991   Congress authorizes the use of force if Iraq does not withdraw by January 15. The Senate vote is 52–47; the House vote is 250–183.

January 17, 1991   The United States begins the air assault on Iraq. For 42 days, the U.S. will average 2,000 sorties a day throughout Iraq and Kuwait.

February 13, 1991   The United States kills 1,500 civilians instantly in its raid on the Al-Amariyah bomb shelter in Baghdad.

February 15, 1991   In a speech at Raytheon Corporation, the manufacturer of the Patriot missile, President Bush urges the Iraqi people to overthrow Saddam Hussein.

February 21, 1991   The Soviets announce that Iraq has agreed to full and unconditional withdrawal from Kuwait. The United States rejects the plan and issues an ultimatum: that Iraq withdraw from Kuwait by noon February 23 or face a ground attack.

February 23, 1991   President Bush orders the ground assault to begin.

February 26, 1991   Iraq announces on Baghdad Radio that its forces are withdrawing from Kuwait. Iraqi forces begin retreating along the Basra road. U.S. planes bomb both ends of the road, and then proceed to attack the long rows of cars along a 7-mile stretch. The U.S. kills thousands in the "turkey shoot," including many civilians fleeing Kuwait.

February 28, 1991   Iraq and the United States agree to a ceasefire.

March 2, 1991   The 24th Mechanized Infantry Division slaughters thousands of Iraqi soldiers in a post-ceasefire battle. No Americans die.

March 1991 U.S.-encouraged rebellions against Saddam Hussein break out in Iraq. Shiite rebellions are quickly quelled. Kurdish rebellions are put down near the end of the month.

May 1992 Over 150,000 Iraqi civilians, mostly children, die since the end of the war as a result of the bombing and ongoing sanctions.

August 27, 1992 With France and Britain, the United States imposes a "no-fly zone" on Iraq, forbidding Iraqi planes to fly south of the 32nd parallel. The U.S. claims it is "protecting the Shiites" from Saddam Hussein, though the heaviest U.S. bombing in the Gulf War occurred in the south of Iraq, where the Shiites live. Neither this demarcation nor the previous imposition of a "no-fly zone" north of the 36th parallel was part of the UN ceasefire agreement, nor were they sanctioned by any UN resolution. These violations of Iraq's sovereignty broke it into three parts, leaving the U.S. in control of the areas with the richest oil reserves.

December 27, 1992 The United States resumes the military war against Iraq, shooting down an Iraqi MIG-25 for flying in the southern "no-fly zone."

January 1993 With George Bush leaving office on January 20, a campaign of attacks on Iraq is waged under two U.S. presidents. This campaign includes an intense revival of anti-Iraq propaganda in the media. Reasons for military actions against Iraq vary from day to day.

The U.S., France, and Britain collaborate on bombings of Iraqi anti-aircraft sites and downing of Iraqi planes in the northern and southern "no-fly zones" on January 13, 17, 18, and 19. These illegal attacks include the use of cluster bombs. The Pentagon announces that these attacks "could proceed without further warning."

The worst attack occurs on January 17, with Navy ships firing 45 Tomahawk cruise missiles at and around Baghdad. Ostensibly aimed at the Zaafaraniya industrial complex outside of Baghdad, one missile hits the Al-Rashid hotel, killing and injuring civilians.

One day after Bill Clinton's inauguration, U.S. planes attack anti-aircraft batteries in Iraq for three consecutive days. U.S. officials claim variously that the planes were tracked by Iraqi radar or fired upon.

April 1993 On April 9, US F-16 and F4-G fighter planes drop cluster bombs on Iraq in the north, claiming they were fired upon. Iraq denies the charge. On April 18, an F4-G fires a HARM anti-radiation missile at a radar site 11 miles below the northern "no-fly zone"; the U.S. complains that Iraqi radar was tracking U.S. planes.

il

June 1993 On June 26, President Clinton orders the firing of 23 Tomahawk cruise missiles at downtown Baghdad. The U.S. says it is a response to an Iraqi attempt to assassinate former President George Bush on his April trip to Kuwait. This charge has since been questioned as highly suspect in the U.S. media. The U.S. invokes Article 51 of the UN Charter giving member nations the right to "self-defense," neglecting to state that the threat must be instant, overwhelming, and leave no room for deliberation.

Many civilians are killed in their homes. Layla al-Attar, a famous Iraqi artist and director of many museums, including the Iraqi National Gallery of Modern Art, is one of those killed, along with most of her family. The U.S. again fires a Tomahawk missile at an Iraqi military site in the south on June 29, charging that Iraqi radar systems were tracking U.S. planes.

THE FIRE THIS TIME

CHAPTER 1

Planning U.S.
Dominion over
the Gulf

THE U.S. government claimed Iraq caused the Gulf War by invading Kuwait. The Bush administration argued that the United States was only responding to the actions of Saddam Hussein who, Americans were told, had invaded his smaller neighbor without provocation or warning. But a careful look at American involvement in the region reveals that the U.S. government, not Iraq, bears prime responsibility for the war, which was planned in Washington long before the first Iraqi soldier entered Kuwait.

The U.S. government used the Kuwaiti royal family to provoke an Iraqi invasion that would justify a massive assault on Iraq to establish U.S. dominion in the Gulf. The Gulf War was fought not to restore Kuwait's sovereignty, as President Bush proclaimed, but to establish U.S. power over the region and its oil.

As Jordan's King Hussein accurately stated in a letter to Saddam Hussein in September 1990:

> The large industrial powers saw in the Gulf crisis a golden opportunity to reorganize the area according to designs in harmony with their ambitions and interests, at the expense of the aspirations and the interests of the Arab peoples, and to put in place a new international order.[1]

The Pentagon has acknowledged this evaluation. A revealing draft of its plan to prevent the emergence of rival powers in the world, reported by the *New York Times* on March 8, 1992, contained the following paragraph about the Gulf War.

> In the Middle East and Southwest Asia, our overall objective is to remain the predominant outside power in the region and preserve U.S. and Western access to the region's oil. . . . As demonstrated by Iraq's invasion of Kuwait, it remains fundamentally important to prevent a hegemon or alignment of powers from dominating the region.[2]

After all of President Bush's impassioned speeches about Iraq's "naked aggression," the Pentagon posed the invasion of Kuwait as a threat to Western oil access — not a violation of Kuwait's sovereignty.

U.S. INTERVENTION IN GULF POLITICS

Iraq has been a target of covert activity by the United States since at least 1958, when British influence in the region began to wane. On July 14 of that year, a popular, nationalist revolution in Iraq led by Abdel Karim Kassem overthrew the Hashemite monarchy, which had been installed by the British in 1921. The new government helped found the Organization of Petroleum Exporting Countries (OPEC), which was formed in 1960 to resist the power of Western oil monopolies. Kassem said: "We are not combating the oil companies for another 7 million dinars a year. We are fighting for the industrialization of our republic and an end to our dependence on the sale of crude oil."[3]

Kassem challenged the absolute stranglehold Western oil companies then held on the marketing of Arab oil. Washington had little tolerance for this challenge to its long-standing intention to succeed colonial Britain and France as the dominant power in the Middle East. Ever since, the United States has planned to weaken Iraq and control its oil.

Shortly after the 1958 revolution, the CIA formed a "health alterations committee" to plot Kassem's assassination. At the same time, U.S. generals in Turkey devised a military plan, code-named Cannonbone, for invading northern Iraq and seizing the oil fields there.[4] In 1963, Kassem and thousands of his supporters were massacred in a bloody CIA-backed coup. Testifying to a Senate committee about the coup, a CIA member joked, "The target suffered a terminal illness before a firing squad in Baghdad."[5]

Ten years before, another CIA-backed operation had overthrown the democratically elected Mossadegh government of neighboring Iran. As in Iraq, the major stimulus for the Iranian coup was that country's attempt to control its own oil industry. Shah Reza Pahlevi was placed on the Peacock throne in Iran, and he then handed over 40 percent ownership of Iran's oil fields to U.S. companies. Kermit Roosevelt, the CIA agent who masterminded the Iran coup, was named vice president of Gulf Oil.[6]

In 1968, the Baathist Party came to power in Iraq, and in 1972, it became the target of covert CIA operations after it nationalized the U.S./British-owned Iraqi Petroleum Company under the slogan "Arab oil for the Arabs." After a May 1972 meeting between President Nixon, National Security Adviser Henry Kissinger, and the Shah of Iran, Washington began to urge Kurdish leaders in northern Iraq to rebel against the Iraqi government. The Kurds were promised that the United States would back them all the way.

The Pike Report, issued later by the House Select Committee on Intelligence, described what followed as a "cynical enterprise, even in the context of clandestine operations."[7] The Shah funneled U.S.-supplied arms to the Kurds, and Kissinger encouraged the Kurdish leadership to reject a Soviet offer to mediate between them and Baghdad.[8] According to the Pike Report, "neither the foreign head of state [the Shah] nor the President and Dr. Kissinger desired a victory for our clients [the Kurds]. They merely hoped to insure that the insurgents would be capable of maintaining a level of hostilities high enough to sap the resources of the neighboring state [Iraq]."[9]

In 1975, Iraq agreed to share control of the disputed Shatt-al-Arab waterway with Iran in an agreement reached in Algiers. The United States and the Shah abruptly terminated their support for the Kurdish insurgents, whose leadership abandoned the struggle and fled the country. But the fate of the Kurds left behind did not concern the U.S. government: as Henry Kissinger explained to an aide, "Covert operations should not be confused with missionary work."[10]

In early 1979 the long struggle of the Iranian people to overthrow the Shah succeeded. That despotic regime, the proudest achievement of the CIA, according to former director William Colby, had been Washington's main ally in the Gulf region. U.S. policy then took another radical turn. Adopting a supportive stance toward Iraq, National Security Adviser Zbigniew Brzezinski publicly encouraged Iraq to attack Iran and take back the Shatt-al-Arab waterway — control of which the U.S. had forced Iraq to share with Iran only four years earlier.[11]

In the fall of 1980, the United States, acting through Kuwait, Saudi Arabia, and other friendly Arab governments, provided Iraq with intelligence reports that Iranian forces would quickly collapse in the face of an Iraqi advance. At the urging of the Emir of Kuwait, Egypt's Anwar Sadat, and other U.S.-backed Arab rulers, Saddam

Hussein followed Brzezinski's advice in late 1980 and unleashed a war with Iran in which hundreds of thousands died.[12]

In contrast to its reaction to Iraq's relatively bloodless entry into Kuwait ten years later, Washington expressed no moral outrage at the 1980 Iraqi attack on Iran. The attack served U.S. interests by weakening both Iran, where U.S. Embassy personnel were still held hostage, and the anti-U.S. influence in the Muslim world of Iran's Islamic government.

Of course, war against the much larger Iran would weaken Iraq as well. Washington did not want either side to win. "We wanted to avoid victory by both sides," a Reagan administration official told the *New York Times*.[13] Henry Kissinger was more blunt about it, being variously quoted as saying,"I hope they kill each other" and "too bad they both can't lose."[14]

Although the United States increased its aid and assistance to Iraq, especially when it appeared Iran might win the war, its overall goals remained the same. It wanted to weaken the Gulf states and eventually establish unchallengeable power in the region. This overriding purpose explains the various strategy shifts by the United States which would lead to Iraq's destruction by U.S. military technology in 1991.

Iraq could not have sustained eight years of war with its much larger neighbor without massive assistance, direct and indirect, from the U.S.S.R., Eastern bloc countries, Kuwait, the United Arab Emirates (UAE), Saudi Arabia, the United States, Britain, France, and West Germany. Throughout the war the Pentagon and CIA provided Iraq with satellite and AWACS intelligence on Iranian forces.[15] Well-informed sources have told Commission staffers that the U.S. sent CIA and Special Forces operatives to train Iraqi commandos. And Washington encouraged and helped funnel billions of dollars worth of arms to Iraq through pro-U.S. Middle Eastern regimes.[16]

Egypt, a major recipient of U.S. military aid, sent troops, tanks, and heavy artillery to Iraq, and authorized Baghdad to draft Egyptians working in Iraq into the army.[17] After U.S. Army Chief of Staff General David Jones visited Turkey in 1980, that military dictatorship — a major recipient of U.S. military aid — sent troops to fight rebels in Iraqi Kurdistan, freeing Iraq's army to concentrate on the war with Iran.

The U.S.-supported regimes in Kuwait and Saudi Arabia provided tens of billions of dollars for Iraq's war effort. Kuwait's contribution alone was over $30 billion. The U.S. sold over $20 billion worth of arms to Kuwait, Saudi Arabia, and other Gulf states during this period. The Reagan administration illegally allowed Saudi Arabia, a major U.S. arms customer, to transfer large quantities of U.S. arms to Iraq during the war.

When Iraq nationalized its oil industry in 1972, the United States placed it on a list of countries that allegedly supported terrorism. However, during the Iran–Iraq War, the Reagan administration removed Iraq from the list. This allowed U.S. companies to sell directly to Baghdad such "dual-use" equipment as jeeps, helicopters, and Lockheed L-100 transports.[18] The Agriculture Department extended $5 billion of credits to Iraq through a program meant for agricultural purchases only, that illegally funded many of these sales.[19] Among the items sold to Iraq were 45 Bell helicopters originally built as troop carriers for the Shah's army.[20]

In 1984 the United States increased its support for Iraq, becoming its principal trading partner by increasing its purchases of Iraqi oil while encouraging Europe and Japan to do the same.[21] The Reagan administration issued a top-secret finding authorizing increased intelligence-sharing with Iraq. The *New York Times* reported that the finding was interpreted as mandating that the United States "do anything and everything" to help Iraq prevail against Iran.[22] That same year Vice President Bush, the State Department, and the CIA began lobbying the Export-Import Bank to begin large-scale financing of U.S. exports to Iraq.[23] And in 1986 the United States dispatched a high-level CIA team to Baghdad to advise the Iraqi military.[24]

Still, the United States was playing both sides against the middle to advance its own interests. In 1983 the *New Statesman* reported that U.S. and Turkish generals had revived Operation Cannonbone, the 1958 plan to invade northern Iraq and seize its oil fields, and were preparing to implement it in the event of an Iraqi defeat.[25] As is now widely known, the United States was until late 1986 funneling large quantities of arms to Iran through Oliver North's activities and bigger covert operations involving Israel and Pakistan.[26] And in 1985, according to testimony at the Iran–Contra hearings, Oliver North told Iranian officials that the United States would try to engineer the overthrow of Saddam Hussein.[27]

Finally, with its 1987 decision to protect Kuwaiti oil tankers in the Gulf, the United States became directly involved in the war on Iraq's side. By flying U.S. flags on Kuwaiti tankers to protect their passage through the Gulf, the United States not only aided Iraq's war effort but found an excuse for a major military presence in the Gulf for itself. Some of the tankers escorted by U.S. ships carried Iraqi oil. Thus Iraq's oil was exported under U.S. protection while Iraqi planes attacked Iranian tankers. The United States also sank Iran's patrol ships and destroyed their oil platforms.

The Iran–Iraq conflict itself didn't provide the United States with the pretext it needed to establish a permanent military presence in the Gulf. So, in August 1988, when Iraq and Iran agreed to a cease-fire, U.S. tactics changed again. With Iran substantially weakened and the Soviet Union unable to react, the United States looked to the Western-manufactured image of a militarily strong Iraq to provide the excuse for intervention in the Middle East.

U.S. MILITARY PREPARATIONS

U.S. planning for military action in the Middle East goes back to the 1970s, when Washington reacted to the upsurge of nationalist feelings in and growing independence of oil-producing countries. Before the formation of OPEC in 1960, Middle East oil was owned primarily by seven U.S. and British companies. These firms determined the level of each country's oil production, for which they paid literally pennies a barrel, and reaped huge profits from the sales. In addition to corporate profits, the United States' increasing control among other Western countries over oil resources gave it greater geopolitical leverage.

By the 1970s, this situation was drastically changed as one oil-producing nation after another asserted authority over resources within its borders. Following the 1969 Libyan revolution, the 1972 nationalization of the Iraq Petroleum Company, and the 1973 Arab oil embargo, oil-producing states took a much greater share of oil revenues. By 1975, even pro-Western regimes in Saudi Arabia and Kuwait had nationalized their oil industries.

In 1973 the Pentagon began an annual training exercise in the Mojave Desert called Alkali Canyon, in which Marines and Army Rangers were pitted against soldiers in Libyan and Iraqi uniforms.[28] Washington strategists openly discussed an invasion of the Gulf designed to seize its oil fields. In early 1974, threatening statements by Secretary of Defense Schlesinger prompted Kuwait and Saudi Arabia to mine their oil fields in preparation for a feared U.S. invasion. And in 1977, Senator Henry Jackson's Energy and Natural Resources Committee warned: "A U.S. commitment to the defense of oil resources of the Gulf and to political stability in the region constitutes one of the most vital and enduring interests of the United States."

A number of factors kept the United States from direct intervention in the region. One was the high risk that it would lead to a military confrontation with the Soviet Union. Another was the still strong antiwar sentiment in the United States left over from the Vietnam War. Such obstacles necessitated a policy known as the Nixon Doctrine, which placed reliance upon regional powers like Israel and Iran to control nationalist challenges to U.S. interests in the area. The Pentagon built the Shah's Iran into the region's major power. In return, the Shah helped fund operations like harassment of Iraq through its Kurdish minority as well as helping to crush a popular uprising against the sultan of Oman.

But in 1979 the Shah fell. His military and intelligence services were wracked by mass desertions and civilian attacks. Planning for a U.S. military operation in the Middle East resumed in earnest at the Pentagon. By 1981, the second year of the Iran–Iraq War, the Joint Chiefs of Staff had drafted a plan for rapid deployment of U.S. troops to the Gulf, presented as a response to the new threat supposedly posed by the Soviet invasion of Afghanistan. Though the Soviets were never actually a threat to the Gulf, their invasion was posed as such to sell Congress and the public on new intervention strategies. This sale was made easier by the powerful anti-Iran feelings that were created in the United States after the supporters of Ayatollah Khomeini took American hostages in Teheran.

Central to the new U.S. intervention strategies was War Plan 1002. It was designed at the beginning of the Reagan administration to implement the earlier Carter Doctrine of meeting any challenge to U.S. access to Middle East oil by military force. In 1983, the Rapid Deployment Joint Task Force became U.S. Central Command (CENTCOM), and began secretly to extend the network of U.S. military and surveillance bases in Saudi Arabia. Though the United States had military installations in Saudi Arabia in the late 1970s, the new facilities were more sophisticated, and would provide essential support for the assault on Iraq.

They also provided the United States with a foot in the door of direct intervention in the Middle East. Prefiguring the scenario of the Persian Gulf War in 1990, President Carter's Secretary of Defense Harold Brown said in late 1979, "I don't believe that American bases as such in that area are the right way to go. A number of countries in the area can maintain bases which, in an emergency in which they asked our help, we could then come in and use."[29]

At the height of a major Iranian offensive against Iraq in 1984, Assistant Secretary of State Richard Murphy and National Security Council staff member John Poindexter visited ruling Gulf families to state that any military intervention on their behalf would require a

9

public invitation and full U.S. access.[30] By 1985, the United States had obtained an open-ended agreement from Saudi Arabia for such access. A classified State Department study that appeared in the September 5, 1985 *New York Times* stated, "Although the Saudis have steadfastly resisted formal access agreements, they have stated that access will be forthcoming for United States forces as necessary to counter Soviet aggression or in regional crises they cannot manage on their own."

In 1987, Army General Norman Schwarzkopf, Jr. was named commander of CENTCOM. Originally the Marines Corps was slated to head CENTCOM, but General Schwarzkopf had a unique background for the assignment.[31] He had known the Middle East since childhood. His father had assisted in the 1953 overthrow of Iran's Mossadegh government.[32] As the United States began its detailed and extensive preparation for war against Iraq, Schwarzkopf was placed at the helm.

The decline of the USSR gave the White House and the Pentagon the freedom to act on their plans. As the Soviet economy disintegrated, it withdrew its forces from Afghanistan and dismantled the Warsaw Pact. Thus, it was no longer a deterrent to U.S. intervention in the Gulf. An emboldened Pentagon now defined a new mission.

With the end of the Iran–Iraq War in 1988, contingency plans for war in the Gulf region posed Iraq as the enemy.[33] In January 1990, CIA Director William Webster testified before the Senate Armed Services Committee on the growing Western dependency on Middle East oil.[34] In February, General Schwarzkopf told the same committee that the United States should increase its military presence in the region, and described new military plans to intervene in a conflict.[35] With Japan and Europe's much greater dependency on Persian Gulf oil, the United States considered control over the region crucial to geopolitical power for decades to come.

The Pentagon's purpose now was to protect U.S. access to strategic resources. In a January 1990 paper titled "A Strategic Force for the 1990s and Beyond," General Carl E. Vuono, Army Chief of Staff, wrote: "The United States must maintain the capability of protecting vital interests wherever they are threatened. That could mean confronting a fully equipped army in the Third World."[36] In January 1992, Representative Les Aspin, chairman of the House Armed Services Committee, felt that the Gulf War had validated this new direction. The *New York Times* reported his view that the Iraq experience should be "transported around the globe" to gauge the relative strengths of other "troublesome regional powers" as a means to plan their defeat. "Mr. Aspin," the *Times* stated, "has dubbed this method 'Iraq equivalents.' "[37]

This new strategy was more than a bolder version of what the United States had always done in the Third World — waging overt and covert war to protect its "vital interests." It was based on the strategic permanent location of U.S. military forces capable of destroying any opposition with sophisticated weapons to secure dominion over a region and its resources. In Schwarzkopf's early 1990 testimony before the Senate, he said that CENTCOM should increase its military presence in the Gulf region through permanently assigned ground forces, combined exercises, and "security assistance," which is really a euphemism for arms sales.[38] Even before this testimony, in 1989, CENTCOM's War Plan 1002 was revised and renamed War Plan 1002–90. In the new version, Iraq replaced the Soviet Union as the enemy.[39] The last two digits of the war plan, of course, stood for 1990. At Schwarzkopf's direction, CENTCOM began devising war games targeting Iraq.

In 1990 at least four war games directed at Iraq, some premised on an Iraqi invasion of Kuwait, were conducted before the invasion occurred. One of the first, a computer exercise called Internal Look, was held in January,[40] and by June, Schwarzkopf was conducting sophisticated war games pitting thousands of U.S. troops against armored divisions of the Republican Guard.[41]

In May 1990 the Center for Strategic and International Studies (CSIS), a Washington-based think tank, had completed a study begun two years earlier predicting the outcome of a war between the United States and Iraq. This study, according to the CSIS's Major James Blackwell (Retired), was widely circulated among Pentagon officials, members of Congress, and military contractors.[42] Thus, far from being a surprise, Iraq's invasion of Kuwait had actually been the scenario for intense U.S. planning.

One would think from all this planning that Iraq posed a grave threat. But Iraq was struggling to recover from eight years of war. Following the ceasefire with Iran, Saddam Hussein announced a $40 billion plan to peacefully rebuild his country. According to "Iraqi Power and U.S. Security in the Middle East," a study issued in early 1990 by the Strategic Studies Institute of the U.S. Army War College:

> Baghdad should not be expected to deliberately provoke military confrontations with anyone. Its interests are best served now and in the immediate future by peace. . . . Revenues from oil sales could

11

put it in the front ranks of nations economically. A stable Middle East is conducive to selling oil; disruption has a long-range adverse effect on the oil market which would hurt Iraq. . . . Force is only likely if the Iraqis feel seriously threatened.

. . . it is our belief that Iraq is basically committed to a nonaggressive strategy, and that it will, over the course of the next few years, considerably reduce the size of its military. Economic conditions practically mandate such action. . . . There seems no doubt that Iraq would like to demobilize now that the war has ended.[43]

It was not Iraq but powerful forces in the United States that wanted a new war in the Middle East: the Pentagon, to maintain its tremendous budget; the military-industrial complex, with its dependence on Middle East arms sales and domestic military contracts; the oil companies, which wanted more control over the price of crude oil and greater profits; and the Bush administration, which saw in the Soviet Union's disintegration its chance to establish a permanent military presence in the Middle East, securing the region and achieving vast geopolitical power into the next century through control of its oil resources.

The Pentagon's challenge was to figure out what would force Iraq, a country more interested in rebuilding than expansion, to take some action that would justify U.S. military intervention. In order to create such a crisis, the Pentagon invoked its special relationship with the Kuwaiti royal family.

KUWAIT AND THE ROAD TO WAR

The *New York Times* has described the emirate of Kuwait as "less a country than a family-owned oil company with a flag."[44] Kuwait was arbitrarily created as a national entity by the British Colonial Office after World War I to exert leverage against Iraq, which was abundantly rich in oil.

In 1918, a tidal wave of nationalist resistance to Great Britain's wartime seizure of Iraq erupted. Britain crushed the rebellions with the first systematic use of aerial bombardment in history. In 1932, facing constant rebellions, Britain gave Iraq nominal independence. But a British-appointed monarch sat on the Iraqi throne, and Iraq's oil fields were owned by the Iraq Petroleum Company, a consortium of British, U.S., and French companies. Furthermore, with a permanent British naval base and a British-selected royal family, Kuwait remained a British protectorate as insurance against Iraq challenging Western ownership of its oil reserves.

To create the country of Kuwait, Britain had separated out a desert area of Iraq around and including the town of Kuwait and the islands of Bubiyan and Warba, which dominated Iraq's access to the Persian Gulf. The borders between Kuwait, Iraq, and Saudi Arabia were drawn by Sir Percy Cox of the British Colonial Office in 1921 and 1923. This flew in the face of the fact that Iraq had historically controlled this coastal territory.

Kuwaitis who wanted to remain part of Iraq were suppressed by British forces. British diplomat Sir Anthony Parsons later acknowledged, "In the Iraqi subconscious, Kuwait is part of Basra province, and the bloody British took it away from them. We protected our strategic interests rather successfully, but in doing so we didn't worry too much about the people living there. We created a situation in which people felt they had been wronged."[45]

When huge oil fields were discovered in Kuwait in 1936, it was to mean big profits for Gulf Oil, which held the Kuwaiti concession. Production from those fields in later years would give the Western oil companies a powerful weapon in their struggle with the oil-producing countries, and finally became a major factor in causing Iraq to invade.

In the early 1950s, when the Mossadegh government in Iran nationalized the holdings of the Anglo-Iranian Oil Company (now British Petroleum), the Big Seven oil companies simply boycotted Iranian oil and opened up unused wells in Kuwait to replace Iranian production. The CIA took advantage of the resulting economic crisis in Iran to engineer Mossadegh's overthrow, and Iran was reopened to Western oil companies.

In 1960, when the Kassem government in Iraq helped organize the Organization of Petroleum Exporting Countries (OPEC) to resist unilateral price cuts by the oil cartels, the oil companies again increased Kuwaiti production and cut Iraq's oil exports. Iraq's economy was crippled and Kassem was overthrown three years later.

Time and again, Kuwait's royal family has acted within OPEC to benefit the oil companies, using their country's vast oil reserves to bludgeon poorer and more populous OPEC members into line when they tried to negotiate fairer prices from the oil companies. They have also recycled billions of dollars from oil sales into U.S. banks. In return, the al-Sabahs' throne is guaranteed by the U.S. military and the CIA.

After the Iran–Iraq War ended, Kuwait was used once again by the United States to embark on a campaign of what CSIS director Henry M. Schuler described as "economic warfare" against Iraq.[46] In his book *Secret Dossier: The Hidden Agenda Behind the Gulf War*, Pierre Salinger observed that Kuwait decided to drastically increase oil production on August 8, 1988, one day after Iran agreed to a ceasefire with Iraq.[47] Both Iran and Iraq desperately needed stable oil prices to finance postwar reconstruction. Kuwait's action, which violated OPEC agreements, sent oil prices into a tailspin. Crude oil prices fell from $21 to $11 a barrel, costing Iraq $14 billion a year, according to the *New York Times*.[48] The price cuts also wrought havoc on the economies of poorer oil-producing countries like Algeria and Nigeria. Then, in March 1989, Kuwait demanded a 50 percent increase in the OPEC quotas. This demand was rejected at the June 1989 OPEC meeting, but Kuwaiti oil minister Sheikh Ali al-Khalifa announced Kuwait would no longer be bound by any quota. Kuwait eventually doubled production to over 2 million barrels per day.[49]

"In particular," wrote Salinger, "[Kuwait] intended to extract more from the oil fields at Rumaila."[50] The Rumaila field, which lies on the disputed Iraq–Kuwait border, was a particular sore spot for Iraq. While Iraq was preoccupied with Iran, Kuwait had moved its border northward, seizing an additional 900 square miles of the Rumaila field. With the help of U.S.-supplied slant-drilling technology, Kuwait was also stealing oil from the part of Rumaila that was indisputably inside Iraq. Thus, at the height of the Iran–Iraq War, when Iraq's ability to export oil was reduced, Kuwait had prospered by selling Iraqi oil to Iraq's customers.

But that was not all. Iraq had incurred a tremendous debt during the Iran war. According to the U.S. Army War College report, "The Baathists argue that they should be allowed to invest in economic recovery and industrialization so that they can become productive again and pay off their debts. The banks want their money now."[51] Kuwait was chief among Iraq's creditors, having provided Iraq $30 billion during the war, mostly after Iran directly threatened Kuwait itself. Kuwait's rulers now demanded that Iraq pay them back. But the war had cost Iraq over $80 billion, and the falling price of oil — a result of Kuwait's own actions — made it impossible for Iraq to pay Kuwait.

From 1988 to 1990, Iraq tried to resolve its differences diplomatically — as the U.S. Army War College study had predicted it would. Time and again it was rebuffed. Kuwait maintained what all observers agreed was an attitude of arrogance and intransigence. The sheikdom's stance was well known in the Arab world. It didn't expect to be repaid, but refused to formally forgive the debt. A senior Bush administration official told *New York Newsday,* "Kuwait was overproducing, and when the Iraqis came and said, 'Can't you do something about it?' the Kuwaitis said, 'Sit on it.' And they didn't even say it nicely. They were nasty about it. They were stupid. They were arrogant. They were terrible."[52]

Kuwait's intransigence perplexed Jordan's King Hussein. The March 13, 1991, *San Francisco Chronicle* reported that he said:

> Over a long period of time — before the end of the war between Iraq and Iran — I had tried my very best to see what could be done. . . . He [Saddam Hussein] told me how anxious he was to ensure that the situation be resolved as soon as possible. So he initiated contact with the Kuwaitis . . . this didn't work from the beginning. There were meetings but nothing happened. . . . To my way of thinking, this was really puzzling. It was in the Kuwaitis' interest to solve the problem. I know how there wasn't a definite border, how there was a feeling that Kuwait was part of Iraq.[53]

Was it mere coincidence that Kuwait's rulers suddenly adopted a belligerent stance toward their bigger neighbor at the same time Pentagon war plans began targeting Iraq? Few Kuwaitis think so. Writing in *The New Yorker,* Middle East expert Milton Viorst quoted Ali al-Bedah, a Kuwaiti business owner and pro-democracy activist, who said, "I think if the Americans had not pushed, the royal family would have never taken the steps that it did to provoke Saddam."[54] Dr. Mussama al-Mubarak, a political science professor at Kuwait University, told Viorst: "I don't know what the government was thinking, but it adopted an extremely hard line, which makes me think that the decisions were not Kuwait's alone. It is my assumption that, as a matter of course, Kuwait would have consulted on such matters with Saudi Arabia and Britain, as well as the United States."[55]

Viorst also interviewed both U.S. and Kuwaiti officials. Kuwaiti Foreign Minister Sheikh Salem al-Sabah told him General Schwarzkopf was a regular visitor to Kuwait after the Iran–Iraq War. Sheikh al-Sabah told Viorst: "Schwarzkopf came here a few times and met with the Crown Prince and Minister of Defense. These became routine visits to discuss military cooperation, and by the time the crisis with Iraq began last year, we knew we could rely on the Americans."[56]

A U.S. official in Kuwait corroborated Sheikh al-Sabah's account: "Schwarzkopf was here on visits before the war, maybe a few times a year. He was a political general, and that was unusual in itself. He kept a personally high profile and was on a first-name basis with all the ministers in Kuwait."[57]

After Iraq occupied Kuwait in the summer of 1990, it submitted to UN Secretary-General Javier Perez de Cuellar a copy of a memo it said its soldiers had captured. Dated November 22, 1989, the memo recounted a meeting between Kuwaiti Brigadier Fahd Ahmed al-Fahd, the director general of Kuwait's Department of State Security, and Director William Webster of the CIA. The memo discussed CIA training for 128 bodyguards for Kuwaiti royalty, and intelligence exchanges about Iraq and Iran between the CIA and Kuwait. The memo also included the following point:

> We agreed with the American side that it was important to take advantage of the deteriorating economic situation in Iraq in order to put pressure on that country's government to delineate our common border. The Central Intelligence Agency gave us its view of appropriate means of pressure, saying that broad cooperation should be initiated between us, on condition that such activities are coordinated at a high level.[58]

The CIA has disputed the memo's authenticity, claiming Iraq was not discussed "at that meeting."[59] But many experts affirm that it is genuine. It is telling evidence, documenting the economic warfare waged against Iraq by Kuwait and the United States — warfare that the United States continues through sanctions long after the Iraqi army has been driven from Kuwait.

By 1990 the Iraqi economy was in worse condition than at the end of the war with Iran. Inflation was at 40 percent and the value of the dinar was plummeting. In a speech to an Arab League summit meeting in Amman in February, Saddam Hussein called for the U.S. fleet to withdraw from the Gulf. He said:

> [I]f the Gulf people, along with all Arabs, are not careful, the Arab Gulf region will be governed by the United States' will. If the Arabs are not alerted and the weakness persists, the situation could develop to the extent desired by the United States; that is, it would fix the amount of oil and gas produced in each country and sold to this or that country in the world. Prices would also be fixed in line with a special perspective benefiting U.S. interests and ignoring the interests of others.[60]

New production quotas were set at a March 1990 OPEC meeting, but Kuwait and the UAE refused to adhere to them and increased their production again.[61] At an Arab League summit in Baghdad in May, Saddam Hussein said that war is usually waged by "sending armies across frontiers, by acts of sabotage, by killing people and by supporting coups d'etat, but war can also be waged by economic means . . . and what is happening [Kuwait's oil policy] is war against Iraq."[62]

In June, Iraq sent envoys to several Arab states with appeals for new quotas that would allow a slight rise in the price of crude. Kuwait refused, and also rejected an Iraqi proposal for a summit of the leaders of Iraq, Kuwait, Saudi Arabia, and the UAE.

Finally, on July 10, a meeting of the oil ministers of these states was held, and quotas that would allow a gradual increase in prices were set. But the next day, after meeting with the Emir, Kuwait's oil minister announced that Kuwait would increase its production substantially by October.

On July 17, Saddam Hussein publicly accused Kuwait and the United States of conspiring to destroy Iraq's economy. He said: "If words fail to protect Iraqis, something effective must be done to return things to their natural course and to return usurped rights to their owners. . . . O God Almighty, be witness that we have warned them."[63] The next day, Iraqi troops began massing on the Kuwaiti border.

Thus, Iraq had made known the seriousness with which it viewed the economic warfare being waged against it. President Bush's August 8 statement that Iraq had invaded Kuwait with neither warning nor provocation was sheer deceit.

Despite Saddam Hussein's warning, Kuwait seemed amazingly unconcerned. Finally, at the repeated urging of King Hussein and Saudi Arabia's King Fahd, the Emir agreed to attend a mini-summit on July 31, in Jidda, Saudi Arabia.[64]

Customarily, Arab nations work out agreements prior to such formal meetings. King Fahd privately assured Saddam Hussein that Kuwait had agreed to compromise in Jidda. Dr. Michael Emery, journalism professor at California State University at Northridge, obtained a copy of the official invitation to the Jidda meeting King Fahd sent to the Emir. Translated from Arabic, it reads in part:

> I would like to refer to the brotherly communications that took place with your Excellence and President Saddam Hussein of Iraq and what you agreed upon regarding the meeting of his excellency Sheikh Saad al-Abdullah al-Sabah and Mr. Izzat Ibrahim in your second country the Kingdom of Saudi Arabia. I have full confidence in your judgment and wisdom in fulfilling all that we are looking for

17

and what your Arab brothers are looking for in overcoming all of the obstacles and confirming the love and friendship between the two brotherly countries.[65]

The Emir wrote a note across the top of the invitation to his Prime Minister, whom he sent in his stead after initially agreeing to attend personally. It included the following:

> We will attend the meeting according to the conditions we agreed upon. What is important to us is our national interest. Do not listen to anything you hear from the Saudis and Iraqis on brotherhood and Arab solidarity. Each of them has his own interest.
>
> The Saudis want to weaken us and exploit our concessions to the Iraqis, so that we will concede to them [the Saudis] in the future the divided [Neutral] zone. The Iraqis want to compensate their war expenditures from our accounts. Neither this nor that should happen. This is also the opinion of our friends in Egypt, Washington, and London.
>
> Be unwavering in your discussions. We are stronger than they think.[66]

Emery has conducted several signature and handwriting checks on the note and even showed it to King Hussein, who made inquiries about the note's origins. He believes it to be authentic.

The Emir's note implies that foreign backing precluded any need to negotiate. This consistent attitude on the part of Kuwait's ruling al-Sabah family was made crystal clear to a Jordanian delegation headed by King Hussein, which went to Kuwait on July 30 to counsel compromise at Jidda. Although by that time Iraqi troops had massed on Kuwait's border, the Jordanians found the Kuwaitis unconcerned and arrogant. When Sheikh Sabah was urged to take Iraq more seriously, he told the Jordanian delegation: "We are not going to respond to [Iraq]. . . . If they don't like it, let them occupy our territory . . . we are going to bring in the Americans." Observers at the meeting reported that Sheikh Sabah apparently realized he had let something slip. He hastily added, "Well, you know what is embarrassing about this . . . what is embarrassing is the Israeli–American dimension."[67]

The Emir's note and his discussion with the Jordanians directly contradict stated U.S. policy at that time. John Kelly, Assistant Secretary of State for Near East and South Asian Affairs, testified before Congress on July 31, 1990, proclaiming U.S. neutrality in "Arab–Arab" conflicts. The note and discussion also reveal United States obstruction of peaceful solutions to Iraq–Kuwait differences.

Palestine Liberation Organization (PLO) President Yasir Arafat told media representatives that at the Arab League summit held on August 9–10, 1990, Kuwait rejected his pleas for a negotiated solution to the Gulf crisis. "They said that, in a matter of days, 'the Americans will solve the problem,' " Arafat reported.[68]

What was happening in July 1990 was quite clear to Arabs, though Americans remained uninformed. On July 20, in an editorial typical of many in the Arab media that month, columnist Mu'nis al-Razzaz said on Radio Jordan:

> From my position as an Arab citizen, and in the name of Arab dignity, I ask Kuwait to denounce the U.S. position supporting it against Iraq because Iraq is a fraternal Arab country. . . . We hope that Kuwait will take a decisive position on the U.S. administration's support for it against a fraternal Arab country. . . . [We] are certain that the brothers in Kuwait will reject the insulting U.S. statements that the United States will defend its friends in the region. . . . This U.S. logic, which Kuwait did not request, will reinforce the U.S. military presence in the Gulf — a presence that is rejected by all the Arab masses.[69]

ISOLATING IRAQ

Not only did the U.S. encourage Kuwait's economic war against Iraq, it engaged in efforts of its own to isolate and economically imperil Iraq. As soon as the Iran–Iraq War ended, the U.S. began a propaganda war against Saddam Hussein and, along with other Western countries, a de facto sanctions campaign. This was evident throughout the Arab world. On February 14, 1991, Algerian Foreign Minister Sid Ahmed Ghozali observed over the radio that Iraq had been under escalating attack for two years.[70]

The ceasefire between Iraq and Iran officially took effect on August 20, 1988. Almost immediately, Iraq's standing in the Western world began to change. On September 8, Washington announced to the world that Iraq had used poison gas against the Kurds. Washington's outrage, however, was a bit delayed; the worst incident, alleged to have occurred six months earlier at Halabja in March 1988, received no U.S. condemnation at the time. Even the Iraqi Kurds' hunger strike held at the UN to protest the incident went unnoticed by Western governments and media.

But in September, the day Iraqi Foreign Minister Sa'dun Hammadi was scheduled to meet with Secretary of State George Schultz,

U.S. State Department spokesperson Charles Redman called a press conference. Without providing evidence, Redman charged, "The U.S. government is convinced that Iraq has used chemical weapons in its military campaign against Kurdish guerrillas. We don't know the extent to which chemical weapons have been used, but any use in this context is abhorrent and unjustifiable."[71]

This was a strange way to greet the foreign minister of a country the United States had just sided with in war. When Hammadi reached the State Department two hours later, he was met with a barrage of questions from reporters about the accusation. Clearly surprised, Hammadi was unable to respond. Within 24 hours of Redman's news conference, the Senate voted unanimously to impose economic sanctions that would cancel technology and food sales to Iraq. Though the bill never became law, it was both a threat and a humiliation that could only be seen in Iraq as hypocritical.

The State Department's attack on Iraq was the beginning of nearly two years of anti-Iraq propaganda. The propaganda intensified in early 1990, concentrating on Iraqi production of illegal weapons. The Western media seized on Saddam Hussein's April 2 statement that Iraq's chemical weapons would "eat up half of Israel" if Israel attacked Iraq. The propaganda covered up two important facts about Hussein's speech. First, it was Israel, financed by the United States, that introduced chemical and nuclear weapons into the region. And second, Saddam Hussein's speech had included his proposal for a nuclear, chemical, and biological weapons-free zone in the Middle East. Iraq, of course, had some reason to feel threatened by Israel, since in 1981 Israel had bombed Iraq's nuclear power complex and in the spring of 1990 had threatened to attack again.

On April 11, British agents heightened public concern by seizing eight steel tubes being exported to Iraq. Although they were listed as petroleum pipes, Britain charged they were actually parts to an Iraqi "supergun." The seized goods were "dual-use" items, of the kind Western governments had been knowingly and illegally shipping to Iraq for years. British officials acted as if export controls had broken down, and the media jumped at the chance to portray Iraq as a military menace. Later, when the BBC *Panorama* series was due to expose the British government's complicity in providing Iraq with the parts, the show was "postponed" indefinitely.[72]

At the very same time propaganda about Iraq's military abuses was carried in the international media, the U.S. Department of Commerce was approving shipments of billions of dollars worth of similar dual-use equipment to Iraq. This must have suggested to Iraq that the U.S. government supported the development of its military.

The Commerce Department altered its records to conceal its acts from Congress and the public.[73]

Western propaganda in the period after the Iran–Iraq War was so obviously false and provocative that the Arab League Council issued a statement on April 5, 1990, saying that it "viewed with extreme concern the political statements and the unjust, hostile and tendentious media campaign against Iraq."[74]

Along with propaganda, Western countries started to institute de facto sanctions against Iraq. Not UN-approved, they nevertheless combined with Kuwait's economic warfare to worsen Iraq's economy. In his meeting with U.S. Ambassador April Glaspie on July 25, 1990, Saddam Hussein referred to these sanctions: "There is nothing left to buy from America except wheat. Every time we want to buy something, they say it is forbidden. I am afraid that one day you will say, 'You are going to make gunpowder out of wheat.' "[75]

Iraqi Deputy Prime Minister Ramadan told the Muhammad Ali peace delegation in November 1990 that hundreds of scientific, engineering, and food supply contracts between Iraq and Western governments had been canceled in the preceding two years. Cuba's UN Ambassador Ricardo Alarcon referred to this isolation in his August 6, 1990 speech before the Security Council. Explaining why he opposed the resolution calling for worldwide sanctions against Iraq, he explained: "We are asked to approve specific sanctions that have already been imposed unilaterally by the principal developed powers of the world."[76]

The United States sent confusing signals to Iraq in the first seven months of 1990. The United States gave private signals of a desire for better relations with Iraq despite the hostile propaganda and economic embargo, and even though War Plan 1002–90 still designated Iraq as the principal threat in the Persian Gulf. General Schwarzkopf told the Senate in February 1990 that "Iraq has the capability to militarily coerce its neighboring states. . . . We in Central Command consider our most dangerous scenario to be the spillover of some local conflict leading to a regional war."[77] Yet on February 13, Assistant Secretary of State John Kelly told Saddam Hussein in Baghdad that he was "a force for moderation" and that the United States wanted better relations with Iraq.[78]

In early April, Kelly helped draft proposals for sanctions against Iraq for Congress. But on April 12, a delegation of U.S. Senators headed by minority leader Robert Dole, while visiting Iraq, sought to reassure Saddam Hussein about a Congressional sanctions bill. "I assume Bush will object to the sanctions. He may veto them unless something provocative occurs." When Hussein complained about

21

the virulent propaganda waged against him in the Western press, Senator Alan Simpson assured him Bush was not behind it, calling reporters "spoiled and conceited."[79]

After the Gulf War, when euphoria from the U.S. military victory subsided and the public slowly learned of the death and destruction rained on Iraq, it became more important than ever to explain away evidence that Iraq was provoked into invading Kuwait. Since that time, efforts have been made, including the selective release of documents, to explain these prewar incidents as Bush's misguided attempts to maintain a working relationship with Iraq after the Iran war. Typical of such explanations was *New York Times* columnist Leslie Gelb's op-ed piece of May 4, 1992. Titled "Bush's Iraqi Blunder," it stated that the "Bush team . . . believed they had to work with [Hussein] because Iraq had become the dominant power in the region. And they thought they could tame him with aid and diplomatic stroking — because he was a 'realist' with whom fellow realists could do business."[80]

This analysis ignores acts by the Bush administration that completely contradict the conclusion it draws. Gelb protrays the Bush administration as determined to sell weapons to Iraq — to the point of pressuring Export-Import Bank presidents for unwise loan approvals and consistently violating export controls — with no apparent motivation other than Bush "thought he could work with Saddam Hussein." Washington supposedly accepted assurances from Saudi Arabia's King Fahd, Jordan's King Hussein, and Egypt's President Hosni Mubarak that Iraqi threats against Kuwait were bluster.

These portrayals leave out crucial facts: that the entire military planning strategy beginning in 1988 had identified Iraq as the central threat to the Gulf region; that having done so, the United States assured Iraq it considered its disputes with Kuwait a regional matter; and that while overtly conciliatory, the United States was working with other Western countries and Kuwait to undermine Iraq through propaganda and economic pressure.

While the idea that Bush blundered in his dealings with Iraq may create domestic political problems for him, it is better for him than that the truth about American dealings with Iraq come out, which is that the United States had sought a justification for intervention in the region to control its resources since the 1970s. The United States was manipulating Iraq into action that would enable the United States to intervene by simultaneously painting Saddam Hussein as a monster and subtly coaxing him into the invasion of Kuwait. This had to be the real purpose for the seemingly conciliatory tone and the remarkable assurances of Assistant Secretary Kelly and Ambassador Glaspie. If the United States was truly interested in "doing business" with Iraq, it would not have acted to economically weaken it. "Doing business" with Iraq was also not facilitated by portraying it as a menace after several years of cooperation.

What was facilitated was military intervention, for which plans were well under way. British columnist John Pilger reported in the *New Statesman* that in May 1990 the National Security Council presented a white paper to President Bush describing Iraq and Saddam Hussein as "the optimum contenders to replace the Warsaw Pact" as the rationale for continued Cold War-level military spending.[81]

POSITIONING FOR WAR

On July 24, 1990, the Pentagon announced that six U.S. warships were beginning "short-notice" maneuvers — Schwarzkopf's "combined exercises" — with UAE forces in the southern Gulf. The July 25 *Wall Street Journal* reported that the move was directly related to the tensions between Iraq and Kuwait.[82] The *Journal* article was one of the few reports in this country that contradicted Bush administration statements that it was not concerned about Iraq. Nothing more would be written until after August 2.

On July 25 — the day after the United States announced Gulf exercises with the UAE, while Iraqi troops were massing on the Kuwaiti border, and as General Schwarzkopf readied CENTCOM for war against Iraq — Saddam Hussein summoned Ambassador Glaspie to his office in what seems to have been a final attempt to clarify Washington's position on his dispute with Kuwait. Glaspie assured him: "We have no opinion on Arab–Arab conflicts, like your border disagreement with Kuwait. . . . [Secretary of State] James Baker has directed our official spokesmen to emphasize this instruction."[83] She was expressing official policy. On July 24, she had received a cable from the State Department explicitly directing her to reiterate that the United States had "no position" on "Arab–Arab" conflicts.[84]

After the war, on March 21, 1991, Glaspie denied this version of her meeting with Hussein. She testified to the Senate Foreign Relations Committee that she had repeatedly warned Hussein that the United States would not tolerate Iraq's use of violence to settle the dispute with Kuwait. She said Hussein must have been too "stupid" to understand how the United States would react.[85]

But in July 1991, Glaspie's cables to the State Department describing the meeting were finally released to the Senate. The cables showed that her Senate testimony was largely fabricated, and that the version released by Iraq was accurate.[86] On July 12, 1991, Committee Chairman Senator Claiborne Pell wrote an angry letter to Secretary of State James Baker demanding an explanation for the inconsistencies between Glaspie's testimony and the cable. Senator Alan Cranston charged that Glaspie had deliberately misled Congress about her role in the Gulf War.

On July 31, the Defense Intelligence Agency (DIA) detected Iraqi forces moving fuel, water, ammunition, and other logistical support from the rear to frontline Iraqi military units stationed on Kuwait's border.[87] That same day, Assistant Secretary of State Kelly gave the last misleading signal in a House subcommittee hearing. He was questioned by Representative Lee Hamilton. The exchange went as follows:

> *Hamilton:* Do we have a commitment to our friends in the Gulf in the event that they are engaged in oil or territorial disputes with their neighbors?
>
> *Kelly:* As I said, Mr. Chairman, we have no defense treaty relationships with any of the countries. We have historically avoided taking a position on border disputes or on internal OPEC deliberations, but we certainly, as have all administrations, resoundingly called for the peaceful settlement of disputes and differences in the area.
>
> *Hamilton:* If Iraq, for example, charged across the border into Kuwait, for whatever reason, what would be our position with regard to the use of U.S. forces?
>
> *Kelly:* That, Mr. Chairman, is a hypothetical or a contingency, the kind of which I can't get into. Suffice it to say, we would be extremely concerned, but I cannot get into the realm of "what if" answers.
>
> *Hamilton:* In that circumstance, is it correct to say, however, that we do not have a treaty commitment which would obligate us to engage U.S. forces?
>
> *Kelly:* That is correct.[88]

On August 2, 1990, Iraq, apparently believing it had U.S. assurances it would not intervene, invaded Kuwait. The United States moved immediately to condemn Iraq at the UN.

One of Washington's first steps in the region after the Iraqi invasion was to pressure Egypt into introducing a resolution condemning

Iraq at the Arab League summit in Cairo on August 2–3 — an act U.S. officials knew would make an Iraqi withdrawal from Kuwait more difficult.

The day of the invasion, Jordan's King Hussein, hoping to forge an Arab solution to the crisis, spoke to Saddam Hussein, who said he was willing to withdraw. However, he said he would be less willing if Iraq were condemned by the Arab League.

The king flew to Alexandria, where he obtained a promise from Egyptian President Hosni Mubarak that his foreign ministers in Cairo would not condemn Iraq. While King Hussein was with Mubarak, President Bush by telephone gave him 48 hours to reach a negotiated solution. The king left Egypt carrying with him an invitation to another Jidda conference, a last-ditch negotiation effort with Kuwait and Saudi Arabia, set for August 5. He presented it to Saddam Hussein at a meeting in Baghdad on August 3.

Saddam Hussein told King Hussein he would attend the Jidda conference. More significant, he also said he would begin withdrawing troops on August 5 if negotiations that day proved fruitful — unless, he cautioned, any of the Arab states issued a condemnation of Iraq. Journalist Pierre Salinger reports that he warned, "If things move in that direction, I'll just say that Kuwait is a part of Iraq and annex it." [89]

Apparently, on August 3 Saddam Hussein was willing to pull out of Kuwait if no condemnation occurred. At the very least, his own words provided a high opportunity for an Arab solution to the crisis.

King Hussein flew back to Amman confident a solution could be arranged, since Mubarak had promised Egypt would not condemn Iraq. That day, Saddam Hussein sent a communique stating he would begin withdrawing Iraqi troops from Kuwait on August 5, two days later. Bush's response to the communique was, "Let's see him haul them out right now, then." [90] But upon arriving in Jordan, King Hussein learned that Egypt had introduced a resolution, adopted by the Arab League, to condemn the invasion of Kuwait. [91]

Egypt, it turned out, was under immense pressure from the United States. According to Salinger, on August 3 Assistant Secretary of State Kelly sent a message to the Egyptian Foreign Ministry:

> The West has done its duty, but the Arab nations are doing nothing. The United States has sold a lot of arms to Arab countries, especially Egypt. If they do not act, if they do not take a firm stand on the Kuwait affair, they can be sure that in the future they will no longer be able to count on America. [92]

Because Bush had given King Hussein two days to achieve a settlement, the Kelly message reveals that President Bush never intended to let him succeed. King Hussein told Dr. Emery he later learned Mubarak had been pressured to pass the condemnation by 5:00 P.M. New York time on August 3 to coincide with the second U.S.-drafted Security Council resolution, this one calling for an economic boycott of Iraq.[93] The Security Council received the text for this resolution, Number 661, at 5:48 P.M. by fax from the U.S. mission.[94] It was only one day after Iraq's occupation of Kuwait.

Cuban UN Ambassador Alarcon, who voted for the first Security Council Resolution condemning Iraq's invasion of Kuwait, told the Security Council on August 6 how the United States used Hussein's decision not to withdraw on August 5 as he had originally planned:

> An attempt is now being made to justify the actions [the sanctions resolution] proposed on the grounds that Iraq has failed to carry out the withdrawal of its forces from Kuwaiti territory or by interpreting various statements made in Baghdad on Sunday [August 5] or what has been said here by the permanent representative of Iraq. But that is not the truth. The plan to impose sanctions on Iraq actually existed before we entered this new phase of Security Council deliberations, at a time when no one even knew about the statement made by the Iraqi government, also on August 3, to the effect that it was going to withdraw its troops from Kuwait.[95]

Thus, the United States manipulated Egypt to get the Arab League to condemn the Iraqi invasion, which resulted in Iraq reversing its willingness to withdraw. Then, Washington used Iraq's refusal to withdraw as a justification to impose sanctions.

The government of Jordan later received a threatening letter similar to the one Egypt received. Signed by President Bush, it read, "It is in Jordan's essential interests that it not be neutral in the struggle between Iraq and the great majority of the Arab states." Asked by Emery how he interpreted this letter, an aide to King Hussein said, "Bullying, intimidating, chauvinistic, and completely unacceptable."[96]

At the August 9–10 Cairo summit, Egypt led the effort for another condemnation of the invasion, and invited Western forces to the Gulf. Many Arab observers, as well as Western journalists who read Arabic, reported that the text of the final communique read awkwardly, as if it had been translated into Arabic from English.[97] A regional agreement among Arab nations was the greatest initial threat to U.S. war plans. By pressuring Egypt and others, and with the vigorous support of the Kuwaiti royal family, the United States successfully frustrated early chances for peace.

The United States moved immediately on the military front, as well. Its first need was to persuade Saudi Arabia to accept troops on its soil. Washington claimed Saddam Hussein was massing thousands of troops on the Saudi border, and that Saudi Arabia had requested a U.S. military presence. But the truth is that Saudi Arabia acceded to U.S. demands to deploy troops there, which it had at first opposed, only after intense U.S. pressure. On August 3, four days before the first U.S. troop deployment was announced, Defense Secretary Dick Cheney and Joint Chiefs Chairman General Colin Powell met with the Saudi ambassador to the United States, Prince Bandar bin Sultan. Bandar was more pro-Western than most in the Saud family, and had been involved in various covert U.S. schemes, including the Iran–Contra scandal.

In making their case to the prince, Cheney and Powell relied heavily on satellite photos they claimed showed Iraqi troops massing on the Saudi border. Bandar then used the photos to win the Saud family's agreement to meet with a U.S. delegation.[98]

On January 28, 1991, *Newsweek* reported what happened on August 4, the day after Cheney and Powell met with Bandar:

> In the middle of the session, the war council got a jolt: "a very authoritative report" from a friendly head of state that the Saudis had decided to reject American troops. The signal contradicted those that Bandar had sent the day before. The president rose, left the room and placed a call to King Fahd. He didn't mention [to Fahd] the tip he had just received. Instead, he told the king he was firmly committed to defending Saudi Arabia, that he didn't want any permanent military bases, that he would withdraw all American troops whenever the king thought the right time had come. . . . He advised the king not even to ask for troops if all he wanted was a token force. The call seemed to help, though the king remained shaky. Bush returned to the meeting and said that the Saudis still seemed willing to accept troops.[99]

On August 5, Cheney, Powell, then-National Security Agency Deputy Director Robert Gates, Defense Department aide Paul Wolfowitz, and General Schwarzkopf flew to Saudi Arabia to intensify the pressure.

Until then, Saudi diplomats did not believe there was any evidence of an imminent Iraqi invasion. Bob Woodward wrote in his book *The Commanders* that before the Cheney delegation arrived, King Fahd sent a team across the Kuwaiti border to look for the Iraqi troops. The team came back empty-handed. "There was no trace of Iraqi troops heading toward the kingdom," Woodward wrote. Fahd was therefore skeptical about the need for a U.S. deployment.[100]

Saudi Arabia initially wanted only air defense and a verbal commitment from the United States that it would defend Saudi Arabia if necessary—not the 100,000 troops the United States wanted to land. But the August 5 Cheney mission proved successful. On August 6, worn down after four days of intense pressure from Washington, King Fahd agreed, in essence, to let the United States use Saudi Arabia as a staging ground for an assault against Iraq. But he asked President Bush to declare in any public announcement that the Saudis had requested U.S. troops to defend their borders.[101]

On August 7, White House Press Secretary Marlin Fitzwater said, "We believe that there is a very imminent threat to Saudi Arabia from the way that they [Iraqi troops] are positioned and located in Kuwait."[102] In a nationally televised speech on August 8, Bush said, "After consulting with King Fahd, I sent Secretary of Defense Dick Cheney to discuss cooperative measures we could take. Following those meetings, the Saudi government requested our help." [103]

A little over a month later, on September 11, Bush would tell Congress 120,000 Iraqi troops with 850 tanks had "poured into Kuwait and moved south to threaten Saudi Arabia" by August 5.[104] But according to the January 20, 1992 *U.S. News & World Report*, the same week Cheney was steamrolling the Saudis into letting U.S. troops land, a U.S. intelligence officer reported from Kuwait that Republican Guard troops were actually withdrawing from southern Kuwait back into Iraq. *U.S. News'* book on the war, *Triumph Without Victory*, quoted a CENTCOM commander who said, "We still have no hard evidence that [Hussein] ever intended to invade Saudi Arabia."[105]

Florida's *St. Petersburg Times* reported on January 6, 1991 that Soviet commercial satellite photos showed there were no Iraqi troops on the Saudi border by August 8, when Bush announced the U.S. deployment. The *Times* employed two defense intelligence experts to review the satellite shots, which included photos taken on September 11 and September 13, when the Defense Department was estimating 250,000 Iraqi troops and 1,500 tanks in Kuwait. One expert was Peter Zimmerman, a George Washington University professor who served at the U.S. Arms Control and Disarmament Agency under Reagan. The other was a former satellite photo specialist for the DIA.

The analysts said the photographic evidence did not support U.S. statements. The August 8 photos show light sand drifts over roads leading from Kuwait City to the Saudi border. Zimmerman said, "It certainly indicates that nobody's been driving over them and that the [Iraqi] military hasn't bothered to clear them for traffic." The drifts on the September photos were larger and deeper, having built up naturally without the disturbance of traffic for a month. While at that point the presence of the 100,000 U.S. troops in Saudi Arabia was obvious, Zimmerman said:

> [W]e don't see anything to indicate an Iraqi force in Kuwait of even 20 percent the size the administration claimed. . . . We didn't find anything of that sort. We don't see any tent cities, we don't see congregations of tanks, we can't see troop concentrations, and the main Kuwaiti airbase appears deserted. It's five weeks after the invasion, and from what we can see, the Iraqi air force hasn't flown a single fighter to the most strategic air base in Kuwait. There is no infrastructure to support large numbers of people. They have to use toilets . . . they have to have food . . . but where is it?[106]

Similarly, the former DIA specialist said: "I simply didn't see what I expected to see. There should be revetments—three-sided berms with vehicles inside, facing the anticipated direction of attack. But they aren't there."[107]

The satellite photos were a very big news story. They showed that the U.S. government lied to justify placing 540,000 troops in Saudi Arabia to attack Iraq. However, the major media almost unanimously refused to cover the story. The only national press mention was a small piece on December 3 in *Newsweek*, noting that ABC had originally shown the satellite photos to the same experts in November, but found them "so bewildering it won't air them."[108] The editors of the *St. Petersburg Times* approached the Scripps-Howard news service and the Associated Press—twice—with the story. Neither was interested.[109]

THE DEMONIZATION OF SADDAM HUSSEIN

Aided by the press, the United States sought to demonize Saddam Hussein in order to sell the war to the U.S. public. After several years of close diplomatic, economic, and military cooperation between Baghdad and Washington during the Iran–Iraq War, Saddam Hussein was suddenly a tyrant "worse than Hitler."

Along with personal abuse emerged other public relations hooks. Oil was an early one. Bush said on September 11: "[W]e cannot permit a resource so vital to be dominated by one so ruthless. And we won't."[110] Still, a significant segment of the United States remained unconvinced. The *New York Times* reported a new approach on November 14, 1990:

> Mr. Baker . . . is said to have grown exasperated with White House speech writers' inability to present the President's Gulf policy in a simple, coherent and compelling fashion so that it will have the sustained support of the American public.
>
> Since the start of the Gulf crisis in August, the President's justifications for sending troops have included everything from "vital interests" being at stake, to the principle that aggression should not be allowed to pay, to President Saddam Hussein of Iraq being worse than Hitler.
>
> Beginning last Friday in Moscow, Mr. Baker first began to say that what was at stake in the Gulf was the "pocketbook" and "standard of living" of every American.
>
> It has become apparent to Administration officials that the eroding support for the administration's Gulf policy, if not stemmed, is going to nullify its entire Gulf strategy.[111]

Thus, Baker introduced a new fear: the loss of jobs. "To bring it down to the level of the average American citizen," Baker said, "let me say that means jobs. Because an economic recession worldwide, caused by the control of one nation — one dictator, if you will — of the West's economic lifeline [oil], will result in the loss of jobs for American citizens."[112] In one stroke, Baker had blamed Saddam Hussein not only for the U.S. buildup in the Gulf, but also for the worsening American recession, which only deepened after the war.

When in the fall of 1990 a *New York Times*/CBS opinion poll showed that 54 percent of respondents believed preventing Iraq from acquiring nuclear weapons would justify military action, Bush found his most effective, if most spurious, argument. It was now incumbent upon the United States to destroy Hussein's weapons of mass destruction. "Every day that passes," he told troops at Thanksgiving, "brings Saddam one step closer to realizing his goal of a nuclear weapons arsenal. And that's why, more and more, your mission is marked by a real sense of urgency. . . . He has never possessed a weapon he didn't use."[113]

Bush exaggerated both Iraq's nuclear capability and its military prowess. It was widely reported that Iraq was close to producing nuclear weapons, but the country lacked — among other things — the essential supply of plutonium. In April 1992, nuclear weapons experts reviewing a years' worth of inspection and analyses by the International Atomic Energy Agency decided Iraq had been at least three years away from developing a single atomic bomb. In any case, the claim was a hypocritical ruse.

Seymour Hersh reports in his book *The Samson Option* that Israel had hundreds of nuclear warheads, and sophisticated rocketry for their delivery.[114] The danger of Israel using nuclear weapons against its neighbors is a great concern in the Arab world, much as Pakistan worries about India's nuclear arms. Israel works vigorously to prevent the Arabs from developing such weapons. But the UN has never felt compelled to send nuclear inspection teams to Israel, India, Pakistan, or other countries believed to have violated the Nuclear Non-Proliferation Treaty.

And what of Iraq's "million-man army"? Of course, Iraq's army had grown during the Iran–Iraq War. The Baathists pressed hard for recruits and conducted a massive conscription program in 1986. The Republican Guard, formerly restricted to residents of Tikrit, Hussein's hometown, was opened to conscripts from anywhere in Iraq. Men were literally drafted off the street.

However, the image of a battle-tested force dedicated to overrunning the Gulf region was illusory. The bulk of the Iraqi troops were draftees, ranging in age from 16 to 42, and with no deep-felt loyalty to the military. The percentage of its armed forces that were well trained and equipped was very low.[115] Despite the hype about Iraq's army, military and intelligence experts put Iraq's real troop strength at only 300,000.[116] No military experts in the West believed it was a first-rate military force.

The most emotionally explosive lie told during this time was the "incubator story." Testifying to the Congressional Human Rights Caucus on October 10, 1990, a 15-year-old girl introduced only as "Nayirah" claimed that she had witnessed Iraqi soldiers taking babies from incubators and "leaving them on the cold floor to die."[117] This story was quickly used by the Bush administration for its push toward war. Bush repeated it in numerous speeches, claiming 312 babies had died this way. Amnesty International reported the story as truth in a December 19, 1990 report.

The story has been thoroughly discredited since the end of the conflict. It was later revealed that witnesses who spoke before the Security Council and the Congress did so under false names and identities. A "Mr. Issah Ibrahim, the surgeon," was really Ibraheem Behbehani, an orthodontist.[118] Nayirah, the 15-year-old who testified that she was volunteering at the hospital when the atrocities al-

31

THE FIRE THIS TIME

legedly occurred, turned out to be the daughter of the Kuwaiti ambassador to the United States, a fact known by organizers of the October 10 hearing.[119]

Amnesty International retracted its support for the story in April 1991. In February 1992, Middle East Watch issued a report stating that the story was "clearly wartime propaganda," as were other stories of mass rape and torture by Iraqis.[120]

WASHINGTON'S "NO NEGOTIATIONS" STANCE

From the beginning of the crisis, President Bush argued that any negotiation with Saddam Hussein would be a "reward for aggression." This posture was more than ironic, taken as it was less than a year after the U.S. invasion of Panama, where thousands of civilians had been killed.

The United States torpedoed early Arab efforts to negotiate a settlement among Arab nations. Yet Iraq continued to seek a negotiated solution. On August 12, 1990, Iraq proposed talks linking withdrawal from Kuwait to comprehensive discussions of Israel's occupation of Palestinian territories and other problems in the region. The proposal included canceling the sanctions and replacing U.S. forces in the Gulf with Arab forces under UN direction. It was ridiculed and loudly denounced by the Bush administration.

When Iraq made another modified proposal to Washington in mid-August, it barely received media notice. This new plan, which did not mention linkage, proposed an Iraqi pullout from Kuwait and release of all Americans and Europeans who were not permitted to leave Iraq. In return, Iraq wanted the lifting of UN sanctions, guaranteed access to the Persian Gulf, and control of the Rumaila oil field.

The State Department denied the proposal was made — an embarrassing lie since the White House simultaneously acknowledged the proposal. The September 10, 1990 issue of *Newsweek* reported that

> *Newsday* . . . said "a former high-ranking U.S. official" had delivered an Iraqi peace plan to Brent Scowcroft, Bush's national-security adviser. . . . The State Department "categorically" denied the story, which made the vacationing Secretary of State James Baker look out of touch when White House officials confirmed that the offer had indeed been brought to Scowcroft by an old friend.

"The proposal," the article continued, "was quickly rejected as a complete nonstarter."[121]

Not everyone thought so. A Congressional summary of Iraq's proposal, prepared in January 1991 by a Democratic staff member for intelligence oversight, argued that serious U.S. consideration of the proposal could have avoided war. The summary stated: "The Iraqis apparently believed that having invaded Kuwait, they would get everyone's attention, negotiate improvements to their economic situation, and pull out. . . . [A] diplomatic solution satisfactory to the interests of the United States may well have been possible since the earliest days of the invasion."[122]

But the Bush administration did not want a negotiated solution. It was preparing for war. Washington quickly moved to quash any signs that agreement could be reached. On August 22, the day after Tariq Aziz again said Iraq was willing to negotiate, Saudi Arabia strongly implied interest in a territorial compromise. Saudi Defense Minister Prince Sultan said the disputed Warba and Bubiyan islands could be part of a negotiated pullout from Kuwait: "Saudi Arabia has said, and says now, that giving rights, including territorial brotherly concessions — given willingly — is a matter of pride for the Arab nation."[123]

The United States responded by getting Saudi Ambassador Bandar to pressure his government to retract the statement. "Bandar reported back to us that the Prince claims he was misquoted," a White House official said after the call. Kuwait and the U.S. then reaffirmed their demand for unconditional Iraqi withdrawal.[124]

After this further rebuff, Iraq continued to try to negotiate. On November 14, Saddam Hussein said in an interview with ABC News in Baghdad that he wanted talks, even hinting that Iraq might eventually leave Kuwait. Two weeks earlier, Soviet envoy Yevgeny Primakov had also reported Iraq wanted talks, noting after his second meeting with Hussein that the Iraqi leader was no longer discussing Kuwait as part of Iraq.

"We are ready to talk to the parties concerned," Hussein had told ABC.[125] He repeatedly emphasized his desire to resolve differences with the United States and Arab countries. His appeals went unanswered.

Instead, many of his efforts were ridiculed. On August 28, Saddam Hussein suggested televised debates between President Bush; U.K. Prime Minister Margaret Thatcher, a chief protagonist; and himself. The state department called the proposal "sick." The United Kingdom called it "pure gimmickry." [126]

On November 18, after I had urged him to permit and assist all foreigners who wanted to leave to do so, Saddam Hussein said he was willing to let all the remaining European and U.S. citizens depart over a three-month period, as long as the United States did not start a war. Washington rejected this as "further cynical manipulation."[127] When Hussein did authorize 14 U.S. and 32 British hostages to leave and announced he would release 330 French nationals, he saw it as a humanitarian gesture. The United States called it "barbaric," accusing Hussein of running a "hostage bazaar."[128] While some hundreds of Westerners were denied the right to leave for a period of months, they were not confined. I spent several hours late one November evening with about 15 U.S. nationals, all men, who were living comfortably in the U.S. Ambassadors' residence. They were free to move around Baghdad, and two drove me back to the Al-Rashid Hotel after midnight. We were not even followed. While all said they wanted to leave, most deferred to others when I said I was sure several would be permitted to leave immediately, perhaps the next day. The two they chose were able to leave two days later. Their common, overriding fear was not of the Iraqis, but what might happen to them if a shooting war broke out.

The one time the United States proposed talks, it was an empty gesture that became a threat. On November 30, the day after the UN authorized the use of force, Bush proposed to send Baker to Baghdad and invite Iraqi foreign minister Tariq Aziz to Washington. Iraq immediately accepted the offer, stating the next day that its government welcomed the chance to talk. The United States then began to back away from the proposal. For over a month, the two countries could not agree on a date for the meetings. Finally, January 9 was chosen, but by then the United States had pulled back on its proposal for dual high-level talks in Washington and Baghdad, and insisted that only one meeting would take place in Switzerland.

Bush set the purpose for the meeting, saying there would be "no negotiations, no compromises, no attempts at face-saving, and no rewards for aggression."[129] And indeed, Baker did not negotiate. He handed Aziz a letter from George Bush to Saddam Hussein promising Iraq's destruction if it stayed in Kuwait. The letter did not discuss Palestine or other issues; instead, it warned, "[W]hat is at stake demands that no opportunity be lost to avoid what would be a certain calamity for the people of Iraq."[130] He had proclaimed in November, "We have only friendship for the people [in Iraq]."[131] But his letter was a direct threat against the Iraqi people:

> [I]t is said by some that you do not understand just how isolated Iraq is and what Iraq faces as a result. . . . But unless you withdraw from Kuwait completely and without condition, you will lose more than Kuwait. . . . This choice is yours to make. . . . Iraq is al-

ready feeling the sanctions mandated by the United Nations. Should war come, it will be a far greater tragedy for you and your country. . . . I write this letter not to threaten, but to inform.[132]

As President Bush intended, the meeting came to naught.

WASHINGTON'S RUSH TO WAR

Rather than send negotiators to Baghdad and elsewhere to find a way to settle the crisis, Washington pursued a war course from the moment it received word of the Iraqi invasion of Kuwait. The military moved with remarkable speed.

At 5:00 A.M. on August 2, President Bush prepared two executive orders that prohibited U.S. trade with Iraq and froze Iraqi assets worth $30 billion.[133] The orders were filed with the Office of the Federal Registrar by 10:00 A.M. that day. The Iraqi invasion of Kuwait was only hours old.

At 5:30 A.M., Bush and Brent Scowcroft met to discuss how to persuade allies to join the United States on sanctions. Later that day, the UN Security Council passed a U.S.-initiated resolution condemning Iraq's invasion of Kuwait and calling for withdrawal. On August 2, the United States dispatched a battle group of seven warships, led by the USS *Independence,* to the region. By August 5, the United States had arranged to add another aircraft carrier in the Mediterranean Sea and send another assault ship to the Gulf region. France added a warship. U.S. and allied naval carriers headed toward the Gulf well before Bush's August 7 announcement that Saudi Arabia had agreed to allow 90,000 U.S. troops to land. Afterward, King Hussein would say that British Prime Minister Margaret Thatcher told him that "troops were halfway to their destination before the request for them to come."[134] Without consulting Congress, 40,000 troops were deployed immediately.

On August 7 — one day after the Saudis agreed to let in American troops — additional warplanes and ships from bases all over the United States headed to Saudi Arabia. The deployment would become the biggest U.S. mobilization since the Vietnam War and the biggest airlift since World War II.

When the United States began its massive buildup in the Saudi desert, it took most Americans by surprise. The forces were far larger from the beginning than the public was told. The United States was able to fly warplanes from all over the world to more than 20 fully operative, hardened military air bases in Saudi Arabia — the bases that had been begun ten years before to facilitate the Rapid Deployment Force. Nine readied ports awaited U.S. warships. Their sophistication, including the most advanced surveillance equipment, allowed the United States to wage the kind of war that it could not have waged elsewhere. Journalist Scott Armstrong in the November/December 1991 issue of *Mother Jones* quoted a military planner who said of the bases, "Nowhere else in the world — not even in the United States — could we fight as successfully as we did in the Gulf."[135]

Bush declared that the buildup was wholly defensive. Yet, from the beginning, news reports showed extensive planning by the United States for offensive military action. On August 11, when 40,000 troops were in the Gulf, the *Los Angeles Times* stated in an editorial, "An anonymous Defense Department source is widely quoted as saying that contingency plans for the Persian Gulf could result in the insertion of up to 200,000 to 250,000 [U.S.] ground forces before it's all done. These are sobering, not to say mind boggling thoughts." [136]

On August 24, the *Los Angeles Times* ran a story headlined "If Pentagon Gets a 'Go,' It'll Be a Massive Strike." The article quoted Air Force Chief of Staff Michael Dugan as saying, "We're postured for a joint attack."

Later, when the United States was using every form of pressure available to build a coalition of countries supporting Desert Shield — relying on the claim that its posture in the Gulf was defensive — Secretary of Defense Richard Cheney removed Dugan from his post after he made similar statements. On September 15, Dugan told reporters that traditional military targets in Iraq were "not enough" to win a war with Iraq. He suggested that Iraqi cities, electrical systems, roads, railroads, and oil production facilities were better targets.[137]

From the first, the buildup was intended to be offensive. The Bush administration barely tried to hide it, though no Congressional authorization was ever obtained and no debate was heard on the matter. By September 4, 100,000 troops were in the Gulf, and that number doubled by mid-October. Then, with no material change in the crisis, on October 30 Bush again doubled U.S. troop levels to 400,000. He waited until immediately after the Congressional elections, however, to make this decision public.[138]

On December 29, President Bush directed General Schwarzkopf to begin his attack on Iraq on January 16 at 7:00 P.M. EST, the day after the UN deadline for withdrawal. And still the public was told that peace was possible.[139]

The buildup continued until by mid-January the United States had 540,000 troops in the Gulf, supported by air or ground forces from the United Kingdom, France, Kuwait, Saudi Arabia, Egypt, and other countries. As late as January 9, with Congress moving toward a vote on whether to support UN Resolution 678 authorizing removal of Iraq from Kuwait by any means necessary, President Bush again insisted he had the authority to attack without either UN or Congressional approval. When midnight January 15 passed at the UN in New York, it was already dawn January 16 in Iraq. While B-52s departed many hours earlier from Barksdale Air Force Base in Louisiana and elsewhere for nonstop flights toward their targets, and cruise missiles were launched from vessels on the Indian Ocean and the eastern Mediterranean hours before, the attack was timed to begin as people living on the east coast of the United States watched prime time evening news on January 16. Nineteen hours after the deadline, Iraq was hit almost simultaneously with hundreds of missiles and bombs. Within an hour, 85 percent of all electric power generation throughout Iraq was destroyed. Several thousand bombing sorties cut the major arteries of the nation's vital services within 48 hours.

The evidence that this assault was planned for years before Iraq invaded Kuwait cannot be doubted. That a decision to provoke Iraq into an act that would justify the execution of those plans is clear beyond a reasonable doubt. The ease with which the Bush administration frustrated all efforts to negotiate a peaceful settlement of the dispute it had created reveals the tragic failure of international peace-keeping mechanisms, the UN, the U.S. Constitution, the media that failed to inform the public, and finally the people themselves, who watched war coming for nearly six months, but did not act to prevent the slaughter.

CHAPTER 2

The Turkey Shoot and Consolidation of Control

I RAQ'S military was essentially defenseless against U.S. techno-logical warfare and offered no real resistance. Casualty figures alone establish this. Iraq lost between 125,000 and 150,000 soldiers. The U.S. has said it lost 148 in combat, and of those, 37 were caused by friendly fire.

Iraqi soldiers endured six weeks of unceasing aerial, missile, and artillery bombardment. U.S. planes pounded troops in the Kuwaiti theater of operations and southern Iraq with carpet-bombing, fuel-air explosives, and other illegal weaponry. Iraq never mustered a single significant offensive strike or any effective defensive action. When the ground attack came, the surviving Iraqis were incapable even of self-defense.

In a news briefing on February 23, the eve of the ground war, General Thomas Kelly said, "There won't be many of them [Iraqi soldiers] left."[1] He believed most Iraqi troops were dead or had withdrawn. When U.S. tanks and armored vehicles finally did roll, the soldiers reported driving for miles without encountering live Iraqi forces.

THE ARSENAL

The salient feature of the slaughter of Iraqi troops is that it was carried out overwhelmingly by aircraft and missiles. There was virtually no risk to U.S. troops, as real ground combat did not even occur. There was no military need for U.S. troops to enter Iraq.

Years of preparation had made this possible. U.S. forces operated out of a network of bases in Saudi Arabia on which the Saudis had spent billions of dollars installing on the United States' behalf during the 1980s. This network included sophisticated electronic tracking and surveillance equipment, and military airfields strung across the desert — complete with hangars, repair shops, and hardened bunkers. Lieutenant General Jimmie Adams, Air Force Deputy Chief of Staff, called the aircraft facilities in Saudi Arabia the "finest I've seen anywhere."[2]

By mid-September 1990, the U.S. Air Force was already in place. U.S. Navy aircraft carriers were able to supplement Air Force presence from the Persian Gulf, Indian Ocean, and eastern Mediterranean in comparable time. All that was needed was a few more months of logistical preparation to occupy Kuwait.

Although the Pentagon portrayed the Iraqi armed forces as a dangerous threat, in fact, Iraq had never been capable of inflicting injury on U.S. forces, or even of defending itself. As retired Israeli Major General Matti Peled wrote:

> The Iraqi Army was not an unknown quantity. After 8 years of war in Iran it was very clear that it was not a threatening army, it was not a first-class fighting force. But the United States spread throughout the world the legend about invincibility of the Iraqi Army, knowing full well that it was not true. But this gave the U.S. a justification for conducting what it called "strategic bombardment" of the entire area of Iraq, demolishing their entire civilian infrastructure.[3]

The United States exaggerated both the number of Iraqi troops in Kuwait and southern Iraq and the quality of their experience and equipment. It has been widely acknowledged that, well before U.S. ground forces moved north, probably fewer than 250,000 Iraqi troops remained in the region, not the 400,000 the United States claimed. The best-equipped troops were kept well inside Iraq, concealed as much as possible from direct U.S. strikes.

The Iraqi command knew from the beginning that it could not resist U.S. arms. For five months before the air war began and for another five-and-a-half weeks during the bombing, Iraq did not mount a single attack except the much-discussed minor skirmish at Khafji. Had Iraq's purpose been aggression and had it dared choose war with the United States, it would have invaded Saudi Arabia in August before U.S. troops could arrive in force.

Regarding Iraq's air force, before he was removed from his post General Dugan accurately observed, "Their air force has very limited military capability."[4] The Iraqi air force never rose to defend Iraqi cities, where the pilots' own families lived. Over 100 of the best planes — 20 percent of Iraq's air force — flew at low altitudes to Iran, the old enemy, and never returned. No aerial defense of the helpless country was ordered because Iraqi military officials knew that exposing its planes in the air would be suicidal.

The Iraqi anti-aircraft fireworks display, shown regularly on CNN, created the impression that ground-to-air defenses were protecting Baghdad. However, this fire turned out to be essentially useless. The Iraqi defenses could not target Stealth bombers or low-flying attack planes; nor could they reach the 40,000-foot altitude from which the B-52s dropped their bombs. Even the Soviet-made mobile SA-6 surface-to-air missiles (SAM), which were early targets of U.S. aircraft, proved ineffective. In sharp contrast to the Vietnam War, in which SAM missiles hit scores of B-52s, not one of the big bombers was lost in combat.[5] In fact, the Pentagon reported that despite the 109,876 sorties flown during the entire war, only 38 aircraft were lost — a rate lower than the normal accident rate in combat training.[6]

THE BOMBING CAMPAIGN

From January 17 to February 24, U.S. pilots systematically killed Iraqi troops wherever they found them. Besides the attack by aircraft, the aerial bombardment also included guided missiles launched from land, sea, and air; extended-range artillery; and even the 16-inch guns of the old U.S.S. *Missouri* and *Wisconsin*. F-llls and F-117s struck from Turkey at the rate of one each hour. B-52s dropping up to 40,000 pounds of bombs in each sortie carpet-bombed battlefield sectors without warning. Hundreds of sorties were flown from the U.S.S. *Midway*, which had sailed to the Persian Gulf from its home port in Okasaka, Japan, to join the "party," as General Powell called the war on national television. Tomahawk cruise missiles were fired from the U.S.S. *Pittsburgh*, among other vessels, in the eastern Mediterranean.

The near-constant roar of U.S. overflights continued for 42 days at an average of one every 30 seconds. Over 80 million pounds of bombs were dropped on Iraqi military placements. In the opening days of the bombing, coalition forces destroyed logistical lifelines to Iraqi troops in Kuwait and southern Iraq. They effectively cut off military supplies, reinforcements, food, water, and medical supplies. Communications systems were severely damaged, so troops under heavy bombardment did not know the fate of supporting units or even of their own personnel. Reconnaissance was eliminated. The Iraqis could hardly attempt to check on U.S. air and troop movements while they tried to avoid around-the-clock battering from an enemy they couldn't see.

On February 20, the *Washington Post* reported that Iraqi troops were "suffering 'horrendous' casualties as U.S. and allied forces pound them with air strikes and artillery barrages."[7] The speedy, systematic destruction of tank units, armored vehicles, artillery pieces, and other mechanized equipment left Iraqi troops fully aware that they had no means to defend themselves. The Pentagon claimed 1,500 tanks were destroyed by F-111s alone, and that this was confirmed by videotape. The Iraqi forces were blind during night attacks; deaf from lack of communications; disoriented from sleeplessness; and weak from hunger, cold, thirst, and tension. Members of Iraqi military units that had been hastily organized and pressed into forward positions, including many Kurds and Shiites, began to desert. General Schwarzkopf estimated desertion rates of up to 30 percent in some Iraqi units by mid-February.

The February 5 *Los Angeles Times* reported that a British defense consultant in Dhahran had calculated that "the tonnage of high explosive bombs already released has exceeded the combined allied air offensive of World War II."[8]

The aerial assault continued until no targets remained that were worth the ordnance. Pilots reported a shortage of targets for days. The number of tanks and other armored vehicles the Pentagon claimed to have destroyed before February 24 actually exceeded some estimates of the totals Iraq possessed. But the bombardment did not stop until it was clear that Iraq had been crippled and U.S. forces could move on the ground without significant risk. The surviving Iraqi troops in Kuwait and southern Iraq were incapable of functioning militarily. There was no military need to move ground forces quickly. Iraq was helpless.

General Schwarzkopf made it clear that he was in no hurry to invade. He insisted, as the *New York Times* reported as early as February 4, that "he was determined to take his time" before ordering a ground attack. "I feel no hot breath down my neck," he said, adding, "I agonize, I agonize. I wake up 15, 20 times in the night. My nightmare is anything that would cause mass casualties among my troops. I don't want my troops to die. I don't want my troops to be maimed."[9]

But from the beginning, the generals must have known serious ground fighting would never occur. Schwarzkopf need not have lost any sleep. In more than five weeks of bombing, 14 frontline Iraqi divisions were pummeled until they were reduced to less then half their original strength.[10] Among the explosives that U.S. planes dropped on troops were napalm bombs, fuel-air explosives (FAEs), and cluster bombs. According to an intelligence expert quoted in the *Los Angeles Times*, the air war alone caused 100,000 deaths:

> We probably killed more than 100,000 people without ever occupying the territory. We didn't take the lines and move forward. We passed over them day after day, and that's a different kind of war historically than we've ever fought.[11]

Injured Iraqi soldiers were doomed. Iraq did not possess sophisticated field hospitals, as the United States did. Communications and transportation were next to impossible, and medical units could move among the trenches and bunkers only at high risk. Therefore, wounded Iraqi soldiers remained where they were hit, without medical aid. The *Washington Post* reported on February 18, 1991 that "wounded Iraqi soldiers were dying for lack of treatment amid conditions that recalled the American Civil War."[12] If wounded soldiers were moved out of the lines, treatment was further impaired because U.S. planes bombed at least five Iraqi military hospitals.[13]

Pounded by the latest in high-tech killing machines, it is no surprise that when the ground war began, the surviving Iraqi troops had neither the capacity nor the will to fight. By February 24 there were probably not 150,000 Iraqi troops left alive in Kuwait and the border area. Tens of thousands had deserted. The soldiers who did remain with their units were debilitated by the constant bombardment, the scarcity of food and water, and the destruction of their armor, artillery, ordnance, and communications. They were incapable of defending themselves, and when attacked, they retreated in disorganized flight.

CASUALTIES DON'T COUNT

When asked his assessment of the number of Iraqi soldiers and civilians killed, General Colin Powell answered, "It's really not a number I'm terribly interested in."[14] General Schwarzkopf's strict policy was that Iraqi dead were not to be counted. And Lieutenant General Pagonis boasted, "This is the first war in modern times where every screwdriver, every nail is accounted for." But as for human beings, he said, "I don't think anybody is going to be able to come up with an accurate count for the Iraqi dead."[15]

Although the Pentagon seemingly didn't care about the number of people that were killed, there was actually intense interest in casualty figures. On May 22, 1991, the DIA placed the number of Iraqi soldiers killed at 100,000. This coincides with what General Schwarzkopf said in early March, before he realized that silence on the matter was more important. Soon after the ground war was over, Schwarzkopf said, "We must have killed 100,000. . . . There's a very large number of dead in these units. A very, very large number of dead."[16] On March 20, 1991, the *Wall Street Journal* reported that figures provided to Congress by Schwarzkopf and his top officers also indicated 100,000 Iraqi military dead.[17] The same number was estimated by a Saudi military official in a CNN interview.

European estimates of military deaths were always higher, reflecting the lack of censorship as compared to the U.S. media. On March 3, 1991, the *London Times* reported that allied intelligence estimated as many as 200,000 Iraqi soldiers dead. "[T]housands of troops," reported the *Times*, "may be buried in bunkers and trenches."[18] A French military intelligence source told the *Nouvelle Observateur* that the military death toll was 200,000.

While the Pentagon's silence on military casualties makes it impossible to know precise numbers, it is reasonable to believe that at least 125,000, and probably closer to 150,000, Iraqi soldiers were killed. Although there were attempts in early 1992 to put the total Iraqi deaths as low as 10,000–30,000, these reports were politically motivated. They came out when public discontent with American actions during the Gulf War was beginning to show. Gulf War veterans were turning up in alarming numbers among the homeless,[19] the country's economy was worsening, and many people were wondering if the war had been worth it.

At the same time, President Bush was talking about renewed attacks on Iraq. Therefore, it was important to downplay the Iraqi military casualties so Americans would think the Iraqi military was still strong. Air Force Lieutenant General Charles Horner told the press, "They [U.S. soldiers] really didn't find a lot of bodies."[20] This differed sharply with Schwarzkopf's statement just after the war that "We . . . found them [dead soldiers] when we went into the units ourselves and found them in the trench lines."[21]

Despite revisionist casualty estimates, the definitive analysis was given by Secretary of Defense Richard Cheney. In the March 8, 1991 *Los Angeles Times*, he almost boasted:

43

If anybody is curious about what we think happened, we think there were a lot of Iraqis killed. Our military effort was aimed specifically at the destruction of those forces that took Kuwait, the destruction of [Saddam Hussein's] offensive capability, the destruction of divisions he used over the years to terrorize his neighbors, and we did it.[22]

WEAPONS OF MASS DESTRUCTION

The arsenal used by United States forces in the Gulf War included some horrifying weapons. While proclaiming adherence to the rules of war, U.S. generals ordered the use of fuel-air explosives (FAEs), napalm bombs, cluster bombs, and the GBU-28 "superbomb" in ways that are inconsistent with international law. The highly destructive weapons that the Pentagon claimed were used to clear minefields were used against human beings as well.

Fuel-air explosives are devices of near-nuclear power. Upon impact, they release a cloud of highly volatile vapors that mix with air and detonate. One type of FAE covers an area over 1,000 feet long with blast overpressures of 200 pounds per square inch (psi). Humans can withstand only up to 40 psi.[23] According to a CIA report on FAEs:

> [T]he pressure effects of FAEs approach those produced by low-yield nuclear weapons at short ranges. The effect of an FAE explosion within confined spaces is immense. Those near the ignition point are obliterated. Those at the fringes are likely to suffer many internal . . . injuries, including burst eardrums and crushed inner-ear organs, severe concussions, ruptured lungs and internal organs, and possible blindness.[24]

Ironically, the press wrote about FAEs as a horrifying Iraqi weapon, an "exotic explosive." On October 5, 1990, the *Los Angeles Times* warned, "Unlike Iraq's arsenal of chemical and biological weapons, there is no ready defense against" the FAE, which the *Times* said "the United States does not have in its arsenal."[25] This was simply propaganda; it is no secret that the U.S. military has been stockpiling FAEs since the Vietnam War.

As it became clear that the U.S. did have FAEs, the scare stories abated. U.S. officers said they used FAEs to clean up minefields in Kuwait. *Washington Post* columnist Michael Kinsley called the FAE a weapon "which at first we didn't have, then would never use except against a chemical attack, then were using to clear minefields and pack down sand."[26]

In fact, U.S. forces did use FAEs against Iraqi troops. The February 23, 1991 *Washington Post* reported, "All of the frontline Iraqi troops have been subjected to extensive bombardment, including many detonations of 10,000-pound BLU-82 bombs, containing fuel-air explosives."[27]

The BLU-82 is actually a 15,000-pound fuel-air explosive with blast overpressures of 1,000 psi. It is called "daisy-cutter" after its use in Vietnam to blast out landing spaces for helicopters in the jungle. According to the July 1992 issue of *Soldier of Fortune,* at least 11 BLU-82s were used between February 7, 1991 and the start of the ground assault, with three dropped in one day on Faylakah Island near Kuwait City.

Napalm bombs are incendiary weapons containing a mixture of gasoline and benzene (a carcinogen), with aluminum or polystyrene soap as a thickener. The materials fire up quickly after they disperse. The burning gel envelops large areas, igniting anything in the way. Pentagon spokespeople denied using napalm against Iraqi troops, and claimed it was used only to burn off the oil that Iraqi soldiers had filled trenches with as a defensive measure. But one Marine officer admitted "napalm was being used against Iraqi troops as it was against the enemy in Vietnam."[28] And according to the February 23 *Washington Post*, it was used to "reach entrenched troops."[29]

Cluster bombs were also used widely in the Gulf war. As Stephen Sackur wrote in his book *On the Basra Road*:

> It was clear that Allied aircraft had attacked the highway [Highway of Death] with cluster bombs — the spent casings were lying all over the area. Cluster bombs are designed to break up into hundreds of little "bomblets" to saturate the target area, spewing out specially formulated metal shrapnel to maximize damage to both man and machine. They leave tell-tale pockmarks in the area of impact. The Basra road was covered in pockmarks.[30]

The Americans and British used cluster bombs on both troops and civilians. A typical cluster bomb was the Rockeye II Mk 20, a 222-kilogram bomb that spreads 247 bomblets over an acre, spewing almost 500,000 high-velocity shrapnel fragments. *Aviation Week and Space Technology* reported in February 1991 that F-16As carried four Rockeye cluster bombs per sortie.[31] Other cluster bombs included what are called "gut-rippers," or "bouncing Bettys," which hit the ground, hop into the air, and explode at stomach level.[32]

Cluster bombs were also used by the United States in its so-called search for mobile Scud launchers. Each such attack was typically carried out by two F-15E Strike Eagles, one of which would contain laser-guided bombs, the other often CBU-87 cluster bombs. When the "smart" bombs missed, the second F-15E would unload its cluster bombs at the target — more often than not a civilian vehicle.[33] In fact, this search overwhelmingly targeted civilian vehicles — taxis, buses, trucks, and Volkswagens. Postwar reports stated that no mobile launchers were hit.[34]

U.S. officials ordered an assassination attempt on Saddam Hussein which entailed dropping two 5,000-pound GBU-28 "superbombs," one after the other, onto a hardened bunker at al-Taji air base. U.S. intelligence thought Hussein would be in this bunker, which had already been hit three times with 2,000-pound bombs. The Pentagon had put a rush on the GBU-28s, with construction beginning on January 19. Nothing like it had ever been seen, and only two were built. Although U.S. officials repeatedly denied targeting Saddam Hussein personally, the *Minneapolis Star-Tribune* reported on January 11, 1991: "U.S. forces will attempt to kill Iraqi President Saddam Hussein during the initial phase of the war with Iraq. . . . According to Defense officials, Bush ordered Colin Powell, Chairman of the Joint Chiefs of Staff, to target Hussein for attack shortly after Iraq's August 2 invasion of Kuwait."[35] And a senior CENTCOM officer told *U.S. News & World Report*, "I'd be lying to you if I told you they [the 5,000-pound bombs] weren't meant for Saddam."[36] Only hours before the ceasefire, at 7:19 P.M. on February 27, U.S. pilots landed at an air base in Saudi Arabia to pick up the two specially made bombs.

MOPPING UP

The United States began the ground war having consistently refused to consider any ceasefire or acknowledge any Iraqi offer to withdraw. President Bush called a February 15 proposal by Saddam Hussein, which was never publicized to the American people, a "cruel hoax," while his air force continued to slaughter Iraqi soldiers and civilians. The last-ditch efforts of international negotiators were met with cruel indifference by Washington. On February 23, Soviet Middle East envoy Yevgeny Primakov announced on U.S. television that Saddam Hussein had agreed to withdraw on February 22, and that it would be possible to resolve the situation within a day or two.

President Bush countered by saying that his own February 22 ultimatum was the last chance for Saddam Hussein to withdraw, but that the Iraqi leader was "redoubling efforts to destroy completely Kuwait and its people."[37] President Bush, apparently fearing an Iraqi withdrawal, ordered the ground action immediately.

British Prime Minister John Major told the House of Commons, "I frankly do not believe that our troops or world public opinion would forgive us if at this stage we permitted the Iraqis to withdraw with their weapons." When the truth is known, world opinion will never forgive Bush or Major for the human slaughter they ordered. For instance, the following testimony came from Mike Erlich of the Military Counseling Network at the March–April 1991 European Parliament hearings on the Gulf War:

> . . . hundreds, possibly thousands, of Iraqi soldiers began walking toward the U.S. position unarmed, with their arms raised in an attempt to surrender. However, the orders for this unit were not to take any prisoners. . . .
>
> The commander of the unit began the firing by shooting an anti-tank missile through one of the Iraqi soldiers. This is a missile designed to destroy tanks, but it was used against one man.
>
> At that point, everybody in the unit began shooting. Quite simply, it was a slaughter.[38]

U.S. generals could discuss their plans openly because Iraq could not respond. For weeks before U.S. ground forces attacked, the flanking movement to the west of Iraqi forces, Operation Left Hook, was portrayed as a brilliant maneuver of which witless Iraqi strategists could not conceive. General Schwarzkopf dwelled publicly on how Hannibal perfected the double envelop at the Battle of Cannae in 216 B.C. But Schwarzkopf did not need any skill at manuevering to kill the surviving Iraqi troops. They were simply burned by FAEs or buried by bulldozers.

When Operation Left Hook began, there was no resistance. Iraqi troops in the area were more an obstacle than a threat. U.S. forces moved as quickly as their armored vehicles and support columns could go over the rough terrain. In John MacArthur's book *Second Front*, Pentagon spokesperson Pete Williams admits in an interview that "there was no fighting up-close in this war."[39]

A Saudi intelligence official quoted in columnist Jim Hoagland's March 3 piece in the *Washington Post* commented on the Iraqi military's ability to defend itself:

They [Iraqi troops] had no idea where the attack on them was coming from. They were blind on the battlefield and were more likely
to hit their own troops than ours. You could see the problem in the
way they moved their tanks, going west when they should have been
moving east, or north for south. They had no spotters, no communications and no plan. And they were being pounded by the American
planes without cease.[40]

On the second day of the ground assault, radar revealed masses of
Iraqi troops clogging roads in a northward dash out of Kuwait. One
thousand soldiers from the 101st Airborne Division were carried
deep into Iraq in 66 Blackhawk helicopters. They were dropped near
Highway 8, which connects Basra and Baghdad. As Iraqi convoys
moved north on the highway — retreating from the war zone — the
U.S. troops attacked them with antitank missiles and mortars. The
Americans were amazed at the devastation the air assault had
wrought and surprised by the absence of Iraqi combat capability.
The Iraqis did not fire on the U.S. troops, who destroyed vehicles on
the highway like ducks in a shooting gallery.

In southeastern Iraq, as First Army Division tanks crashed into a
Republican Guard unit, the U.S. commander radioed his deputy,
who was with the forward troops, "Understand we are engaging the
Medina Division." The reply was: "Negative, sir. We are destroying
the Medina Division."[41] The same could be said about every Iraqi
unit encountered. As one soldier said, it was like slaughtering animals in a pen.

The *Toronto Globe and Mail* carried an early Reuters dispatch on
the ground action entitled "Getting Blown to Bits in the Dark" on
February 25:

The first high-tech video of ground fighting in the Persian Gulf war
shows terrified Iraqi infantrymen shot to pieces in the dark by U.S.
attack helicopters.

One by one they were cut down, bewildered by an enemy they
could not see.

Some were blown to bits by exploding cannon shells. Others,
jarred from sleep, fled their bunkers under a firestorm.

The tape was shot through the night-vision gunsights of the
Apache Ah-64 attack helicopter, which turn pitch dark into ghostly
day.

Reporters and even hardened soldiers held their breath when the
first video was shown in a briefing tent of the 18th Airborne Corps,
whose chopper crews had begun carrying the war to the Iraqis.

Combat reporters permitted to see the video did not say where or when the engagement took place. No casualty count was given. Reports from the front are subject to U.S. military censorship.

Apaches — equipped with cannons, laser-guided missiles, and infrared optics — have led several lightning strikes behind Iraqi lines in recent days, raiding bunkers and taking prisoners.

The pilots of the 6th Cavalry exult in their prowess.

"I just didn't quite envision going up there and shooting the hell out of everything in the dark and have them not know what the hell hit them," said one Balak of Beemer, Neb.

"A truck blows up to the right, the ground blows up to the left. They had no idea where we were or what was hitting them," he said.

"When I got back I sat there on the wing and I was laughing. I wasn't laughing at the Iraqis. I was thinking of the training, the anticipation. . . . I was probably laughing at myself . . . sneaking up there, and blowing this up and blowing that up.

"A guy came up to me and we were slapping each other on the back and all that stuff, and he said, 'By God, I thought we had shot into a damn farm. It looked like somebody opened the sheep pen.' "[42]

Reuters thus confirmed not only that Iraqi soldiers were totally unable to see the enemy or defend themselves, but that U.S. troops quickly realized this.

A report from William Branigin in the March 3, 1991 *Washington Post* described what the 1st Cavalry Division encountered as it moved into Iraq:

By the side of a dirt road in Iraq's south-eastern desert sat a truck belonging to President Saddam Hussein's elite Republican Guard. In and around it lay the bodies of eight Iraqi soldiers. The immediate area was cordoned off with white tape like a police crime scene.

The headless corpse of one of the soldiers was on its back a short distance from the truck. Another body was wedged inside the engine compartment. Two more lay face up in the bed of the truck, their feet sticking grotesquely over the side.

This was the gruesome face of the Persian Gulf War, a facet of the conflict not previously seen by many of the young American soldiers who took part in the allied ground offensive against Iraq this week. After weeks of a high-tech war waged largely from the sky, the horrors on the ground took some of the troops by total surprise.

. . . Already, units of the Army's 1st Cavalry Division that had suffered no combat casualties in their unopposed drive through southern Iraq have seen several of their number killed or wounded by bombs or mines in the area they are holding. . .

. . . A couple of miles away from the vehicles, a large expanse of desert that apparently had been a Republican Guard training area was devastated by aerial bombardment well before the U.S. armored units swept through. . .

. . . The entire area was littered with pieces of ordnance, including hundreds of unexploded individual yellow cluster bombs sticking into the sand.[43]

Even Iraqi units with operational tanks and the will to resist were helpless. Here is how the April 8, 1991 *New York Times* reported one slaughter:

. . . The battle, which raged on February 27, the day before a ceasefire went into effect, was a showcase for the superiority of American weapons. But it was also the sort of one-sided victory that some American soldiers who tasted combat for the first time say they will not want to talk about a lot when they get home.

The sky was overcast and it was raining as the Americans approached the ridge around noon.

When the battle began the American tanks generally fired from a safe distance of about 2,500 yards. Unable to find the Americans with their targeting system in the overcast weather, the Iraqis aimed their guns at the muzzle flashes of the guns of the American tanks, and their rounds fell well short.

Other soldiers said the biggest fear was not the Iraqis but the worry that the American tanks might be hit by other allied units in the battle.[44]

The psychological effect on the few American troops who actually witnessed this massacre will be important to monitor. Many will be casualties of the horror — psychological victims of American firepower.

Reports by the U.S. press, although censored by the Pentagon and approved by the military, still could not help but reveal the war crimes committed against Iraq's armed forces. *New York Newsday* published a graphic, lengthy summary of the "ground war" — really just a mop-up after the bombing — on March 31, 1991. It portrayed the attack upon an army that did not want to fight. It described "one-sided carnage," vehicles with white flags of surrender being destroyed, and "dazed and starved frontline Iraqi conscripts happily surrender[ing] by the thousands." It spoke of how U.S. pilots called the assault a "turkey shoot," and carrier crews frantically reloaded attack planes so they could shoot "fish in a barrel." [45]

New York Newsday reported yet another slaughter of Iraqi soldiers that was approved by General Schwarzkopf two days after the ceasefire. According to U.S. military officials, it was the biggest clash of the Gulf War ground campaign, yet no Americans were killed.

. . . The battle occurred March 2 after soldiers from the 7,000-man Iraqi force fired at a patrol of the 24th Mechanized Infantry Division. . . .

"We really waxed them," said one American Desert Storm commander who asked not to be identified. . . .

. . . Although the number of Iraqi troops killed is still unknown, *New York Newsday* has obtained Army footage of the fight showing scores of Iraqi President Saddam Hussein's elite soldiers apparently wounded or killed as Apache helicopters raked the Republican Guard Hammurabi Division with laser-guided Hellfire missiles.

"Say hello to Allah," one American was recorded as saying moments before a Hellfire obliterated one of the 102 vehicles racked up by the Apaches.

. . . Although McCaffrey's division was equipped with loudspeakers mounted on helicopters, they were never used to broadcast word of the ceasefire. "There wasn't time to use the helicopters," said [Operations Chief Lieutenant Colonel Patrick] Lamar.

Instead, after the 6:30 A.M. Iraqi attack, McCaffrey assembled attack helicopters, tanks, fighting vehicles, and artillery for the assault, which began at 8:15 A.M. According to Lamar, the attack ended after noon, with the wreckage strewn over a couple of miles of Route 8, the main Euphrates River valley road to Baghdad.

A senior Desert Storm commander said details about the post-ceasefire attack were withheld at the time even though officials in Riyadh and Washington knew the extent of the damage shortly after the battle ended.

. . . "We knew exactly [what the damage was] but it didn't look good coming after the ceasefire," the Desert Storm officer said. . . .

. . . The combat film of the March 2 attack shows the Apaches destroying vehicles to create a roadblock so that the Hammurabi could not escape on the highway, which is elevated above the nearby Haw al Hammer swamp. "Yee-HAH," said one voice. At one point, an Iraqi soldier runs in front [of] a tank just as the Hellfire explodes, hurling the soldier and chunks of metal into the air.

The Pentagon has documentary evidence, including hours of videotape, of this deadly assault on a defenseless unit.[46]

Months later, on September 12, 1991, *Newsday* broke perhaps the most horrifying story of all. Thousands of Iraqi troops had been buried alive in the first two days of the ground offensive.

The U.S. Army division that broke through Saddam Hussein's defensive frontline used plows mounted on tanks and combat earth movers to bury thousands of Iraqi soldiers—some still alive and firing their weapons—in more than 70 miles of trenches, according to U.S. Army officials.

In the first two days of ground fighting in Operation Desert Storm, three brigades of the 1st Mechanized Infantry Division— "The Big Red One"—used the grisly innovation to destroy trenches and bunkers being defended by more than 8,000 Iraqi soldiers, according to division estimates. While 2,000 surrendered, Iraqi dead and wounded as well as defiant soldiers still firing their weapons were buried beneath tons of sand, according to participants in the carefully planned and rehearsed assault.

"Once we went through there, other than the ones who surrendered, there wasn't anybody left," said Capt. Bennie Williams, who was awarded the Silver Star for his role in the assault.

The unprecedented tactic has been hidden from public view. . . .

"For all I know, we could have killed thousands," said Col. Anthony Moreno, commander of the 2nd Brigade that led the assault on the heaviest defenses.[47]

The article said that after the first wave of bulldozers incapacitated the Iraqi defenders, a second wave filled the trenches with sand, ensuring that none of the wounded could survive.

THE HIGHWAY OF DEATH

Many of those massacred fleeing Kuwait were not Iraqi soldiers at all but Palestinians, Sudanese, Egyptians, and other foreign workers. They were trying to escape to save their lives. As *Newsday* reported,

The vast majority of the vehicles photographed were cars, buses and military and civilian trucks apparently carrying Iraqi soldiers and some civilians, as well as their rifles and large quantities of goods they had looted from Kuwait. Reporters described one section of the highway as a virtually unbroken wall of wrecked and fire-blackened vehicles, piled on top of each other in a jumble of charred, twisted metal; truck cabs crushed, cars flattened underneath buses, other cars flipped upside down, tank guns pointing crazily skyward while the rest of the tank lay on its side.

Less than 10 percent of the vehicles in the one section photographed were tanks, personnel carriers or artillery. . . . [48]

North Carolina GI Mike Ange described what he saw:

> I actually went up close and examined two vehicles that basically looked like refugees maybe trying to get out of the area. You know, you had like a little Toyota pick-up truck that was loaded down with the furniture and the suitcases and rugs and the pet cat and that type of thing, all over the back of this truck, and those trucks were taken out just like the military vehicles.[49]

This was an "outrage," an Air Force analyst proclaimed, yet the White House persisted in justifying the slaughter. "These were the torturers, the looters, the rapists," it said of the dead along the highway.[50] And on March 11, 1991, the *Washington Post* reported on the Pentagon's effort to portray the "Highway of Death" slaughter as militarily justified.

> . . . As the day wore on, senior officers with the U.S. Central Command in Riyadh became worried about what they saw as a growing public perception that Iraq's forces were leaving Kuwait voluntarily and that U.S. pilots were bombing them mercilessly, according to U.S. military sources. Relaying these worries to the Pentagon as they prepared for Tuesday's scheduled televised news briefing, senior officers agreed that U.S. spokesmen needed to use forceful language to portray Iraq's claimed "withdrawal" as a fighting retreat made necessary by heavy allied military pressure.
>
> The strategy became evident at 4:45 P.M. Tuesday in Saudi Arabia (8:45 A.M. in Washington) when President Bush stepped into the Rose Garden in Washington to make a brief and hastily arranged televised statement saying the war would continue despite Baghdad's withdrawal announcement, that Iraq could not be trusted, that Iraqi troops were retreating under pressure, not voluntarily withdrawing, and that Saddam Hussein was attempting to achieve a political victory from a military rout. Bush vowed that the Iraqi president would not be permitted to achieve such a propaganda victory. . . .
>
> . . . In fact, however, tens of thousands of Iraqi soldiers in and around Kuwait City had begun to pull away more than 36 hours before allied forces reached the capital.
>
> While the Iraqi troops may have pulled out because they were battered by allied bombing and fearful of a ground attack, they did not move out under any immediate pressure from allied tanks and infantry, which still were miles from Kuwait City. . . . [51]

Thus, the Pentagon attempted to silence reporting about the "Highway of Death," and then distorted the facts. Finally, President

Bush simply proclaimed that there was no Iraqi withdrawal, although he knew the withdrawal had been ordered and was underway.

Reporter Bob Drogin of the *Los Angeles Times* described another aerial slaughter of retreating Iraqis, apparently all soldiers. It was discovered on the road to Umir Quaar in Kuwait 10 days after the ceasefire.

> For 60 miles, hundreds of Iraqi tanks and armored cars, howitzers and anti-aircraft guns, ammunition trucks and ambulances are strafed, smashed, and burned beyond belief. Scores of soldiers lie in and around the vehicles, mangled and bloated in the drifting desert sands.
>
> Most were retreating on this two-lane road before midnight February 25, one of two huge Iraqi caravans to flee ravaged Kuwait City as their army collapsed under the fast-approaching allied blitzkrieg.
>
> Both convoys were caught by allied warplanes. The remains of the other convoy, which received widespread coverage last week, sit farther west, on the main highway north to Safwan. Many of the vehicles there collided or were simply abandoned in panic, and the loot of Kuwait City was strewn throughout. At least 450 people survived to surrender.
>
> Not in this convoy. Largely unnoticed by the media so far, the tableau stretches for miles. Every vehicle was strafed or bombed. Every windshield is shattered. Every tank is burned. Every truck is riddled with shell fragments. No looting by the dead soldiers was evident. No surviviors are known or likely.
>
> . . . At one spot, snarling wild dogs have reduced two corpses to bare ribs. Giant carrion birds claw and pick at another; only a boot-clad foot and eyeless skull are recognizable.
>
> One flatbed truck has nine bodies. Each man clutches the next. Their hair and clothes are burned off, skin incinerated by heat so intense it melted the windshield onto the dashboard. . . . [52]

This war crime was reported long after it occurred. The Pentagon, unable to resort to calling these soldiers thieves and looters, has not tried to justify or explain it. This slaughter has simply been ignored. The media has failed to investigate the region for other evidence. The world must wonder how many war crimes are covered by the desert sands. And how many human bodies are buried there.

POSTWAR OPERATIONS AGAINST IRAQ

Throughout the Gulf crisis, President Bush made many well-publicized calls to the Iraqi people to revolt. In a February 15, 1991 speech, he said, "There's another way for the bloodshed to stop, and that is for the Iraqi military and the Iraqi people to take matters into their own hands, and force Saddam Hussein, the dictator, to step aside." [53]

Washington has made a great show of concern for the plight of the Kurds. But the evidence shows that the United States cynically encouraged the Kurds' postwar rebellion for its own purposes, just as it had in the 1970s. The result of the encouragement and covert aid to Kurdish rebels was death, hunger, and despair for thousands, and displacement for hundreds of thousands of others. Bush did not really want Kurdish uprisings in Iraq to succeed, for this might have incited the more than 10 million Kurds oppressed by the government in Turkey, a staunch U.S. ally. Turkey hosts 16 U.S. bases and is Washington's third largest military aid recipient.

Iraq's large Shiite population, concentrated in the south, was also prodded into rebellion, with disastrous results. An even greater threat to U.S. strategy than Kurdish success was the risk of successful Shiite uprisings, for an intervention by Iran, itself overwhelmingly Shiite, would threaten Kuwait and Saudi Arabia, both Sunni nations. The royal families dreaded a strong Shiite fundamentalist movement in southern Iraq aligned with Iran. After the war, the United States sent an Iraqi exile with CIA contacts to meetings of Shiite opposition leaders to offer U.S. backing, while warning that Washington would not tolerate fundamentalist Muslim regimes if a Shiite movement successfully toppled Saddam Hussein. [54] Though less publicized than the Kurdish revolt, the cost in life and property of the Shiite uprising was enormous and borne overwhelmingly by the Shiites themselves.

After these rebellions were crushed, the Bush administration claimed the Kurds and Shiites "misunderstood." But U.S. actions and statements were very clear. Washington allowed arms sales to the Kurds before the war, as retired Colonel Jim McDonald admitted on the PBS *Frontline* broadcast "The War We Left Behind." British special operations forces operated deep inside Iraq during the war, contacting Kurdish and other resistance groups. [55]

Besides Bush's repeated calls for uprisings, the United States appealed directly to the Kurds to rebel on a radio station called the Voice of Free Iraq (VOFI), broadcast into Iraq in the Kurdish language. Kurdish expatriates often made the broadcasts. [56] This clandestine station was funded and operated by the CIA in concert with Saudi intelligence. Many of the broadcasts immediately after the war were aimed directly at the Kurdish people, and strongly implied military support would be provided to the rebels. *London Times* journalist Hazir Temourian told Bill Moyers on PBS's "Special Report: After the War" that the broadcasts said in Kurdish and Arabic, "Rise! This is your moment! This time, the allies will not let you down!"[57]

A transcript from the U.S. government's Foreign Broadcast Information Service has a VOFI broadcaster declaring: "We are with you in every heartbeat, in all your feelings, and in every move you make. . . . We stand by you in whatever you carry out and whatever step you take."[58]

On April 16, 1991, the *New York Times* reported that in an effort to broaden the revolt beyond uprisings by Shiites in the south and Kurds in the north, an April 6 VOFI broadcast had exhorted "brother Iraqis" to liberate Baghdad. A March 20 broadcast extolled martyrdom: "The Iraqis have never felt such enthusiasm, joy, and a desire to take part in the revolution or be martyrs."[59]

The broadcasts, continued after the war, are part of a covert anti-Iraq campaign that began as early as August 1990, when President Bush signed the first of at least three authorizations designed to overthrow Hussein's government—one of which called for smuggling thousands of small transistor radios into Iraq for the VOFI broadcasts. These findings, the first of which was signed in August 1990, also authorized broad CIA-sponsored propaganda and deception; CIA cooperation with Army Special Operations forces to supply and support guerrilla fighters in Kuwait; destabilization of the Baath Party government; and CIA aid to rebel factions inside Iraq.[60] The Associated Press reported that one order, signed in January 1991, granted "broad and general authority" for clandestine activities to undermine Hussein and support the efforts of opposition forces.[61]

Thus, it is clear that the United States knowingly fomented revolt in Iraq. The indifference to life was appalling. That Washington never intended the Kurds or Shiites to succeed simply exposes how the United States cynically manipulated these minority peoples in order to weaken Iraq. This activity added directly to the terrible refugee problems after the war.

U.S. forces stayed in southern Iraq until May 9, 1991. Checkpoints in southern Iraq provided food, water, and medical supplies to refugees from the Shiite uprisings, who were then told to move on. But if the refugees had participated in the rebellions, they could not go back to Iraq. If they tried to flee to Kuwait, they were met with hostility.

In the March 31, 1991 *Manchester Guardian Weekly*, Simon Tisdall reported on the desperate situation in southern Iraq:

> Along the roads leading from al-Nasiriyah, Suq ash Shuyukh, Basra, and other southern Iraqi towns, women and children, bundled up in blankets and plastic sheeting on the back of flatbed trucks, appeal to U.S. troops for shelter. Nobody wants them; there is no help; and they dare not go home.
>
> "Let me explain something," says Captain Anthony Phillips to Sa'ad, a fugitive from al-Nasiriyah whose wife, children, and worldly possessions are crammed into a battered Toyota taxi. . . . "I can give you food," he says. "I can give you water. I can give you medical aid. But I cannot run a collection point for refugees. It's dangerous here. This morning I got a child with her leg blown off." But, as Sa'ad knows, it is dangerous everywhere.
>
> "We went to the Red Crescent Camp in Kuwait [across the border from Safwan]," Sa'ad says. "They treat us very badly. They say they cannot receive anyone who is Iraqi. We have been traveling for 15 days. I don't know what to do."[62]

By mid-April 1991 there were 30,000 refugees wandering in the desert. It was not until April 24 that Saudi Arabia announced it would protect and shelter these refugees. The U.S. flew 8,400 refugees to Saudi Arabia and 2,000 to Iran. It gave the rest five gallons of gasoline and all the food and water they could carry.

In the north, once the Kurdish refugee situation had reached its worst point, the United States implemented a belated aid program. On April 9, 1991, the U.S. office of the High Commissioner for Refugees estimated that 750,000 Iraqi Kurds had gone to Iran and 280,000 had gone to Turkey.[63] In mid-April pallets of food were airlifted and dropped into Kurdish refugee camps in Cukurca, Turkey. Some fell on and killed Kurds.

In the April 21, 1991 *Manchester Guardian/Le Monde Weekly*, David Hearst reported that a Turkish military official was "incandescent with rage." He said: "I told the Americans, 'You threw bombs on these people in Iraq and killed them, and now you throw aid on them and still kill them.' "[64]

Ostensibly to control this situation, U.S. Marines took control of the Iraqi city of Zakho on April 20. By April 23, 2,000 Marines and several hundred French and British troops occupied a zone stretching 24 miles into Iraq and 35 miles along the Iraq–Turkey border.

On May 2, the allies extended their presence to Amadiya, 45 miles east of Zakho. By May 8 they had moved south to Dohuk. At the peak of the occupation in mid-May, there were 21,700 allied troops in northern Iraq.[65] Eventually, the United States established a zone of occupation that continues under UN control: northern Iraq is occupied to the 36th parallel, a line 30 miles south of Mosul and, at some points, 100 miles from the Turkish border. And finally, in August 1992, the United States, Great Britain, and France — to "protect the Shiites," whom the United States bombed mercilessly during the war — proclaimed they would shoot down any Iraqi aircraft flying south of the 32nd parallel, threatening to break off the bottom third of the country.

Washington's feigned concern for the people of Iraq was actually a propaganda tool to weaken the country and reduce problems for Turkey and Saudi Arabia. The Kurds were presented as victims of the Iraqi leader's brutality, but the United States created the misery by encouraging the rebellion, implicitly promising military support, and then letting the rebels fail. By summer, Turkey had begun military raids against Kurdish villages in Iraq. The Turkish government had long oppressed the Kurds in Turkey, with even more brutality and violence than the Kurds have faced in Iraq. Now it extended its campaign to Kurds in Iraq, including Iraqis and exiles from Turkey.[66]

The United States has supported Turkey in its long-standing repression of Kurdish people. It strongly supports Saudi Arabia and Kuwait, who feel threatened by Iran and Iraqi Shiites on their borders. It aided these governments, who are essential to its dominion in the Gulf, by manipulating the failed Shiite and Kurdish rebellions and weakening Iraq in the process.

CHAPTER 3

War Crimes Against Iraq's Civilian Population

E ARLY on January 17, 1991, the United States began an un-precedented missile and bombing campaign across Iraq. Starting with 2,000 aerial sorties a day, total U.S. overflights would exceed 109,000 in the 42-day assault. Most were bombing runs. More than 88,500 tons of explosives were dropped on Iraq.[1]

This massive bombing operation was primarily a war against civilian life.

Despite Pentagon assertions that everything possible was done to avoid civilian casualties, that the bombings were "surgical strikes," the bombing unquestionably targeted civilians. When the level of civilian damage is measured, to claim the bombs were accurate only proves they were aimed at Iraq's civilian population. The surgical strike myth was a cynical way to conceal the truth. The bombing was a deadly, calculated, and deeply immoral strategy to bring Iraq to its knees by destroying the essential facilities and support systems of the entire society.

TARGETING INFRASTRUCTURE AND LIFE-SUPPORT SYSTEMS

The bombing of Iraq's cities and infrastructure had nothing to do with driving Iraq from Kuwait. It was intended to cripple a developing Third World country that was a politically independent military power in the region; and that was rich in oil and committed to its own economic development. Before the Gulf crisis, Iraq was making considerable economic progress, despite the ravaging effects of its war with Iran. Commission members Adeeb Abed and Gavrielle Gemma, who traveled widely in Iraq from April 3–14, 1991, made this report:

> Although it varied in different parts of the country, again and again people described to us the following: the entire country was electrified (we saw that even in more rural towns and farms there were electrical lines direct to people's homes). . . . Since 1982, eighteen major hospitals had been built. Some were renowned in the Middle East. Medical care was basically free with a token payment of half a dinar upon admission and one dinar each day regardless of care. Illiteracy had been substantially reduced; education was universal and free through college. Water was supplied to all parts of the country. Prenatal and postnatal care and vaccinations for children were available throughout the country including in rural areas. The social position of women was advancing. Food was abundant and inexpensive. . . . Low-interest loans were provided by the government, which had also started a program to give land to people who promised to produce within five years. Doctors had not seen cases of malnutrition in Baghdad for over a decade.[2]

The physical infrastructure was modern and growing. Thousands of miles of modern highway; major dams and modern hydroelectric, flood control, and irrigation systems; efficient telephone service, electric grid networks, and other facilities evidenced a rapidly developing country.

The social position of women stood out in stark contrast to the oppression women experience in Kuwait and other Gulf nations. The Iraqi government in 1969 established the General Federation of Iraqi Women (GFIW) to advance women's causes. The GFIW has organized women's conferences, training courses, and literacy campaigns. In 1983 it started a four-year plan to encourage women to work outside the home. In Baghdad it opened four employment offices for women.

Like U.S. planning against the Iraqi military, plans to bomb Iraq's civilian sector can be traced to before Iraq's invasion of Kuwait. July 1990 war games at Shaw Air Force Base in South Carolina identified 27 strategic sites in Iraq, based on a "Southwest Asia contingency" projecting Iraq as the aggressor. On August 7, the list was expanded to 57 (and later, 87) strategic targets. These did not include the Iraqi military in Kuwait.[3]

Pentagon statements about plans to bomb civilian sites appeared in the press in August and September 1990, outlining air strikes against industrial sites, power plants, water treatment plants, and similar facilities. The August 5, 1990 *Los Angeles Times* described another war game conducted at the Naval War College in July, in which participants were asked to determine the most effective U.S. response to an Iraqi invasion of Kuwait. The "realistic options" fell into three categories: (1) an attempt to assassinate Saddam Hussein; (2) "punitive raids on such economically vital targets as refineries, pipelines, and power plants"; and (3) committing ground troops with air support to the Arabian peninsula.[4] In reality, each option was pursued.

Then, in September, Air Force Chief of Staff Michael Dugan told reporters that, as far as targets went, the "cutting edge would be downtown Baghdad. If I want to hurt you, it would be at home, not out in the woods someplace." Referring to a list of strictly military targets, Dugan said, "That's a nice list of targets . . . but that's not enough." The *Washington Post* reported that Dugan proposed an additional list — one which included Iraqi power systems, roads, railroads, and "perhaps" domestic petroleum production facilities.[5]

Within days of that statement, Dugan was fired. Secretary of Defense Dick Cheney called his statements "inappropriate," but the real reason for his firing was that Dugan jeopardized both domestic and international support for military action against Iraq. President Bush had been insisting that the U.S. military buildup in Saudi Arabia was strictly defensive, but Dugan's statements revealed that Washington was not only planning an offensive, but would target civilians. In late January 1991, the *London Times* observed that allied bombing was closely following Dugan's description, "with the liberation of Kuwait as only part of the overall plan."[6]

The overall plan was described in the June 23, 1991 *Washington Post*. After interviews with several of the war's top planners and extensive research into how targets were determined, reporter Barton Gellman wrote:

> Many of the targets were chosen only secondarily to contribute to the military defeat of [Iraq]. . . . Military planners hoped the bombing would amplify the economic and psychological impact of international sanctions on Iraqi society. . . . Because of these goals, damage to civilian structures and interests, invariably described by briefers during the war as "collateral" and unintended, was sometimes neither. . . . They deliberately did great harm to Iraq's ability to support itself as an industrial society.[7]

Col. John A. Warden III, whom Gellman quoted, made the additional point that damage to Iraq's life-support systems would make Iraq economically dependent on Western help: "Saddam Hussein

cannot restore his own electricity. He needs help. If there are political objectives that the UN coalition has, it can say, 'Saddam, when
you agree to do these things, we will allow people to come in and fix
your electricity.' It gives us long-term leverage."

One Pentagon planner was quoted in the article explaining the
relationship between the bombing and sanctions:

> People say, "You didn't recognize that it was going to have an effect
> on water and sewage." Well, what were we trying to do with
> sanctions — help out the Iraqi people? No. What we were doing with
> the attacks on the infrastructure was to accelerate the effect of
> sanctions.[8]

The evidence shows that the Pentagon intended the bombing to
destroy Iraq's civilian economy and make the country dependent on
the West. The bombing of Iraq's citizens was central, not collateral,
to U.S. strategy.

The most accurate missiles and laser-guided bombs were used to
destroy key elements of Iraq's infrastructure — communications systems, oil refineries, electric generators, water treatment facilities,
dams, and transportation centers — to inflict maximum hardship on
the Iraqi people. The nature of the bombing of industrial and other
priority sites showed calculated planning. As an illustration, Commission members inspected a bombed textile weaving plant in Babylon. Next to it was a new building that was to replace it once the
equipment was moved over. On January 19, 1991, missiles hit the
old plant — the one with equipment and civilian workers inside —
and left the new, empty building intact.[9]

U.S. bombers knew what weapons would be needed to destroy the
targets. On March 25, 1991, the BBC *Panorama* television documentary titled "America's Secret War" reported that the British provided
original construction plans that helped the allies destroy a "strategic"
building in Baghdad. Most major, sophisticated construction in Iraq
was designed and built by European architectural, engineering, and
construction firms. Many provided plans to the Pentagon that gave
detailed information for bombardiers.

The use of precision weapons reflected the Pentagon's priorities.
When Air Force General Merrill McPeak reported that only 6,520
tons of the total 88,500 tons of bombs dropped — only 7 percent —
were "smart," he spoke of the bombs directed at important targets.[10]
More of the early bombing was electronically controlled, much of it
laser-guided from F-117 Stealth bombers. Most key targets in Iraq's
infrastructure, especially in Baghdad, were hit in the first weeks of

the air war. As the war progressed, less accurate, free-falling bombs were used, as bombs with directional controls were too expensive for the low-priority targets that were left. Basra and other areas with fewer prime targets suffered more from free-falling bombs and carpet-bombing.

U.S. and British agents placed many homing devices near targets early in the bombing, enhancing their accuracy. The commando missions that placed these devices "remained partly cloaked in secrecy," as the March 1, 1991 *New York Times* reported:

> American special forces operations were barely mentioned during the six-week Persian Gulf war. . . . Reporters who learned of some of their activities inside Iraq were urged not to write about them until the end of the war, and special forces commanders turned down interview requests.[11]

At a dinner in early May 1991, British Prime Minister John Major boasted about his country's secret Special Air Service (SAS), which played a major role in placing the homing devices. The *London Times* termed Major's remarks "unprecedented," since the super-secret SAS is not usually mentioned in public.[12] Shortly before the ground war started, a British intelligence officer speaking anonymously told U.S. reporters how the SAS was operating:

> The SAS man fires his hand-held laser pistol at the target and "warms" it long enough for the "smart" bombs to be guided in. . . . The SAS is crawling all over Iraq doing very nasty things. They're dressed as Arabs, they speak as Arabs, and they look like Arabs.[13]

Hundreds of sorties were directed against Iraq's electrical plants, using Tomahawk cruise missiles, laser-guided GBU-10 Paveway II bombs, and unguided bombs. On June 23, 1991, Patrick Tyler reported in the *New York Times* that the United States had designed a weapon specifically to shut down Iraq's electric power. Tyler based his report on interviews with government analysts who saw a classified report on the effects of the war against Iraq. He reported the allies had "developed a still-secret weapon that dropped thousands of metallic filaments onto the electrical network at key points to create huge short-circuits and blackouts on the night of January 17, when the war began."[14] To make repair hazardous, unexploded fragmentation mines were dropped over the same areas.

More than 90 percent of Iraq's electrical capacity was taken out of service in the first hours. Days after the war started, the damage was so severe that Iraq shut down what little remained of its power grid. As one U.S. planner put it, "Not an electron was flowing."[15]

U.S. air attacks destroyed all of the country's 11 major electrical power plants, as well as 119 substations. The Al-Taji turbine plant was attacked with missiles and cluster bombs, and at least one person was killed and many were injured. The power plant at Al-Hartha was struck by missiles 13 times, with one attack on the last day of the war.

And yet, the three-volume Pentagon report issued in April 1992 claimed that the long-term crippling of Iraq's electrical grid was an accident — that the allies had meant only to temporarily damage the grid.[16] But if the United States had really wanted Iraq to be able to restore its electrical power, it would have lifted sanctions after the war to allow Iraq to buy parts to repair the damage. And the damage to Iraq's infrastructure was comprehensive. Electric power was only one part of the overall targeting.

WHAT WAS BOMBED

After their fact-finding trip to Iraq, Commission members Gemma and Abed reported:

> In every city we visited, we documented severe damage to homes, electrical plants, fuel storage facilities, civilian factories, hospitals, churches, civilian airports, vehicles, transportation facilities, food storage and food testing laboratories, grain silos, animal vaccination centers, schools, communication towers, civilian government office buildings, and stores. Almost all facilities we saw had been bombed two or three times, ensuring that they could not be repaired. Most of the bridges we saw destroyed were bombed from both ends.[17]

Dr. David Levinson, who visited Iraq immediately after the war with the International Physicians for the Prevention of Nuclear War, said, "There were many direct civilian casualties from the bombings, but these numbers do not reflect the true horror of this war."[18] Compounded by sanctions, the damage to life-support systems in Iraq killed more after the war than direct attacks did during the war.

As Levinson testified at Commission hearings in San Francisco and Los Angeles, "It was clear that the bombing war against Iraq has been a war directed against the civilian population through massive destruction of the country's infrastructure."[19]

Iraq's eight major multipurpose dams were repeatedly hit and heavily damaged. This simultaneously wrecked flood control, municipal and industrial water storage, irrigation, and hydroelectric power. Four of Iraq's seven major water pumping stations were destroyed. Bombs and missiles hit 31 municipal water and sewage facilities; 20 were hit in Baghdad alone. Sewage spilled into the Tigris and out into the streets of Baghdad, adding water-borne disease to the list of killers. In Basra, the sewage system completely collapsed. Water purification plants were incapacitated nationwide. Those that were not damaged could not function without electricity. For many weeks, people in Baghdad — without television, radio, or newspapers to warn them — were getting their drinking water from the Tigris in buckets. The Iraqi News Agency and Baghdad Broadcasting Station lost six wireless broadcasting stations, 12 television stations, and five radio stations. Without electricity, even undamaged radio transmitters and receivers were useless.

Iraq's telephone system was put out of service in the first few days of the war. The International Telecommunications Union's (ITU) fact-finding trip to Iraq in June–July 1991 reported that 400,000 of Iraq's 900,000 phone lines had been destroyed. Fourteen central exchanges were irreparably damaged, with 13 more put out of service indefinitely. The ITU reported that as late as July 1991, "no reliable telecommunications exist[ed] in Iraq."[20]

Lack of communications frustrated attempts to conduct any activity, including caring for the sick and injured. The destruction of transportation links compounded the problem. In a country built around two great rivers, 139 automobile and railway bridges were either damaged or destroyed, including 26 in the Basra province alone. Major highways and other roads were hit, too, making travel a nightmare. Road maintenance stations were bombed to prevent repairs. All kinds of civilian cars, trucks, buses, and even taxis were attacked along Iraq's major highways.

Iraq's agriculture and food-processing, storage, and distribution system was attacked directly and systematically. Half of Iraq's agricultural production came from irrigated lands, and all of the irrigation systems serving them — including storage dams, barrages, pumping stations, and drainage projects — were attacked. Farmers lost the ability to flood or drain land, cutting food production in half and causing widespread saltwater intrusion in Basra province. At least three food warehouses in the Baghdad province were hit, seven were struck in the Basra province, and all of Iraq's General Company of Foodstuffs warehouses in the Al-Qadissiya province were destroyed. Important pesticide storage was destroyed. Three separate facilities of the Iraqi Dates Company were damaged. Iraq's baby milk powder factory at Abu Ghraib, unique to the region, was attacked on January 20, 21, and 22. Although the Pentagon claimed it was a chemical plant, the attacks were simply part of the deliberate targeting of Iraq's food production. The Al-Ma'mun Vegetable Oils Factory and the sugar factory in Meisan Province were hit. In Al-Taji, a small town near Baghdad, the country's biggest frozen meat storage and distribution center was destroyed. It was bombed three times in one day — at 8:00 A.M., 3:00 P.M., and 8:00 P.M. Farm herds were decimated — 3½ million sheep from a total of 10 million and 2 million cattle — primarily from feed shortages. Ninety percent of the country's poultry production was destroyed.

Grain silos across the entire country were hit methodically, and hundreds of farms and farm buildings were attacked. The nation's tractor assembly plant and major fertilizer plant were destroyed in bombing raids that took 16 lives.

In June 1992, more than a year after Iraq was driven from Kuwait and with sanctions still in place, the United States bombed grain and wheat fields with incendiary bombs near Mosul in northern Iraq. There was no UN resolution to condemn this open and unprovoked attack on Iraq's ability to feed itself.

U.S. bombing hit 28 civilian hospitals and 52 community health centers. Zubair Hospital in Basra province totally collapsed from bombing. At Al-Rashad Mental Hospital, southwest of Baghdad, ceilings collapsed on patients' beds. At Ulwiyya Maternity Hospital, shrapnel and broken glass hit babies and mothers. The student health clinic and school in Hilla was bombed. Five of Iraq's military medical facilities were also damaged.

Allied bombs damaged 676 schools; 38 were totally destroyed. Eight of those hit were parts of universities. Nor were mosques or historic sites immune from U.S. attacks, though the Pentagon stressed that they were not targeted. In fact, they were hit all across the country. Iraq reported that 25 mosques in Baghdad alone were hit, and 31 more were reported damaged around the country. During the first week of February, I saw six badly damaged mosques, with two more in Basra totally destroyed, and three damaged Christian churches. The 900-year-old Church of St. Thomas — in Mosul, more than 1,000 miles from Kuwait — was attacked, as was the Mutansiriya School, one of the oldest Islamic schools in Iraq.

Bombers hit civilian government office buildings in Baghdad, including the Baath Party headquarters, City Hall, the Supreme Court, the Justice Department, the Ministry of Defense, the Ministry of Justice, the Ministry of Labor, the National Palace, and the central post office. Baghdad's impressive new convention and conference center, built to host the annual Non-Aligned Nations meeting, was extensively damaged.

Many manufacturing plants were hit. Seven textile factories sustained damage, as did five engineering plants, five construction facilities, four car assembly plants, three chlorine plants, a major ammonia export facility, and 16 chemical, petrochemical, and phosphate plants. A major hypodermic syringe facility in Hilla was destroyed by laser-guided rockets. All major cement plants were hit. Twelve industrial contracting companies reported extensive damage to their facilities. The Baghdad factories of the Al-Sa'ad Company, the Al-Balsam Cosmetics Company, the Baghdad Razors Company, the Akad Clothes Factory, and the Muwaffak J. Janna Factory were all totally destroyed.

Iraq's oil industry was a priority target. U.S. planes hit 11 oil refineries, five oil pipeline and production facilities, and many oil tankers. Three oil tankers were sunk and three others set on fire. Bombs hit major storage tanks, the gas/oil separators through which crude oil passes to refineries, the distilling towers and catalytic converters critical to modern refineries, and the important K2 pipeline junction near Beiji, which connected northern oil fields, an export pipeline to Turkey, and a reversible north-south pipeline inside Iraq.

Saddam International Airport and Al-Muthana Airport were attacked, along with parked passenger and cargo planes. Rail stations and yards, transportation hubs, bus stations, and car lots were systematically attacked everywhere.

As the infrastructure and life-support systems were being bombed, Iraqi civilians were killed by the thousands. Attacks on life-support systems assured that many more thousands would perish, even though they were not in the direct line of fire.

Dr. Q. M. Ismail, director of Baghdad's Saddam Central Children's Hospital, was on duty the night U.S. bombs began to fall. Forty infants were in incubators, their mothers at their sides. When the electricity went out, the incubators stopped working. With the thunder of war all around them, the desperate mothers grabbed their children and rushed them into the basement.

Six hours later, 20 of the children were dead. "Those 40 mothers nearly went crazy," Dr. Ismail recalled. "I will never forget the sight of those women."[21]

BOMBING CITIES

Seventy-two percent of Iraq's population lives in cities. U.S. claims that it spared civilians through pinpoint bombing are false. There is no way to bomb densely populated cities day after day and not kill civilians.

The whole of Basra was bombed mercilessly. Paul Walker, director of the Institute for Peace and International Security at the Massachusetts Institute of Technology, testified at Commission hearings in New York and Boston that "there was no pretense at a surgical war in this city."[22] He quoted from an article in the February 5, 1991 *Los Angeles Times* — by coincidence, a day I was in Basra — which reported:

> a hellish nightmare of fires and smoke so dense that witnesses say the sun hasn't been clearly visible for several days at a time. . . . [The bombing is] leveling some entire city blocks . . . [and there are] bomb craters the size of football fields and an untold number of casualties.[23]

In the fourth week of bombing, U.S. military officials announced that they no longer considered Basra off-limits to area bombing. Since area bombing — any bombardment that treats a number of clearly separated and distinct military targets within a city as a single military target — violates Article 51 of Protocol 1 additional to the Geneva Convention, U.S. officials had to justify such activity. On February 11, General Richard Neal told reporters, "Basra is a military town in the true sense. . . . The infrastructure, military infrastructure, is closely interwoven within the city of Basra itself." Neal also said no civilians were left in Basra, only military targets.[24]

In fact, 800,000 people lived in Basra, Iraq's second largest city. When I was there, during and after the bombing, I saw whole neighborhoods — schools, homes, a post office — destroyed. San Antonio, Texas has a higher presence of military facilities than Basra. It is appalling to think anyone might claim the whole city of San Antonio is a legitimate target. Postwar visitors to Basra were no less appalled.

Baghdad, with far less damage than Basra and other southern cities, nevertheless was hit for 39 consecutive days. "We're going after hard targets in Baghdad," Lieutenant General Thomas Kelly told reporters. "Therefore, it takes more bombs on each target in order to be successful."[25]

On February 12, journalists in Baghdad reported more than 25 explosions in the central part of the city. Six days later, the allies launched a fierce two-hour bombardment of Baghdad that began at 11:00 P.M. A journalist wrote of the raid:

[M]issiles began skimming past the windows of the al-Rashid hotel. Against a background roar of high-flying aircraft, the hum of a cruise missile was heard every 10 minutes or so, followed by a terrific explosion that shook the entire hotel.[26]

On February 27 at 1:35 A.M., two nights before the ceasefire, Radio Baghdad broadcast Iraq's pullout from Kuwait. Seemingly in response, Baghdad was subjected to another fierce raid, described by a resident as "a sleepless night of horror."[27]

In mid-February, missiles accounted for at least 200 reported civilian deaths and 500 more injured in the town of Falluja. The actual death toll is certainly higher. These deaths were the result of two separate attacks, allegedly on bridges. Eyewitness reports have corroborated these attacks, one of which the British Royal Air Force has claimed resulted from precision-guided bombs missing their targets.

However, witnesses disagree, calling the bomb placement intentional. Hamid Mehsan, a Falluja merchant, who lost his son, brother, and nephew in one of the attacks, saw the bombs from one attack hit a market. He said, "This pilot said he had come to hit the bridge, on the television, and it was a mistake. But we're a distance of 1½ kilometers from the bridge. In our minds, we are convinced that the attack was to the market, to kill our people."[28] Palestinian truck drivers later confirmed that a nearby Egyptian hotel was also leveled in the attack. Two hundred people died.

The other attack destroyed a row of modern concrete five- and six-story apartment houses near another bridge, as well as several other houses nearby. As Middle East Watch described it, "All buildings for 400 meters on both sides of the street, houses and market, were flattened."[29] Simply living near a bridge during the bombing placed civilians in jeopardy. Hundreds were killed in Baghdad in buildings near bridges, and the bridges themselves were not legitimate military targets.

The nature of the U.S. bombing campaign against the Iraqi infrastructure makes the term "collateral damage" inapplicable. The Pentagon has admitted it targeted civilian structures both to demoralize the populace and exacerbate the effects of sanctions. Many attacks were carried out in daytime, when Iraqi civilians would undoubtedly be present. A textile weaving plant in Babylon, for example, was bombed three times on January 19, 1991, and two women were killed at their work stations. Sixteen people were killed on February 18, 1991 when a telephone relay station was bombed twice, destroying the surrounding shops and homes. Scores died in attacks on bridges. None of these facilities were military targets.

THE AMARIYAH SHELTER BOMBING

Baghdad was the site of one of the air war's most horrific attacks. Probably 1,500 civilians, mostly women and children, were killed when the Amariyah civilian bomb shelter was hit by two bombs in the early morning hours of February 13, 1991. One bomb opened a hole in the shelter's roof. The second bomb, much bigger and more powerful, traveled through the hole and blasted its way through one floor to the bottom floor of the shelter, where it exploded. The explosion from the second bomb shattered doors and windows in homes around the neighborhood.

The first bomb hit at 4:30 A.M. It did not kill everyone. Neighborhood residents heard screams as people tried to get out of the shelter. They screamed for four minutes. Then the second bomb hit, killing almost everybody. The screaming ceased.

There were at most 17 survivors.

The U.S. public saw sanitized, heavily edited footage of the bombed shelter. But the *Columbia Journalism Review* reported in its May/June 1991 issue that much more graphic images were shown on news reports in Jordan and Baghdad. The scenes were so devastating that hundreds of enraged Jordanians surrounded the Egyptian and U.S. embassies, shouting pro-Saddam Hussein slogans, throwing stones, and attacking Western journalists. The *Review* obtained the footage via unedited CNN feeds and Baghdad's WTN, and described it as follows:

> This reporter viewed the unedited Baghdad feeds. . . . They showed scenes of incredible carnage. Nearly all the bodies were charred into blackness; in some cases the heat had been so great that entire limbs were burned off. Among the corpses were those of at least six babies and ten children, most of them so severely burned that their gender could not be determined. Rescue workers collapsed in grief, dropping corpses; some rescuers vomited from the stench of the still-smoldering bodies.[30]

Media and Iraqi government accounts report that 300–400 people were killed in the shelter. However, personal visits by Commission staffers, Palestine Human Rights Information Center Director Louise Cainkar, and the Gulf Peace Team (GPT) revealed that the number killed was closer to 1,500. Neighborhood residents told the Commission the shelter's capacity was 2,500, and that at night, there were usually 1,500–1,800 people using it.

Still others contradicted the official death toll. Dr. Beladune Mouloud, president of the Algerian Red Cross, testified at the

March–April 1991 European Parliament hearings on war crimes in the Gulf that he personally counted 415 dead children at Amariyah.[31] GPT members interviewed a woman who had served as the shelter's doctor until two weeks before the attack. She said that on the night of the attack a sign-in book for the shelter contained 1,000 names. But people stopped signing in after that, so the total number was actually higher.

The shelter housed 500 triple-decker beds. GPT interviews with neighborhood residents revealed it was very crowded that night. February 13 was an Islamic holiday; occupants of the shelter held a celebration. Some of the 17 survivors were people who had slept in a hallway because of overcrowding.

U.S. briefers claimed the shelter was being used as a military facility. But the shelter, bombed just two weeks before the end of the war, had been used by civilians for weeks. Neighborhood residents said it was unbelievable that the United States did not know the shelter was being used mostly by women and children. Hundreds of civilians entered the shelter each afternoon and left every morning, and the neighborhood was subject to frequent air surveillance during this time.

Abu Kulud, who lost his wife and two daughters in the shelter, said: "It was impossible for them not to know there were only civilians in the shelter. Their air [communications] were everywhere." Sura, who lost her mother and two sisters in the raid, said: "It is not possible that they did not see with their satellites women and children entering the shelter. . . . How could they not know? They had to know. They had the satellite over our heads 24 hours a day, as well as photographs the planes took before they bombed."[32]

Abu Sabah Hameed, who lost his wife of 42 years and six other family members in the shelter, told the GPT: "You know, seven people went out of this house and they never came back. They went out at sunset, around 4:30 P.M. that day. When they brought me the news — you know, it wasn't easy to hear. It's one of the hardest things that could happen to a person.[33]

Mohammed Khader, a Palestinian who lived in the Amariyah neighborhood, lost his wife and four daughters in the shelter. He testified at the February 29, 1992 War Crimes Tribunal in New York City that 1,500 people died in the shelter bombing.

Earlier that week, Khader had tried to leave Iraq for Jordan. But when he arrived at the border it was closed. Just driving to the border was a terrifying experience:

Bombs were falling around us everywhere. When we reached a city near the border called Rutba, nearly about 100 kilometers from the border, we arrived there about 11:00 at night. We tried to take some rest at a hotel. I heard a big explosion. It was a rocket from an American airplane exploding nearby. My daughters were crying, and they were afraid. I tried to make them quiet, not so afraid. And then the planes came back.

After an hour or so, at 3:00 A.M., the airplanes came back again and bombed the area another time, and my daughters started crying again. . . . During our return [to Amariyah] I saw many places in the road that were bombed, and the driver tried to get to the other side. . . . After we passed one bridge, a half hour later it was gone.[34]

Back in Amariyah, Khader arranged for his wife and daughters to stay in the shelter while he and his son stayed home. On February 12, he tried to arrange for a car to make another attempt to leave the country. He was unable to find one, and his family went back to the shelter that night.

Khader was awakened by an explosion at 4:30 in the morning. Like so many other Amariyah residents, it did not cross his mind that the civilian shelter had actually been hit. He testified:

After one hour, a neighbor came to my house, knocked on the door and told me that the shelter was bombed. . . . When I went there, I found terrible things. . . . The plumes came out from the shelter. All the doors of the shelter were closed, because of the pressure created by the bomb. After two hours, I think, they opened one of the doors and tried to take out the bodies, the dead bodies of the people who were in the shelter. You couldn't distinguish any of the dead, because some were burnt, some cut.

I didn't even find my wife. I didn't find the body of my wife or my daughters. Nearly all the people in the same area, they also didn't find their families.[35]

BOMBING HIGHWAY TRAFFIC

Other direct attacks on civilians received less news coverage than the bombing of the Amariyah shelter. Among the most notable were the regular search-and-destroy missions against civilian highway traffic. Many of these attacks took place on the Baghdad–Amman highway. Civilian vehicles on this road were intentionally strafed. When I was in Iraq during the bombing, we drove the length of the highway twice. All along the way were bombed-out carcasses of passenger buses, trucks, vans, taxis, and cars — all civilian vehicles. Victims also included truckers transporting humanitarian shipments. Ships and vehicles carrying medicine and food — supposedly exempt from both the U.S. and UN embargoes — were bombed, boarded, or otherwise prevented from entering Iraq. It was an attack on transportation designed to paralyze and terrorize the country, prevent civilian flight, and cut off imports.

In a February 7, 1991 letter, Jordan's ambassador to the UN informed Secretary General Javier Perez de Cuellar that 14 Jordanian civilians had been killed and 26 wounded on the Baghdad–Amman highway from January 29 through February 5. The letter said the casualties resulted from "bombing by United States and allied aircraft of trucks and tankers belonging to Jordanian companies." The letter said 52 vehicles had been damaged or destroyed during the eight-day period. The ambassador requested the letter be circulated as a Security Council document.[36]

Commission of Inquiry members met with the widow and seven children of a Jordanian truck driver who was bringing UN-approved frozen meat into Iraq. His truck was bombed and his relief driver was burned in the cab. When he fled the truck, he was strafed and killed.

Najib Toubasi, a Palestinian, was driving a bus filled with 57 civilian passengers on February 1, 1991, when the rear of the vehicle was hit by a bomb. Najib told the Commission that after a second bomb hit the bus and the passengers fled, "People were running away and the planes followed them and strafed them with machine guns. . . . I was wounded in my right leg. I was holding onto a woman with my right hand and a child in my left hand. We were running across the desert. The woman got hit, and the child was screaming, 'I don't want to die! I don't want to die!' " Many did die.

The *New York Times* reported that a Jordanian Red Crescent official witnessed a Jordanian family's two infants die in a highway strafing attack.[37]

Middle East Watch interviewed Dr. Samir A. Qwawasmi, who was sent to Baghdad by the Arab Medical Committee for Emergencies. At 5:15 A.M., after a short stop at a parking area for dawn prayers, Dr. Qwawasmi got into his car and allied planes immediately attacked. MEW reported, "Dr. Qwawasmi . . . was injured with lacerations on his face, nose, cheek and hands. Tossed against the side of the car, he was still suffering pain in his left shoulder when he was interviewed by MEW."[38]

Qwawasmi believes he was hit by pieces of a cluster bomb, illegal under international law even for use against troops. Leaving the scene in a four-wheel-drive vehicle that towed his car, Qwawasmi passed many burned cars and passenger vans. A half-hour after his car was attacked, while he was still on the road, Qwawasmi saw a 40-foot refrigerator truck hit by a missile.

The vehicles on the Baghdad–Amman highway came in all colors, shapes, and sizes. Eyewitnesses reported seeing everything from orange buses to red Volkswagens attacked or damaged. In daylight, when many were hit, these could not have been mistaken for military vehicles. In fact, though the United States sometimes claimed it was searching for Scud launchers, most of the Baghdad–Amman highway killings took place with no military targets within the vicinity. Bernd Debusmann of Reuters reported, "Of at least half a dozen burned or damaged vehicles on the desert highway, only one vehicle was clearly a military vehicle. . . . local residents told me the bombing of the road was frequent, and the targets almost always seemed to be civilian trucks or private cars."[39] Highway bombing and strafing occurred throughout Iraq.

INDISCRIMINATE BOMBING

Thousands of civilians were victims of indiscriminate bombing by B-52s and other aircraft. This result was inescapable when thousands of bombing sorties targeted densely populated areas. Most news reports focused on F-117 Stealth fighters, equipped with more accurate bombs. But B-52s, which drop free-falling, unguided bombs, carried out the bulk of the bombing.

Paul Walker testified that "B-52s were used from the first night of the war to the last. Flying at 40,000 feet and releasing 40–60 bombs of 500 or 750 pounds each, their only function is to carpet bomb entire areas."[40] After the first days of the bombing, the B-52s flew at very high altitudes.

At the Montreal Commission hearing on November 15, 1991, journalist Paul William Roberts, who traveled with Bedouin tribes in Iraq during the bombing, testified on his experience. He said the air attack was unlike anything he witnessed as a war correspondent in Vietnam. He recalled

> three waves of bombing a night. And I experienced bombing in Cambodia, but this was nothing like that. . . . After 20 minutes of this carpet-bombing there would be a silence and you would hear a screaming of children and people, and then the wounded would be dragged out. I found myself with everyone else trying to treat inju-

ries, but the state of people generally was one of pure shock. They were walking around like zombies, and I was too, because the disorienting effects of the blasts themselves formed a psychological warfare if you like . . . but if you've been kept awake every night for the past 10 days as everyone had, you begin to lose your perspective on reality.[41]

SANCTIONS: A CONTINUING CRIME AGAINST HUMANITY

The other major instrument used to wage total war against the Iraqi people was economic sanctions. The war against Iraqi civilians started with sanctions before a single bomb was dropped, and the sanctions have continued long after the shooting stopped. The effects of the bombing compounded by the sanctions have brought unimagined misery to the entire Iraqi nation. That suffering continues unabated.

Iraq's citizens had enjoyed a relatively good and rising standard of living. The country was developing and its oil resources and industrial base offered a prosperous future. Now Iraq is trapped in poverty similar to that found in the poorest countries.

The bombing deprived the Iraqi people of the most basic supports of modern life, stripping the country not only of electric power, communications, and other life-sustaining facilities, but of food, clean water, and medical services. The destruction made it impossible for Iraq to care for its people during the bombing. The sanctions prevented Iraq from restoring vital services, providing basic needs, and mounting an effective national recovery program. Together, bombing and sanctions have reduced Iraq to a pre-industrial state. When I returned to Iraq in February 1992, potable water was delivered by trucks in Basra. Sewage and sanitation systems were ruined. Many communications systems remained inoperable. Transportation was limited. Airports were still closed. Health care facilities were dysfunctional, with hospitals able to operate at only 25 percent capacity. Famine and disease were claiming hundreds of Iraqi lives each day.

The sanctions were never intended as anything but a war strategy. Even before the United States manipulated the Security Council to levy worldwide sanctions against Iraq, Western countries had instituted a selective, de facto sanctions campaign. After the Iran–Iraq War concluded, U.S. companies still sold to Iraq, but also collaborated on an economic squeeze. By 1990, hundreds of scientific, food, and engineering contracts had been canceled by Western companies.[42] UN-sponsored sanctions imposed in early August made Iraq far more vulnerable before the bombing began, reducing medical supplies, impairing health conditions, eroding food reserves, and effectively shutting down much of its economy.

Oil made up 90 percent of Iraqi exports and generated the bulk of the country's revenue. As foreign ports rejected Iraqi ships and foreign tankers stopped filling up with Iraqi oil, Iraq's foreign income was cut off. This affected Iraq's food supply, as oil revenue had previously been used to import food. Before August 1990, Iraq imported approximately 70 percent of its food. With foreign assets frozen and no oil revenue, food purchases became increasingly difficult.

Washington knew this. One month before the invasion of Kuwait, the U.S. Embassy in Baghdad had prepared a confidential report that detailed Iraq's dependence on food imports. According to the *Los Angeles Times,* which obtained a copy in August 1990, the report estimated stockpiles of two months' worth of wheat, nine days' worth of corn, and 38 days' worth of barley.[43] Corn and barley were crucial as farm feed.

Iraq turned to Turkey, once one of its main food suppliers, to provide emergency food aid for children. Turkey refused the request, and it also stopped allowing Iraqi oil to flow through its pipeline. By late August, Iraqis were standing in breadlines, and the Iraqi Ministry of Trade was forced to ration food. In September, the ministry cut the monthly allocation of staple food items provided to the public from 343,000 tons to 182,000 tons. The allocation was further reduced to 135,000 tons in January 1991 – a 60 percent drop in only four months.[44]

In October 1990 the *Washington Post* reported there was no feed left for farm animals. "[T]hey are slaughtering the dairy cows and the egg-laying chickens," one Iraqi said, "because there will be no [feed] for them, and when this is all eaten up, life will begin to get difficult."[45] With staple food items rationed and insufficient, families were forced to buy more food in the markets — where prices doubled, tripled, and sometimes quadrupled.

UN Resolution 661, which imposed sanctions against Iraq, allowed food "in humanitarian circumstances." Paragraph 6 established the Sanctions Committee of the Security Council, which upon the September 13, 1990 passage of UN Resolution 666, assumed the power to determine what constituted humanitarian circumstances. The committee, controlled by the United States, was consistently hostile to Iraq. Importation of food and medicines was severely curtailed.

From August 6, 1990 to March 22, 1991, efforts t(
to Iraq through the Persian Gulf were militarily
Secretary of the Navy Dan Howard defended a vi..
zure of the *Ibn Khaldoun*, a ship carrying humanitarian .
to Iraq, in a letter to Senator Slade Gorton. Howard wrote:

> Foodstuffs were included in the embargo by Resolution 661, except
> "in humanitarian circumstances." Pursuant to resolutions 661 and
> 666, the Security Council Sanctions Committee was established to
> determine when there was an urgent humanitarian need to supply
> foodstuffs to Iraq. Until Security Council Resolution 687 (adopted
> April 3, 1991) exempted foodstuffs altogether from the embargo, all
> ships carrying food to Iraq were diverted, unless their shipment had
> been approved by the Sanctions Committee. *Ibn Khaldoun* never
> received the approval of the Sanctions Committee to transport food
> to Iraq.[46]

But international law unambiguously provides the right of free
passage for medical and humanitarian foodstuffs to countries at war,
regardless of any sanction or blockade. James Fine of the University
of Pennsylvania's Office of International Programs wrote in his study
"Exceptions to the UN Trade Embargo Against Iraq" that Security
Council member states had the obligation under international law
to "agree to arrangements for the free passage of the foodstuffs
needed to eliminate the shortages." [47]

E. Faye Williams, staff counsel for U.S. Representative Mervyn
Dymally, was a member of the peace team aboard the *Ibn Khaldoun*. Williams testified at the New York Commission hearing that
U.S. raiding parties beat women on the ship, used stun guns, and
smashed video recording equipment. As she walked with her hands
up, one Marine screamed at her to get out of his way "or the next
word I say will be a bullet through his [the captain's] head."[48]

Medical supplies, also supposedly exempt from sanctions, were
blocked, too. By December 1990, Iraqi hospitals were experiencing
serious shortages. A delegation from the International Physicians for
the Prevention of Nuclear War (IPPNW) visited Iraq December
14–22, and documented that at Saddam Central Pediatric Hospital
in Baghdad, infant mortality had already doubled. At the two hospitals the doctors visited, supplies of essential medicines like intravenous penicillin, pediatric vaccines, gamma globulin, insulin,
and potassium chloride for intravenous use had been depleted. Older
patients were being taken off hemodialysis, reported the IPPNW, an
act "tantamount to letting them die."[49] On February 8, 1991, the

Iraqi Red Crescent informed me that while Iraq needed 2,500 tons a month of infant formula, it had been able to import only 17 tons since November 1990 and had no raw milk for domestic production of formula.

Sanctions against Iraq were never the merciful alternative to military action. Ann Montgomery of the GPT was in Baghdad on January 7, 1991. She testified at the Commission's New York hearing that the hospital situation had already become acute then, even before the bombing had begun.

> The doctors told us that 40 babies were dying a day, not from wounds, not from any extraordinary illness, but because there was no milk and no very simple medications. Nothing extraordinary, just simple medications, especially for diarrhea. You know how little it takes to get rid of diarrhea if you just have what it takes. . . . But the doctor was very angry, and his words to us were, "Please tell them not to make war on children." It was as plain as that.
>
> Whenever I hear that we should have let the embargo work, that's what I think of. The embargo was war, the embargo still is war when you hear about these ships being stopped.[50]

AFTER THE CATACLYSM

Under optimum conditions with a massive relief and rebuilding effort, years would be required to restore Iraq's facilities and services. But with continued sanctions, it is impossible for Iraq to begin rebuilding itself, or even to supply its people with the simplest needs — medicine, basic food staples, spare parts, generators for water pumps, and tractors.

The bombing destroyed 9,000 homes and left 72,000 people homeless. The ruined electrical system, disabled water pumping and purification systems, and damaged sewage pumping and treatment systems all created emergency needs. Raw waste filled city streets and the rivers from which people obtained their water.

Some neighborhoods in Baghdad and many rural areas went without water for months. In Basra, water is still trucked in for the entire civilian population. Because of sanctions, the chlorine needed for water purification remains generally unavailable.

Iraq could have instituted more effective stop-gap water measures if the electrical system had not been obliterated. Before the bombing, Baghdad used 9,000 megawatts of electricity daily. For more than three months after the bombing, the city was reduced to 700 megawatts per day. No electricity was available for municipal water pumping and purification, nor for private consumption. Sanctions prevented Iraq from buying the equipment and spare parts needed to rehabilitate its power grid.

The lack of electricity and fuel was nationwide, affecting every facet of life in Iraq. A UN delegation to Iraq March 10–17, 1991 led by Marti Ahtisaari reported, "[F]ood that is imported cannot be distributed; water cannot be purified; sewage cannot be pumped away and cleansed; crops cannot be irrigated; medicines cannot be conveyed where they are required; needs cannot even be effectively assessed."[51] The total breakdown of telecommunications worsened the crisis.

Sanctions also meant that Iraq could not rebuild its productive facilities. The factories that remained were mostly idled, as the domestic market had collapsed and no exports were allowed. The Ahtisaari team reported that Iraq's industrial workers "have been reduced to inactivity and will be deprived of income as of the end of March."[52] People were out of work everywhere. For those who still had jobs, wages had dropped to less than 7 percent of prewar levels.

Iraq was also unable to feed its people. Children were hit the hardest. Child mortality tripled through 1991 and in some areas quadrupled. The Harvard International Study Group visited Iraq in August–September 1991, and concluded that 1 million Iraqi children were malnourished, with 120,000 suffering severe and acute malnutrition.

On August 7, 1991, the *San Francisco Chronicle* reported the case of an Iraqi woman whose son was malnourished:

> Satanya Naser sits helplessly by her emaciated son Hamid, who cries at the slightest touch. Since January, she has been able to feed him only rice water. Now a year and a half old, he weighs 15 pounds and has the blotchy skin and distended belly characteristic of kwashiorkor, a severe protein deficiency caused by malnutrition that doctors say has not been seen in Iraq since the late 1950s.[53]

Satanya's son was a victim of acute malnutrition, with food scarce and priced out of reach for the poor. Hyperinflation in food prices rose as high as 2,000 percent. The *Chronicle* article went on:

> Satanya's husband, a day laborer, earns 120 dinars a month; a tin of powdered milk, which cost 3 dinars before the war, now costs 35 — over $100 at the official exchange rate. Flour costs 48 times what it did a year ago, rice 22 times, and vegetable oil 20 times.

Some items — chicken and often powdered milk — are simply not available.[54]

Monthly food rations allocated by the government after the war only covered one-third of average consumption and typically ran out after 10 days. Iraqis hoped that domestic farmers could help make up for food deficits and mounted an ambitious program in the fall of 1990 to produce more of its own food. But there were widespread crop failures in the 1991 summer harvest because of the inability to irrigate adequately and sanctions-induced shortages of spare parts for farm equipment, seeds, seedlings, fertilizer, and pesticides.

The only veterinary vaccination facility in the country had been bombed, leaving farm animals vulnerable to disease. Without grain to eat, the overall livestock population was reduced by 50 percent. The poultry industry was nearly destroyed.

Severe malnutrition was not restricted to the children of poor people because the sanctions had left the entire country without many needed items. The above August 7 *Chronicle* article reported the case of the rich farmer's one-year-old son who had been severely malnourished and sick with diarrhea for six months. Though his parents could afford it, they could not buy special nonallergenic infant formula because it was unavailable.[55]

Even when food was available, its benefits were often lost to diarrhea and other sicknesses. The bombing created ideal conditions for epidemics: poor sanitation, no communication, lack of food and medicine, lack of transportation, and contaminated drinking water. These contributed directly to high levels of cholera, typhoid, dysentery, diarrhea, and thousands of cases of marasmus and kwashiorkor. Hospitals were ill equipped to deal with these conditions. Without electricity, medicines, supplies, or spare parts, they were unable to treat patients or use diagnostic and therapeutic equipment.

Even though medical supplies were allowable under the UN sanctions resolutions, many supplies and medicines ordered before August 2, 1990 had still not reached Iraq by May 1991. With funds frozen, and no oil revenue, it was difficult for Iraq to pay for the medical supplies that were available.

Diabetics didn't have insulin. There was no medication to be had for hypertension. Anesthetics remained scarce. Antibiotics, sedatives, and common medicines were often unavailable. Hundreds of people with pacemakers knew that when the batteries died, replacement in Iraq was not possible.

The lack of electricity idled some medical resources and destroyed others. Medical technicians could not provide laboratory services, dialysis for kidney patients, or culture media. Nor could they sterilize equipment, store medicines, or give radiography treatment. Three to four thousand bags of blood spoiled at Iraq's Kindi Hospital because they could not be refrigerated. After the bombing halted, overburdened hospitals began to see more cases of burn victims who, with no electricity, were injured using kerosene to light their homes.

During my trip to Iraq in February 1991, Dr. Ibrahim Al-Nouri, head of the Iraqi Red Crescent, told me there had been 3,000 infant deaths since November 1, 1990. He attributed them entirely to shortages of infant milk formula and medicines.

The medical supplies that were received immediately after the war came entirely from UN relief organizations and through nongovernmental agencies like the Red Cross and the Red Crescent. But they met only 2.5 percent of the country's medical needs. In February 1992, only about 10 percent of Iraq's medical needs were being covered.

After the war, media accounts focusing on Baghdad reported that life had returned to normal in Iraq. The truth is that Iraq has been crippled for years to come. As Ahtisaari reported, "[We] were fully conversant with media reports regarding the situation in Iraq and, of course, with the recent WHO/UNICEF report on water, sanitary and health conditions. . . . It should . . . be said at once that nothing we had seen or read had quite prepared us for the particular form of devastation which has now befallen the country."[56]

At various times since the war, the U.S. government has attempted to pass responsibility for the destruction wreaked by the bombing onto clashes between rebel forces and the Republican Guard that occurred in March 1991 after the ceasefire. However, independent observers on the scene tell a different story. On their fact-finding trip to Iraq in April 1991, Commission members Adeeb Abed and Gavrielle Gemma found that though rebellions had caused damage, the decimation wreaked by bombing and sanctions was far more severe and constituted an incomparably greater long-term threat. Most areas of the country were unaffected by the uprisings, but none escaped U.S. bombing. The superficial damage caused by rebels' small-arms fire could not begin to compare with the heavy damage caused by U.S. bombing. According to Abed, in those cases where "Iraqi guides could have misled us," they did not. The guides pointed out damage caused by the rebels, referring to them as "hooligans." Even the Iranian devastation of Basra with artillery fire left the sewage system and all other major facilities operable. U.S.

bombing has left Basra crippled, without sewage disposal and having to truck in its water for at least several more years.

On March 22, 1991, the Sanctions Committee finally determined that humanitarian circumstances in Iraq permitted the importation of food and medicine, but nothing changed. The U.S. bombing had already crippled the country, and disease and malnutrition were ravaging the population. Iraq remained unable to purchase enough food and medicine to remedy its situation because of interference with shipments, the freeze on its assets, and the ban of oil sales.

ONE YEAR AFTER THE CEASEFIRE

The fact that Iraq has the second-largest oil reserves in the world and a determined government and population would seem to make reconstruction of the shattered country a certainty. Yet, long after the war, the nation remains gripped by poverty, malnutrition, water-borne disease, massive unemployment, despair, and daily death. Sanctions are paralyzing the country's ability to rebuild from the ruins caused by U.S. bombing.

The situation is getting worse, not better. Doctors and relief agencies report that the daily death toll continues to rise. In late January 1992, a funeral procession in Baghdad mourned the deaths of 10 children who had died in one hospital within one 10-hour span.[57] Though electricity has returned to much of Iraq, lack of cash limits supplies of food, medicine, and other requirements of life.

Touted as the nonviolent way to force Iraq to accede to UN demands, sanctions were still killing Iraqi children under the age of five at the rate of 300 per day in April 1992.[58] The embargo remains firmly in place, even though it was ostensibly imposed to remove Iraq from Kuwait. Requirements for lifting the sanctions continually change, and always involve billions of dollars in reparations that Iraq would find difficult to pay even if the sanctions were dropped.

Saduddrin Aga Khan, who led the second UN mission to Iraq June 29–July 13, 1991, said:

> None of us could overlook a glaring paradox: at a time when the international community is beset with disasters of daunting dimensions around the globe, we continue to appeal to the same donors to fund emergency programs in Iraq that the country could pay for itself. With considerable oil reserves in the ground, Iraq should not have to compete for scarce aid funds with a famine-ravaged Horn of Africa, with a cyclone-hit Bangladesh.[59]

A combination of factors — the embargo on foreign trade, billions in frozen assets, the ban on oil sales, and Iraq's outstanding $80 billion debt from the war with Iran — have prevented Iraq from importing more than small amounts of food and special medicine. Countries have refused to sell Iraq food staples like wheat and rice because they know Iraq does not have the revenues with which to pay. In May 1991, the Thai Rice Exporters Association turned down an Iraqi request for 200,000 tons of rice because of Iraq's $67.5 million debt to that country. As of July 1991, Australia was withholding the 1 million tons of food Iraq had requested in May until Iraq could prove it could both pay for it and settle its outstanding $470 million debt.[60]

CIVILIAN DEATHS

The devastating six-week bombing and the destructive long-term sanctions have killed tens of thousands of Iraqi civilians. Commission research shows that probably more than 150,000 civilians have died as a result of the U.S. assault on Iraq. This includes at least 100,000 postwar deaths, a figure used by many who have direct knowledge of the situation — Iraq's health minister, Dr. Umaid Midhat Mubarak, and Catholic Relief Services, to name two. Many estimates are higher. Based on infant mortality rates, UNICEF estimated in December 1991 that 87,000 children alone would have died by the war's anniversary.

On my trip to Iraq during the bombing, what I saw and the numbers of deaths I was able to verify directly due to bombing led me to estimate that there had been 15,000 civilian deaths by that time. The heaviest bombing occurred during the last three weeks, including the tragedies at Falluja and Amariyah. Based on all evidence available to the Commission, I estimated at least 25,000 Iraqi civilians dead as a direct result of bombing. Other estimates are in this range, or higher, though the Iraqi government, Greenpeace, and Middle East Watch have given estimates in the low thousands, which are unsupportable.

I met with the Iraqi Health Minister on February 2, 1991 and the Red Crescent on February 8, 1991. They gave figures that, when totalled, show 7,000 civilians had died by those dates from contaminated water, lack of infant food supplement, and medicine shortages alone. Total indirect deaths as of that date were probably above 12,000. The death rate was rapidly accelerating during the first week of February. Considering all evidence available to the Commission,

I estimate 25,000 civilians had died from indirect effects of the bombing, embargo, shattered infrastructure, and damaged safety and health services by March 1, 1991. Adding 25,000 indirect deaths, 25,000 bombing deaths, and at least 100,000 postwar deaths makes total civilian deaths in excess of 150,000.

And the death toll continues. Diseases arising from the disasters of war, malnutrition, contaminated water, dysfunctional medical services, inadequate medicines, and the debilitation of the population combine to cause hundreds of preventable deaths daily. The sanctions still deprive the Iraqi people of many essentials for human life. They constitute a continuing crime against humanity.

CHAPTER 4

Washington's Continuing Effort to Control the Middle East

THROUGH continued sanctions, demands for excessive reparations, and creation of a permanent military presence in the
Persian Gulf region, the United States seeks to advance its policy to
establish unchallengeable control of the Middle East's oil.

The United States, through the Security Council, has insisted that
sanctions remain in force until Iraq complies with the ceasefire resolutions. This is not a political bargaining position to trade for Iraqi
concessions. The sanctions are the centerpiece of Washington's continuing war against Iraq. They have contributed to the greatly increased death rate — thousands of Iraqis are dying each month — and
are designed to further cripple the country and reduce its ability to
resist American domination.

The brutal sanctions levied against democratic Iran in 1951,
which culminated in the CIA-backed installation of Shah Reza
Pahlevi, illustrates the strategy currently at work against Iraq. The
New York Times reported on January 19, 1992 that Bush administration officials felt it possible to take advantage of what they perceived
as weakening support for Hussein brought about in part by sanctions
that are strangling the Iraqi economy.[1]

At the same time, the American media was full of speculation
about how and when the United States would resume military oper-
ations to topple Hussein. William Safire wrote in the *New York
Times*: "An October 'surprise' would be too obviously political.
. . . [S]ome of our spooks expect a balloon up in April or May."[2] On
January 19, the *Times* ran a front-page story with the headlines
"Saudis Press U.S. for Help in Ouster of Iraq's Leader," "A Plan to

Back Uprisings," and "White House Considers Steps to Topple Hussein Before U.S. Presidential Vote."[3]

The U.S. plan to topple Hussein was no mere reelection ploy. Government officials had been planning for it since 1988, and openly discussing it from the first day of the sanctions in 1990. The March 22, 1991 *New York Times* article about the apocalypse in Iraq included this observation: "Ever since the trade embargo was imposed . . . the United States has argued against any premature relaxation in the belief that by making life uncomfortable for the Iraqi people it will eventually encourage them to remove President Saddam Hussein from power."[4]

Despite their many public protests that their goal in the war was not to topple Saddam Hussein, U.S. officials often undercut their denials with statements that made it clear they hoped he would be deposed one way or another. President Bush's February 15, 1991 call to the Iraqi people to rise up against Saddam Hussein was neither the first nor the last such message.

While Hussein's continuing support among Iraqis has thwarted attempts to remove him, this is also useful for the Bush administration. His presence justifies sanctions and reparations, and eliminates any rush of sympathy for the Iraqi people. Many observers believe that when those uses are adequately served, Hussein will be removed. It is largely a matter of time.

Months after the war, Bush continued to plan to overthrow Saddam Hussein. Much of the planning was done by the so-called Deputies Committee, a collection of senior officials from the Pentagon, the State Department, the CIA, and the National Security Council. A subcommittee under National Security Council auspices was expressly formed to plan covert operations.[5] Among its early efforts was a massive injection of counterfeit currency into Iraq's economy.

In November 1991, long after the first wave of postwar rebellions in Iraq had been crushed, the Deputies Committee requested military plans from the Joint Chiefs of Staff on aiding rebellions in Iraq. At the same time, Bush wrote to Saudi Arabia's King Fahd that he was determined to see Saddam Hussein overthrown, and that he would continue to provide arms for that purpose.[6] As summer 1992 approached, the Bush administration remained determined to further weaken and punish the Iraqi people and replace Saddam Hussein with a surrogate of its choice. The President continued to promote this policy even though, as U.S. experience in Iran and Latin America has shown, it is doomed to ultimate failure and creates a legacy of suffering and hatred.

REPARATIONS

The issue of reparations has received less attention than other aspects of the assault on Iraq. But reparations demanded of Iraq total upwards of $100 billion.

Reparations are always demanded of the defeated by the victor. This seems particularly perverse in the case of Iraq. The damage to Iraq far exceeded all the damage, casualties, and costs of all other countries involved in the war. Knowledgeable sources have placed the cost of rebuilding Iraq after the massive bombing onslaught in the hundreds of billions of dollars. Iraqi Minister of Trade Mohammed Mohdi Saleh has estimated Iraq needs $200 billion to rebuild. *Los Angeles Times* reporter Tom Furlong reported the cost of rebuilding Iraq was $100 billion to $200 billion.[7] Under these conditions, reparations amount to exacting tribute from a badly crippled victim.

Historically, reparations have not always been paid by the defeated in war, and rarely have they been paid in full. But they serve a purpose other than the reimbursment of injured parties. By imposing demands for reparations, the victors gain control over the vanquished. Thus, by seeking to enforce such payments, the United States can maintain a stranglehold on Iraq. With such control, Washington can exploit Iraq's oil wealth, keep the country poor, foster dependence on Western countries, and promote instability that may result in the creation of a compliant regime in Iraq.

It is through UN Resolution 687 — the ceasefire agreement signed on April 3, 1991 by Iraq and the United States — that Washington wages this aspect of the continuing war against Iraq. The resolution stipulates that Iraq is liable for "any direct loss, damage, including environmental damage and the depletion of natural resources, or injury to foreign governments, nationals and corporations" and must pay reparations. The agreement created U.S. control over Iraq principally through reparations, weapons destruction, and a UN commission to decide border demarcation.

Washington continues to demand that Iraq pay for damage to Kuwait that was caused largely by the U.S. military. It even demands that Iraq pay for the U.S. occupation of northern Iraq in violation of Iraqi sovereignty.

Kuwait seeks $60 billion in reparations from Iraq, nearly $30,000 per capita for its prewar population, a population that had a prewar per capita income eight times higher than the people of Iraq. Saudi Arabia requested compensation for Gulf cleanup costs. Immigrant workers who had to flee their jobs and homes asked compensation, which they ought to receive from governments responsible for their losses. The United States demanded payment for the Kurdish relief effort. When all of these demands are added up, the total reparations demanded of Iraq is estimated at $70–$100 billion.

The $300 billion combined cost of rebuilding and reparations, not to mention Iraq's prior $80 billion debt, is nearly seven times the $45 billion annual gross national product of Iraq before its destruction. A burden of that magnitude is unprecedented and impossible for any society to bear. There is no chance of it being paid. It is clearly intended to impoverish the Iraqis while others exploit their resources.

The UN proposal to allow Iraq limited oil sales was designed to further this policy. It permitted only enough sales to let Iraq purchase some of its food and medical needs, with insufficient funds to rebuild infrastructure. It seeks to exact reparations in the presence of systemic hunger and to fund challenges to Iraqi sovereignty by UN inspection teams as well as a UN commission to delineate an Iraq–Kuwait border.

The UN arrangement for the sale of oil stipulated that Iraq would be able to sell $1.6 billion worth of oil in six months. The proceeds would go into a UN-controlled escrow account. Of that amount, 30 percent would go toward reparations, with an additional 5 percent funding weapons destruction and border decisions. Iraq would then have had $1.04 billion for food and medicine over a six-month period.[8]

This amount was grossly insufficient for Iraq's food and medicine needs. Even UN Secretary General Perez de Cuellar, who recommended the 30 percent ceiling for reparations, advised the Council that an additional $800 million was needed to meet Iraq's humanitarian needs.[9] Iraqi UN Ambassador Abdul Amir Anbari reminded the Security Council of this recommendation on September 19, 1991, but to no avail.[10]

Cuba and Yemen, both of which had courageously voted in 1990 against authorizing the attack on Iraq, opposed the oil sales proposal. Iraq rejected the terms as a violation of its sovereignty.

In May 1991 Iraq had estimated it needed $1 billion for four months for food needs alone;[11] these funds did not even address the shattered medical system. Leaving the food and medical issues aside, the $1.6 billion figure was not enough to rebuild Iraq's infrastructure, nor was it even 1 percent of the amount needed for that task. The *New York Times* reported on June 3, 1991 that Iraq's most pressing problem — its destroyed electrical system — would require a "major infusion" of $1.5 billion.[12] This figure shows how irrelevant the oil sale arrangement was for meeting Iraq's needs.

The same day the *Times* article appeared, State Department

spokesperson Margaret Tutwiler told reporters, "We do not think that the 30 percent level suggested is adequate to compensate on a timely basis Kuwaitis and the others who have suffered so grievously at Iraq's hands." The United States said the rate of reparation payments from Iraqi oil sales should be 50 percent instead.[13]

Washington tried to downplay Iraq's desperate need to rebuild. U.S. estimates for the reconstruction of Iraq ranged from the CIA's figure of $30 billion up to a maximum of $50 billion.[14] In comparison, Kuwait — much smaller than Iraq, and with its infrastructure intact — demanded $60 billion in reparations. As Tom Furlong wrote in the *Los Angeles Times*, "If the cost of rebuilding Kuwait is staggering, it pales next to the likely price tag for repairing Iraq."[15]

The United States designed its postwar demands to strengthen its domination of the Middle East. A Bush administration official, quoted anonymously in the February 7, 1992 *New York Times*, revealed the real purpose of the ceasefire stipulation that Iraq destroy certain weapons. The official said that with more intrusive UN inspections and demands for information, the United States and its allies were trying to push Saddam Hussein into a humiliating corner, hoping he would lash out and provide justification for a military blow fatal to his regime. "The whole program of the inspection regime is to keep putting sand in his shorts," the official said.[16]

Much sand was shoveled in April 1992, when the UN committee established to determine the Iraq–Kuwait border awarded a larger portion of the disputed Rumaila oil field to Kuwait, along with part of Umm Qasr port, Iraq's major access to the Persian Gulf. Through the UN, the United States deprived Iraq of oil resources and effectively landlocked the country. Recalling the actions of the British in drawing the original lines between Iraq, Kuwait, and Saudi Arabia, this decision shows that Western countries still exert arbitrary power over the geography of the Middle East.

Thus, reparations is simply one more aspect of Washington's postwar strategy to recast Iraq as a subservient client state. This strategy includes overthrowing Saddam Hussein. To this end, Secretary of State Baker has said reparations claims against Iraq would be dropped if the Iraqi people overthrow Saddam Hussein.[17] As of summer 1992, the U.S. government was planning covert operations for precisely that purpose.

PERMANENT U.S. BASES IN THE GULF

The Gulf crisis provided a golden opportunity for the United States to reinforce its military presence in the region. Before and during the crisis, Washington moved to establish itself as a regional force. This was the culmination of years of U.S. planning and policy in the region, the centerpiece of which was and continues to be U.S. geopolitical control and allocation of oil resources. In early 1990, General Schwarzkopf testified before the Senate that the new strategy to implement this control should be a permanent U.S. military presence in the Middle East.

Fifty percent of the world's known oil reserves are in the Middle East. The United States annually imports nearly 15 percent of its oil from the region, while Western Europe imports 50 percent from there and Japan 70 percent. The "seven sisters" — the world's largest oil companies — include some of the wealthiest U.S. corporations. Twenty-five percent of U.S. profits from the Third World come from oil — most of it from refining and selling oil.[18] Oil wells in the Middle East are much more productive than U.S. wells, and contract workers from Asian and African countries make less than $100 per month in the Gulf sheikhdoms. Thus, it is much cheaper to extract oil in the Gulf than in the United States.

Cheap oil is pumped to Western industries and the astronomical profits are invested in Western economies. Any regime or movement that threatens to use oil resources for the benefit of the people of the Middle East — building homes, schools, hospitals, local industries, mass transit, and so on — will become a target of U.S. enmity and violence, as the people of Iraq have learned.

This is why the U.S has maintained a naval and military presence in and around the waters of the Persian Gulf since 1949, and has supported surrogate military governments.

In 1990 — six months before Iraq invaded Kuwait — General Schwarzkopf told Congress:

> Middle East oil is the West's lifeblood. It fuels us today, and being 77 percent of the Free World's proven oil reserves, is going to fuel us when the rest of the world has run dry. . . . Our allies are even more dependent on Middle East oil. Japan gets almost two-thirds of its oil from the area while our allies in Europe import over one-quarter.[19]

Schwarzkopf went on to say that any "local conflict can become a threat to our interests and warrant the commitment of U.S. forces." He warned that "Iraq is now the pre-eminent military power in the Gulf. . . . [It] has the capability to militarily coerce its neighboring states should diplomatic efforts fail to produce the desired results."[20]

Schwarzkopf saw the need to change the American strategy for enforcing its oil interests in the Middle East, then known as the Carter Doctrine. He explained that this doctrine stipulated that any threat to U.S. "vital interests" in the Middle East would be repelled by any means necessary, including military force. The Rapid Deployment Joint Task Force, capable of quick military action in the Middle East, was formed in 1981 to implement this strategy.

As Schwarzkopf went on to explain, the United States has always had a strategy for safeguarding its oil interests in the region. The Carter Doctrine had replaced the Nixon Doctrine, which Schwarzkopf told the Senate "stated that the U.S. would provide military and economic assistance to any nation whose freedom was threatened, but the nation would be expected to assume primary responsibility for its own defense."[21] This neatly summarizes U.S. support for surrogates or proxy governments like the Shah's Iran or Israel to control nationalist or other struggles that would impede U.S. "vital interests." When the Iranian revolution overthrew the Shah in 1979, the United States adopted the Carter Doctrine, which promised more direct action.

In 1990, with Iran weakened and the Soviet Union no longer a deterrent to U.S. action in the Middle East, Schwarzkopf outlined to the Senate a strategy designed to place a permanent U.S. military presence in the Gulf. He based it on "three pillars": "security assistance, U.S. presence and combined exercises." It was no longer sufficient to maintain mere readiness for intervention, as the Rapid Deployment Joint Task Force contemplated. Now, Schwarzkopf proposed, the U.S. military should keep its own troops in the Middle East. Six months later, Schwarzkopf was commander of the buildup in Saudi Arabia that allowed the United States to get its foot in the door.

In May 1991, Defense Secretary Dick Cheney arranged with various Gulf state leaders to quietly but forcefully install U.S. presence in the region. He sought approval from Saudi Arabia's Defense Minister Prince Sultan for a permanent deployment of troops in the Saudi superbase. Cheney presented the idea to Sultan while suggesting that his kingdom would not have to admit to a U.S. presence; it could be covered up. Scott Armstrong, reporting on the meeting in the November/December 1991 issue of *Mother Jones*, wrote:

> In their meeting, Cheney promised Sultan that Special Forces units would hardly be noticed by residents or, for that matter, by other regional powers such as Iran and Syria. If the increased presence were noticed, it could be explained away as a "routine rotation," he

suggested. There would be no admission of a permanent U.S. base; there would be no public treaty. There would be no announcement of any kind. Everything would, as usual, remain secret.[22]

On May 7, 1991, the *New York Times* reported this meeting was part of a four-day tour of the Gulf region "to muster support for the Administration's plan for a postwar presence." It also reported ways to cover up the U.S. military presence in the Gulf:

> Some Gulf nations, wary of being criticized by Islamic leaders and others for their close ties to the Americans, also appear to prefer that some aspects of their military cooperation with Washington remain hidden. . . . Mr. Cheney appears to be calculating that some Gulf states will find the administration's plan more acceptable if different arrangements are established with different countries, and no gulf nation is singled out for working with Washington."[23]

The *Times* reported Cheney as saying steps the U.S. could take "to improve its military position in the region might include moving aircraft carriers in and out of the Persian Gulf and shifting an amphibious force to the area from time to time."[24]

The Gulf War provided the U.S. military with the chance to establish a major permanent presence in the Middle East. The United States deployment to the Gulf included 542,000 troops, 108 warships — including six aircraft carriers — and 1,800 fixed-wing combat aircraft. This constituted 50 percent of all U.S. military resources worldwide.[25] During and after the war the U.S. made or strengthened agreements for bases in Saudi Arabia, Egypt, Turkey, Bahrain, the UAE, Kuwait, Pakistan, and Oman. Although Gulf exercises have been conducted for over a decade, the size of U.S. Navy battle groups have increased substantially since the 1991 war. As of spring 1992, the aircraft carrier *Eisenhower* and its battle group remain in the Gulf.

Before the invasion of Kuwait, the United States spent approximately 15 percent of its total military budget maintaining forces and firepower for intervention in the Middle East. During the course of the war it used bases in Saudi Arabia, Egypt, Turkey, Bahrain, the UAE, Kuwait, and Oman, among other countries. The Pentagon's "superbase" in Saudi Arabia, built during a ten-year period before Iraq's invasion, proved crucial to the allied performance against Iraq. An adviser to Defense Secretary Dick Cheney said that without the superbase network, the U.S. Air Force, radar, and missile systems would have operated with "less than one-quarter the efficiency and accuracy" they did.[26]

It is difficult to find reliable information on actual U.S. troop strength and bases currently in the Middle East. According to Scott Armstrong, the United States now has over 100,000 troops in the Middle East — including about 15,000 in Saudi Arabia, 30,000 in the other Gulf Cooperation Council states, 20,000 in Egypt, and 30,000 in Turkey. This does not include U.S. military installations in Morocco, Tunisia, Sudan, Somalia, Kenya, and other North and East African countries, or the 5,000 U.S. troops in Guadar, Pakistan.

U.S. arms sales to the Middle East, enormous to begin with, have increased and are expected to skyrocket. Before the Gulf War, Israel, Egypt, Turkey, and Pakistan together received $10 billion in annual U.S. military and economic aid. In the last decade, the U.S. sold over $40 billion in arms to the Gulf states, more than U.S. sales to all other Third World countries combined. A sale of 72 F-15s to Saudi Arabia is in the pipeline. If the sale goes through the Saudis have promised to buy all their military equipment from the U.S. In 10 years U.S. military sales to Saudi Arabia alone could exceed $50 billion.

Besides greatly increasing arms sales in the region, the Gulf War has also radically changed arms sales patterns. Until 1990, the former Soviet Union was the top arms supplier in the region. But in May 1992, Representative Lee Hamilton said in a House Foreign Affairs subcommittee that the five permanent members of the Security Council — the United States, Russia, England, France, and China — accounted for 90 percent of the arms business in the Middle East in 1991, with the United States selling two-thirds of the total.[27]

While profoundly damaging every human interest and the future of the United States as well as the Gulf region, the assault against Iraq accomplished every strategic objective Schwarzkopf outlined in his Senate testimony.

CHAPTER 5

The War Against the Environment

HIGH-TECHNOLOGY warfare damages the environment and threatens life in ways that cannot be measured. It is clear, however, that modern warfare is the most reckless and dangerous threat to the habitability of the planet that human abuses of technology have produced. The Gulf War is a case study of the ecological perils of war. To count the ways weapons kill in our technologically advanced times, you must look far beyond battlefield casualties. Deadly radiation is released from bombed nuclear power plants and toxins are released from chemical and biological factories. Radioactive shrapnel from uranium-tipped missiles and shells render whole regions uninhabitable. The crush of thousands of tanks and heavy armored vehicles and the concussion from thousands of tons of high explosives pulverize fragile ecosystems. And the massive fires that result from bombing oil refineries and storage tanks, and the ignition of crude oil at wellheads pollute the atmosphere around the world. Whole water systems are destroyed and polluted, and sewage systems crushed beneath the earth ooze cesspools throughout cities and towns. Full-scale modern warfare attacks life on the planet.

The direct human costs of the assault against Iraq are clear: tens of thousands of people died in the war, and many thousands more will die from the starvation and dislocation that have followed. What is not so obvious is how pervasively the environmental damage the war caused will injure and shorten people's lives around the globe. Most of these effects will be realized only in the long term, in illness and lower life expectancy for whole generations.

PREMEDITATION

Long before the war began, U.S. officials were well aware of its environmental dangers. In August 1990 the Pentagon and the White House signed an agreement to waive National Environmental Protection Act requirements for U.S. military operations in the Gulf. The act mandates that the federal government must fully study any environmental effects of a proposed project, and must then allow review by the public. Keith Schneider would later write in the *New York Times,* "Concerned that war efforts could otherwise be hampered, the White House has waived the legal requirements for assessments of the effect that Pentagon projects have on the environment."[1]

By waiving the law's requirements, the Pentagon could ignore the environmental impact of its massive mobilization and assault. The waiver also set a precedent endangering other environmental laws. According to the *Times,* a Pentagon spokesperson admitted the agreement "could be the first in a wider program seeking suspension of other Federal environmental statutes."[2]

On November 6, 1990, at the Second World Climate Conference in Geneva, Switzerland, Jordan's King Hussein warned, "A war in the Gulf would not only result in devastating human death and injury and tremendous economic loss and prolonged political confrontation between Orient and Occident, it could also lead to an environmental catastrophe that would be swift, severe, and devastating." In presenting the conclusions of Jordanian scientists, Hussein said, "The impact of a war on the 50 million barrels of oil that Kuwait produces, set in flames, could increase atmospheric carbon dioxide from these fires and the result would cause a global warming and result in lower food production."[3]

His predictions turned out to be accurate. The summer 1991 issue of the *Earth Island Journal* reported on a postwar study (released anonymously for fear of jeopardizing federal research grants) showing that carbon released from the war-related oil fires exceeded 10 percent of the 2.5-billion-ton annual increase in atmospheric carbon.[4] This undermined international plans to reduce carbon emissions by 20 percent by the year 2005.

A conference of environmental organizations in London on January 2, 1991 — two weeks before the war started — reinforced the predictions. With oil industry representatives, members of the British Parliament, the Iraqi ambassador, and invited representatives of other Middle Eastern countries present, Dr. John Cox of the British Campaign for Nuclear Disarmament and other participants forecast, "The burning of 3 million barrels of oil would release 15,000 tons of black smoke a day into the atmosphere."[5] The smoke-release figure reported after the war by the World Meteorological Organization was actually closer to 100,000 tons a day.[6]

Nine days later, on January 11, environmentalists met in New York City. At a news conference hosted by the Arms Control Research Center, they discussed the potential disaster of the coming war. Dr. Abdullah Toukan of Jordan predicted vast environmental damage caused by smoke from oil well fires. Richard Golob, editor of *Golob's Oil Pollution Bulletin*, warned, "A series of well blow-outs could develop into the largest spill in history, quickly dwarfing that of the *Exxon Valdez*."[7]

The Bush administration knew the environmental consequences war would bring. Two federal studies released in January 1991 showed the government had been evaluating the war's environmental impact for some time. These two reports predicted oil fire smoke, but they downplayed any major worldwide environmental effects. After the war, on October 16, 1991, the Gulf Environmental Emergency Response Team reported that pollution from the oil fires had already circled the globe three times.[8]

Sandia Labs conducted the first study, involving Livermore and Los Alamos National Laboratories, for the Department of Energy. The report, titled "Potential Impacts of Iraqi Use of Oil as a Defensive Weapon," concluded:

> Based on information we have received, a 20 million barrel crude oil spill to the Persian Gulf is possible near Kuwait's coast. Ten million barrels could be released in the first 24 hours, followed by another 10 million in the next 36 hours. The potential source is a combination of tankers and on-shore storage tanks located near Kuwait's coast. The magnitude of this potential oil spill exceeds, by a factor of five, any previous spill. Such an oil spill could disrupt the important fishing industry in the Gulf, shut down water desalinization plants in Kuwait, Saudi Arabia, Bahrain, and Qatar that supply a large share of the area's water, and cause long-term damage to the Gulf's ecology.[9]

The other report—"Environmental Impact of Damage to Kuwaiti Oil Facilities"—was released on January 11, 1991 by Pacific Sierra Research for the Defense Nuclear Agency. It stated:

> This would be a massive and unprecedented pollution event. It would impact the ecology of the Persian Gulf and fallout on a wide

swath across Southern Iran, Pakistan, and Northern India. The impact on human population and desert ecosystems from such a prolonged soot fallout is unknown. . . . Destruction of the Kuwaiti oil fields is promised.[10]

The Bush administration understood the potential harm of the war, for an Associated Press report revealed that U.S. companies knew to order cleanup material two months before the U.S. started dropping bombs. According to the AP, T. B. O'Brien, president of OGE Drilling, a cleanup company working in the Gulf, was in June 1991 "still waiting for heavy construction bulldozers, backhoes, cranes, more than 300 trucks and a host of specialized smaller tools" ordered in November 1990.[11]

Although it was aware of the danger, Washington prevented negotiation of a peaceful settlement, commenced an aerial assault on Iraq, and failed to take preventive and control measures. This resulted in environmental disaster for the Persian Gulf, India, the rest of Asia, and beyond.

NUCLEAR AND CHEMICAL FALLOUT

All forms of environmental destruction that occurred during the Gulf War were foreseen, and perhaps none more so than the effect of bombing nuclear, chemical, and other inherently dangerous facilities. International laws had prohibited such acts for years, but they did not deter the Pentagon.

Anticipating the problem in the Gulf, the UN on December 4, 1990 passed a resolution specifically prohibiting attacks on nuclear facilities. Yet when the war began the next month, General Schwarzkopf said that nuclear, biological, and chemical weapons factories were primary bombing targets. On January 23, 1991, General Powell said "[Iraq's] two operating reactors . . . are both gone. They're down. They're finished."[12] On January 30, Schwarzkopf said allied forces had attacked 18 chemical, 10 biological, and three nuclear plants.[13]

The results of these attacks were observed within days. As early as January 22, 1991, a Czechoslovakian antichemical unit found traces of chemical weapons agents that the bombing had released. On February 4, a French military spokesperson said that chemical fallout was being detected throughout Iraq.[14] The German newspaper *Frankfurter Rundschau und Handlesblatt* reported that allied raids had caused the release of toxic vapors that were killing scores of civilians. Michael Sailer of the Ecological Institute in Darmstadt told the *Rundschau* that portions of Iraq would remain polluted, useless desert long after the war.[15]

Other bombed plants also released toxins. For example, the International Study Team found chemical fallout from bombed asbestos factories, a sponge and rubber factory, and many textile mills. These bombed sites released sulfur, carbon dioxide, and nitrous oxide into the atmosphere for at least 30 days after they were hit. Much wildlife in the area, especially birds, died.[16]

THE THREAT OF RADIOACTIVITY

By far the most dangerous substance rained on Iraq during the assault was radioactive debris from shells fired by a variety of sophisticated U.S. weapons. Along with the cloud of toxic, carcinogenic smoke, the people of the Gulf region will have to face the effects of radiation poisoning for years to come.

The United Kingdom Atomic Energy Authority (UKAEA) prepared a secret report in April 1991, which the *London Independent* obtained. The report confirmed that U.S. ground forces fired between 5,000 and 6,000 rounds of advanced depleted uranium (DU) armor-piercing shells. In addition, U.S. and British aircraft launched approximately 50,000 DU rockets and missiles. The result is tons of radioactive and toxic rubble in Kuwait and Iraq.[17]

Countless Iraqi soldiers were either killed outright by these shells or exposed to their radiation. In the January 15, 1991 *Village Voice*, James Ridgeway described the effect when hardened DU shells pierce tank armor:

> When fired, the uranium bursts into flame and all but liquifies, searing through steel armor like a white hot phosphorescent flare. The heat of the shell causes any diesel fuel vapors in the enemy tank to explode, and the crew inside is burned alive.[18]

The DU shells were fired primarily from M-1A1 Abrams tanks, A-10 attack planes, and Apache helicopters. Army Colonel David Weisman confirmed how lethal they are when he said, "If you set the Abrams up correctly, you will kill what you aim at."[19]

But the effects of DU shells do not stop at human incineration. The fire creates uranium oxide, which spreads and contaminates bodies, equipment, and the ground. The UKAEA report noted:

The DU will be spread around the battlefield and target vehicles in varying sizes and quantities, from dust particles to full-size penetrators and shot. It would be unwise for people to stay close to large quantities of DU for long periods and this would obviously be of concern to the local population if they collect this heavy metal and keep it. There will be specific areas in which many rounds will have been fired where localized contamination of vehicles and the soil may exceed permissible limits and these could be hazardous to both cleanup teams and the local population. Furthermore, if DU gets in the food chain or water this will create potential health problems.[20]

The uranium-238 used to make the weapons can cause cancer and genetic defects when inhaled. Uranium is also chemically toxic, like lead. Inhalation causes heavy metal poisoning or kidney or lung damage. Therefore, Iraqi soldiers who were pinned down in their bunkers during the assault almost certainly were poisoned by radioactive dust clouds. In fact, anyone who came in contact with the DU weapons was affected. The Food and Drug Administration assessed the exposure of troops in vehicles loaded with DU shells as equal to one chest X-ray for every 20 or 30 hours.[21] Although this level is well within Nuclear Regulatory Commission limits, it is undesirable. Most nuclear experts agree that any radiation exposure poses a health risk. But the effects will not appear for five to 10 years.

Army investigators reported that most of the armored vehicles struck by "friendly fire" were hit by DU rounds. Included among those killed was Specialist Anthony Wayne Kidd, 21, of Lima, Ohio. In the November 10, 1991 issue of *New York Newsday*, Patrick Sloyan reported:

> On the night of February 26, [Kidd's] company was raked by "friendly fire" from a nearby U.S. tank unit in southern Iraq. The Bradley was hit by a sabot round, a two-foot steel dart tipped with dense depleted uranium. It travels almost a mile a second. . . . M1A1 Abrams tank gunners call it the "Silver Bullet."
> When Skaggs tried to stand Kidd upright, the injured soldier began screaming. It took a while for Skaggs to realize the Silver Bullet that tore through his Bradley had sheared both feet from Kidd's legs. Skaggs, also a trained combat lifesaver, suddenly assumed the burdens of an overwhelmed physician as he treated wounded from two other Bradleys hit by friendly fire.[22]

Skaggs escaped immediate death, but his proximity to the DU explosion and scattered uranium dust makes him a likely candidate for radiation poisoning.

The effects of the uranium-tipped shells were not unknown. DU weapons testing grounds in Minnesota and New Mexico have been left permanently radioactive. Radiation expert Geoffrey Sea told environmental expert John Miller, "Depleted uranium munitions have caused serious contamination problems in every community in which they have been tested."[23] Saudi researchers have reported elevated levels of radioactivity along their country's northern borders.

According to the UKAEA report, 40 tons of radioactive debris in the desert could cause 500,000 deaths. Uranium-238 remains radioactive for millions of years. Thus, entire regions in Iraq and Kuwait may be deadly and uninhabitable forever.

THE OIL SPILLS

On January 25, 1991, the Pentagon reported an alarming oil slick spreading in the Gulf. Washington accused Saddam Hussein, announcing that Iraq had caused the supposedly newly discovered oil slick—actually first sighted on January 19—by opening spigots at the Sea Island Terminal and on nearby tankers at Mina al-Ahmadi. U.S. officials expressed shock and outrage. Bush called it "kind of sick."

A closer look shows what really happened. On January 24, the day before President Bush accused Saddam Hussein of deliberately spilling oil into the Gulf, Baghdad Radio announced U.S aircraft had hit two of its oil tankers in the Persian Gulf.[24] On January 25, Iraqi diplomats to the UN reported the allied bombing of Iraqi tankers, and issued an international call to environmental groups to denounce "this criminal act."[25]

U.S. bombing purposely targeted oil tankers and storage facilities in the Gulf. Saudi scientists estimated that 30 percent of the oil spill was attributable to this bombing.[26] Kuwaiti oil facilities on the shores of the Gulf also came under heavy attack.

The Gulf-based Regional Organization for Protection of the Marine Environment provided a breakdown that attributed the spill to the following sources:

Damaged oil tankers at loading terminals in Kuwait: 4.5 million barrels

The Kuwaiti loading terminal at Al-Ahmadi (including Sea Island Terminal): 2–3 million barrels

The Iraqi port of Mina-al-Bakr: 0.7 million barrels

   Damaged Saudi storage tanks at Khafji: 0.1 million barrels
   Unidentified discharges and spills: unknown[27]

According to this report, the 2–3-million-barrel spill from the Sea Island Terminal — where the U.S. accused Saddam of opening the
spigots — was smaller than spills from damaged oil tankers at other
Kuwaiti loading terminals.

   The United States has admitted responsibility: On January 30,
General Schwarzkopf admitted the U.S.-led coalition had attacked
Mina-al-Bakr earlier in the war.[28] Yet no one challenged Pentagon
spokesperson Pete Williams when he said the spill was an Iraqi "act
of environmental terrorism."[29]

   The front page of the January 26 *New York Times* carried a photograph of an oil spill on the coast of northern Saudi Arabia. The article, which blamed Iraq, included a picture of a cormorant struggling
in oil-clogged waters off the Gulf coast. In fact, these photographs
showed an earlier oil spill that was caused by allied bombing.[30] (Both
U.S. and Saudi oil officials admitted this in a briefing.) Yet the *Times*
prominently quoted President Bush, who said: "Saddam Hussein
continues to amaze the world. . . . Now he resorts to environmental damage."[31]

   The next day, the *Times* did mention Iraq's claim that the main
spill resulted from allied bombing of two tankers. But it gave the
most prominent play to U.S. accusations, comments, and speculation about why Saddam Hussein would commit such an act. In contrast, Britain's ITN Channel Four News reported on January 28 that
the oil pollution on Saudi Arabia's northeast coast was the result of
U.S. military action.[32]

   What actually caused the damage to Kuwaiti facilities is unknown, but the U.S. could easily clarify matters with an open accounting of its actions. Instead, Washington has maintained silence
on the issue since its initial accusations against Iraq. The government
has also silenced anyone who might be in a position to expose the
Pentagon's culpability. In January 1991, for example, when a team
of researchers from the National Oceanic and Atmospheric Administration (NOAA) went to the Gulf to investigate the spill, they were
promptly ordered by Washington not to discuss their findings
publicly.[33]

   On March 4, 1991, Greenpeace reported that U.S. secrecy was actually hampering cleanup efforts. The U.S. military refused to share
reconnaissance information about the spill. Bahrain Petroleum coordinator Derek Brown told Greenpeace, "We've been fighting the
spills with a blindfold on."[34]

Friends of the Earth International has reported the following:

> The oil spilled into the Gulf was at least twenty times greater than the *Exxon Valdez* spill. Although about one-sixth of the oil was re-covered, the remainder has contaminated mangrove and wetlands areas along 200 miles of coast. The spill is estimated at 6.8 million barrels, the largest in history.[35]

More recent figures estimate the spill at 7.5 million barrels and rising.

The slick has killed tens of thousands of birds. Dolphins have left the area. Flamingos were found soaked with oil. Saudi shrimp fishing was rendered practically impossible. The marine food chain, the seagrass beds, and algal mats of photosynthetic bacteria have all been damaged. Layers of tar that laid under the sand of the Gulf shores have sunk to the Gulf floor to form an asphalt-like paving, destroying much sea life. In March 1991, Japanese scientists reported "many, many small tar balls" coming ashore on Bahrain's east coast.[36]

THE OIL FIRES

Smoke from oil fires contributed significantly to the damage in the Gulf region and beyond. Sulfur from the fires brought acid rain, which in turn increased the size of the Gulf oil slick. By early February 1991, there were few horizons in Iraq that did not contain clouds of black smoke from fires at refineries, oil storage facilities, and even gas stations. U.S. and allied bombing of oil refineries caused many of the eventual total of 800 oil fires.

On February 22, 1991, President Bush accused the Iraqis of torching 140 wells as they began to retreat from Kuwait. But long before this, Washington knew that the allied bombing was causing many of the fires, which sent oily black rain to Iran as early as January. In fact, smoke clouds arose from all over Iraq before the air assault was 24 hours old.

A delegation from the International Study Team, which visited Iraq August 23–September 5, 1991, interviewed the assistant director of the Basra refinery. He told them it was set on fire by allied aerial attacks starting January 17. The Study Team's report of the interview states that "Some family members of employees were killed in the attacks, some were killed by suffocation from the massive fires."[37]

102

According to a Nuclear Defense Agency report, Iran experienced repeated black rain events starting on January 22 — a month before Bush accused Iraq of torching the wells and only five days after the bombing of Basra began.[38] On March 5, Joni Seager reported in the *Village Voice* that "oil-well and refinery fires . . . have been burning since the first week of war."[39]

On February 13, the *San Jose Mercury News* recounted a Pentagon report that 50 fires were already burning, covering Kuwait with a pall of smoke. Rear Admiral Mike Cornell told reporters the smoke could be a result of either Iraqi action or allied bombing: "There is an advantage from their point of view [to] starting a fire. It . . . makes it difficult for us to find targets. . . . And then there's the possibility that some of our strikes may have had some collateral damage to start a fire."[40]

On February 23, the Iraqi government denied responsibility for the fires. As with the oil spills, there has been no adequate effort to fix responsibility, though the Pentagon must have evidence. Iraq's Revolutionary Command Council called on the Security Council to "get acquainted with the degree of [allied] civilian and economic destruction . . . in Kuwait."[41] But the Security Council refused to investigate. That same day, oil fires erupted in the Rumaila oil field in Iraq following intense U.S. bombing and the first reported U.S. use of napalm.

The United States moved early to suppress information about environmental damage. On January 25, the Department of Energy issued a gag order for its researchers. *Scientific American* obtained the memorandum from scientists at the Livermore National Laboratory, and published it in its May 1991 issue. The memorandum read:

> DOE Headquarters Public Affairs has requested that all DOE facilities and contractors immediately discontinue any further discussion of war-related research and issues with the media until further notice. The extent of what we are authorized to say about environmental impacts of fires/oil spills in the Middle East follows: "Most independent studies and experts suggest that the catastrophic predictions in some recent news reports are exaggerated. We are currently reviewing the matter, but these predictions remain speculative and do not warrant any further comment at this time."[42]

The reference to "fires" along with "oil spills" is revealing, coming as it did almost one month before Bush accused Iraq of setting the fires.

According to *Scientific American*, the White House specifically ordered researchers to withhold satellite images and other information on the Gulf region after the war ended. John Cox said the satellite images revealed that allied bombing of Iraqi refineries and oil reserves had "created an appalling smoke cloud."[43] And in July *Scientific American* confirmed that as early as mid-February photographs from the Landsat-5 and NOAA-11 satellites showed smoke plumes several hundred kilometers long issuing from different regions in Iraq;[44] yet the fires burning north of the Iraq–Kuwait border have received little attention. These fires resulted from allied bombing of Iraqi refineries and storage tanks.

The suppression of information continued after the war. Officials were particularly sensitive about evidence that oil fires were detected before Bush's February 22 accusation. After the January 25 gag order, government agencies stifled two NOAA studies about the oil fires.[45] In May, Joyce E. Penner's supervisors at Livermore told her not to present a computer simulation of Kuwaiti oil fires at a scientific conference in Vienna.[46]

In March 1992, Australian author and oil consultant O. J. Vialls, who has maintained contact with U.S. firefighting teams in the Gulf, wrote in the *Australian Guardian* that "in a minimum of 66 known cases in Kuwait" allied strikes blew the wellheads off oil wells.[47] *Life* magazine had provided evidence of this in June 1991, reporting that firefighters found unexploded ordnance from allied bombing "everywhere" while trying to put out the Kuwaiti oil fires. "We've seen them in the hundreds," said firefighter Mike Miller. "And because they're covered with oil, it would be very easy to run over one. There was a camel in our area who stepped on one and blew himself to pieces."[48]

Vialls argued that Iraq would not have been able to ignite the wells under prevailing circumstances. Explosions of wellheads alone will rarely set oil wells on fire; indeed, they are often used to extinguish fires. The intense temperature required for ignition could come from flamethrowers or napalm. Flamethrowers require a dangerous proximity, and napalm must be dropped from aircraft.

Vialls wrote in an October 29, 1991 letter to the Commission that 5,500-degree napalm fire would be hot enough to bring to white heat the small bore oil pipes that leave the wellheads. At that point, the weakened metal would burst under the internal pressure of the napalm-ignited oil.[49]

At the time Iraqi soldiers in Kuwait supposedly torched oil wells — between February 16 and 22 — they had been pounded from the air by U.S. bombing for four weeks. Most survivors were pinned down in their bunkers. Their communications systems had been destroyed. They had had no air defense since the start of the war. It was impossible for Iraq to drop napalm from aircraft under the circumstances.

U.S. forces, on the other hand, had and used napalm. In fact they used it to bomb Iraqi soldiers in trenches. On February 16, 1991, U.S. Marine AV88 Harrier ground-attack aircraft started flying missions with napalm. Vialls wrote:

> This fact was confirmed by one of [the U.S.] pilots when interviewed by the media in Saudi Arabia on February 23rd while the aircraft were filmed with the napalm pods being fused after loading onto the four wing hard-points of each AV88. The marines flew missions with napalm for a period of one week.[50]

THE IMPACT OF OIL FIRES AND OIL LAKES

For months, flames from hundreds of burning wells in Kuwait and Iraq polluted the landscape. Black soot rained on the desert. Sooty clouds blocked the sunlight. Oil that continued to flow from oil wells and bombed tankers covered the ground in pools. Metal rusted faster as a result of moisture released from constantly burning fires. Butchers found that slaughtered sheep had black lungs.

The smoke from the fires — more than twice as bad as Abdullah Toukan had predicted — covered parts of Kuwait, Iraq, Turkey, and Iran. Air pollution levels were reported 17 times higher than normal in Teheran. Soot particles and gases released from the fires brought acid rain over a vast region stretching from southern Bulgaria and Romania to Pakistan and Afghanistan. The black rain even fell on the Soviet Union, Eastern Europe, East Africa, and China.

Skiers in the Himalayas reported that black oily goo two inches thick covered the snow. Scientists found traces of the soot as far away as Hawaii, Japan, and Germany.

Researchers at the University of Wyoming found unusually high particle concentrations over the continental United States. Particle concentrations increased tenfold over Wyoming between early February and late March 1991. And particles were at 100 times their normal level in the upper troposphere — 20,000–30,000 feet up.[51]

In August 1991, U.S. astronauts detected a black-edged stratospheric haze hovering over the world.[52]

The Gulf Environmental Emergency Response Team (GEERT) reported in late 1991 that half of Iran's crops had been wiped out by black rain. According to GEERT, the oil fires emitted 100,000 tons of soot, 50,000 tons of sulfur, and 850,000 tons of carbon dioxide a day:

> By mid-March 1991, satellite images showed that heavy pollution from Kuwait's burning oil wells extended for hundreds of miles; the smoke was 50,000 square kilometers (19,300 square miles), stretching from Kuwait to Karachi in Pakistan and out over the Indian Ocean. Gulf regional daytime temperatures fell to 20–30 degrees below normal, because of the blockage of the sun by soot particles.[53]

Yet the Environmental Protection Agency (EPA) minimized the oil fires' effects. The EPA claimed pollutants were not "at levels of concern." EPA task force head Bill Hunt told reporters, "I don't think we've found anything that alarming."[54]

According to a later GEERT report, a health survey of 1,400 residents in eight districts close to the Burgan oil fields found many babies had "oil rashes from the inside of their bodies out." Fifty percent of the respondents had trouble breathing. Over 80 percent wanted to be evacuated.[55]

U.S. soldiers were also subjected to the toxic fumes. Army reservist Don Mentele was stationed near the fire for two weeks. A week after the EPA study was released, he told reporters: "They're telling us there's nothing wrong with the air. Come on, man, you can taste it in your mouth." Sergeant John Brandon, Jr. of the Third Armored Division agreed: "We're not stupid. They say the pollution is no worse than New York City. That's a bunch of crap. I've been to New York, and it doesn't look anything like this."[56]

At an international conference on the Kuwaiti oil fires, held in Cambridge, Massachusetts, Harvard physicist Richard Wilson estimated that 50,000 people in the region between Basra and Bahrain would have their lives "shortened in some way" by the smoke.[57] And while the EPA maintained the smoke was not harmful, the National Toxics Campaign went to Saudi Arabia and found levels of dichlorobenzene — a chemical that attacks the liver, kidneys, and respiratory system — were 200 times higher than U.S. standards.[58]

The World Conservation Monitoring Centre at Cambridge, England, supported by the UN Environmental Program and the World Wide Fund for Nature, warned that "burning wells cause less pollution damage than nonburning gushers."[59] Conservative Kuwaiti estimates say that 35 million barrels of oil were standing in surface lakes in Kuwait. U.S. Corps of Engineers technicians, as well as NOAA's chief scientist, Dr. John Robinson, put the figure closer to 150–175 million barrels.[60] At 42 gallons a barrel, that amounts to as much as 7 billion gallons of oil. By now, many small lakes have run together in Kuwait to form vast networks of oil that stretch for many kilometers. Hydrocarbons continue to evaporate into the air from these lakes, and the lakes will pollute the groundwater underneath for decades. These oil lakes also kill directly. Three vehicles crossing a pool of oil were incinerated as sparks from the cars ignited the gases underneath. Five people died.[61]

THE DESERT ECOSYSTEM AND THE TOXIC TIME BOMB

Many people think of the desert as a vast wasteland that does not contain life. But the desert actually sustains a vast and delicate ecosystem alive with species ranging from spiders, snakes, and scorpions to camels, sheep, and gazelles.

The surface of a desert is held together by microorganisms. In Iraq and Kuwait, the movement of 800,000 allied troops and thousands of tanks destroyed this fragile protection. Without it, seeds from desert brush cannot take root. And without vegetation, the top sand blows away, speeding erosion and bringing sandstorms.

Tragically, as with so much about the war, this too was predictable, for there are many precedents showing how troop maneuvers cause erosion in desert sands. In Libya, the desert still bears heavy scars from the World War II mechanized divisions of Rommel and Montgomery. The U.S. Geological Survey has studied California's Mojave Desert, where General George Patton trained a million troops during World War II. The geologists say vegetation there still has not recovered.[62] The chain of ecological events that occurred in the desert as a consequence of the allied troop movements will take centuries to correct.

In the Gulf War, allied troops left human waste behind — 10–12 million gallons of sewage per day, according to an estimate by the Arms Control Research Center[63] — as well as other debris. On March 5, 1991, the *Los Angeles Times* reported how the head of the Global Environment Monitoring System of the Nairobi-based UN Environmental Program reacted to a wartime stopover at the allies' Dhahran air base in Saudi Arabia: "I never saw so much junk floating around in my life. Packing crates and material, cleaning solutions and solvents of all types, paint for camouflage, some of which we know is toxic. It was all contained, but it will have to go somewhere."[64]

The military is at war with the environment even in peacetime. Researchers at the University of Toronto's Science for Peace Institute have found that up to 30 percent of "all global environmental degradation can be attributed to military activities."[65] U.S. nuclear arms facilities, weapons, and warheads are the greatest source and risk of nuclear radiation on earth. The Pentagon generates more than five times the toxic waste produced by the five major U.S. chemical corporations combined. Germany's air force is responsible for 58 percent of the air pollutants generated by aircraft in German air space. An F-16 jet fighter consumes nearly twice as much gas in one hour as the average American car uses in a year. Oil bought by the Pentagon, the largest U.S. consumer, could fuel all public transit systems in the United States for 22 years. Armed forces release almost two-thirds of all ozone-depleting CFC-113 that enters the atmosphere.[66]

In wartime, the military threat to the environment is far more dangerous, and its supreme indifference to environmental consequences is uncontrollable. We must recognize in the Gulf War, in which such a vast array of technologically advanced weapons and vehicles were used for an assault of unprecedented intensity, a warning to the world of the threat that militarism poses to life on the planet.

CHAPTER 6

The War and Human Rights

WAR and its threat have always been the greatest and most pervasive assailants of human rights. The Gulf crisis proved no exception. As awful as the human rights records of the governments in the region were, the crisis made them worse. The U.S. assault on Iraq greatly worsened the violations of human and civil rights not only in the Gulf region, but far beyond.

Oil and democracy don't mix. Oil has never enhanced democratic institutions or economic justice where it has been found. The industrial countries' unquenchable thirst for Middle East oil and the concentration of wealth it has spawned has always been antagonistic to democracy and human rights throughout the Arab world.

U.S. policymakers have understood that democracy in the oil-producing countries of the Middle East would end U.S. domination of the region. It would also mean that oil revenues would be invested in Arab economies. Together these would mean higher oil costs and the loss of mammoth profits and capital for the Western economies.

In this region with 50 percent of the world's oil reserves, the economic inequalities are staggering. The kingdoms of Saudi Arabia, Kuwait, and the UAE, created by European colonialism and backed by U.S. might, possess the lion's share of the region's oil and have relatively small populations. The per capita income of these countries is amongst the highest in the world. Iraq and Iran, although having large oil reserves, have larger populations. Egypt, Jordan, Syria, and Yemen have very little oil, and correspondingly low per capita income. Worldwide, Muslim countries have more than one billion people, including many of the poorest on the planet. The difference in conditions between these hungry millions and the vast wealth of the keepers of Mecca is irreconcilable with their shared faith.

The U.S.-backed kingdoms not only ensure the cheap flow of oil to the West, they also funnel oil revenues into U.S. and European corporate coffers. For example, since the mid-1980s Kuwait's revenue from investments in Western Europe and North America have exceeded its oil revenue. Joe Stork and Ann M. Lesch reported in the November/December 1990 issue of *Middle East Report* that in 1988 Kuwait's oil revenue totaled about $6 billion while its investment revenue was approximately $7.8 billion.[1]

Therefore, the oil-rich monarchies have a material interest in the prosperity of Western economies. High oil prices and investment of oil revenues in the Middle East rather than in the West would destabilize Western economies. To ensure the flow of cheap oil and huge investments to Western economies, existing inequalities must be maintained. This requires repressive governments in the oil-producing states; thus the U.S. support in the Gulf for some of the world's most repressive regimes.

During and after the Gulf War, the United States sent a strong message to those who dared question its policy toward Iraq. Arab Americans have been harassed in the U.S., almost a million Yemenis were expelled from Saudi Arabia, millions of poor laborers from many countries were driven from the Gulf, and Palestinians in Kuwait were subjected to collective punishment. The message was clear: The United States intends to increase its domination of the region and its resources by any means necessary.

REPRESSION IN KUWAIT

Before the war, Kuwait denied basic human rights to citizens and immigrant workers alike. Only some 750,000 of its population of about 2 million were Kuwaiti citizens. Political parties were banned. On the rare occasions when Kuwait held "elections," only Kuwaiti men whose forebears lived in Kuwait before 1920 could vote. Kuwaiti women were denied suffrage. Searches of homes, arrests without warrants, summary deportations, torture, imprisonment, and executions without judicial process were normal in prewar Kuwait.

Workers from other countries were denied citizenship even if they were born and raised in Kuwait. Non-Kuwaiti children, on turning 18, lost the right to live in Kuwait even if their parents were working in the country. In most instances immigrant workers were not allowed to bring their spouses and children into the country.

Before the war more than 300,000 Palestinians resided in Kuwait, and much of Kuwait's economy and government depended on their labor and expertise. These Palestinians were major providers for their families, who either lived under Israeli occupation in the West Bank and Gaza or were displaced by the Israeli occupation and resided in Lebanon, Jordan, or elsewhere.

During the war about 150,000 Palestinians left Kuwait. Most went to Jordan because the Israeli government wouldn't allow them into the occupied territories. Tens of thousands of Palestinians from Kuwait have become refugees, living in tent camps in Jordan or being confined in virtual concentration camps in mine-infested desert strips within Kuwait.

After the war, Kuwait became a living hell for the remaining Palestinians, Iraqis, Bedouins, Jordanians, and others, many of whom have toiled in that country most or all their lives. The government canceled residence and work permits for all non-Kuwaitis, who then had to reapply for residency. For a Palestinian to be considered for a residence permit, he has to obtain signatures from at least five Kuwaiti citizens who vouch for his character.

Tragically, the Palestinians lost whether they stayed in Kuwait or left. Almost all those who left were banned from reentering Kuwait. In many cases, Kuwaiti landlords confiscated their property. The 150,000 Palestinians who remained in Kuwait at least for a time after the war were collectively accused as "collaborators." Based on reports in newspapers, by human rights organizations and fact-finding teams, and from hearing testimony, the Commission estimates that as many as 200 were summarily executed. Others were tortured by the Kuwaiti police, military, and government-backed paramilitary squads. Today only an estimated 30,000 Palestinians remain in Kuwait. Palestinians living in the occupied territories are losing an estimated $100 million in remittances per year[2] from family members who no longer work in Kuwait. The impact, aggravated by other losses arising directly from the war, has been devastating for the families and for the economy of the occupied territories.

The *London Times* reported on March 26, 1991 that the roads leading into Hawalli, the largely Palestinian section of Kuwait, had been blocked at the end of the war. Gun-toting teenage Kuwaitis checked the credentials of anyone entering or leaving the area:

> What better way to begin the obliteration of a people than by blacking out the road signs which lead to its home district? Hawalli, the Palestinian district of Kuwait City, becomes harder to find each day. And locating Hawalli is not the same as entering it, because its access

111

> roads are blocked with concrete slabs and wrecked cars. . . .
> There seems to be only one entrance, through barriers into the guns
> of teenage Kuwaitis, who may or may not be soldiers. . . . [3]

My application for a visa to enter Kuwait in March 1991 was rejected, as had been my application in 1987. Apparently, the first application was rejected because of my criticism of Iraq throughout its war with Iran; the second because of my trip to Iraq during the bombing. Only two other countries — South Africa and Taiwan — had previously denied me entry out of more than 100 countries.

Middle East Watch was allowed to send two fact-finding missions to Kuwait after the war. According to MEW's September 1991 report, "A Victory Turned Sour: Human Rights in Kuwait Since Liberation," hundreds of Palestinians, stateless Bedouins, Iraqis, Sudanese, Egyptians, Tunisians, and others have been tortured, murdered, or deported, have suffered loss of property, and have been confined in camps under harsh conditions. Top Kuwaiti government officials, including Emir Sheikh Jaber Al-Ahmed Al-Sabah, not only condoned but encouraged such violations of human rights. [4]

Kuwait unleashed a deadly and unrestrained vengeance on Palestinians and other oppressed groups in Kuwait. More than 1,200 Bedouins, fearing retribution at the hands of Kuwaiti forces, fled to Iraq for safety rather than return to their homes in Kuwait. [5] Mass graves of unidentified victims killed by the Kuwaiti military and police were discovered. According to the MEW report, most of the killings "were committed by official security forces or by irregular armed groups working closely with official forces." [6]

New York Newsday reported on March 29, 1991 that according to Western diplomats, "members of Kuwait's ruling family were involved in the killings of Palestinians and other people suspected of collaborating with the Iraqi occupation." [7] Torture was widely reported by human rights groups, fact-finding missions, and reporters. Torture methods included beatings with canes, rods, electrical cables, and rifle butts; electric shock treatment; and having cigarettes extinguished on parts of the body. [8] Such atrocities, as well as the "trials" of suspected collaborators, violated among other laws the Fourth Geneva Convention and its Protocol I.

THE UNITED STATES' ROLE

Kuwait's actions went hand-in-hand with U.S. policy in the region. The American press reported U.S. soldiers watching, or even protecting, Kuwaiti groups as they assaulted and killed Palestinians and others. Press members who tried to interfere were themselves threatened. The *New York Times* reported on April 3, 1991 that the U.S. Civil Affairs Command and Special Forces troops worked closely with the Kuwaiti police and had "taken over much of the day-to-day running of Kuwait."[9] Special Forces troops advised Kuwaiti soldiers at police stations and roadblocks. Members of the 10th Transportation Battalion worked as longshoremen on the docks. The *New York Times* reported that these activities were run out of the Defense Restoration Assistance Office, whose head reported directly to Secretary of Defense Cheney. The U.S. government is therefore responsible for human rights abuses in Kuwait under the Third and Fourth Geneva Conventions and the International Laws of Belligerent Occupation.

President Bush had based his authority to "liberate" Kuwait on the duty to preserve and enforce international law. Administration officials stressed that the reason the President was reluctant to pressure the Kuwaiti government to be more democratic was that he didn't want to interfere with Kuwait's sovereignty. One administration official said: "Of all the countries not to mess around in, Kuwait is at the top of the list. After all, the war was fought over that very issue: another country forcing its will on Kuwait."[10] But the U.S. government did more than just stand aside; it condoned Kuwait's violations of international law and encouraged the illegal conduct.

President Bush not only ignored human rights violations in Kuwait and restored its antidemocratic government, he repeatedly encouraged vigilante violence there. The *Orange County Register* reported on June 17, 1991 that, after highly publicized trials in Kuwait resulted in death sentences for crimes such as wearing a T-shirt bearing Saddam Hussein's picture, the President told Kuwait's ambassador, "We didn't fight this war for democracy or those trials. Don't be intimidated by what's going on."[11] At a July 1, 1991 news conference, Bush compared the situation in Kuwait to post-World War II Europe. He said: "The people that were liberated did not take kindly to those that sold out to the Nazis. . . . I think we're expecting a little much if we're asking the people in Kuwait to take kindly to those that had spied on their countrymen that were left there, that had brutalized families there and things of that nature."[12]

In Kuwait, Bush's remarks condoning the death squads made front-page headlines in Kuwaiti newspapers and encouraged indiscriminate killings and torture. The day after the President's news conference, headlines in *Sawt Al Kuwait*, a Kuwaiti government newspaper, announced: "Bush Declares His Understanding of

Kuwaitis' Attitude Toward Collaborators: 'We Would Be Asking a Lot If We Asked Them to Show Mercy,' He Says."[13]

The United States fully endorsed the Kuwaiti government's treatment of all Palestinians as collaborators and terrorists. On February 25, 1991, Pacific News Service reported that a declassified 200-page Pentagon white paper planned for the United States military to take over rebuilding and running Kuwait after the war. Under the heading "Assumptions," the paper states, "Terrorist action is expected from stay-behind Palestinians or Iraqi personnel."[14]

The Pentagon paper shows that the United States had planned before the end of the war to assume full control over Kuwaiti affairs following the expulsion of Iraq from Kuwait, stating that martial law would be in effect for as long as a year. The document also outlined the logistics for the U.S. military in rebuilding Kuwait, covering everything from providing potable water and emergency food, to repairing the airport and restoring the flow of oil, to guarding government documents and capturing subversives.[15] Thus, while Kuwaiti death squads were rounding up and executing Palestinians and other "undesirables" in violation of international law, U.S. forces were busy refurbishing the Emir's palace.

Robert Fisk of the *London Independent* reported that he and another journalist physically stopped three Kuwaiti soldiers from beating up a Palestinian boy on a bicycle. When he asked a U.S. officer standing there why he did not intervene, he was told to get lost. "You having a nice day?" the U.S. soldier asked Fisk. "We don't need your kind around here with your dirty rumors. You have a big mouth. This is martial law, boy."[16]

GUEST WORKERS

Before the war there were about 4 million immigrant workers in the Persian Gulf region. Many were born and brought up in Kuwait, Saudi Arabia, and the other monarchies, but had no right to claim citizenship in these countries. The vast majority of these workers came from South Asia, North and East Africa, and other Middle Eastern countries. There were 350,000 Egyptians and 145,000 other North Africans in Kuwait alone.

During and after the war, the majority of these workers in Kuwait were expelled.[17] This wreaked havoc on their families and on the economies of their homelands. Those expelled were invariably barred from taking their savings and other property with them. They were instantly impoverished after they had toiled for low wages for decades in the monarchies. North African nations were adversely affected by the expulsion of guest workers from the region. Dr. Samad-Matias, Professor of African and Caribbean Studies at the City University of New York, reported: "Many have disappeared and are still missing. Many lost their health or are incapacitated. Others left whatever properties or savings they may have had in Kuwait, Saudi Arabia, or Iraq. In most cases, they were forced to leave with nothing but what they were wearing on their backs."[18]

Samad-Matias quoted figures from the International Monetary Fund in her testimony to the New York Commission hearing: "Sixty-five nations of the world were negatively affected and impacted by the crisis. And Sub-Saharan African countries, being the poorest, were among the worst affected. They had about a $4 billion loss due to, and as a direct result of, this war."[19]

According to Samad-Matias, about $2.7 billion in losses was caused by increased oil prices during the war. Other factors included "the loss of exports and imports, the cancellation of international contracts, transportation, tourism, and the absence of expatriate remittances coming from these guest workers who were expelled or displaced."[20]

After the war, guest workers in Kuwait continued to suffer grave mistreatment at the hands of their Kuwaiti employers. According to American GIs in Kuwait, the government paid Bangladeshi workers small sums of money to clear mines. These "mine-sweepers" were forced to walk through mine-infested areas using bamboo poles to detonate land mines. And on January 3, 1992, the *New York Times* noted:

> Many Kuwaitis, who felt the sting of mistreatment by their Iraqi occupiers, have failed to translate that experience into compassion for the 500,000 menial laborers, most of them from Asia, who do everything from sweep their streets to cook their food.[21]

The small country of Yemen, which had infuriated the United States by abstaining or voting against U.S.-sponsored Security Council resolutions against Iraq, paid dearly for its independence. Washington cut all U.S. aid to Yemen after it voted against Resolution 678 in October 1990, and Saudi Arabia expelled virtually all of the more than one million Yemeni workers from the country.

Returning Yemeni workers complained of having even food—rice, sugar, grain—confiscated at the Saudi–Yemen border.[22] Yemeni business owners in Saudi Arabia were told to find Saudi partners and Saudi employers to sponsor them if they wanted to remain, or to sell their businesses to Saudis. On October 30, 1990, the *New York Times* quoted one man who had owned a tire shop in Saudi Arabia for 12 years and complained that he could find no buyer: "Why should they buy it when they can take it for free after I have gone?" The *Times* commented:

> Yet because so many of those coming back to Yemen have lived in Saudi Arabia for years—some for all of their lives—the disruption caused by this migration is in many ways more profound than the exodus to Jordan. The burden placed by these returnees on this fragile economy threatens its very stability.[23]

Today only a few thousand Yemenis remain in Saudi Arabia. The loss of income from relatives working there has been a huge blow to Yemen's economy. Before, remittances sent home to Yemen each year totaled around $2 billion, constituting the country's single largest source of income. And with no housing to accommodate them, returning workers were living in tent camps in Sana and Haradh for extended periods.[24] Other countries, including Bangladesh, Sri Lanka, India, Pakistan, the Philippines, and Iran, also suffered adverse economic effects when their workers had to leave the Gulf.

TREATMENT OF WOMEN

Kuwaiti women themselves have no civil rights, and the treatment of immigrant women is abominable. Nurses, nannies, maids, and other domestic servants in Kuwait are imported from the Philippines, Sri Lanka, Pakistan, Bangladesh, India, and other impoverished countries. They are lured with promises of a decent life and guarantees of relatively good pay and housing, and a chance to save money.[25]

What they confront in Kuwait is a nightmare. This is especially true for domestic servants. Upon arrival at the employer's house they find that their salaries are but a fraction of what was promised. Frequently Kuwaiti employers refuse to pay any salary at all to maids and other servants.[26]

It is commonplace for domestic servants in Kuwait to be beaten, sexually abused, and otherwise humiliated with virtually no legal recourse. Their airfare and agency fees, which their Kuwaiti employers initially pay, become a mammoth debt they must pay back before they can attempt to terminate their contract. Their employers can withhold their passports, and the Kuwaiti government will not allow them to leave the country without their employers' permission. "This job of a houseboy or a maid in Kuwait is almost like slavery," Mir Abdel Hossain, First Secretary of the Bangladesh embassy in Kuwait told the *New York Times.*[27]

My interviews with women in the Philippines who had responded to advertisements for good jobs as nannies in Kuwait confirmed that they are often whisked away to jobs as maids, in which they labor under horrible conditions. The *New York Times* reported on January 3, 1992:

> Once in her employer's home, Mrs. Castro was refused permission to leave for even a few minutes. She could not receive letters or phone calls, even from her family. Her work began before dawn and ended long after midnight.
> If she failed to respond fast enough, she was beaten. She was never paid her $130 a month salary. Then, she recounts, she was raped by her employer.[28]

The Philippine, Indian, Bangladesh, and Sri Lankan embassies are commonly crowded with women seeking refuge after having escaped from their employers.

One Filipina maid who had taken refuge with 130 other women in the Philippine embassy tried to kill herself rather than return to her employer, a military official. The *Times* reported: "The maid, who contends she was frequently beaten, said the colonel followed and struck her with his car as she tried to flee from the house. The colonel says, 'She had an accident trying to escape.' "[29]

Since the war hundreds of Third World women have been raped by members of the Kuwaiti military as well as by civilians. More than 100 Filipinas alone have said they were raped by Kuwaitis since the war. So too were Sri Lankan, Indian, Pakistani, Palestinian, Lebanese, and Iraqi women.[30] Naimat Farhat, a Palestinian living in Kuwait, was raped and shot by Kuwaiti soldiers after they killed her father and brother. Her surviving brother, Naim, filed a complaint and contacted the U.S. ambassador to Kuwait, Edward W. Gnehm. Gnehm replied that Kuwaiti authorities said they had no record of any complaint having been filed by the Farhats.[31]

ANTI-ARAB RACISM IN THE UNITED STATES

During the Gulf Crisis, the U.S. government distinguished the "good Arabs" of Kuwait, Saudi Arabia, Egypt, and Syria from the "bad Arabs" of Iraq, Palestine, and Yemen in international circles. Yet for the government and the mainstream news media inside the United States, all Arabs were bad.

Every time the United States attacks a Middle Eastern country, or when the U.S. government merely steps up its racist rhetoric against Arabs or Iranians, anti-Arab racism in the United States escalates dramatically. During the Gulf crisis, President Bush and other leaders made statements equating Saddam Hussein with Hitler. The long-standing racist stereotyping of Arabs in the American news media and Hollywood films intensified. The FBI conducted an extensive harassment campaign against Arab Americans. The combination of these factors generated scores of attacks against Arab Americans in the United States.

Arab Americans were the target of physical and verbal assaults, death threats, job discrimination, and ridicule on radio and television talk shows. Pan American Airlines instituted a policy of refusing to sell tickets to anyone who had an "Arab-sounding" name. Other airlines subjected Arab passengers to lengthy interrogations and security checks before allowing them to board aircraft.

The FBI's massive harassment campaign was nationwide. Publicly, the FBI sometimes said it was questioning Arab community and political leaders for potential information about anti-Arab violence. In reality, agents questioned hundreds of Arab Americans about their political affiliation — for example, whether they belonged to the PLO — and knowledge of or involvement in "terrorist activities." Most of those interrogated were not community leaders.

The purpose of the FBI campaign was to intimidate the Arab community, to deter Arab Americans from participating in the antiwar movement, and to obtain information on the antiwar movement. FBI agents accused many Arab Americans of minor violations of their visa status. Some agents brought Immigration and Naturalization officials to questionings, with the implied threat that lack of cooperation would bring punishment of visa violations.[32]

In a January 31, 1991 letter to Arab American organizations, the Center for Constitutional Rights wrote:

> The FBI is acting on the unfounded, illegal assumption that Arab Americans are likely to know something about terrorism, just because they are Arab, or because they are opponents of U.S. government policy. . . . Our experience with FBI tactics in the past leads us to conclude that the agency is playing upon fears of terrorism as an excuse to collect information about constitutionally protected political activity, and to harass and disrupt attempts to organize protests against U.S. policy.[33]

The FBI campaign was partially successful. Intimidated by the threat and fact of surveillance as well as by racist attacks, many Arab Americans who would have otherwise come to antiwar rallies and meetings stayed away.

Antiwar organizations were also subject to FBI and other police surveillance and harassment. Telephones of many groups and their members were tapped. Offices were vandalized. Antiwar activists were questioned. Some received death threats. Evidence strongly suggests that these incidents were conducted by the FBI.

REFUSING TO FIGHT

Perhaps the one domestic development that most frightened the U.S. government was the growing number of resisters in the armed forces — conscientious objectors (COs) and others who refused to fight in the Gulf. The government was clearly concerned that such resistance might escalate and jeopardize its war plans. The military was cautious early in the crisis, determined to avoid bad publicity like that during the Vietnam War. However, after the assault on Iraq, it came down hard on hundreds of those who had resisted or filed for CO status.

Sixty percent of American troops sent to the Gulf were people of color. Most of the others were poor whites. Many had joined the army when they were 17, trying to find a way out of their poverty-stricken lives. They'd been influenced by slick television commercials urging them to "be all that you can be; join the army" and promising them a college education. Others wanted tuition subsidies for college and medical school tuition.

Many either decided in the course of their training that they were unwilling to kill at all, or realized the war in the Gulf had nothing to do with U.S. national security. Resistance to fighting in the Gulf grew, not only among troops in the United States, but also among U.S. troops stationed in Germany and elsewhere overseas.

At first the services reacted by trying to threaten COs into dropping their requests for discharge. When this didn't work and the numbers of COs swelled, some branches said COs could petition for discharge only after they had arrived in Saudi Arabia. Some U.S. soldiers in Germany who filed for CO status were actually shipped to Saudi Arabia in handcuffs and leg irons.[34]

Eric Larsen, a young Marine, was one of the most prominent COs. He became deeply involved in the antiwar movement and spoke at scores of rallies around the United States. After being AWOL for a month he turned himself in to military authorities. According to Larsen's lawyer, Robert S. Rivkin: "Normally, such an offense would be dealt with by imposing nonjudicial punishment. At worst, it might trigger a special court-martial and a 30-day prison sentence, and maybe even a Bad Conduct Discharge. . . . Almost incredibly, the Marine Corps has charged Larsen with desertion in time of war, a potential death penalty offense."[35] He later served a short prison sentence.

Tahan Jones was the first African American to claim CO status during the war. When he filed his application for discharge, his sergeant threatened him with bodily harm if he took his case to the media. Jones told the *San Francisco Bay Guardian*, "Because I'm an African American he saw me as a dangerous example that other minorities in the military might follow." He added: "It's morally wrong to kill thousands of Arabs to protect America's interests. And minorities shouldn't die for it. I was too naive when I enlisted to understand that it's minorities that get screwed by a war."[36]

Dr. Yolanda Huet-Vaughn, a family doctor and Army reservist, refused to go to Saudi Arabia or perform military duty that aided the war effort. She was convicted after the war in a highly publicized court-martial at Ft. Leonard Wood and served a prison sentence away from her patients, her husband, and her three small children. She is one of the hundreds of resisters punished by the U.S. government for not participating in its violence. Perhaps she and others had come to share Martin Luther King, Jr.'s realization that "the greatest purveyor of violence on earth is my own government." Our national character will be measured by how the American people treat these heroes.

CHAPTER 7

The Role of the American Media in the Gulf Crisis

O N ITS two-hundredth anniversary in 1991, the First Amendment to the Constitution, which was originally intended to protect a free press, offered nothing to an American people desperately in need of facts and diverse opinions. The U.S. government and the American media were committed to a common cause in the Persian Gulf. The most powerful capacity for propaganda and the most sophisticated technology for death in history acted in concert to slaughter an army, cripple a nation, name it liberty, and call for a celebration.

When the Bill of Rights was ratified in 1791, the provision protective of all rights, that Congress shall make no law abridging the freedom of the press, had been, in the words of Zechariah Chafee, included "to . . . make further prosecution for criticism of the government . . . forever impossible in the United States of America."[1] The press, watchdog for the people, was expected to vigorously scrutinize and criticize government without fear of prosecution. It was a major milestone in the long road toward freedom. Before, the government was supreme, the king could do no wrong, and to demean government or blame officials was blasphemy. A long line of heroic editors and writers had paid terrible prices for printing unpleasant facts about the government or holding opposing opinions.

Freedom of the press was understood to mean, as Alexander Meicklejohn wrote, that "the citizens of the United States will be fit to govern themselves under their own institutions only if they have faced squarely and fearlessly everything that can be said in favor of those institutions, everything that can be said against them."[2]

The tension between the government and the press was very real. The press offered the principal restraint on arbitrary and despotic government. William Penn, Peter Zenger, John Wilkes, and the pseudonymous Junius were all seen by the people as champions of liberty because they dared criticize the crown. On the other hand, government saw the press as the most dangerous sower of the seeds of rebellion, because it fertilized the inarticulate germs of public opinion.

Whether the government was popular or not, the press was a thorn in its side. Before and during the Revolution, as Leonard Levy shows in *Legacy of Suppression*, his great study of freedom of speech and the press in early American history, the revolutionaries outmatched the Tories in destroying presses. Benjamin Franklin in his autobiography referred to scurrilous press attacks on the government as an "infamous disgrace." Concerned for ratification of the new Constitution in 1789, Franklin said of writers who attacked the government's reputation: "we should, in moderation, content ourselves with tarring and feathering and tossing them in a blanket."[3]

President George Washington grumbled threateningly about "that rascal Freneau," whose newspaper constantly criticized his administration. Sturdy John Adams signed the infamous Alien and Sedition Laws and approved prosecutions of journalists under them for criticizing his government. Thomas Jefferson, who had sworn eternal hostility to every form of tyranny over the mind of man, wrote in 1803, "I have . . . long thought that a few prosecutions of the most prominent offenders would have a wholesome effect in restoring the integrity of the presses."[4]

Now, however, no longer made up of publishers who set their own type, hand-pressed the sheets, and then hawked their own papers, giant corporate business media monopoly was determined, with the government, to peddle the official line, demonize the enemy, and stifle any voice that said anything against the U.S. assault on Iraq. Highly paid media celebrities working in pools, entertainers who would strike dramatic poses in Deserta Arabia, read lines largely written by the Pentagon for national television audiences. They replaced the Tom Paines, Mathew Bradys, and Ernie Pyles of bygone years who looked at war for themselves and tried to tell people what they saw and thought.

There was no hope for sedition prosecutions against the American media for its coverage of the Gulf crisis because there was no media criticism of government conduct. The watchdog had become more than a lap dog of the Pentagon; it had become a cheerleader for the war. There was no struggle between a heroic press determined to denounce war and a domineering government determined to do its will. The press rendered First Amendment protection meaningless, because its wealthy owners uncritically supported the government as it destroyed Iraq. It barely reported dissent; when it did, it ridiculed, misrepresented, or marginalized those who criticized U.S. intervention in the Gulf. TV coverage of the Gulf crisis from August 1990 through March 1991 was more a long-running commercial for war, weapons systems, and militarism than news reporting.

THE AMERICAN MEDIA AND WAR

The American media has a long history of promoting war. William Randolph Hearst boasted that he caused the Spanish-American War. As the legend goes, Hearst hired the famous artist Frederic Remington to go to Cuba and draw pictures of battle. When Remington cabled that there was no war, Hearst is said to have wired back, "You provide the pictures and I will provide the war." Even so, scores of independent papers across the country opposed the war. There was a lively debate, a variety of opinions, a choice for the people.

Closer to our time, the role of the media in the Vietnam War was terribly deficient, despite its ultimately decisive function in forcing American withdrawal. Throughout the Kennedy–Johnson years the press was largely hostile to civil rights and Great Society programs, but it overwhelmingly favored military spending and the arms race, support for NATO, stationing U.S. troops around the world, and intervention in Vietnam. Media support for the Tonkin Gulf resolution was as high as support in Congress, where not a single Representative and only two Senators dared vote no. No journalists were assigned to investigate whether North Vietnamese ships had attacked U.S. vessels. It was only after public opposition had reached fever pitch that the media began to question the war seriously.

News film footage from Vietnam, with graphic print reporting, helped persuade major segments of the public that U.S. violence in Vietnam was wrong. Every night the news was full of violence, new U.S. casualty reports, and Pentagon body counts. But the press showed little interest in Vietnamese casualties. Rolling Thunder, B-52s carpet-bombing villages, the Phoenix extermination program, Agent Orange, and the extensive use of napalm did not bring critical news or editorial coverage. The My Lai massacre went unreported, presumably undiscovered, for many months. Finally, it was forced on the media, not found by it.

No U.S. media reported from North Vietnam. They wanted to, but until 1972, North Vietnam would not let them in. Several articles from Hanoi in December 1966 by the courageous Harrison Salisbury were an exception, and they earned him hostile personal attacks for years. As a consequence, reporting on civilian casualties in the North was extremely difficult. When I traveled to North Vietnam in August 1972, ABC and Time-Life subsidized my trip. I carried a video camera and a tape recorder. The film I took was not good, but short clips were used on the national news on my return. Several hours of audiotapes were played on ABC and its affiliates and a 30-minute cassette was played many times. Still pictures I took with a Time-Life camera were run by *Time* and used with an essay I wrote in a feature article for *Life* magazine.

While in Hanoi I persuaded Pham Van Dong to accept one American camera crew. This professional footage from a CBS crew, the ABC radio reports, and my *Life* article were the first substantial media coverage of the war from within North Vietnam used by major U.S. media. Had reporting been extensive earlier, it might have saved many lives.

Although it used my accounts, the American media overwhelmingly condemned my trip. The Nixon administration threatened me with prosecution under the Logan Act, an unused statute of Alien and Sedition vintage, presumably to deter others from gathering information on how American bombing was affecting North Vietnam.

Other experiences I have had demonstrate that the media coverage of international events that conflict with U.S. foreign policy interests is extremely limited. My 1971 trip to South Africa as the guest of separate black and white national student organizations, during which I severely criticized apartheid and U.S. policy supporting it, was extensively covered by South African and other African press, but was ignored by the U.S. press despite my long involvement in civil rights. My trips to Chile after the coup in 1973 and attendence at show trials there went virtually unreported in the American press. Repeated trips to Iran in support of human rights before and during 1978 went unreported while the Shah was in power. There can be little doubt that these trips would have been reported by the U.S. media if, as most U.S. public figures who traveled to these countries, I had supported the Shah, Pinochet, apartheid, and others protected by American foreign policy.

When President Carter asked me to go to Teheran immediately after the U.S. embassy staff was taken hostage in November 1979, the press rushed to interview me before I left. They never ceased pursuing me for interviews until after my return from Turkey, where I had worked for more than a week to obtain permission to travel to Iran. Yet a few months later, when I went to Teheran at the urgent request of the Iranian government to plead for the hostages' release while condemning U.S. interference in Iran's internal affairs, the major media reported nothing about my trip except the Carter administration's announcement that it was conducting a criminal investigation to determine whether I had violated the 1920 Trading with the Enemy Act.

Among many such experiences, it was the invasion of Grenada in 1983 that most dramatically revealed to me the near total identity of action between the U.S. government and the American mass media. The Pentagon excluded the media from the island for a week after the invasion, but the media barely complained. The press accepted unchallenged Pentagon stories that the surviving leadership of the New Jewel Movement had ordered the execution of Prime Minister Maurice Bishop, and then danced and chanted "Central Committee gives order, order carried out" on his death. It adopted the presentations of military psychological warfare units that the surviving Defense Minister, Hudson Austin, was a "Caribbean Idi Amin" and that Deputy Prime Minister Bernard Coard was a "Stalinist-Leninist Moscow puppet." It perpetuated the myth that the airfield being built at Point Salines by a British company was to be a Soviet bomber base and that American medical students were endangered.

By contrast, the American media rarely mentioned Grenadian casualties of U.S. aggression. It barely reported the mental hospital destroyed by a Navy jet, leaving more than 20 dead. It has never interviewed a single surviving New Jewel leader imprisoned by the United States, turned over to Grenada for trial by U.S.-paid prosecutors and judges, and condemned to death. The invasion of Grenada was one of the biggest news stories of 1983. But soon after, Grenada, condemned to another generation of poverty by the U.S. invasion, slipped from media attention. When death sentences for 14 wrongfully convicted leaders of Bishop's government were commuted in August 1991, the U.S. media, which had ignored the trial and appeals over an eight-year period, did not report the fact. The American public was unaware that U.S. forces took several thousand Grenadians prisoner, compelled prosecution of the surviving leaders, and paid millions of dollars for their imprisonment, the prosecutors, and the special courts. Half a dozen news conferences called to report significant developments in the proceedings were ignored by the press. A lengthy petition filed with the Inter-American Human Rights Commission supported by eyewitness affidavits asserting the innocence of the 14 people on death row and the Commission's cable to Grenada requesting a delay in executions were all ignored by the major U.S. media. Even the dramatic commutation of the sentences went unreported because the U.S. government was the principal player in the drama and was determined to cover up its role.

Following the U.S. bombing of Tripoli and Benghazi in April 1986, I was asked by Libyan families to visit survivors in hospitals in Vienna, Zurich, and Rome, and thereafter to investigate deaths and injuries in Libya and file suit for damages for the families of those killed and seriously injured. The U.S. media covered the raid live by radio in Tripoli from downtown hotels. It knew civilians were killed. Yet there was no challenge when Defense Secretary Caspar Weinberger said it was "impossible" that civilians were killed. The media did report the death of a small child and other injuries in Colonel Qaddafi's house when the Libyan government held a press conference to show the destroyed home, office, and tent of its leader. Yet even then the U.S. media showed more skepticism over whether the child had been legally adopted by Qaddafi than concern for her death. And when I filed suit months later in U.S. District Court for 340 persons killed or injured in the raids, alleging deliberate bombing of civilian areas and an attempt to assassinate the head of state, both facts unarguable and the evidence available, no major media attended. Nor did the press report a series of news conferences called at various stages of the proceedings.

The contrast with intense media coverage of U.S. and British demands that Libya surrender two of its citizens indicted in the United States for the destruction of Pan Am 103 over Lockerbie, Scotland, shows how the media advances U.S. policy. The press never demanded that the United States explain why it had earlier charged Palestinians, Syrians, and Iranians with the crime, or that it produce evidence against the Libyans. The demand that Libya, not even charged in the indictment, pay damages to families of the dead got supporting editorials from papers that never reported the dismissal of the claims of the 340 Libyan civilians killed or wounded by American bombs. In addition, my law office was sanctioned $20,000 to intimidate other lawyers who might dare to file such claims.

I flew to Panama on the first day commercial flights were permitted to operate after the U.S. invasion in December 1990. Surveying devastated neighborhoods; finding a 120 × 18-foot mass grave; talking with Red Cross, hospital, and morgue workers, and religious, human rights, labor, student, and other leaders, I readily counted hundreds of civilians dead. The press, however, initially asked no questions about civilian casualties. When eventually prodded in early January, General Stiner repeatedly stated that 83 civilians were killed, and the media faithfully reported that number.

A press conference I held before leaving Panama, like a number held thereafter by a private commission formed to investigate and report on Panama, was virtually ignored by the mass media. Estimates of casualties from that commission and many other religious, human rights, and health groups ranged from 1,000 to 7,000 dead. By 1992 a consensus was emerging around 4,000 Panamanians killed. Yet the media used only the final Pentagon figure of 345 Panamanian deaths when it explained why angry crowds disrupted President Bush's visit to Panama in June 1992. It was clear that the major American media did not intend to report casualty figures that conflicted with Pentagon estimates.

The handful of incidents I've described are only a few of many occasions on which I witnessed the U.S. media refuse to report facts and opinions that impact critically on U.S. foreign policy. Often I have been the only person, or part of the only group, investigating and reporting on such instances. Many times American correspondents abroad and reporters in the United States have turned off their cameras, laid down their pens, and frankly said their networks or newspapers would not use the story. More often they have admitted they stayed away from interviews or press conferences of people who criticize U.S. actions and policies. Some reporters have said they would be fired if they submitted a story based on such critical reports. Thus, the American people are deprived of information and opinions that are necessary for democratic institutions to be meaningful.

The effect of this media failure on the lives of people in foreign countries and on the opportunity for a U.S. foreign policy that seeks peace is enormous. Since the United States overthrew the Arbenz government in Guatemala in 1954, the military regimes established and supported there by the Pentagon have practiced systematic killings against the Indian majority and other Guatemalan dissidents. The Thai military slaughtered hundreds of students at Thammasat University in Thailand in 1976 and the U.S. media ignored the story. The United States supported the Thai military government. In contrast, when Chinese troops killed students in Tiananmen Square after exercising much greater tolerance and with less directed gunfire and violence than in Thailand, the incident became a defining moment for U.S. foreign policy, after which China was isolated in the international community.

The United States gave the Indonesian government thousands of names of suspected communists in 1966, and the Indonesians slaughtered hundreds of thousands shortly thereafter using the U.S. lists in part. Indonesia accelerated its assaults on East Timor in 1983 and slaughtered thousands, continuing its killing through 1992 with virtually no U.S. media coverage. In each case, the media served U.S. policy, condemning its enemies, often demonizing them, while covering up for dictators the United States supports. When Salman Rushdie, threatened with death by Iran for his book *The Satanic Verses,* sought support in Washington in March 1992, Washington rejected him for fear of antagonizing Iran. Few questions are nearer the hearts of writers and the media than freedom to publish without fear of reprisal, but the major media raised no outcry.

The U.S. media has ignored a virtual civil war in southeast Turkey in which Turkish forces have killed thousands of Kurds in both Turkey and Iraq while holding millions under martial law. Yet the media inflames passions against Iraq regularly for its acts against Kurds.

Over the years, I have come to focus more and more on the deaths and injuries that result from war, military actions, foreign policies, and natural disasters as the most important facts for world opinion to consider. How many people were killed by foreign military interventions in Vietnam, Afghanistan, Tibet, and East Timor? By typhoons in Bangladesh, earthquakes in Iran, famine in Ethiopia, and AIDS in Africa? We ought to carefully study what American presidents and the media knew about such unimaginable tragedies as the Holocaust in the dark years of World War II and the deaths of 20 million or more from famine in the People's Republic of China from 1959 to 1962. Above all, the public must learn that it is not adequately informed and demand access to the truth and vigorous debate over policies. Otherwise, democratic planning and action to deal with such human disasters will remain nonexistent. Had the American people understood that their wars would cost hundreds of thousands of Filipino lives in the first years of the century and over a quarter of a million Iraqi lives in 1991, perhaps they would have demanded peace then and thereafter.

In 1991 the major media, primarily the TV networks, consumed hours of people's lives daily. It monopolized public access to the events that make the news. Its intimate financial relationships with the military and weapons industries, its dependence on major corporate advertising, its political campaign contributions, its close alliances with political parties and leaders, the celebrity status and huge salaries of the major TV news readers identified as friends of the famous, made the American media virtually one with the government. The media exerted its power to persuade the public to support war while it demonized Saddam Hussein and portrayed George Bush as a courageous leader determined to liberate an innocent Kuwait. Even so, the strong undercurrents of doubt clearly present across the country, the outbursts of passionate opposition to preparation for war, the belated debate and vote of the Congress, strongly suggest that a modestly open, accessible, and fair media presenting dissenting fact and opinion would have stimulated resistance that might have prevented the exercise of imperial power which devastated Iraq.

The capacity of the mass media to present facts is enormous. Its power to control and limit information is dangerous. It can help the people see the world as it is, know themselves, analyze democratic choices, form opinions, and face the problems of the planet. It is the greatest disservice to country and self-interest to do otherwise. It is a form of treason to conceal the truth and condone the wrongful conduct of a country you love.

CONDUCT OF THE MEDIA DURING THE GULF WAR

Nothing I had experienced prepared me for the conduct of the media during the Gulf crisis. Military censorship, self-censorship, uncritical acceptance of Pentagon stories, suppression of dissenting voices, perpetuation of false stories, each present and inexcusable in and of itself, were minor offenses. What occurred was not merely the presentation of a false picture or the failure to adequately inform the public. Instead, there was a massive media campaign to persuade the public of the righteousness of the American cause and conduct, including an intense promotion of U.S. military actions. It required justifying violence by creating hatred toward and dehumanizing Iraq, and concealing or misrepresenting anything that conflicted with that purpose.

While this sounds extreme, it is demonstrably true. What else could cause any people to celebrate the slaughter of tens of thousands of defenseless human beings, ignore continuing crimes against humanity that are taking thousands of innocent lives each month, and then blame those who are dying for their plight?

The media saturated the American public with good stories about U.S. military operations and bad stories about Iraq. The United States bombed with surgical accuracy, we were told. On the first day of the bombing, Charles Osgood called it "a marvel."[5] The next day, Jim Stewart of CBS told Americans there had been "two days of almost picture perfect bombing."[6] Ted Koppel, in a typical comment, assured millions of viewers on ABC that "great effort is taken, sometimes at great personal cost to American pilots, that civilian targets are not hit." These newsmen were not in Iraq, so the only basis they could have for such statements was that the Pentagon told them so, and their standing as newsmen lent credibility to the Pentagon reports. Now we know 38 U.S. aircraft were lost, none in air combat. Military experts have shown that only 7 percent of the bombs and missiles used had directional control systems. Tens of thousands of Iraqi civilians were killed by the bombing. Civilian targets were systematically selected and destroyed to cripple the country. Planes searched for and strafed civilian cars, taxis, buses, and trucks traveling alone on highways between Amman and Baghdad and elsewhere. Despite this mass destruction, Howard Stringer, president of CBS Broadcast Group, observed after the war, "There are more people routinely killed across the spectrum of American television in a given night than you saw in any of the coverage of this war."[7]

More TV time was given to film taken in Israel of Scud attacks than was given to all attacks on Iraq taken within Iraq. Fewer than 40 Scuds were fired at Israel, and two Israelis died as a result. There were nearly 110,000 U.S. aerial sorties against Iraq. More than 50,000 Iraqi civilians died during the bombing. One evening before the U.S. ground forces attacked, Walter Cronkite told the CBS audience, "We knocked out one of their Scuds." This "we–they" formulation is a way of taking sides. The program noted that the only event in the war that day was one Scud fired at Tel Aviv. Yet that day there were more than 2,000 aerial sorties against Iraq which undoubtedly killed hundreds of people.

Robert Fisk, a correspondent for the London *Independent*, recounted an incident in which an Air Force colonel, to "honor" reporters, gave them all a small American flag and told them, "You are warriors, too." In the same article Fisk referred to a *Philadelphia Inquirer* pool dispatch from the U.S.S. *Kennedy* that described bombers taking off to bomb Iraq as "paving the way for new dawn of hope." He observed, "Journalists are now talking of Iraq as 'the enemy,' as if they themselves have gone to war which, in a sense, they have."[8]

Dan Rather wrapped it up for the newsgatherers, when he said of the U.S. assault on Iraq, "Congratulations on a job wonderfully done."[9] There were hundreds of such comments in prime time before major radio and TV audiences, as the media continued to be a flack for U.S. aggression.

Through the press, the Bush administration characterized Iraq, its recent beneficiary, as an evil, outlaw state. It portrayed the invasion of Kuwait as completely unprovoked. The media never analyzed the enormous volume of evidence that the United States planned the destruction of Iraq long before August 2, 1990. It never speculated on the vast amount of evidence showing that the United States, with help from Kuwait, was trying to provoke Saddam Hussein into an attack. When a federal court, at government insistence, in April 1992 refused to order the State Department to release Ambassador April Glaspie's memorandum of her July 25, 1990 meeting with Saddam Hussein just before Iraq's invasion of Kuwait, the media did not cry "coverup" and demand the memo. Instead, it ignored the story. It falsely claimed Iraq planned to invade Saudi Arabia to dominate world oil reserves, and it frequently repeated claims that Iraq used chemical weapons in the Iran war, had a huge chemical warfare stockpile, and was on the verge of developing atomic weapons. Iraq was constantly described as a powerful military dictatorship with the fourth largest army in the world, although its population is only 6 percent of the United States'. It was accused of atrocities against the Kuwaiti people that never occurred.

The demonization of Saddam Hussein was a continuing process by the government and the media from early August 1990. On August 9 Marjorie Williams wrote an article in the *Washington Post* describing press vilification of Saddam Hussein. The headline was "Saddam Hussein: Monster in the Making." The subtitle was "From Unknown to Arch-Villain in a Matter of Days."[10] Later Jack Anderson wrote a syndicated column entitled "The Demonization of Saddam Hussein" in which he described CIA and DIA efforts "to see who can trump whom with the most outrageous Saddam story."[11] Among the contenders were the claim Saddam Hussein was a murderer at age 10, that he preferred to shoot victims in the back, and that he kept a vat of acid to dispose of the bodies. President Bush set the tone by comparing Hussein to Hitler. *The New Republic* took the cue and ran a doctored cover photo of the Iraqi leader with a Hitler mustache.[12] On August 7, liberal columnist Mary McGrory referred to him as a "beast." By August 20, Saddam Hussein had become a "monster" to *Newsweek*. *Time* magazine was more dramatic, writing, "On first meeting him, a visitor is first struck by his eyes, crackling with alertness and at the same time cold and remorseless as snake eyes on the sides of dice. They are the eyes of a killer."[13] Columnist George Will wrote, "It is tempting, but misleading, to compare the strutting Saddam Hussein to Mussolini. . . . Hussein radiates a more virulent and personal viciousness than Mussolini did." Later Will decided "Saddam Hussein is not Hitler, but the dynamism of his regime is Hitlerism."[14] During the war, on January 24, CBS correspondent Allen Pizzey labeled Hussein "psychologically deformed."[15] The media saturated the country with such presentations. Few public figures dared suggest that Saddam Hussein or even the Iraqi people might be human.

Such propaganda has always been used to dehumanize an enemy so that their deaths seem desirable. It is essential to emotionalize soldiers to kill. Thus, a U.S. helicopter gunship crew crying "Say hello to Allah!" as they blasted helpless Iraqi troops can be understood as the moral price of war. But what is to be said when top media news personalities ask, as Tom Brokaw did on NBC, "Can the United States allow Saddam Hussein to live?"[16]

THE POOL SYSTEM: CONTROLLING THE NEWS

The media was aware of the near total control the Pentagon exerted over its reporters. *San Francisco Chronicle* reporter Carl Nolte, one of the few journalists to stray from the pool system, reported on January 23:

> Critics back home have begun to notice that the first war ever shown live on television around the world has turned out so far to be an illusion, carefully staged by the military.
>
> From here, it is like a hall of mirrors. No one can tell what is real and what is not.
>
> To anyone who has ever been in any army, it defies belief. But the pool reports, written by some of the best journalists in the world, are banal and upbeat like papers handed in at a sophomore feature writing class back in journalism school.
>
> Of course, the reports are cleared by military censors, and the reporters, who spend weeks at a time in the field wearing flak jackets and combat helmets, are rooting for the home team.
>
> No one in the rear can go to the front. It is forbidden. What is left is what the world is seeing and reading.
>
> And that, most of the journalists admit, is what the American military and the Saudi government wants the world — and Iraq — to see and read.[17]

Two days later, in a column written by Liz Trotta and reprinted in the *Chronicle*, she said, "We are seeing a Hollywood version of war."[18] And Maria Mann, director of photos for Agence Press, with 14 combat photographers assigned to her but none permitted in a pool, said that photographers were unable to take negative pictures.[19]

The inadequacies of the Pentagon briefing system and the control it permitted over news coverage were clearly understood by the media. Walter Cronkite testified in a Senate Government Affairs Committee hearing that military briefings from Saudi Arabia were "ridiculously inadequate." He spoke of U.S. military "arrogance" in controlling news. He argued the media must be free to roam the battlefields.[20] Other TV personalities, though invited, avoided the hearings.

The *Christian Science Monitor* ran a detailed story entitled "Pool System Inadequate, Western Journalists Say," by Peter Ford. It described press dissatisfaction, quoting Philip Shenon of the *New York Times* as saying, "The system is working very poorly. . . . My paper has had a reporter in the field in only five or six days" during the first four weeks of the bombing. Jean-Michel Thenaid of the Paris daily *Liberation* voiced a more common experience, saying that at the current rotation rate "it will be ten months before I get into a pool."[21]

Christopher Hanson wrote of his service as a combat pool correspondent in the *Columbia Journalism Review*. He described Captain John Koko, a six-foot-four former Army Ranger, who apprehended reporters attempting to get to the front without permission: "He dutifully, if reluctantly, stopped Americans, but truly gets a charge out of busting French and especially Italian reporters, because in his view, neither country is contributing enough to the war effort." When Hanson tried to talk with soldiers, Koko came over and rebuked him "for talking to troops without a military escort."[22]

He described his big chance in the pool on February 23.

> Word is that the Second Armored Cavalry does not want reporters along on the ground offensive. But the regimental spokesman, Captain Bob Dodson, says this restriction applies only to TV crews. He can take one "pencil" and agrees to take me, but only if I agree to his terms—I can go only where Dodson goes and must never venture out by myself. No other escorts are available. Koko and Botkins will be returning to headquarters. Reluctantly, I agree to the terms. The alternative is sitting out the war in the rear. Captain Dodson is now my assignment editor.[23]

Censorship was complete. When the ground war began, a general 48-hour news blackout was imposed. But scores of individual reporters had their own blackouts. AP journalist Fred Bayles was held for six hours by U.S. forces. *Time* photographer Wesley Bocxe was seized, searched, held overnight, blindfolded, and driven 60 miles, where he was "lectured" by a public affairs officer for photographing tanks in Saudi Arabia. Military police covered television camera lenses to prevent the filming of American casualties being removed from a barracks hit by a Scud or Patriot missile in Saudi Arabia.[24] Tom Brokaw questioned on the air whether the media should cover the return of U.S. casualties from the Gulf when the first caskets arrived at Dover, Delaware,[25] as the painful pictures could create opposition to the war. Cameras were kept away from the U.S. troops burying Iraqi dead, preventing the filming of violations of the Geneva Convention.

A small group of publications in the United States decided to fight the Pentagon's press rules. *The Nation,* the *Village Voice, Harper's Magazine,* and others sued to test the constitutionality of the rules, but no establishment news organization joined the action. And the shortness of the war made any outcome of the suit moot.

The total control of information from the Gulf enabled the Pentagon to tell more than one family that their loved one died from enemy fire, heroically defending freedom, when death was actually caused by mistake. To learn the truth later, as some families did, usually from other soldiers in the unit who saw what happened, burdened the deep sorrow of the loss with an embitterment toward a government that would lie like that about a precious life.

A principled reporter would have rejected a pool assignment altogether. It provided no free opportunity to observe combat, see war damage, or interview soldiers or civilians, and all news copy and film footage had to be approved by military censors before publication. Most correspondents in the region were never confronted with the ethical dilemma, because they never had a chance to be in a pool.

If a reporter's story cleared the military censors, it was then subjected to censorship by media officials. This was by far the more severe limitation on the news. Reporters lost much of their desire to get film or write stories that were critical of the Pentagon, showed heavy casualties, or described military conduct that was improper, because they knew their employers would not use them. While many reporters would take and even enjoy the risk of getting cut off from access to Pentagon sources and being excluded from pools for negative reports, knowing that their stories would be rejected by their employers left them without any choice but to go along.

CHECKING OUT ON THE FIRST AMENDMENT

One moment on the day before the bombing of Iraq began best illustrates how the American press covered the crisis. The deadline for

Iraq to withdraw from Kuwait was hours away, and standing in line at the cashier's desk of the Al-Rashid Hotel in Baghdad were some of the most famous and highly paid personalities in the U.S. media. A very major news event was about to occur, the biggest part of which was bound to be in Baghdad and the rest of Iraq. There must have been times over the years, as they dreamed of their futures, that those reporters yearned for just such a moment: like Murrow in London, Shirer in Berlin, Hemingway in Barcelona. And they were checking out. The media was not going to report what would happen to Iraq.[26]

Why would the press leave? Supposedly, management ordered many to leave because of the danger. No one wanted to have to explain a death to surviving families and friends. Some reporters chose to leave on their own. And yet hundreds of freelance reporters in Saudi Arabia and Jordan wanted to enter Iraq to cover the story.

What about the news? Must the world wait for the postmortems to know what happened? Certainly everyone has a right to refuse to face danger, but you should not choose dangerous work if you are not willing to take the risk. You know what would happen if the fire department decided to check out when your home was in flames.

If the media really left from fear, they must have believed the United States planned to bomb civilians in Baghdad. If they believed this, they were right. But they should have known the Al-Rashid was the safest place in town. If the media did not believe it was too dangerous to remain in Baghdad, then they must have left because they knew they would not report what they saw there.

Peter Arnett of CNN chose to remain in Baghdad, and he reported what he saw. What he saw was not much, because he was only one man and his travel was restricted by Iraqi officials, but he both provided vital information and opinion and fulfilled his duty to the American people and the First Amendment.

What was revealed about the media and the U.S. government by Arnett staying in Baghdad was worth more than his reporting. Almost immediately he was the center of a controversy over whether Saddam Hussein was using him for propaganda purposes. Although virtually the entire American media was prostituted as an unpaid public relations firm for the Pentagon, the question it raised was whether Peter Arnett was aiding and abetting the enemy. The inaptly named organization Accuracy in Media sent out 100,000 postcards asking its supporters to call for Arnett to be removed from Iraq, and called his reporting a "betrayal of the [American] troops." Nothing he could have said or shown on TV could have helped Iraq, but his pictures did not lie, and his judgments were overwhelmingly sound. He gave a glimpse of what was happening in Iraq, primarily around Baghdad: the nightly anti-aircraft fire, the important interview with Saddam Hussein, the baby milk plant bombing, the horror of the Amariyah bomb shelter. This was the unimpaired view that the American people needed to do their duty as citizens in a democratic society. But their own government and the mass media overwhelmingly deprived them of it.

Right now the Pentagon knows exactly what it did in Iraq. It has film of much of the assault. The media knows this, yet does not demand this vital information. But questions by the media about Peter Arnett's role persist, and the polls say the public favors censorship on such occasions.

When it became clear to me from the nature of the bombing reports that Iraq was suffering heavy civilian casualties, I asked the Iraqi Ambassador to the UN, whom I had never met, to obtain permission for U.S. network television to enter Iraq or, if this was rejected, permission for me to enter Iraq with a camera crew. I never received an answer about network TV crews, but permission came quickly for me to proceed. On February 2, 1991, at the beginning of the third week of the air assault, I entered Iraq accompanied by Jon Alpert, Maryann DeLeo, and Mohammed al-Kaysi. Jon had won seven Emmy awards for documentary films from Afghanistan, Angola, El Salvador, Vietnam, and elsewhere. He had worked closely with NBC for 12 years.

My primary purpose was to witness and report on civilian casualties and damage. I hoped to cause the U.S. Air Force to use greater care and avoid bombing civilian areas. Jon and Maryann were to film and photograph civilian damage and civilian life. Kaduri, as al-Kaysi is called, would use his familiarity with Iraq, his many contacts there, and his fluent Arabic to find places where damage and casualties were greatest and act as an interpreter. Together and separately we traveled more than 2,000 miles across Iraq as far south as Basra. Jon was the first foreign cameraman to film bomb damage in heavily hit Basra and elsewhere in the south. He took more than six hours of videotape during the week, much of it filmed without Iraqi officials present. He was always free to film any civilian damage and interview anyone. No one viewed his film in Iraq. The Iraqi government did not see it or ask for a copy. This material was uncensored, and was the first footage of civilian damage from U.S. bombing of southern Iraq. It was a major scoop.

The film was never shown by the mass media in the United States. *NBC Nightly News* wanted to use it. According to *Variety* magazine, anchorman Tom Brokaw was anxious to include excerpts on his show. After a crucial two-day delay it was rejected by NBC News President Michael Gartner, who had not seen the film.[27] Don Brown, the second-ranking official at NBC News, fronted for Gartner. He used what he called the "Clark mission" as his excuse. He did not suggest what he thought my mission was; or, if I had one, why it wasn't news. He knew I had never met Alpert before the trip, and that Jon was famous throughout the media for his independence. He said, "We're not going to prostitute ourselves like that" when asked why the film was not shown. Unfortunately, the Pentagon had long before prostituted the media.

A senior CBS correspondent was on our plane from Amman to Amsterdam when we returned. He expressed a strong desire to buy the rights for the film. But CBS, and then every major U.S. TV organization including PBS, rejected the footage.

Later, *The McNeil-Lehrer News Hour* ran a short segment of the film. Jon made a videocassette called *Nowhere to Hide* and several thousand copies were sold. The cassette was shown to scores of live audiences, on some cable channels, and overseas on many major stations. However, its total exposure in the United States was insignificant compared to even 60 seconds on national network news.

Before the war, the very limited opportunities for opposition voices to be heard in the major media were swamped by the hostile context in which they were presented. When I appeared on the *Today Show* in the late fall of 1990, I described my November meeting with Saddam Hussein and my belief that Iraq was ready to negotiate "everything." Without any notice to me, Congressman Hunter Duncan was interviewed in the same segment of the show, and he introduced the allegation that over 300 infants had been killed in Kuwait when Iraqi soldiers removed them from incubators. With no knowledge of the source or truthfulness of this charge, I was compelled to spend my few remaining moments reacting to the worst atrocity story of the war, which we now know was false. John Chancellor, a former NBC anchorman, wrote, "it never happened."[28] Human rights groups, including Amnesty International, which had originally partially validated the story, later helped establish its untruth. But President Bush proudly waved the report of the story for TV cameras. The hatred generated toward Iraq in this way was spread also to those who sought peace and who seemed insensitive to such a shocking story.

Another way the media avoided examination of the critical issues was by strictly limiting the scope of interviews. Before the war, both Leslie Stahl during my appearance on *Issues and Answers* and Connie Chung during her magazine program restricted the scope of the interview to avoid discussion of whether the United States was seeking war with Iraq, whether the President was usurping Congressional powers, and whether bribery of UN members for their votes was wrong. They asked questions such as whether Saddam Hussein was insane. Thus the media, while seeming to present opposing views, actually prevented presentation of facts and opinion on the important issues that needed airing.

When I met Peter Arnett my first morning in the Al-Rashid Hotel during the bombing, he asked immediately for an interview. Since I had arrived in the dark, I had seen nothing so far except fires. We agreed he would interview me later in my trip. After I returned from Basra several days later, he caught me in the lobby and said he had live air time at 4 and 7. We agreed to meet at 3:45 outside the hotel, where CNN had a generator that powered transmissions. When I came downstairs, Arnett was waiting for me. He looked dejected.

"They will only give us one minute," he said. Knowing I was the first American eyewitness to the destruction of Basra, he told me he would ask one quick question: "You've just returned from Basra, Mr. Clark. What did you see?" Arnett urged me to talk as fast as I could to get as much said as possible. I was describing the damage we had seen and filmed when I heard through my earplug, "That is one man's opinion." I assumed we were off the air and answered angrily that it was not an opinion; it was an eyewitness account. The voice was that of reporter Reed Collins from the United States. He then challenged my statement that we had seen extensive damage, all civilian.

Later, I learned that just before my brief interview CNN had quoted Iraqi Foreign Minister Tariq Aziz as estimating Iraqi civilian casualties in the hundreds. CNN was trying to discredit my descriptions of extensive civilian damage by juxtaposing my interview with Aziz's and interrupting me with Collins's remarks. For its own reasons, Iraq has consistently understated the numbers of civilians killed by the bombing. When Iraqi statements helped the United States portray its bombing as having killed few civilians, the estimates were deemed trustworthy. The next day at a Baghdad news conference I spoke of thousands of casualties and estimated 15,000 civilians dead. As it turned out, this figure, based on estimates by the Red Crescent, the Iraqi Health Ministry, civilian defense, and my own extensive travels, was actually low.

After my brief interview, CNN went live to a U.S. Air Force general in Saudi Arabia, who was asked for his comments on my statement that we saw only civilian vehicles damaged and destroyed on the highways. Surprisingly, the general admitted that Iraqi military vehicles stayed off the highways because they knew they would be attacked. However, no one asked why the civilian cars, taxis, buses, and trucks were destroyed.

Since there was no TV reception in Iraq, it was only when we returned to Jordan that I learned how the CNN interview had been sandwiched. The short clip was shown over and over in Jordan. I was recognized everywhere. I thought my description of the bombing in Basra was what would impress Arab people. Not at all. They were overjoyed to see someone stand up to a pious American TV personality and try to tell the truth. They knew about the disasters of the war from the flood of refugees and a small stream of drivers and persons fleeing Iraq.

SELF-CENSORSHIP, DISINFORMATION, AND PROPAGANDA

Even on the homefront, commentators who voiced the wrong opinion ran into trouble. Warren Hinckle of the *San Francisco Examiner* was placed on a three-month "vacation" for his known views against the war. Dr. Orlando Garcia, a popular talk show host on New York Spanish-language station WADO, was dismissed for his "unbalanced view of the war." Editor Joe Reedy of the Kutztown (PA) *Patriot* was fired for writing an editorial "How About a Little Peace?" just before the bombing started. In an editorial explaining why Reedy was fired, two weeks into the bombing, the paper said "the time for debate has passed."[29]

The Pentagon went to great lengths not only to prevent and distort news coverage, but to create and direct it. James Le Moyne of the *New York Times* wrote, "three Pentagon officials in the Gulf region said they spent significant time analyzing reporters' stories in order to make recommendations on how to sway coverage in the Pentagon's favor."[30] *New York Times* correspondent Malcolm Browne told *Newsday* on January 23, 1991, "I've never seen anything that can compare to it, in the degree of surveillance and control the military has over the correspondents. When the entire environment is controlled, a journalist ceases to be a reporter in the American or Anglo-Saxon tradition. He works a lot like the PK (Propagandakompanien, the Nazi propaganda corps)."[31]

The *Toronto Star*'s Linda Diebel, in a column dated February 24, 1991 and headlined "Pentagon Exerts Total Control over News," quoted an expert's comment on a Pentagon press conference the day before: "It couldn't be done any better." She found the Pentagon

presentation and press acceptance "a display that should have shattered, for anyone watching the televised performance, one of the
biggest myths of the war — that there's a gulf between the U.S. military and the media. And, with the land war beginning just hours
later, it was an ominous signal of how little information was going
to be available — except what the Pentagon wants us to know."

Diebel quoted Michael Deaver, whom she described as the
"former Ronald Reagan staffer and news manipulator," as saying
"The Department of Defense has done an excellent job of managing
the news in an almost classic way. If you were going to hire a public
relations firm to do the media relations for an international event,
it couldn't be done any better than this is being done."

As an illustration of Pentagon thoroughness, the military showed
film footage of a U.S. helicopter assault to selected reporters to measure how they would react. The screen test "showed frightened, disoriented Iraqi infantrymen being shot to pieces in the dark by U.S.
attack helicopters. One by one they were cut down in the middle of
the night by an enemy they could not see. Some were blown to bits
by bursts of exploding 30-millimeter cannon shells."[32]

Reporting on the private showing, an AP-Reuters dispatch said,
"The combat reporters permitted to see the video did not mention
where and when the engagement took place, and no casualty count
was given. . . . TV viewers won't see the footage: censors ruled it
too brutal for general audiences."[33]

Of course, the real reason the film was not shown on TV was not
its violent nature. for American TV audiences see violence constantly. The film showed the truth, a truth reporters were kept from
seeing, that the glorified U.S. ground war was a "turkey shoot," a
slaughter of defenseless Iraqis, a war crime. That the majority of
American "combat reporters" did not write about the film, demand
its release, and demand to know when and where it was taken shows
how useless they were for informing the public. The Pentagon has
hundreds of hours of such film including contemporaneous pictures
of the aerial bombardment of civilians. This film is direct evidence
of criminal actions, and the media and Congress know it but do
nothing.

A column in the *San Jose Mercury-News* in April 1991 discussed
Pentagon audience reaction testing. "Neatness counts when marketing war, or the appearance of neatness, and the administration
knows it. Katherine Boo wrote in the April (1991) *Washington
Monthly* that Pentagon officials 'allowed a select group of reporters
to screen-test a videotape of Iraqis being mowed down by [U.S.]
Apache helicopters. The reporters blanched. The Pentagon shelved

the film,' essentially reediting the plot line like the producers of *Pretty Woman*, sparing American audiences a sour ending. Perhaps concerned with neatness themselves, those journalists didn't challenge the tenor of celebratory coverage by reporting on the screening."[34]

The extent to which the media would accept any falsehood of the Pentagon, and indeed say whatever it was asked to say, is illustrated by a weird episode that began on January 7, 1991, 10 days before the bombardment of Iraq began. The Defense Department announced that six Iraqi helicopter crews had defected and flown into Saudi Arabia. The *New York Times* dutifully announced that American officials called it "one of the most significant defections of Iraqi military officers since Iraq's invasion of Kuwait."[35] Iraq denied the story. The next day the Pentagon retracted the story, saying it could not confirm the regional Saudi report.[36] The retractions were strange because U.S. intelligence digests that announced the defections also identified the aircraft as Soviet Mi-8-Hips helicopters,[37] and a senior official had said U.S. electronic tracking confirmed the reports. *Newsday* had been told the Iraqis had been asked to identify themselves and their purpose before reaching Saudi soil. But despite the wealth of detail about the story, the media accepted the Pentagon retraction. Michael Wines of the *New York Times* then wrote that apparently some U.S. officers had accepted Saudi propaganda beamed at Iraq as fact, but the *Times* was assured the helicopter story "never happened."[38]

Later it was learned the helicopters existed. They were Soviet-built craft painted with Iraqi markings piloted by Americans dressed as Iraqis. They were flying missions into Iraq to plant smart bomb homing devices, among other things, and were coordinated by the CIA. U.S. troops, unaware of their true identity, had fired on the helicopters as they returned to Saudi Arabia, causing American casualties and at least one helicopter to crash. The original defection story was created to cover up what had happened. And what happened violated the Geneva Convention, which prohibits the wearing of uniforms and insignia or the use of equipment to deceive enemy forces about your identity.[39]

The U.S. media, as solicitous of the Pentagon as Polonius was of Hamlet, printed whatever it was told.

> *Hamlet.* Do you see yonder cloud that's almost in shape of a camel?
>
> *Polonius.* By the mass, and tis like a camel, indeed.
>
> *Hamlet.* Methinks it is like a weasel.

Polonius. It is backed like a weasel.

Hamlet. Or like a whale?

Polonius. Very like a whale.

What the media failed to report was far more harmful than the propaganda it carried for the Pentagon. A peaceful resolution of the dispute would have been virtually assured if the American people had known how effective the sanctions against Iraq were, and how Saddam Hussein was offering, indeed urging, a negotiated settlement. Ninety-six percent of Iraq's exports were stopped by the embargo, but there was no informed media debate of this issue. Twenty-four of the 25 largest newspapers in the United States editorially supported the use of force against Iraq as opposed to economic sanctions in the months before the bombing began. They did not inform the public that the sanctions were working and that negotiations were possible.

Iraq repeatedly sought comprehensive negotiations after a statement by Saddam Hussein and a detailed proposal in mid-August 1990. The *New York Times*, which supported military action, had the story for 10 days without mentioning it. Only after *Newsday* ran a report of the offer did the *Times* print it. The press ridiculed the Iraqi offer and presented President Bush as seeking peace despite his oft-repeated statement that there would be no negotiations and no compromise. The urgent efforts of scores of international leaders to achieve negotiations or some agreement were largely ignored or presented as merely meddlesome, if not worse. The media effectively cut off consideration of peaceful alternatives, even attacking the patriotism of some who sought such a solution.

Any information that challenged the Pentagon account of the situation was ignored. For example, in late August 1990, the Pentagon reported that 150,000 Iraqi troops and 1,500 tanks were in Kuwait. In late September, it claimed that 265,000 Iraqi troops and 2,200 tanks were there. ABC bought five satellite pictures of eastern Kuwait and southern Iraq taken in mid-September from the Soviet commercial agency Soyuz-Karta that showed virtually no Iraqi military presence as claimed by the Pentagon. But ABC simply refused to air the photos after retaining two experts, formerly with the DIA and the U.S. Arms Control Agency, who confirmed that there was no visible Iraqi presence of any size in the pictures. All they could see in "crystal clear detail was the U.S. buildup in Saudi Arabia." Questioned at the time, the Pentagon said "it sticks by its num-

Bodybag in the sand. © *1991 Kenneth Jarecke/Contact Press Images*

One of the hundreds of thousands of Iraqi casualties.
© *1991 Kenneth Jarecke/Contact Press Images*

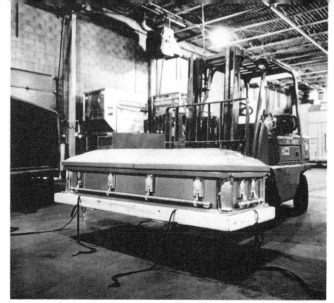

Soldier, killed in action, returns for funeral in Milwaukee.
© *1992 Kenneth Jarecke/Contact Press Images*

An oil-fire-fighter team in
action. © *1991 Steve
McCurry/Magnum Photos*

One of many Kuwaiti shop windows which displayed photos of Bush. © *1991 P.J. Griffiths/ Magnum Photos*

Dying bird, in an oil spill off the coast of Saudi Arabia. © *1991 Steve McCurry/ Magnum Photos*

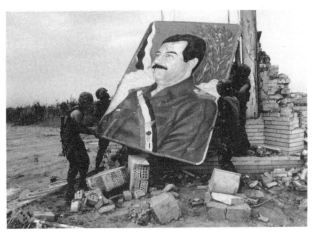

In Iraq, U.S. soldiers tear down a portrait of Saddam Hussein. © *1991 Steve McCurry/Magnum Photos*

Survivors of the bombing of Baghdad's Kadahmiya district. © 1991 Rick Reinhardt, Impact Visuals

One of the defining images of the war. © 1991 T.L. Litt, Impact Visuals

A show of popular support for Saddam Hussein. © *1991 Henrik Sakgren, Impact Visuals*

General Norman Schwarzkopf. © *1991 Donna Binder, Impact Visuals*

Dick Cheney, Colin Powell, and Norman Schwarzkopf applauding themselves. © *1991 Donna Binder, Impact Visuals*

The ecological aftermath of the war. © *1991 Bill Gasperini, Impact Visuals*

Desert in flames. © *1991 Bill Gasperini, Impact Visuals*

Dead Iraqi soldier, Southeast Iraq. © *1991 Kenneth Jarecke/Contact Press Images*

Captured Iraqi soldiers. © *1991 Kenneth Jarecke/Contact Press Images*

Refugees fleeing Iraq. © *1991 Tomas Muscionico/Contact Press Images*

Lone Iraqi prisoner of war faces bleak landscape. © *1991 Kenneth Jarecke/Contact Press Images*

In Safwan, Iraqi women wash clothing and dishes in a ditch filled with dirty water. © *1991 Jim Lukoski/Black Star*

Former residential area in Babylon province. Seventeen people, including 4 children, were killed in the bombing. *Commission of Inquiry*

Children — the real victims of U.S. intervention. *Commission of Inquiry*

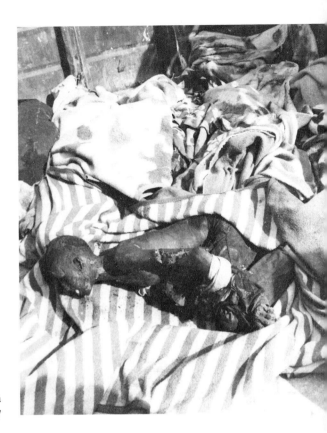

Child burned to death in the Allied bombing of El-Amerijah shelter. *Commission of Inquiry*

Women in Kuwait City, waiting for gas. © *1991 Abbas/Magnum Photos*

A Kuwaiti poses in front of the charred body of an Iraqi. © *1991 Abbas/Magnum Photos*

Oil wells out of control. © *1991 Sebastiao Salgado/Magnum Photos*

A common scene throughout Iraq, due to power outages.
Commission of Inquiry

Survivor of "mistaken" bombing of civilian neighborhood. Seven houses destroyed and forty people killed. © *1991 Rick Reinhardt, Impact Visuals*

The excessive use of force on the infamous "Highway of Death" was in direct violation of international law. *Commission of Inquiry*

One of the Middle East's most influential artists, Layla al-Attar also headed several Iraqi museums and fought for women's rights. She and others were killed in the June 1993 U.S. bombing of Bagdad.

Telephone exchange in Baghdad. Civilian communications centers were key targets in U.S. bombing. *Commission of Inquiry*

Ramsey Clark addresses the first hearing of the War Crimes Tribunal, May 11, 1991. © *1991 Brian Palmer, Impact Visuals*

A young Ramsey Clark attends the Nuremburg War Trials. *Photo courtesy of Ramsey Clark*

Clark meets with Saddam Hussein. The man in the middle is their translator. *Photo courtesy of Ramsey Clark*

bers."[40] End of story, until the *St. Petersburg* (FL) *Times* reopened it three months later.

The media faithfully reported and rarely criticized the major propaganda effort of the Pentagon to convince the American people of Saddam Hussein's power, the size of his military, and the sophistication of his arms. There has been no recognition by the media that Iraq was defenseless: not a single Abrams tank nor B-52 bomber was hit by enemy fire, not a single significant military engagement took place, there were 42 consecutive days of unrestrained bombing after which targets were hard to find. The real military story from the Gulf campaign was that technology now permits the United States to destroy nearly any country on earth without the risk of casualties from enemy fire. It can send missiles and planes that cannot be intercepted, and bomb at will. The media has never told that story.

ABANDONING THE TRUTH

For me, the most important human concerns about war are how many people does it kill and injure, and what does it do to the survivors? The U.S. media has never tried to tell the American people how many Grenadians, Libyans, or Panamanians were killed by U.S. military actions against those countries in the 1980s. It has never meaningfully reported about the effect on the survivors. There have been no human interest stories about a permanently crippled victim, no surveys of the devastation to the countries or the effects on health or the crushing poverty.

The media has barely inquired about Iraqi casualties. It accepted General Schwarzkopf's assurance in early February that "We will continue to be deliberately conservative in what we tell you and the American people, we don't want a credibility gap,"[41] and accepted accounts of the destruction of Iraqi tanks, armored vehicles, artillery pieces, and troops that were palpable propaganda. While it carried contemporary estimates of more than 100,000 Iraqi military casualties by Pentagon officials, this was presented as the triumph of war rather than as human tragedy. The comparison to 148 U.S. combat casualties, many from friendly fire, was never made. The media never criticized Powell or Schwarzkopf for declining to give Iraqi casualty figures later. It marginally reported the DIA estimate of 150,000, and General Horner's later estimates of 10,000, 20,000, or 30,000 — which the media referred to as the first "official" estimate.

There was no press criticism of Pentagon statements that Iraqi casualties would not be reported. Even General Colin Powell's insensitive statement that the number of Iraqi casualties was "not a number I'm terribly interested in" escaped press attacks. The media accepted without notice or comment the July 1991 Pentagon disclaimer that "the Department does not have accurate assessments of the collateral damage and casualties suffered as a result of operation Desert Storm among the civilian population of Iraq."[42] When the Pentagon issued its three-volume report on the Gulf War in April 1992, glorifying its conduct and pointing toward future military needs, it never discussed Iraqi civilian casualties. It was as if they never happened, or didn't matter. The "watchdog" U.S. media never criticized this outrageous omission, and never raised the issue of civilian deaths. It called the destruction of Iraq a clean war.

Whatever history agrees upon concerning Iraqi casualties, we know that during the war the Pentagon wanted us to believe that it had killed over 100,000 soldiers, that there were not many left alive to fight when the ground war started. Now it does not want the war to seem so bloody, and it will fight fiercely any suggestion of serious civilian casualties.

The media covered reports by UNICEF, the Harvard Medical Team, Greenpeace, Middle East Watch, and others concerning sickness, hunger, and the failure of the medical system in Iraq, with each group predicting as many as 150,000 civilian deaths among infants, children, the chronically ill, and the elderly. But there was no suggestion in major media reporting that the United States was responsible for these deaths, or that the aerial bombardment was causally related. Often the stories argued that the fault was with Iraq for refusing to sell oil as the UN authorized in order to pay reparations and purchase food and medicine. But there was no recognition that this U.S.-compelled requirement in effect held Iraq's health hostage unless reparations were paid.

While it was clear that the combination of the effects of the bombing on food supply, water quality, infant formula, medicines, and availability of medical services plus the effect of the sanctions on the availability of needed food and medicine were causing thousands of deaths each month, there was no major media investigation or news reporting of this human tragedy. The U.S. media remained determined to ignore anything that might create sympathy for the enemy. One consequence was the American public, being largely unaware of what was happening, did not protest their government's insistence on the continuation of the sanctions.

Although the media's near-total failure to report on the Commission of Inquiry cannot be equated with its refusal to cover the devastation of Iraq, both instances reveal its power to reject coverage of issues and events as editors see fit. The Commission held over 30 hearings and meetings in the United States, and sponsored hearings and meetings in 20 other countries. On February 29, 1992, the International U.S. War Crimes Tribunal, presided over by a panel of internationally recognized human rights leaders, judges, politicians, and lawyers, took place in New York City. The *New York Times* sent a reporter, but didn't print a word about it. One well-known columnist told Commission staffers he would "lose his job" if he wrote about the Tribunal.

The uniqueness of a public hearing in a nation in which its citizens and others accuse the President and high officials of war crimes would seem to be almost irresistible to the media. Nothing like it had ever happened before. But for most Americans, the hearings and final Tribunal did not occur, because they never heard about them. Is it possible that a free and open press would have ignored such a story?

Had the media pointed to the facts, or raised a question in the public mind about the legality of the war, the corruption of the UN, the United States' interference with the peace process, the systematic destruction of civilian facilities and life, the defenselessness of Iraq and the vast death and suffering there, the American people would never have tolerated the war and would never have celebrated the slaughter.

A year after Iraq was left bloody and broken, the U.S. media referred to the war as "ancient history." Public concern was directed to other issues. There were references to the "victory" and the "good feelings" Americans shared about the war, and the public was reassured that the Vietnam syndrome was dead.[43] On January 16, NBC, which is owned by major defense contractor General Electric, questioned whether the United States had enough effective modern weapons to fight "another Desert Storm."[44] The main flaw with the war was repeatedly described as the failure to kill Saddam Hussein. The *Houston Post* editorialized on the anniversary of the opening of the air bombardment that Hussein remained a "bully and butcher" that the "world cannot tolerate."[45] ABC's *Nightline* presented Pentagon videotapes of U.S. military training exercises, not combat footage, and host Ted Koppel praised the "efficiency and humanity" of the U.S. troops, proclaiming, "It was, in military terms, a work of art." The program went so far as to call the slaughter of Iraqis, Kuwaitis, and others on the "Highway of Death" a "tribute to the efficiency and humanity of those who planned the attack."[46]

There was not a word of pity or sorrow for, or even a mention of, the Iraqi dead. The greatness that enabled Abraham Lincoln in the depths of the Civil War to mourn the dead on both sides and say "with malice toward none, with charity for all" was totally absent. Now we praised the military for efficiency and humanity as if no one had really been hurt.

Having convinced the American people of the nobility of the slaughter of Iraq, the media turned its efforts to new preparations for war. The first order of business was eliminating remaining foreign nuisances. In a column on February 27, 1992, William Safire of the *New York Times*, discussing "How Weak Is Bush," asked, speaking of Saddam Hussein, Muammar Qaddafi, and North Korea's Kim Il Sung, "Does it strain credulity that one of these three dictators is going to get zapped?" He added, "I think not." He concluded that if President Bush's "stern warnings to three dictators about threatening the peace turn out to be empty posturing — then and only then would President Bush reveal himself too weak to deserve re-election."[47] The next day on the same page, A. M. Rosenthal said Saddam Hussein "alone is responsible for any shortage of food and medicine in Iraq," as if that justified tens of thousands of preventable deaths. But he made his pleas for more militarism this way: "One day the U.S. will try to separate his head from his shoulders. Not just for his crimes — they sat well enough with the West before the Kuwaiti invasion. But his refusal to reveal the size and location of his nuclear, chemical and germ-war capacity will eventually make him just too dangerous to be allowed to remain on his throne of skulls."[48] If the role of the media is to present a rational, balanced view of an issue, no commentators from the major media were as consistently unprofessional in their cries for war and as disgraceful in their disregard for truth, their hatred, or their lack of humanity and justice. And none were more intimately related to power in government and the media as these two men.

As the destruction of Iraq slipped from memory with new threats by the United States toward Cuba, Pakistan, Liberia, Syria, Libya, Japan, and Iraq, the media sang in harmony with U.S. foreign policy. It justified to the American people, in all the ways used against Iraq, the means and ends sought by powerful U.S. economic interests, the U.S. government, and the military, ready as the enforcer. With the Cold War between two nuclear superpowers largely behind, the new plan, the new world order, was for a one-superpower world. Having seen what its military could do, knowing of its virtual monopoly on weapons of mass destruction and its long lead in sophisticated military technology, the United States was developing a policy to prevent any rival for power from emerging. The strategy called for military supremacy to insure economic and political domination. By March 1992 outlines of the plan were carried in the press, though careful observers could see for several years in the conduct of the government more than the contours of the plan as the Soviet Union declined. The Gulf War itself was a key element in the plan, securing control over Gulf oil and domination of the region.[49]

The American people, their economy faltering, their wealth more concentrated in a plutocracy than in any other rich country, were going to be told to forego health care, repairs to a crumbling education system, and other essential needs. With the decay of life in central cities, the disappearance of the family there, and police and fear of crime as the principal social controls, the resources of the country, $1.5 trillion within a few fiscal years, were to be devoted to a new military capacity to control the planet.[50] Those expenditures, paid by the middle class and poor, would line the pockets of the plutocracy that controlled politics, the government, foreign policy, the economy, and through the media, public opinion. The $1.5 trillion would also buy militarism and seek to dominate the planet for the greater wealth and security of the American plutocrats. The victims of war, to be sure, will be dark-skinned people from poor countries and Americans who live in poverty.

The media, owned by the wealthy, speaking for the plutocracy, has the dual role of anesthetizing the public to prevent serious consideration or debate of such staggering human issues as world hunger, AIDS, regional civil wars, environmental destruction, and social anarchy, and emotionalizing the people for aggression, all without a serious military threat in sight. In the light of its past performance, the odds seem high that it will succeed.

THE SEARCH FOR TRUTH

It is very painful for a person who has been inspired by the history and possibilities of the ideas embodied in the First Amendment to see what has become of that dream. Surely most American journalists are such people. They know the truth can make us free. And as surely they recognize what has happened. All know that access to vital information, the ability to parse out the truth, is essential to human understanding, happiness, and survival. We can recall the first session of the UN General Assembly in 1946 when freedom of information was called "a fundamental human right and the touchstone of all freedoms to which the United Nations is consecrated." And yet the American media, guardian of the First Amendment, has abandoned its ward in favor of Mammon.

All know what is needed: unrestrained adversarial access to information from and about government without which democracy is a roll of dice, pure chance, ignorant of truth and consequences; hard investigation of important facts all over the world; a broad participation in developing and presenting the facts by the people directly involved. Equally essential are diversity in analysis, uninhibited examination of the most sensitive issues; encouragement of the poor to report on their condition, their needs in the slums and rural poverty of America and from the poor countries around the world where most American-generated violence occurs; and an implementation of the long-repressed and ostracized report by Sean McBride for UNESCO named *Many Voices/One World*,[51] which sought reforms to bring essential knowledge to people everywhere.

We need to give a voice in a technologically advanced world to the people who will never otherwise be heard beyond the narrow range of the spoken word, however often repeated, and who are suffocating with the desire to be heard, while the TV pundits prattle on to tens of millions who have few other sources of fact or opinion. We need heroes in the press, journalists who will dig for stories, take risks to get them and tell them articulately, and owners who will not fire these people for this necessary work. We need editors who encourage reporters to get the important facts the people need to know about real issues and reward reporters who succeed, who insist on reporting stories power wants suppressed. We need publishers who believe in great journalism, who want their papers to break the important stories, who recognize their duty to inform the people, who let the journalists run the paper, and who take greater pride in circulation increased by good coverage than in revenues from running more ads.

The media, in all its forms, must be used to speak to and for all people around the world, to provide vigorous debate on subjects of human concern. And finally, we must share the faith that guided Thomas Paine: "convinced as I am, that where opinion is free, the truth shall finally and powerfully prevail."[52]

CHAPTER 8

The Trashing of the UN Charter and the U.S. Constitution

T HE Charter of the United Nations and the Constitution of the United States were corrupted to become instruments of war in the fall of 1990. Both were easily subverted to authorize unrestrained power and unlimited military aggression.

The peoples of the world watched submissively as the United Nations approved the murder of tens of thousands of Iraqis and the crippling of the whole nation, and assented to the deaths of tens of thousands more from contaminated water and intentional deprivation of food and medicine because of sanctions. The people of the United States watched in general silence or outright approval as President Bush seized absolute power to assault a defenseless people, glorify U.S. violence, dehumanize a whole nation, and celebrate the slaughter of its people. No dictator was ever less restrained.

The two great charters had promised more. The preamble to the UN Charter expresses a determination to "save succeeding generations from the scourge of war." And the authors of the Constitution, painfully aware of the propensity of the executive for foreign military adventures, vested the power to wage war in Congress.

The UN Charter and the U.S. Constitution failed totally to achieve their most important purposes — the prevention of war and the rule of law.

UNEQUAL ACCOUNTABILITY AT THE UN

Iraq invaded Kuwait on August 2, 1990. The Security Council was called into emergency session immediately at the request of U.S. Am-

149

bassador Thomas Pickering on instructions from the White House. It passed Resolution 660 the same day, condemning the invasion, demanding an immediate withdrawal, and calling for direct negotiations between Iraq and Kuwait. The vote was 14–0, with Yemen abstaining. Many who had decried the paralysis of the UN during the long Cold War which had dominated its existence hoped that finally the UN was becoming an effective agency for peace.

The years have seen many invasions, occupations, and similar violations condemned by the UN in words, but supported and condoned by members through deeds. The decades of violations by South Africa, against both its own people and other countries, in the face of UN resolutions and International Court of Justice decrees was rewarded by billions of dollars of investments from the United States, Great Britain, and others who profited handsomely from apartheid.

The Israeli occupation of the West Bank, East Jerusalem, and Gaza since 1967 defies UN resolutions, and only the United States' veto has protected Israel from condemnation by the Security Council. Israel's grim repression of the Palestinians in Israel and the occupied territories, its invasion and continued occupation of southern Lebanon, its assaults on refugee camps throughout Lebanon in defiance of international law and UN resolutions has earned it annual financial aid from the United States equaling $1,000 per person.

In recent years, China brutally occupied Tibet, the Soviet Union invaded Afghanistan, and Indonesia seized East Timor without UN reprisals. The United States invaded Grenada, bombed Libya, and supported military activities against other UN members in Africa, Central America, and Asia. While the General Assembly and Security Council have protested, they have not acted.

On December 20, 1989, the United States invaded Panama, killing hundreds and probably several thousand. That invasion, less than eight months before Iraq invaded Kuwait, was condemned by the UN General Assembly. No action was taken, although the United States violated all the international laws later violated by Iraq when it invaded Kuwait, plus a number of Western Hemisphere conventions and the Panama Canal Treaties.

Instead of taking firm, united action toward Iraq based on negotiation with pacific intent and by peaceful means, the UN was quickly and easily converted into an instrumentality of war. When the assault began, the UN abided and even abetted the crimes against peace, war crimes, and crimes against humanity committed by the United States.

In the wake of the awful assault it authorized, there is a crippled, bleeding people and no effort by the UN to alleviate their suffering or to address the longstanding problems of the region. Instead UN members continue to support sanctions against Iraq, contract for even greater arms purchases, and ignore the plight of the huge Kurdish population that is being abused in Turkey, Iraq, Iran, and Syria. Lebanon remains occupied by Syria in the east and Israel in the south.

The question of Palestine, which nearly all agree is the key to peace in the Middle East, has been abandoned by the UN to the not so tender mercies of powers that intend Palestine no good. The United States, which never sought a peace conference between Israel and the Palestinians in the years when the Palestinians could bargain as a near equal, suddenly has sought to force a settlement independent of the UN. Yet these inherently unfair negotiations offer little hope for peace. The Palestinians cannot even choose their own negotiators, as Israel can veto any choice they make. Every day of the negotiations Israelis rush to seize more land from Palestinians, take their homes by force, and build new settlements in their territory. With no apparent concern, or risk, of alienating world opinion, Israel has bombed deep inside Lebanon on the eve of new peace conference sessions, one strike killing twelve people. The United States appeared at the UN Human Rights Commission in Geneva before the peace session in Moscow in early 1992 and urged the commission to ignore Israeli human rights violations against Palestinians, arguing "Let's give peace a chance." The failure of the UN to enforce equal accountability for its powerful as well as its weak members must be corrected if that body is to fulfill its charter.

SMOTHERING INTERNATIONAL DEBATE ON IRAQ

The United States used its power to control the media to persuade the world that Iraq's invasion of Kuwait was unprovoked, and that Iraq intended to invade Saudi Arabia as well. Actually, Washington had covertly encouraged Kuwait to take a tough line with Iraq, which the Bush administration hoped would push Saddam Hussein into invading. As to the invasion of Saudi Arabia, when Bush was pledging American commitment to defend the Saudis on August 3 and 4 — a commitment the Saudis did not solicit — the President knew Iraq was pulling units back from southern Kuwait.[1]

To stir up international fervor against Iraq, stories of atrocities committed by Iraqi troops began immediately after Iraq occupied Kuwait and were systematically and pervasively disseminated. They were all almost entirely false. Rumors emblazoned in the media about young girls being hung by wire until they were dead and children being shot were never substantiated, but helped create the level of hatred necessary to destroy Iraq.

President Bush contributed mightily to inflaming international opinion. He repeatedly referred to the fabricated story of 312 incubator babies being killed by Iraqi troops. He used his Thankgiving message to tell U.S. troops in the Gulf that Saddam Hussein was "a dictator who gassed his own people, innocent women and children," ignoring an Army War College study and many other intelligence reports that contradicted him.[2] His apparent compassion for the innocent Iraqis he claimed Saddam Hussein gassed did not extend to the tens of thousands of Iraqi civilians he had to know American bombing and the international embargo would kill.

The propaganda campaign was the centerpiece of a successful effort to prevent discussion, negotiation, and a peaceful resolution. Throughout the crisis, President Bush maintained that there could be no negotiations, no compromise with Saddam Hussein. Efforts by other countries, notably Jordan, France, and the USSR, and by individual leaders to open talks were frustrated by Washington. Iraq's many offers to negotiate were mostly ignored by the United States and the UN. When reference was made to Iraqi efforts to settle the dispute peaceably, its proposals were ridiculed as a "cruel hoax" by President Bush. As late as January 9, 1991, President Bush announced, though it was not true, that Iraq had rejected a diplomatic solution.

SHORT-CIRCUITING A PEACEFUL RESOLUTION THROUGH THE UN

By placing the dispute before the Security Council, the United States was able to prevent any meaningful role by the General Assembly, whose membership represents most of the countries of the world. Article 12 of the UN Charter prohibits the General Assembly from making any recommendation regarding a dispute before the Security Council unless the Security Council requests it to do so.

The 15-member Security Council was much easier to control than the 150-plus-member General Assembly would have been. The five permanent Council members include Britain and France (who had dominated the Gulf region during most of the century and still have substantial interests there), the United States, the Soviet Union, and China — the victors of World War II. The Soviet Union was too debilitated to exercise any initiative in the Security Council, and China was too isolated. While both had veto power, neither had the will or the interest to exercise it.

Article 24 of the UN Charter vested primary responsibility for maintaining international peace in the Security Council, reflecting the power of the major postwar allies. The same article also required the Council to act in accordance with the principles and purposes of the Charter. Foremost among these purposes were the maintenance of peace and the effective exercise of powers imposed by Chapter VI to achieve the "pacific settlement of disputes."

Article 33, the first provision in Chapter VI, requires that "first of all" parties shall seek a solution by "negotiation, inquiry, mediation, conciliation, arbitration, judicial settlement, resort to regional agencies or arrangements, or other peaceful means of their own choice." It also provides that the Security Council may at any stage recommend appropriate procedures for peaceful settlement.

Under pressure from the United States, the Security Council completely failed in its duty to seek a peaceful settlement. On August 6 it imposed a trade and financial embargo on Iraq, and created a Special Sanctions Committee to monitor it. For the next four months, the Council ignored efforts by Saddam Hussein and other international leaders, including Mikhail Gorbachev, Francois Mitterand, and UN Secretary General Perez de Cuellar, to reach a settlement. It busied itself through November 28 with the passage of an unprecedented eleven separate resolutions against Iraq, further ostracizing Iraq in world opinion. No Council member dared vote against the United States, though Cuba and Yemen abstained on several of the votes, primarily those dealing with the embargo. And in the General Assembly, economic dependency on the United States, fear of sanctions against themselves, and even fear of military assault silenced Iraq's closest friends. Great Britain, to a lesser degree France, and a handful of other rich countries actively supported the United States, some countries were hostile to Iraq, and most simply did not want to clash with the United States over something that did not seem important to them.

THE CORRUPTION OF THE UN

In order to obtain votes on November 29 for the crucial Resolution 678, which would authorize member states "to use all necessary means" to force Iraq to withdraw from Kuwait if it failed to do so by January 15, 1991, the United States engaged in open bribery, blackmail, and coercion.

Ethiopia and Zaire were both provided new aid packages, World Bank credits, and rearrangements of International Monetary Fund grants or loans after they voted for the resolution. The Ethiopian government, which the United States knew to be on the verge of defeat by rebels, was given new military aid after years of being denied arms. This aid doubtless cost more lives in the tragic Ethiopian civil war before the government fell. Colombia, a major U.S. military aid recipient, was offered an increased aid package, including both economic and military components.

China was awarded $114 million dollars in deferred aid by the U.S.-dominated World Bank less than a week after it abstained from the vote on Resolution 678. The evening before the vote, Secretary of State Baker met with Chinese Foreign Minister Qian Qichen.[3] The day after the vote President Bush held a highly publicized conference with Qian Qichen at the White House. These were the first such meetings since the Tiananmen Square massacre 18 months earlier, and they restored international diplomatic acceptance for China. These were the two acts known at the UN to be most desired by the Chinese, and they got them both after not exercising their veto power. Other loans were also processed after China's abstention.

The Soviet Union, in economic disintegration, was provided $4 billion dollars in loans and emergency aid by Saudi Arabia, Kuwait, and the UAE after it voted for the resolution. Iraq had long ties to the USSR, and it seems highly probable, though not part of any public record, that the USSR was promised a real effort for a negotiated settlement would be made. Certainly the Soviets tried until hours before the assault began to secure an agreement.

Malaysia was subjected to enormous pressure. Predominantly Muslim, its vote for Resolution 678, even after initially resisting U.S. pressures, was widely criticized by its people.

Cuba and Yemen were subjected to both entreaty and punishment. The first meeting of the foreign ministers of Cuba and the United States in three decades occurred in a Manhattan hotel on the eve of the November 29 vote when James Baker and Isidoro Malmierca sat down together. The press barely noted the meeting, and U.S. diplomats described it as an ordinary discussion between acting Security Council President Baker and a Council member. Almost surely, however, Baker was measuring the feasibility of persuading Cuba to stop its efforts to enlist opposition to UN authorization for an assault on Iraq. Cuba courageously voted against the resolution.[4]

Yemen, which had frequently abstained during votes on earlier resolutions, was expected to abstain on Resolution 678. Enormous pressure was brought to bear on the only Arab country on the Coun-

154

cil. Economically troubled and still politically unsettled after the unification of the two Yemens only six months earlier, it was particularly vulnerable. Within minutes after he voted against Resolution 678, Yemen's Ambassador, Abdallah Saleh al Ashtol, was told that this would be "the most expensive 'no' vote you ever cast."[5] Three days later the United States canceled its $70-million aid package to Yemen, and soon some 900,000 Yemeni workers were banished from Saudi Arabia, including several hundred who were removed from hospital beds.

Countries like Egypt, an economic basket case dependent on U.S. aid, which supported the United States with troops and votes, fared better. The United States forgave $7 billion in Egyptian debt. Saudi Arabia canceled another $4 billion in Egyptian debt and other Gulf states wrote off an additional $3 billion. These, too, were bribes paid for support in the UN.

The United Nations itself profited from its own prostration. The United States paid $187 million, or more than half of the debt it owed the UN in past dues, as a show of appreciation. These funds, previously wrongfully withheld from the UN, were now wrongfully paid to secure support.

Resolution 678 was itself utterly lawless. Having already invoked sanctions in violation of the requirement of Articles 33 and 36 that pacific means be tried first, the Security Council invoked war powers under Article 42 without giving real consideration to whether its sanctions had "proved to be inadequate." When the Security Council authorized member nations "to use all necessary means," it conferred absolute discretion to achieve its stated goal. This action is the negation of law. As Supreme Court Justice William Douglas wrote:

> Law has reached its finest moments when it has freed man from the unlimited discretion of some ruler, some civil or military official, some bureaucrat. Where discretion is absolute, man has always suffered. At times it has been his property that has been invaded; at times, his privacy; at times, his liberty of movement; at times, his freedom of thought; at times, his life. Absolute discretion is a ruthless master. It is more destructive of freedom than any of man's other inventions.[6]

Not only did the resolution confer absolute discretion to remove Iraq from Kuwait, it conferred it on all UN members indiscriminately. It was a complete abandonment of UN duty, an open and unlimited assignment of all its power. It conveyed authority to begin

155

the very act the UN was created to end — waging war. The Security Council delegation of power was so complete, that in addition to giving no guidance and imposing no limitation, it required no reporting. The Security Council did not even ask to know what was done on its authority and in its name. Any nation without consulting or coordinating with any other could act as it chose to oust Iraq from Kuwait.

It was clear that the United States would conduct the war. Other countries would participate as directed by Washington. Germany and Japan were coerced into making major monetary contributions. The Japanese contribution violated Article 9 of its Constitution. The USSR would stay out. Turkey, Saudi Arabia, Syria, and Egypt were pressured to provide troops or permit the use of bases, assuring a legacy of hostility in the region. Israel was ordered by the United States to stay out of the conflict.

The Military Staff Command contemplated by the UN Charter to advise the Security Council on military questions and provide strategic direction for any armed forces at the disposal of the Council remained nonfunctional. General Schwarzkopf was in command. The Secretary General was not even informed when Desert Storm was to begin. In effect, the United States superceded the UN.

The first act of aggression, aerial bombardment of Iraqi cities from Mosul, more than 600 miles from Kuwait, to Basra near the Kuwait border was clearly beyond the scope of action needed to drive Iraq from Kuwait. The United States never reported conduct of the war to the Security Council, and it was never questioned by the members as they watched what was happening on CNN with the rest of the world. The UN was a bystander as the American-led coalition committed grievous war crimes against a defenseless country in its name.

IGNORING THE CONGRESS AND THE CONSTITUTION

Article I of the U.S. Constitution vests power over war and peace in the Congress. President Bush usurped these powers to wage his war. Among other Congressional powers, Article I, Section 8 of the Constitution provides:

> The Congress shall have Power to lay and collect taxes, duties, imposts, and excises, to pay the debts and provide for the common defense and general welfare of the United States;

To declare war, grant letters of marque and reprisal, and make rules concerning captures on land and water;

To raise and support armies;

To provide and maintain a navy;

To make rules for the government and regulation of the land and naval forces;

To provide for calling forth the militia to execute the laws of the Union, suppress insurrections and repel invasions:

To provide for organizing, arming, and disciplining the militia, and for governing such part of them as may be employed in the service of the United States, reserving to the states respectively, the appointment of the officers, and the authority of training the militia according to the discipline prescribed by Congress.

The President's constitutional powers as commander in chief of the armed forces are all delegated to him by a single phrase in Article II, Section 2 of the Constitution. Those powers are defined and limited by laws enacted by Congress. As commander in chief, the President can act only as authorized by Congress. Colonial experience with the arbitrary power of British kings to commit their sons to foreign wars left the authors of the Constitution in no doubt that the legislative branch should control powers of war and peace. The President would only have troops and weapons provided, authorized, and financed by Congress. He could use them only in war declared by Congress and in accordance with provisions of law. James Madison, the most influential delegate at the Constitutional Convention in 1787, wrote Thomas Jefferson on the subject of war powers in 1798: "The Constitution supposes, what the history of all governments demonstrates, that the executive is the branch of power most interested in war, and most prone to it. It has, accordingly, with studied care, vested the question of war in the legislature."[7]

The major means by which President Bush frustrated Congressional action and violated the Constitution was by usurping legislative authority and not consulting Congressional leadership. He totally ignored his statutory duties under the War Powers Act of 1973 to report to and consult with Congress on emergency military matters. He used deception and disinformation to avoid Congressional challenge.

Congress was heading for its Labor Day recess when the crisis broke. Conditioned to arbitrary executive action in foreign affairs, it showed little interest in exercising its constitutional duties. Without prior notice to Congress, the President ordered 10,000 troops to Saudi Arabia during the first week of August. On August 8, to allay

157

alarm he described his purpose as "wholly defensive." In fact it was the beginning of an unbroken movement to crush Iraq.

Congress returned from its Labor Day recess to assurances from the President that his purpose was to defend Saudi Arabia. Still acting unilaterally, the President announced an increase in American troops in Saudi Arabia to over 200,000. This appeared to be consistent with a defensive position. Then, within a month of its return, Congress was almost completely involved in the November elections.

Only after the elections on November 2 did the President reveal to Congress that he had earlier ordered more than 400,000 military personnel to the Gulf.[8] No longer could his purpose be claimed to be wholly defensive. Still Bush argued that Congress should stay out of the matter, that the appearance of division within the United States would only embolden Saddam Hussein.

Hate propaganda was systematically used by members of Congress who favored war. In an appearance on the *Today Show* in November, I was suddenly confronted by Congressman Hunter Duncan from San Diego with the charge that Saddam Hussein had caused the death of incubator babies in Kuwait City. While I questioned the reasonableness of the report and observed it would be the acts of individual soldiers and officers if it occurred, having never heard the charge before, it was impossible to reject out of hand even so improbable a claim. The congressman's fury must have created hatred toward Iraq among many of the several million viewers. This must have been his motive, as it most likely was President Bush's when he repeatedly used the same false story thereafter.

On January 9, President Bush reasserted his view that he needed no Congressional authorization to attack Iraq. He reinforced his earlier claims to presidential power with responsibilities created by UN Resolution 678, though in any other context he would never concede that international law would impose duties superior to the U.S. Constitution. But by January the administration was working vigorously to win a vote in the Congress approving presidential use of U.S. armed forces.

Political expediency had caused the debate in Congress to be framed between military aggression and sanctions. This sort of debate is much like the one between the death penalty and life imprisonment without the possibility of parole. The warhawks were in favor of killing Iraqis outright. The supporters of sanctions, although seemingly voices of moderation, were actually advocating starving Iraqis to death. With oil by far its major export, Iraq was particularly vulnerable to sanctions because it was relatively easy to stop shipments through the Persian Gulf and pipeline transmissions through Turkey or across Jordan to Aqaba. In addition, Iraq imports a large majority of its food supply. In early January, CIA Director William Webster testified before Congress that the embargo had reduced Iraqi exports by 97 percent and imports by 90 percent. The Bush administration, being able to focus media attention on what it wanted reported, was able to obscure the effectiveness of sanctions in its drive for war. The vote in Congress for economic sanctions failed.

When Congress finally acted, each member knew that 540,000 Americans in uniform in the Gulf and their families and friends at home were looking to see who supported the troops overseas. The Bush administration strategy of securing UN authority first also put great pressure on the Congress to support the President. A member voting against war was confronted with the political cost of failing to back the President in the community of nations after he had obtained Security Council approval for Resolution 678. The eleven nations that supported the President included strong allies of the United States.

Administration supporters in the Congress placed a bill to authorize use of U.S. armed forces pursuant to Resolution 678 on floor calendars only days before the UN deadline. Congressional inaction through the fall of 1990 had undermined its ability to do its duty. Republican leadership, in the person of Senate Minority Leader Robert Dole, was able to argue that Congress should not interfere "now, at the 11th hour, having been AWOL, for these three or four months, and try to change the direction of the policy that President Bush has so patiently and successfully put together."[9]

Key House Democrats, like Representative Stephen Solarz of New York, an ardent supporter of Israel, and seven southern Senators urged party members to vote with them for President Bush's war. On January 11, the Senate voted 52–47 to authorize enforcement of Resolution 678. The vote in the House of Representatives was 250–183 for approval.

On January 16, 1991, the day President Bush ordered the bombing to begin, Congressman Henry Gonzalez of Texas spoke to the House of Representatives in a great act of individual courage, conscience, and vision:

> Mr. Speaker, it is with great sadness, yet with great conviction, that I introduce today a resolution of impeachment of President Bush. At a time when our nation is deeply divided over the question of war, we find ourselves on the brink of a world war of such magnitude that our minds cannot fully comprehend the destruction that is about to

be leveled. The position we are in is a direct result of the actions of one man and the reactions of another. The Iraqi people are as opposed to war as are the American people — the difference is that the Iraqi people have no choice but to support their country's leader, but the American people not only have the right to oppose and speak out in disagreement with their President, but they have the responsibility to do so if our democracy is to be preserved.

When I took the oath of office earlier this month, as I had numerous times before, I swore to uphold the Constitution. The President's oath was the same — to uphold the Constitution of the United States. We did not pledge an oath of allegiance to the President, but to the Constitution, which is the highest law of the land. The Constitution provides for removal of the President when he has committed high crimes and misdemeanors, including violation of the principles of the Constitution. President Bush has violated these principles.

My resolution has five articles of impeachment. First, the President has violated the equal protection clause of the Constitution. Our soldiers in the Middle East are overwhelmingly poor white, black, and Mexican-American.

Article II states that the President has violated the Constitution, federal law, and the United Nations Charter by bribing, intimidating, and threatening others, including the members of the United Nations Security Council, to support belligerent acts against Iraq. It is clear that the President paid off members of the U.N. Security Council in return for their votes in support of war against Iraq.

Article III states that the President has conspired to engage in a massive war against Iraq, employing methods of mass destruction that will result in the killing of tens of thousands of civilians, many of whom will be children.

Article IV states that the President has committed the United States to acts of war without Congressional consent and contrary to the United Nations Charter and international law. From August 1990 through January 1991, the President embarked on a course of action that systematically eliminated every option for peaceful resolution of the Persian Gulf crisis. Once the President approached Congress for a declaration of war, 500,000 American soldiers' lives were in jeopardy — rendering any substantive debate by Congress meaningless.

Article V states that the President has conspired to commit crimes against the peace by leading the United States into aggressive war against Iraq in violation of Article 2(4) of the United Nations Charter, the Nuremberg Charter, other international instruments and treaties, and the Constitution of the United States.[10]

There was a time when presidents respected the constitutional limitations on their power over the military. An early episode involving the Barbary pirates is instructive. After the Bey of Tunis declared war on the United States, President Jefferson, having insisted on and obtained specific legislative authority from the Congress, sent a squadron of frigates to the Mediterranean to protect American shipping. As the ships entered the Mediterranean, a tender schooner, the U.S.S. *Enterprise,* was attacked by a Barbary cruiser from Tripoli which it overwhelmed and captured.

Reporting on the incident, President Jefferson in his first annual message to Congress on December 8, 1801 said:

> Unauthorized by the Constitution, without the sanction of Congress, to go beyond the line of defense, the vessel, being disabled from committing further hostilities, was liberated with its crew. The Legislature will doubtless consider whether, by authorizing measures of offense also, they will place our force on an equal footing with that of its adversaries. I communicate all material information on this subject, that in the exercise of this important function confided by the Constitution to the Legislature exclusively their judgment may form itself on a knowledge and consideration of every circumstance of weight.[11]

By the mid-twentieth century, presidents had become used to asserting war powers without deference to the Constitution or Congress. In the absence of a declaration of war, President Truman, having secured UN authorization, sent U.S. forces to Korea. He later seized steel mills to prevent labor strikes from impairing the war effort. The U.S. Supreme Court ruled the President had no such power even when a large American military force was engaged in an active ground war. Justice Jackson warned:

> But no doctrine that the Court could promulgate would seem to me more sinister and alarming than that a President whose conduct of foreign affairs is so largely uncontrolled, and often even is unknown, can vastly enlarge his mastery over the internal affairs of the country by his own commitment of the Nation's armed forces to some foreign venture.

He observed such power "belongs in the hands of Congress, but only Congress itself can prevent power from slipping through its fingers."[12]

Less than a decade after the Korean War, U.S. presidents began a buildup of U.S. forces in Vietnam that finally reached more than 500,000 men and women. The major Congressional authorization for this, the Tonkin Gulf Resolution, passed the Senate with only two

161

dissenting votes and the House with none. This infamous Congressional resolution, not even a law, had no constitutional force and was founded on the false premise that North Vietnamese boats had attacked U.S. warships in the Gulf of Tonkin. Some years after, the last Navy pilot to search the area where the attacks were said to have occurred for the aggressor Vietnamese naval vessels wrote in his autobiography that there were no boats.

Campaigning in New Hampshire in January 1992, President Bush boastfully told voters, "When I moved those [Desert Storm] forces I didn't have to ask Senator Kennedy, or some liberal Democrat whether we were going to do it. We just did it."[13]

The blood of 38,000 American servicemen remains in Vietnamese soil. More than 40,000 U.S. troops remain stationed in South Korea. The U.S. military dominates the Persian Gulf. Millions of Third World people lost their lives in these three military actions of the United States.

Congress has tragically failed to muster the will to exercise its constitutional powers over war and peace. The American people must demand that it do so if they want to restore integrity to constitutional government and live in peace.

CHAPTER 9

Crimes Against Peace, War Crimes, and Crimes Against Humanity

W AR is the most violent crime that humanity inflicts upon itself. Other conduct does not approach its horror. History leaves no doubt of this.

Law reaches its highest potential for good when it addresses crimes against peace and war crimes. The very names of the places associated with the major conventions addressing war and its conduct fill us with both hope and dread — The Hague, Geneva, Nuremberg. We know those statutes were written with the blood of millions who died in the wars from which these lessons were learned. The highest commitment of law to peace must be in their faithful, equal, and fair enforcement.

If society wants to prevent war, control and punish those who cause it, address its excesses, and avoid its consequences, then it must take action to enforce laws designed for such purposes. Until the most powerful military forces and their highest officers are held equally accountable with the powerless for crimes related to war, the rule of force will remain paramount. And the world will remain, as the Athenians said it was, a place where the powerful do as they will and the weak suffer as they must.

THE RULE OF LAW VERSUS THE REIGN OF FORCE

The concept of war crimes presents the choice between the rule of law and the reign of force. When principle is chosen, all are equally accountable. If we are to live in a world of principle, then we must apply those principles to all, including our own country.

In an interview during the Nuremberg trials, Hermann Goering, the highest-ranking Nazi defendant, said of war crimes trials, "The victors will always be the judges, the accused the vanquished." At Nuremberg, defendants shouted, "What about Dresden? What about Hiroshima?" Yet despite the universal principles of the Nuremberg Charter, and the assurance of the Chief Prosecutor for the United States, Robert H. Jackson, that it would apply to all including those sitting in judgment, the Nuremberg court accused only the vanquished and only the victors sat in judgment.

Tragically, the victors in World War II did not submit themselves to the rule of law, or even maintain the Nuremberg Tribunal they had created and under whose mandate enemy leaders were put to death. Had they done so, nuclear proliferation, the arms race, and military conflict which dominated life on the planet for the next generation might have been limited. Instead, immediately after the worst war ever, the victorious nations quickly began the Cold War, which caused an arms race, spawned armed conflicts around the world, was responsible for the deaths of millions, and resulted in the impoverishment of hundreds of millions by the displacement of people, destruction of property, consumption of wealth, and glorification of violence. This is the greatest crime against humanity yet committed.

Effective enforcement of international principles preventing and controlling war is as essential to peace and human survival as effective enforcement of domestic criminal codes is to the prevention and control of crime in neighborhoods where people live. For over 200 years, the people of the United States have acted on the assumption that the rule of law is essential to insure domestic tranquility. Indeed, all people living in politically organized societies have shared that assumption for several thousand years. Common experience has suggested to most that personal safety depends on the enforcement of principles designed to protect individuals from the violence, lust, greed, and cunning of others.

Nearly all who live in the United States believe their lives, their fortunes, and their sacred honor depend on the police department, the criminal courts, and the district attorney. Americans believe the rule of law and its effective enforcement is essential to their physical safety. They would be terrified at the prospect of a society without police, prisons, and criminal laws. A large part of popular dissatisfaction is with the assumed failure of these institutions to protect society.

Experience shows that international tranquility depends on the enforcement of an international rule of law. More than 700 years ago, Thomas Aquinas wrote, "War is inevitable among sovereign nations not governed by positive law," and the observation has been around for several millennia. War and lesser forms of international violence and coercion have been the dominant experience of nearly every generation in nearly every society on the planet throughout recorded history.

In this last generation, the technology of war and the expanding capacity for mass destruction have become so horrific that assured peace is no mere amenity, but necessary for moral, mental, economic, and physical survival. The need for international law and its enforcement is as urgent for the world community to prevent omnicide as local law and police are to a family whose home is surrounded by a mob bent on arson and murder.

Yet in the face of this inescapably dangerous environment, the public overwhelmingly yawns, shrugs, or blinks at the suggestion of world law as a means to peace. They have accepted nuclear arms as their protector. Lawyers themselves consider the subject of international law as too exotic, if not embarrassing, to contemplate. Powerful national governments proclaim it unpatriotic or treasonous.

Discussions about domestic law and order fill the electronic and print media, as well as daily conversations among friends, family, and casual acquaintances. Rarely is any notion of world law mentioned; and when it is, it is usually derided as the province of dreamers. The courts, our citadels of law, are worse. A U.S. court of appeals which addressed the argument that international law is part of the supreme law of the land in 1989 found it "fanciful," "idiosyncratic," "far-fetched." Most courts decline to consider the argument at all.

However, this attitude simply ignores the incontestable fact that international law is woven into the fabric of American law. Article VI of the U.S. Constitution includes international treaties in the supreme law of the land. Common law processes absorb customary international law into the domestic corpus juris. Yet the courts, legislatures, government executives, and lawyers relegate issues of war and peace that threaten all life to international anarchy.

Law in theory has always recognized and often glorified its role in the quest for peace. The Pax Romana was said to be founded on Roman law. Hugo Grotius, in his great work on international law, *The Law of War and Peace (De Jure Belli ac Paces)*, first published in 1625, wrote, "This care to preserve society, which we have here roughly outlined, and which is characteristic of human intelligence, is the source of all law which is properly so called." The very purpose of law is peace. A major international lawyers' association created during the early years of the Cold War calls itself World Peace Through Law. Literally hundreds of organizations seek to create systems of laws they believe will bring peace.

Those who wield power naturally oppose international law because such law would impose limits on the use of power and require peaceful resolution of disputes. Power prefers to have its way. In reality, the media in the United States is an instrument of power: while the media may preach principles and occasionally even the rule of international law, it urges the exercise of power in practice. When international law challenges the privileges of power the media overwhelmingly derides the law and justifies force.

That the American people acquiesce in this rejection of international law exposes a failure of our democratic institutions. Surely a knowledgeable people guiding their own destiny through democratic processes based on principles of law would wrest power from such governance as a preliminary act toward self-preservation.

Unwilling to assert outright that there is no international public law binding the United States, federal courts often invoke the "political question" doctrine when confronted with international issues. This doctrine holds that courts are not competent to judge questions of war and peace. It finds that the political branches, the Congress and the President, are delegated authority by the Constitution over activity involving foreign relations. This is tantamount to declaring the absence of law in the crucial area of war and peace, or at least an absence of law that can be enforced against the political branches by the courts. Such a doctrine places the executive above the law when it acts in the foreign policy area, even if the result is the slaughter of hundreds of thousands, assassination of foreign leaders, invasion of foreign countries, or military raids without authority of domestic or international law, treaty, or declaration of war.

The position U.S. policy makers take is that Congress can alter, amend, repeal, or ignore any international law. This is a declaration of independence from the world community and a warning that the United States will not be bound by any international rule not to the liking of Congress. Little wonder then that few lawyers are willing to spend much time or thought on international law, since however important we say international law is, in action it is near impotent. It may be a helpful political argument, and it may even reinforce public opinion outraged by despicable acts. But it has little power to fulfill its promise against the will and force of the nations involved in a controversy.

While nations do abide by decisions of the International Court of Justice, which was established by the UN Charter, such obedience is largely a matter of choice, at least for the powerful nations. A prime example of this was the U.S. refusal to acknowledge the Court's jurisdiction when the Sandinista government of Nicaragua claimed damages for U.S. military aggression against it. The United States had battered Nicaragua with direct attacks, Contra warfare, and severe economic sanctions, and had spent close to $48 million to create an artificial unified opposition political party, stealing an election in utter contempt of democratic principles. A first act of the Chamorro government after its election in Nicaragua ousted the Sandinista government was dismissal of the suit against the United States. Its reward was the further debilitation of international law and democracy.

Another international court is the Inter-American Court for Human Rights at San Jose, Costa Rica. It has a history of inaction and little power to enforce any disputed decision. Its major weakness stems from the lack of participation of the United States, the region's preeminent power. One consequence of this is widespread human rights violations throughout the hemisphere. In contrast, the European Court at Strasbourg is a highly effective tribunal for the enforcement of international human rights principles within Europe. It has successfully ordered Germany, France, Italy, Spain, and the United Kingdom, among others, to stop violating human rights.

Few national courts have considered enforcing international principles concerning war and peace against their own governments. Until they do, national courts cannot restrain militarism. The history of litigation in United States courts seeking enforcement of international public law principles against the government is spotty and ambiguous. While there are a few heroic court decisions over the years, the most recent growing out of the Korean War, U.S. legal history contains huge voids because claims are not asserted against the government in spite of terrible injuries inflicted by war crimes. The law is undeveloped, and few lawyers are willing to mount serious lawsuits in the face of the bleak prospects for success.

An illustration of the difficulties facing suits against the United States based largely on international law involves claims arising from the U.S. bombing of Libya in April 1986. I brought suit in federal district court in Washington, D.C. for hundreds of civilians injured by this attack and the families of those killed. The suit alleged that the bombing was an attempt to assassinate a foreign leader and randomly kill civilians to terrorize the people into overthrowing their government. The claims were based upon international law, U.S. constitutional and statutory law, the laws of armed conflict, and U.S. criminal law. Motions to dismiss on behalf of the United States, the United Kingdom, Margaret Thatcher, and the chain of command from President Reagan to the pilots of the assaulting aircraft were filed. The court accepted the allegations of the complaint as true, thus conceding the attempts to assassinate Colonel Qaddafi and to kill civilians. Yet it dismissed the claims — being later affirmed by the court of appeals — on the basis of sovereign immunity, ignoring all arguments based on international law. The court added, "the case offered no hope whatsoever of success, and plaintiff's attorneys surely knew it." The United States and the United Kingdom both sought monetary sanctions against my law office for daring to bring the action. The court called the action "not so much frivolous as audacious," and refused to punish counsel. The court of appeals reversed without opinion on the merits and ordered sanctions. The sanctions issue remains in the courts. The chilling effects on future claims will further diminish the role of law in war.

Meanwhile, the United States demanded and Iraq paid $36 million in damages to families of U.S. servicemen killed and injured when the U.S.S. *Stark* was torpedoed by an Iraqi jet in the Persian Gulf during the Iran–Iraq War. The United States paid nothing in reparations to the families of people killed in its invasions of Grenada and Panama, or to the 270 families of persons killed on an Iranian commercial airliner shot down by the U.S. while on a scheduled flight from Shiraz to Bahrain in 1987. Power prevailed, and as a result, in the very field of most urgent need and greatest importance, positive international law seems largely dormant, if not dead, at the hands of military supremacy.

International law, as practiced by American foreign policy makers, is not a coherent set of principles and procedures. Instead, it is what these policy makers will accept — principles that are thoroughly politicized, then savaged by discretionary actions. Enforceability of international rules against the United States is not even contemplated by its foreign policy establishment, or presently imaginable to its courts. The position of the U.S. government reflects the determination of power not to be accountable. Therefore, true international law, applied equally to the entire world community as it must be, offers slender hope for the establishment of a peaceful world order.

And for those who believe that law is what the courts say it is, the problem with international public law is clear. For most questions, there is no court to say what the law is. The International Court of Justice can decide only a narrow range of cases between nations. Individuals and organizations have no standing. Few cases are brought and the issues are rarely of great importance. There is no substantial body of international case law creating patterns of principles to guide conduct and future decision making. And no court has the power to enforce its order.

With an imperial President uncontrolled by domestic law or public opinion and free to interpret international law as he chooses, there is little limitation on his arbitrary decision to go to war, or the arbitrary use of military force to destroy an enemy.

Few presidential acts in American history have been as dangerous, unreasoning, or arbitrary as President Bush's decision to send troops to the Persian Gulf. In August 1990 he abandoned all pretense of constitutional authority, made no gesture to obtain approval of the Congress, offered no explanation of the source of his power to unilaterally commit American military forces to foreign territory half a world away. A military dictator could not have been less restrained.

The question of constitutionality, of law and democratic institutions, does not seem to arise when the President wants war. President Bush did not even deem it necessary to invoke the usual and usually false justification that military action was necessary to protect American citizens. The depth of the administration's commitment to that canard is revealed by its failure to take steps to protect the several thousand Americans in Iraq and Kuwait before acts were committed that might — and did — put them in jeopardy.

The Constitution delegated war powers to the Congress. Its authors were aware of the consequences to the lives of citizens who lived under a monarch capable of committing a country to war at his will. Despite the clarity of the Constitution and the known importance of placing such crucial power in the legislative branch, President Bush claimed power to act alone without congressional or UN authority. He restated his views as late as January 9, a week before the bombing began.

The fig leaf of UN approval was a fraud. The Security Council resolutions were secured by what would constitute criminal bribes, coercion, and extortion in any system of government desiring integrity in voting. The delegation of authority to unnamed nations to use any means necessary is as lawless as legislation can be. It was no ordinary discretion that was delegated by the Security Council. It was undefined, unlimited, and unsupervised. The United States misused that mandate to kill civilians, cripple Iraq, and destroy most of Iraq's military power. Yet not a word of the resolution authorized any attack on Iraq itself.

Even if the President had been empowered under the Constitution and authorized by the UN to attack Iraq, there can be no claim that war crimes were, or could have been, authorized by the Congress or the UN. Nor can there be any doubt that specific and binding international laws applied directly to military acts committed under the orders of President Bush. As the Supreme Court noted in a famous case protecting Confederate property from superior Union force after the Civil War, "No man in this country is so high that he is above the law."

That President Bush thought he was above the law was revealed in many ways. A sad illustration was when the press reported Pentagon sources saying Bush had ordered General Powell to target Saddam Hussein for assassination shortly after August 2. We now know that an attempt to carry out this order was made by dropping "super bombs" on a command shelter in February 1991, and we may never know what other efforts were made. Of course, the assassination of a foreign head of state, even in time of war, is prohibited by laws. Article 23 of the Hague Regulations, the Convention on the Prevention and Punishment of Crimes Against Internationally Protected Persons, and even U.S. Presidential Executive Order 12333 prohibit assassinations.

THE LAWS OF ARMED CONFLICT

During the American Civil War, President Lincoln appointed Columbia College Professor Francis Lieber to draft a code of military conduct to govern the actions of Union troops. The Lieber code of 1863 became a part of subsequent international treaties limiting military conduct in war. Geneva Conventions of 1864 and 1906 provided protection for soldiers wounded in action. The Hague Conventions of 1899, revised in 1907, were the first international codification of the laws of armed conflict.

In Part IV, Section 22, the Hague Convention established the principles that the means of injuring the enemy are not unlimited and barred weapons that cause unnecessary suffering. Founded on the principle of proportionality, the Convention concluded that the amount of force used must be proportional to a legitimate military objective. Excessive force was prohibited. The other basic principle provided that military operations must be directed at military objectives. Civilians and civilians facilities must be protected.

The Hague Convention for the Pacific Settlement of International Disputes of 1907, to which both the United States and Iraq are parties, established procedures for mediation with a mandatory cooling off period in "case of a serious difference endangering the peace." It was ignored. The Geneva Protocol of 1925, reflecting the terrible experiences of World War I, prohibited the use of chemical and biological weapons.

The Charter of the United Nations

The horrors of World War II brought whole new treaties of international law into being, with the United States playing a central role in their creation. These treaties were bought with the blood of the millions who died, and are the promise of those who survived to live by their words. The Charter of the United Nations, signed in San Franciso in June 1945 as war still raged in the Pacific, has a preamble stating its first purpose: "We the Peoples of the United Nations determined to save succeeding generations from the scourge of war, which twice in our lifetime has brought untold sorrow to mankind. . . . "

Article I of the Charter expands on the purposes of the United Nations. Section 1 begins:

> The Purposes of the United Nations are:
> 1. To maintain international peace and security, and to that end: to take effective collective measures for the prevention and removal of threats to the peace, and for the suppression of acts of aggression or other breaches of the peace, and to bring about by peaceful means, and in conformity with the principles of justice and international law, adjustment or settlement of international disputes or situations which might lead to a breach of the peace. . . .

Article II, Section 3 requires that "All Members shall settle their international disputes by peaceful means in such a manner that international peace and security, and justice, are not endangered."

Chapter VI, titled "Pacific Settlement of Disputes," begins with Article 33, which provides:

> 1. The parties to any dispute, the continuance of which is likely to endanger the maintenance of international peace and security, shall, first of all, seek a solution by negotiation, enquiry, mediation, conciliation, arbitration, judicial settlement, resort to regional agencies or arrangements, or other peaceful means of their own choice.

President Bush announced in early August 1990 and repeated until Iraq was destroyed that there would be no negotiation, no compromise, no facesaving, no reward for aggression. He deliberately frustrated all efforts for a peaceful solution. His words and his deeds were contemptuous of the UN Charter. The essential requirements of Chapter VI were violated by a President who had ordered the U.S. invasion of Panama less than eight months before Iraq invaded Kuwait. The invasion of Panama violated all the principles of international law violated by Iraq in its invasion of Kuwait, and in addition the Charter of the Organization of American States, the Pact of Rio de Janeiro, and the Panama Canal Treaties of 1977. More Panamanians died in the U.S. invasion than Kuwaitis died in Iraq's invasion.

The Nuremberg Tribunal

After World War II, the first among new international conventions addressing war was what became the Charter of the Nuremberg Tribunal. Ironically, it was promulgated in London on the day Nagasaki was incinerated by the second atomic bomb.

We ought to see the fumbling effort at Nuremberg, though clearly victor's justice, as a major milestone in the human struggle for peace. If it is remembered as a quaint sideshow to the glorious drama of battle, peace will have little chance. Its words deserve careful scrutiny, continuing respect, and fair and equal enforcement.

The Nuremberg Charter set forth the following acts punishable as crimes under international law:

Principle VI

(a) Crimes against peace:
  (i) Planning, preparation, initiation or waging of a war of aggression or a war in violation of international treaties, agreements or assurances;
  (ii) Participation in a common plan or conspiracy for the accomplishment of any of the acts mentioned under (i).
(b) War crimes:
  Violations of the laws or customs of war which include, but are not limited to, murder, ill-treatment or deportation of slave-labor or for any other purpose of civilian population of or in occupied territory, murder or ill-treatment of prisoners of war, of persons on the seas, killing of hostages, plunder of public or private property, wanton destruction of cities, towns, or villages, or devastation not justified by military necessity.
(c) Crimes against humanity:
  Murder, extermination, enslavement, deportation and other inhuman acts done against any civilian population, or persecutions on political, racial or religious grounds, when such acts are done or such persecutions are carried on in execution of or in connection with any crime against peace or any war crime.

The universal principles of the Nuremberg Tribunal which recognize the essential role of accountability include the following:

Principle I

Any person who commits an act which constitutes a crime under international law is responsible therefore and liable to punishments.

Principle II

The fact that internal law does not impose a penalty for an act which constitutes a crime under international law does not relieve the person who committed the act from responsibility under international law.

Principle III

The fact that a person who committed an act which constitutes a crime under international law acted as Head of State or responsible Government official does not relieve him from responsibility under international law.

Principle IV

The fact that a person acted pursuant to order of his Government or of a superior does not relieve him from responsibility under international law, provided a moral choice was in fact possible to him.

To read and believe the findings set forth in this book is to know that the United States committed crimes against peace, war crimes, and crimes against humanity. The planning of aggression against Iraq to destroy its army and cripple the society, the murders of defenseless soldiers, the wanton destruction of cities, towns and villages, the wide range of violent acts against the civilian population are all Nuremberg crimes. The International War Crimes Tribunal found that the UN sanctions constituted a continuing crime against humanity. President Bush and those who participated in the criminal acts have violated the principles of the Nuremberg Tribunal and ought to be held accountable.

The Geneva Conventions

International law protecting civilians from the ravages of war developed as technology exposed civilian life to greater threats of destruction. In earlier times, while civilians were always in jeopardy when undefended, combatants overwhelmingly suffered the largest violence of arms. With the advent of airplanes, extended range artillery, and missiles, a whole society was exposed to attack while its military forces remained intact. Sophisticated laws protecting civilians have been developed, and their application removed from the emotion, confusion, and emergency nature of military combat and "necessity" is clear.

Protocol I of 1977 Additional to the Geneva Conventions of 1949 provides the most sophisticated and specific statement of international law protecting civilians. Both Iraq and the United States are signatories. The basic rule is set forth in Part IV, Article 48:

> In order to ensure respect for and protection of the civilian population and civilian objects, the Parties to the conflict shall at all times distinguish between the civilian population and combatants and between civilian objects and military objectives and accordingly shall direct their operations only against military objectives.

President Bush ordered an attack against Iraq that crippled the nation. Evidence that this was precisely his purpose is overwhelming.

Article 51 provides more specific protection for the civilian population in the following language:

1. The civilian population and individual civilians shall enjoy general protection against dangers arising from military operations. To give effect to this protection, the following rules, which are additional to other applicable rules of international law, shall be observed in all circumstances.
2. The civilian population as such, as well as individual civilians, shall not be the object of attack. Acts or threats of violence the primary purpose of which is to spread terror among the civilian population are prohibited.
3. Civilians shall enjoy the protection afforded by this Section, unless and for such time as they take a direct part in hostilities.
4. Indiscriminate attacks are prohibited. Indiscriminate attacks are:
    (a) those which are not directed at a specific military objective;
    (b) those which employ a method or means of combat which cannot be directed at a specific military objective; or
    (c) those which employ a method or means of combat the effects of which cannot be limited as required by this Protocol;
    and consequently, in each such case, are of a nature to strike military objectives and civilians or civilian objects without distinction.
5. Among others, the following types of attacks are to be considered as indiscriminate:
    (a) an attack by bombardment by any methods or means which treats as a single military objective a number of clearly separated and distinct military objectives located in a city, town,

174

village or other area containing a similar concentration of civilians or civilian objects; and

(b) an attack which may be expected to cause incidental loss of civilian life, injury to civilians, damage to civilian objects or a combination thereof, which would be excessive in relation to the concrete and direct military advantage anticipated.

President Bush and the U.S. military forces that carried out his orders to bomb Iraq made civilians the direct object of their attack in tens of thousands of aerial sorties and missile launchings. From taxis and public buses on highways to farms, markets, offices, hotels, mosques, and private homes, civilians were attacked. Article 52 protects civilian facilities and property:

1. Civilian objects shall not be the object of attack or of reprisals. Civilian objects are all objects which are not military objectives as defined in paragraph 2.
2. Attacks shall be limited strictly to military objectives. Insofar as objects are concerned, military objectives are limited to those objects which by their nature, location, purpose or use make an effective contribution to military action and whose total or partial destruction, capture or neutralization, in the circumstances ruling at the time, offers a definite military advantage.
3. In case of doubt whether an object which is normally dedicated to civilian purposes, such as a place of worship, a house or other dwelling or a school, is being used to make an effective contribution to military action, it shall be presumed not to be so used.

Facts found by the Commission leave no doubt that President Bush ordered the destruction of civilian facilities and property throughout Iraq. Included were schools, hospitals, bridges, cement plants, TV and radio stations, bus and railway depots, shops, restaurants, and homes.

Article 53 protects cultural objects and places of worship. It was not able to prevent widespread destruction by U.S. bombardment of irreplaceable historical sites, museums, ancient monuments, religious shrines, and active mosques, churches, and synagogues.

Article 54 protects objects indispensable to the survival of the civilian population:

1. Starvation of civilians as a method of warfare is prohibited.
2. It is prohibited to attack, destroy, remove or render useless objects indispensable to the survival of the civilian population, such as foodstuffs, agricultural areas for the production of foodstuffs, crops, livestock, drinking water installations and supplies and ir-

rigation works, for the specific purpose of denying them for their sustenance value to the civilian population or to the adverse Party, whatever the motive, whether in order to starve out civilians, to cause them to move away, or for any other motive.

No explanation of the importance to life of such a provision is needed. Yet the United States destroyed all public water supply systems in Iraq. Its assault on the chain of food production, storage, processing, and distribution was intensive, destroying 90 percent of the poultry, half the animal herds, and most fish farming.

The environment is protected by Article 55:

1. Care shall be taken in warfare to protect the natural environment against widespread, long-term and severe damage. This protection includes a prohibition of the use of methods or means of warfare which are intended or may be expected to cause such damage to the natural environment and thereby to prejudice the health or survival of the population.

Commission findings detail the deliberate assault on the natural environment of the Persian Gulf, and consequently its neighbors. Through the unleashing of 88,000 tons of explosives; scattering of radioactive debris; firing of refineries, fuel storage tanks, oil wells, and filling stations; and total destruction of the sewage treatment facilities and sewer systems, the air, earth, and water were polluted.

Installations containing dangerous forces are protected by Article 56:

1. Works or installations containing dangerous forces, namely dams, dikes and nuclear electrical generating stations, shall not be made the object of attack, even where these objects are military objectives, if such attack may cause the release of dangerous forces and consequent severe losses among the civilian population. Other military objectives located at or in the vicinity of these works or installations shall not be made the object of attack if such attack may cause the release of dangerous forces from the works or installations and consequent severe losses among the civilian population.

The United States highlighted attacks on what it labeled chemical warfare plants and nuclear arms research and nuclear power and storage sites throughout the bombing of Iraq. It proclaimed the destruction of all secret nuclear research and storage sites after the bombing, only to declare later it had missed some. It openly threatened renewed attacks against alleged nuclear sites into the summer of 1992. It relished the debate over whether an infant milk formula plant it destroyed was actually a chemical weapons plant. It flaunted the law prohibiting such attacks, ignored the consequences to people who live in such vicinities, and lied about the targets.

Because prevention is the best protection, Article 57 requires the military to take precautionary measures to spare civilians from the disaster of war:

1. In the conduct of military operations, constant care shall be taken to spare the civilian population, civilians and civilian objects.
2. With respect to attacks, the following precautions shall be taken:
    (a) those who plan or decide upon an attack shall:
        (i) do everything feasible to verify that the objectives to be attacked are neither civilians nor civilian objects and are not subject to special protection but are military objectives within the meaning of paragraph 2 of Article 52 and that it is not prohibited by the provisions of this Protocol to attack them;
        (ii) take all feasible precautions in the choice of means and methods of attack with a view to avoiding, and in any event to minimizing, incidental loss of civilian life, injury to civilians and damage to civilian objects;
        (iii) refrain from deciding to launch any attack which may be expected to cause incidental loss of civilian life, injury to civilians, damage to civilian objects, or a combination thereof, which would be excessive in relation to the concrete and direct military advantage anticipated;
    (b) an attack shall be canceled or suspended if it becomes apparent that the objective is not a military one or is subject to special protection or that the attack may be expected to cause incidental loss of civilian life, injury to civilians, damage to civilian objects, or a combination thereof, which would be excessive in relation to the concrete and direct military advantage anticipated;
    (c) effective advance warning shall be given of attack which may affect the civilian population, unless circumstances do not permit.

The Commission findings show beyond a reasonable doubt that General Dugan's statement in September 1990 about targeting cities and terrorizing civilians was exactly what the United States intended and exactly what it did. The violations of international laws resulted in the deaths of more than 150,000 civilians. In early 1992, it was widely reported that 5,000–6,000 civilians were dying every month as a direct result of the bombing compounded by shortages of food, medicine, and medical services caused by the sanctions.

Military Application of War Crime Rules

The 125,000 military casualties suffered by Iraq also resulted from crimes against peace and war crimes.

Applying these laws to combat can be difficult because of the emotion and confusion involved in war and the life-and-death nature of the struggle. However, it is relatively easy to do so in the case of the Gulf War because there was no combat. While a few skirmishes can be identified, with rare exceptions Iraqi troops were defenseless against the murderous assaults that intended their liquidation.

Crimes against the Iraqi military included violations of the Nuremberg Charter, the Hague Conventions, the Geneva Conventions and Protocols, the international laws of armed conflict, and the U.S.-prescribed Rules of Engagement. They included killing tens of thousands of essentially defenseless soldiers, soldiers withdrawing without weapons, and soldiers seeking to surrender; burying soldiers alive; using illegal weapons; disrespect for the dead; and many others. The combat death toll alone — 125,000 Iraqi deaths to 148 American — reveals the defenselessness of the Iraqis and the dimension of the crime. This was certainly a violation of the Hague Convention requiring that force used be proportional to a legitimate military objective.

The Final Act of the Geneva Conventions of 1949 recognized the importance of accounting for enemy casualties. Article 16 provides: "Parties to the conflict shall record as soon as possible in respect of each wounded, sick or dead person of the adverse Party falling into their hands, any particulars which may assist in his identification." Article 17 of the Final Act requires that the enemy dead be "honorably interred" wherever possible "according to the rites of the religion to which they belonged" and that parties exchange lists describing "the particulars of the dead interred."

U.S. forces buried thousands of Iraqi soldiers alive, wounded, dying, and dead. Miles of trenches with Iraqi troops in them were bulldozed over with sand. The United States refused to count, locate, identify, or honor the dead. General Powell said of the death count that it was "not a number I am terribly interested in."

Guidance for the U.S. armed forces is set forth in service manuals which must observe international treaties and customary international law. These manuals include rules of engagement imposed by the United States as well as international laws of armed conflict.

Each of the U.S. services has books full of honorable-sounding rules. The U.S. manuals sometimes impose greater restraint than established international law.

The efficacy of these restraints during the U.S. operations in the Gulf is placed in question by the lawyers assigned to advise the military commanders on their application. In the cover story of the December 1991 *American Bar Association Journal* entitled "Lawyers in the War Room," the reader is told, "Desert Storm was the most legalistic war we've ever fought." It would be better if the fight had been legal.

The article describes international law as seeking "a balance between military necessity and humanitarian concerns."[1] But "balance" is not a standard applied in murder cases. "Necessity" cannot compromise. And "concerns" are vague, undefined and pliable. The very choice of words reveals a commitment to military authority.

The author identifies the role of lawyers as purely advisory, leaving the military commander free to act as he chose. He discusses attacks on vehicles on the Amman-to-Baghdad highway, claiming mobile Scud launchers were indistinguishable from civilian vehicles:

> "Once a commander realized civilians were being injured when we went after the launchers, he had to weigh the issues," says Hays Parks, special assistant for Law of War matters in the Office of the Judge Advocate General [JAG] of the Army.
>
> "He's going to ask the JAG, can I do it? Is it legal? And the JAG will say, yes, you can. But any good commander, and especially one as smart as Gen. Schwarzkopf, will ask, is this the way we want to fight a war?" Parks says. "It underlines the fact that few legal decisions are made in a vacuum. They are often fraught with political and moral considerations."[2]

It is interesting that the military lawyer quoted would admit that the JAG would say "yes, you can" to attacks that injured civilians. Obviously, you cannot shoot everything moving on a public highway because you cannot distinguish Scud launchers from civilian vehicles. By indicating that civilians were being injured shows that civilian vehicles could be distinguished from military vehicles. And his suggestion that civilians were being "injured" rather than killed when hundreds were killed in these attacks, and that commanders look beyond the law to political and moral considerations, reveals the propaganda nature of the piece. Completely whitewashed were atrocities such as the Highway of Death, the crippling of an entire nation, the use of fuel-air explosives, and the destruction of an armored division deep in Iraq 48 hours after the ceasefire.

The Vietnam syndrome was kicked once and for all by the military lawyers as well as by President Bush, according to the *ABA Journal* article:

"Lots of people came out of Vietnam thinking things were illegal when they were not," Parks says. "It has been very important to get commanders to realize that there's a crucial distinction between political decisions and the law. I've given hundreds of lectures on how we could have done in Vietnam everything we did in Iraq, but that policy, not law, restricted us."

These misconceptions do not die easily. In the Gulf, lawyers sometimes had to tell commanders that it was okay to do something the commanders had assumed was illegal.[3]

This is an argument by Pentagon counsel for unlimited discretion in the conduct of war, and a gross distortion of what happened during the Vietnam War, when carpet-bombing, village massacres, napalm, and Agent Orange were used against civilians.

And here is the *ABA Journal*'s evaluation of the destruction of the Amariyah bomb shelter:

It is perhaps surprising that in one of the most tragic incidents of the war—the U.S. attack on an Iraqi bunker that, according to Baghdad, killed several hundred civilians—there were really no thorny legal issues to contemplate. . . .

"From a legal standpoint, it was very clear-cut," Parks says. "It was known that the target had been converted to a command-and-control center during the Iran–Iraq War. Barbed wire had been put around it; armed guards had been put on the doors; and it had been camouflaged, which is not something you do for air raid shelters."[4]

Thus the deadliest single missile attack against Baghdad is disposed of. The military law advisers ignored the facts that the bomb shelter was known to have been used by civilians and that the hundreds of dead were nearly all women and children. When this is considered, it is unthinkable that this tragic destruction of a civilian bomb shelter could have raised no legal concerns.

The President, other high officials, and the massive Pentagon propaganda machine engaged in a continuous campaign to convince world opinion and the American people of the legality of their acts. The *ABA Journal* article and similar law journal publications fed into this campaign. Designed for general consumption, they help to persuade lawyers with no knowledge of the law or facts that U.S. conduct was legal. They corrupt the hope that law may help us on the road to peace.

Both President Bush and UN Secretary General Perez de Cuellar were put on notice by my letter delivered February 12, 1991 that war crimes were being committed. In part the ten-page letter stated:

> The bombing constitutes the most grievous violation of international law. It is intended to destroy the civilian life and economy of Iraq. It is not necessary, meaningful or permissible as a means of driving Iraq from Kuwait.
>
> No UN resolution authorizes any military assault on Iraq, except as is necessary to drive Iraqi forces from Kuwait. The bombing that has occurred throughout Iraq is the clearest violation of international law and norms for armed conflict, including the Hague and Geneva Conventions and the Nuremberg Charter. It is uncivilized, brutal and racist by any moral standard. With few if any exceptions we witnessed, the destruction is not conceivably within the language or contemplation of Security Council Resolution 678/44.
>
> The use of highly sophisticated military technology with mass destructive capacity by rich nations against an essentially defenseless civilian population of a poor nation is one of the great tragedies of our time. United States annual military expenditures alone are four times the gross national product of Iraq. The scourge of war will never end if the United Nations tolerates this assault on life. The United Nations must not be an accessory to war crimes.

War inherently knows no principle. Still, societies have struggled for generations to place limits on how commanders conduct war. In the destruction of Iraq, the U.S. military placed no limits on bombing civilians or soldiers. Its purpose was the destruction of the Iraqi military and crippling of the economy of the whole society. Its means were the measured death and destruction of civilians and their life-support systems.

The slaughter of Iraqi civilians and soldiers was a continuing war crime from the first bomb on the morning of January 17 through the last destructive assault on a retreating army division 48 hours after the ceasefire on March 3. The crimes took the lives of tens of thousands of defenseless people by direct violence and more than that number by the foreseeable consequences of destroying facilities essential to human life and the embargo on the importation of necessary food, medicines, and parts and equipment for restoration of facilities and health delivery systems.

Even greater than war crimes are crimes against peace, for if there are no crimes against peace, there is no war. U.S. crimes against peace began no later than 1989, with the planning of the assault on Iraq, and continued until the bombing began in January 1991. The United States planned to destroy Iraq and worked to avoid any negotiation that would prevent its purpose.

For such acts there must be accountability if the world is to know justice and peace.

CHAPTER 10

The Quest for Peace and Accountability

AFTER Iraq invaded Kuwait on August 2, 1990, President Bush secured immediate UN condemnation of Iraq and pressured Saudi Arabia to accept U.S. troops on its soil, while telling the world that their presence was "wholly defensive." His true purpose would not become known for several months, but his bellicosity was unmistakable.

THE PEACE COALITION

In reponse, alarmed peace activists met in New York in mid-August to form the Coalition to Stop U.S. Intervention in the Middle East. On August 24, my op-ed piece in the *Los Angeles Times*, titled "Peril from an Imperial Presidency," charged President Bush's rush to war ignored all restraints imposed by law. In it I demanded immediate withdrawal of U.S. forces from the Gulf, renunciation of any desire for military bases in the area, and full U.S. support for regional, Arab, and UN efforts to peacefully resolve the disputes that plagued the area. The article reflected the early goals of the Coalition.

Above all, I pleaded for the President to respect the Constitution, observing, "He has abandoned all pretense of constitutional authority, made no gesture to obtain approval of Congress, offered no explanation of the source of his power to unilaterally commit American military forces to a foreign territory half a world away. A military dictator could not be less restrained."

The Coalition held meetings and major rallies against the U.S. intervention in the Gulf from coast to coast during August, September,

183

and October, drawing 20,000 people each in New York and San Francisco. It supported my trip to Baghdad in November to evaluate the situation then and meet with Saddam Hussein. The Coalition helped stimulate the steady growth of antiwar organizing all over the country through February. Representative Henry Gonzales joined the Coalition's call for President Bush's impeachment for usurping Congressional powers at its Washington press conference in early January. A series of press conferences, scores of individual meetings with UN delegates, and many protests by the Coalition were held at the United Nations from October into March.

On the evening of January 16, the Coalition sponsored a rally that was broadcast live for 2 hours over 40 radio stations. The U.S. bombing of Iraq actually began then, giving the broadcast a somber, anguished tone rarely heard on American radio. On January 19 the Coalition held its largest rallies, with more than 100,000 people at Lafayette Park in front of the White House and a larger crowd at San Francisco's Civic Center. Prominent speakers from all walks of life spoke to these deeply hurt and angry crowds. An even larger demonstration organized by the Campaign for Peace was held in Washington the following week. But the movement had failed; the bombing had begun.

The media gave scant coverage to the antiwar protests. When reported, they were almost always described negatively and offset by pages of prowar stories. As much notice was given the few hundred who occasionally protested in favor of the war. For example, the handful of prowar protesters in Washington on January 19 were given equal coverage on TV and in the press as the tens of thousands who gathered in Lafayette Park and later marched toward the Capitol.

The Coalition was formed by people and organizations who earlier in 1990 had joined to investigate and protest U.S. intervention in Panama. It grew quickly by networking among known opponents to war. Unlike the invasion of Panama, which was a fait accompli before opposition could develop, the Gulf crisis presented an important opportunity to test democratic institutions and prevent war. Early participants included opponents of the Vietnam War, antinuclear organizations, Central American peace activists, and traditional pacifists. Religious leadership and organized church groups were the largest elements from the beginning, having shown a higher commitment to peace and greater perseverance in the years following Vietnam when so many efforts had been disbanded. Civil rights and civil liberties associations, labor unions, Arab-American

Committees, student groups, and environmentalists in unprecedented numbers joined as the threat of war grew.

The antiwar movement was ignored by the media and lacked essential funds for organizing and advertising. There was no shooting war to resist, there was a widespread belief that war would not happen, and the government manipulated events and controlled information. Yet the outpouring of opposition to the war was impressive. It seems probable that if citizens had been given a chance to know the facts and have access to real diversity of opinion, and if there had been more resources to organize the antiwar opposition, the American people would have prevented their government's assault on Iraq. The close vote in Congress on the eve of the deadline set by President Bush for Iraq to withdraw from Kuwait is compelling evidence that there was much stronger opposition to war than the media led the American people to believe.

The bombing of Iraq began during East Coast prime time evening news on January 16, just as the 1986 raid on Libya did, to assure maximum impact on public opinion. As the number of U.S. bombing sorties against Iraq approached 10,000, it became clear civilian casualties would be high. I then urged Iraq to invite U.S. and European news media to travel throughout the country to assess civilian casualties and damage, offering to go myself with a camera crew if the media were not acceptable.

Four days later, I received permission to visit Iraq with a camera crew. Jon Alpert and Maryann De Leo, who have filmed war's destructiveness in Asia, Africa, and Central America joined me and Abdul al-Kaysi, an American citizen born and raised in Iraq. Entering Iraq after dark on February 2 by road from Jordan, we traveled over 2,000 miles viewing civilian casualties and destruction from Baghdad to Basra and beyond.

We left Iraq on February 9 with over six hours of important, uncensored videotape, hundreds of still pictures, and vivid personal impressions of the aerial war directed at the civilian population. Alpert gave NBC first option on the tape because he had worked with them for 12 years. *NBC Nightly News* viewed segments and knew they had a scoop, the first footage of war damage from Basra and other cities in the south. However, NBC News President Michael Gartner, who had not seen the film, ordered its rejection.

Men with the professional ethics of Gartner have no place in a communications organization that wants to inform the public. They had in their hands uncensored film from inside Iraq showing civilian damage from U.S. bombing and they refused to show it. Instead they projected the Pentagon myth of surgical accuracy and repeatedly headlined Scud missiles striking Israel and Saudi Arabia. After NBC's rejection, no U.S. television network accepted Alpert's film.

While U.S. television rejected Alpert's film and showed practically no footage of the destruction of Iraq's cities, each of the 85 Scud missiles fired by Iraq at Israel and Saudi Arabia was treated as a major news event with extensive live footage from the sites where those that were found fell. Much was made of the Patriot missile which was presented by the media as a miraculous defender against the Scuds. A year later the Patriot was authoritatively branded an "almost total failure" by MIT expert Theodore A. Postol.

On February 12, my letter describing civilian casualties, suffering, and damage to civilian property was delivered to President Bush, UN Secretary General Perez de Cuellar, and the Iraqi UN Mission for President Saddam Hussein. It called for UN relief funds, or the release of frozen Iraqi funds, so that Iraq could purchase 2,500 tons a month of infant formula and medical and sanitation supplies, and so Iraq could begin to restore its municipal water and purification systems. The letter was announced at a press conference at the International Church Center across the street from the UN. It observed that no UN resolution authorized the bombing of Iraq and charged war crimes and described the clearest violations of international law and norms for armed conflict, including the Hague and Geneva Conventions and the Nuremberg Charter. It urged the creation of an investigative body to examine the effects of the U.S. bombing. Most urgently, it sought a ceasefire to stop the bombing of the cities and the civilian population.

THE COMMISSION

In March, within days of the end of the assault on Iraq, the Commission of Inquiry for the International War Crimes Tribunal was formed and announced. An outgrowth of the Coalition and its activities, the Commission was located in Coalition space in New York City. It gathered Coalition files and data; began new research activity; organized and sent a small investigative team to Iraq and Jordan; and encouraged, helped form, and aided other investigative efforts. By May, an initial complaint against President Bush and others stating 19 criminal charges was prepared on the basis of preliminary inquiry and evidence. The complaint was forwarded to President Bush with the invitation and request that he assign officials to provide documentation and information, answer questions, and present any defense. It remains unanswered.

The concept for the Commission was unique in history. Its search for facts of crimes against peace, war crimes, and crimes against humanity was unprecedented in scope and magnitude as an international peace effort. Simply put, the Commission wanted to obtain all possible evidence of government crimes committed during the Gulf crisis, and it intended an exhaustive and continuing effort to get the facts. It wanted to have those facts fairly and impartially evaluated by an international private tribunal made up of people of different backgrounds and experience from around the world. It intended to obtain an informed judgment of guilt or innocence on each of its 19 charges. After the judgment, it intended to seek the widest possible circulation of the evidence and judgments, believing that truth is the greatest energizer of popular actions. Finally, it wanted to distill from all it learned some lessons that might help humanity avoid the repetition of such tragic, violent conduct.

Early in its endeavors, Commission participants studied prior private efforts similar to its endeavor, where government misconduct had caused people to create forums to study or judge its actions. The experience of six were analyzed. Most important and helpful were the several Bertrand Russell Tribunals beginning with the Vietnam War. These reports were reviewed and several people intimately involved in the Russell Tribunals advised the Commission throughout.

The Commission focused on the United States because it was begun there by United States citizens and because the growing evidence revealed that the United States was the real transgressor, provoking Iraq and being supported in minor ways by a few nations that would not have acted except for the United States. The importance of the idea that peace largely depends on the people of nations capable of aggression controlling their own government grew throughout the Commission work. Never before had so many people within a country made so great an effort to secure evidence that showed their own government's guilt. Never before had any war crimes tribunal initiated by citizens of the principal country accused involved so vast an effort to gather evidence, so many hearings, or so many people from so many countries. No private tribunal in the past compared in magnitude to the Commission's activity.

The Commission held the first U.S. hearing in New York City in May 1991. The rest of the year, hearings were held in over 30 cities in the United States, with Commission-sponsored meetings in many more cities. Commission hearings or presentations were also held in more than 20 different countries, including Canada, in which five such hearings were held; England and Turkey, four each; Germany, two; and 18 other nations. Over the course of eight months I brought back evidence on the Gulf War from hearings or sessions in Europe, North America, North Africa, the Middle East, Asia, and Central America.

Every hearing considered evidence concerning the 19 charges. Nearly every hearing in the U.S. and all those abroad were independently organized, planned, financed, and conducted by local people. The charges were translated into their languages, and additional languages, by participants or for foreign publications. In addition to European languages, Commission charges were translated into Arabic, Urdu, Hindi, Malay, Chinese, Japanese, and Turkish, among others. The Commission provided printed materials, nearly always in English, for the organizers of all hearings and sessions. It sent representatives from the United States to almost all foreign hearings, in most cases at Commission expense. The Commission wanted each hearing to reflect the independent efforts of its organizers and to secure evidence available to them, but it did provide reports and occasionally access to witnesses, particularly experts on law, weapons systems, and the environment. All evidence was shared, if requested and possible, with the organizers of all hearings.

Each hearing developed new evidence through additional witnesses and reports. Most were attended by 300–600 people. The audiences at several exceeded 1,000, though large audiences were not the objective. Nearly all included Arab people with direct knowledge about the bombing.

The Commission's commitment to international law attracted support not only from peace groups but also from various countries' trade organizations and unions, including national lawyers' and jurists' associations, international medical and scientific study groups, journalists' associations, and student groups. In Hong Kong, the Asia Students Association (ASA) organized a press conference, a public forum on the work of the Commission, and a meeting with UN nongovernmental organizations based in that country. ASA represents 40 student organizations in 28 countries in Asia, and sent a student delegation to Iraq before the bombing.

In many countries, the Commission had the support of government figures or acting or former members of parliament. In India, for example, three former members of the Indian Supreme Court served on the Commission hearing panel, with the event itself organized by retired Chief Justice Hardev Singh.

With few exceptions, the hearings outside the U.S. received extensive media coverage, including reports on TV, radio, newspapers, and magazines. National or major reporting of U.S. hearings was virtually nonexistent, though some coverage was usually given in local newspapers and on radio.

The purposes in each hearing were to present evidence obtained by the Commission to the audience, to hear new evidence from experts and witnesses available to the sponsors of the hearing, and to organize for future action on a final report. One of the surprises was how evidence that could not be anticipated was presented in nearly every hearing. A city like Detroit was a nearly inexhaustible source of evidence because of its Arab-American population of more than 250,000, including 40,000 Iraqis and Iraqi Americans, most of whom have families and friends in Iraq. Many made or helped arrange trips to Iraq; many more had communications with people there. In Santa Rosa, California, a direct contact with medical personnel in Kuwait City hospitals was identified.

Commissions in other countries proved invaluable sources of information. Unique eyewitness testimony was provided at the hearing in Montreal by journalist Paul William Roberts, who spent 10 days traveling in Iraq disguised as a Bedouin. Roberts, who had experienced bombing in Vietnam and Cambodia, described the U.S. bombing: "Remember [in Vietnam], the North Vietnamese actually won that war. They stood a chance; these people had no chance. There was not any possibility of defending themselves or any possibility of protecting themselves or resisting it."

Commission hearings were conducted in many ways. In Pakistan, from which the first formal Commission report was issued, the Awami People's Tribunal was convened in Lahore, where it tried George Bush as representative of the 28-nation coalition for war crimes, crimes against peace, and crimes against humanity. When the defendant did not answer the call to appear, he was provided with defense counsel to speak on his behalf. Upon examination of the evidence presented against Bush, a 12-person jury found Bush's war crimes as serious as those committed by war criminals of World War II. Presiding in Lahore was Sheikh Mohammed Rashid, who would later serve as a judge at the Tribunal. His service to Pakistan spanned the history of the nation from its birth in 1948. Only a handful of national leaders have contributed as much to Pakistan in as many ways, including his service as Deputy Prime Minister during the Bhutto crisis. None has emerged with greater respect from the people for integrity and service.

Many of the foreign hearings indicted their own governments' role in supporting the U.S. offensive. A major issue for the Commission in Malaysia was why the Prime Minister, Dr. Mahathir bin Mohammed, submitted to U.S. pressure to support UN Resolution 678, which led to the assault. Members rejected Dr. Mahathir's claim that Malaysia had always supported small countries against powerful ones and therefore sided with Kuwait against Iraq. They showed that, among other things, Malaysia's vote for Resolution 678 won it over $1 million a year in U.S. military aid.

The hearing in Japan coincided with the lawsuit filed by almost 1,000 citizens against their government for its participation in the Gulf War. Claimants sought to prevent their country's $9 billion payment for the U.S. assault on Iraq as a breach of Article 9 of Japan's constitution, which renounces participation in all war. I attended the first of the court hearings on September 10, 1991; Tokyo District's largest courtroom was packed. Later that evening, over 1,000 people filled Yamanote Church for the Commission hearing. Japanese TV, radio, and magazines gave prominent coverage to both events. The case is still in litigation.

One of those present, Suzumu Ozaki, a man who has devoted his life to peace, later became a judge at the Tribunal. Serving as a judge in Japan in 1937, he protested Japanese aggression against China and was imprisoned. Protesting the Japanese attack on Pearl Harbor, he remained in prison until 1945. Thereafter he again sat as a judge and worked as a lawyer in peace activities.

The Japanese Commission hearing also coincided with the arrival of the U.S.S. *Independence* at its new home port in Yokasuka. The day after the hearing, I was in one of more than 50 small boats filled with antiwar activists protesting the arrival of this awesome nuclear-attack-capable aircraft carrier.

Yuriko Okawara, an organizer of the Japanese Commission, spoke at the Tribunal on February 29, 1992. The Japanese delegation was present, carrying a huge banner that read "Peace Now! We Won't Pay Taxes for Wars!" Okawara testified, "We firmly believe that (1) the Japanese Constitution's renunciation of force as a means of settling disputes should be the basis for resolving international conflicts, (2) people not only in Japan but all over the world have the right to live in peace as an important fundamental human right, and (3) we have the right to suspend government attempts to spend taxpayers' money and use national resouces in an unconstitutional manner."

Hearings at the Philippines' Commission focused on that country's debate over the future of U.S. bases in the Philippines. Commission members met with activists there who stressed the similarities between the U.S. attack against Iraq and the Philippine-American War nearly a century earlier. Historians estimate more than 200,000

Filipinos were killed, and another 900,000 died primarily from dengue fever as the result of the five-year war for control of the Philippine archipelago and the region. Testimony was also given on the difficulties faced by many of the tens of thousands of Filipinos who worked in the Gulf during the war.

This was the theme in many poor, Third World countries who exported labor to the Gulf. In Egypt, the Commission's testimony included interviews with some of the many Egyptian workers who had been in Iraq and Kuwait during the war, and who had endured bombing and postwar persecution in Kuwait or hardship in desert refugee camps. Members also discussed the devastating economic effects of the war on the already impoverished Egyptian working class. This evidence, like so much received from foreign hearings, was available only in that country.

Dr. Nawal El-Saadawi, president of the Arab Women's Solidarity Organization, and an internationally known author, testified on the increasing poverty of women and children due to inequalities in the Middle East fostered by U.S. policies. Dr. Sherif Hetata, also a writer, spoke on the economic pressures that forced Egypt to support the Gulf War. Hetata, who spent 14 years as a political prisoner in the 1950s and 1960s, later served as one of the Tribunal judges. Among a number of former high officials of the Egyptian Foreign Ministry present were three ambassadors, including one to the United States.

In Australia, Commission hearings focused on the fact that some of the more than 30 U.S. military bases in Australia facilitated the attack against Iraq. The Commission concluded that Australian bases, most notably the sophisticated Nurrungar, Pine Gap, and North West Cape monitoring facilities, were instrumental to the kind of assault waged against Iraq, where a wealth of continuous surveillance data allowed bombers to target Iraq's infrastructure with no danger to themselves. Members additionally charged that "the Australian Government, with no reference to the Australian people or our elected Paliaments, permitted the United States bases to be used for these purposes."

In Belgium, the Commission held three days of hearings beginning in June 1991. Held in facilities of the European Parliament, there was in-house equipment for simultaneous translation, which was provided in four languages. The organizers brought more than 20 witnesses from Iraq, Jordan, and the Gulf states who presented a wide range of evidence of war crimes.

Testimony indicted the western press for its biased, pro-U.S. coverage of the war. For instance, Journalist Georges Kazolias of

Radio France International (RFI) testified that his editor refused to broadcast the numbers of demonstrators against the war. Typical of the partisan coverage was a story describing journalists' cries of victory when the British fleet destroyed Iraqi "vessels," which were only Zodiac inflatable boats, and about the complete blackout about the police repression of an antiwar demonstration in Paris. TV, radio, and newspaper coverage of the Brussels hearing itself, however, was extensive in French, Flemish, Dutch, German, Arabic, and English.

In Italy, a series of seminars and public inquests on the Gulf War were conducted in Naples, Milan, and Rome. The main Commission hearings took place in Rome on January 17–18, 1992. Commission members charged that the Italian government obscured its military deployments by portraying them as police actions to fulfill UN resolutions. In fact, members charged, these were acts of war, which Item 11 of the Italian Constitution forbids.

I made a presentation for the Commission at a major meeting in Berlin on November 29, 1991. It was followed by hearings the next day in Stuttgart and later in Erfurt in January 1992. The Stuttgart meeting was highly emotional because that city is the key U.S. military center in Europe. Hundreds of American peace activists were present among a greater number of Germans, including prominent German political figures. Participants became so committed to the idea of the War Crimes Tribunal that they decided to charter a plane to fly to New York for the Tribunal hearings. Unfortunately, our capacity to house, provide hospitality for, and seat in the Tribunal auditorium such a large group from one city was not adequate. In the end, ten people came from Stuttgart and made a fine contribution at the Tribunal, with Dr. Alfred Mechtersheimer serving on the Tribunal panel.

In Stuttgart, Dr. Mechtersheimer, along with other Germans, addressed the U.S. role in a "new world order," arguing that the United States is not capable of leading the world to peace because it tops the list in every category of social problem. Peace researcher Johan Galtung observed that the United States has intervened internationally some 200 times since 1804, and has experienced at most only 20 consecutive years without war.

The hearing was almost entirely in German. The weather was chilly, with a heavy ground fog. Forty-five years earlier, less than 100 miles away and under similar conditions, I had observed the Nuremberg trials as a young marine. That memory filled me with profound concern for human destiny as I listened to German voices condemn my country for war crimes.

The London December 1991 hearing was in that city's Turkish

Kurdish Center in the heart of a large, predominantly Middle Eastern neighborhood. A crowd of over 1,000 jammed into the hall and hundreds more milled around outside for hours. The proceedings were translated simultaneously into Kurdish for the several hundred Kurds present, and the hearing had strong support from the community. The Turkish and Kurdish communities were aware that in Turkey itself, Kurds and others had risked their lives to take part in Commission hearings. The eyewitness testimony included some very painful accounts of death, destruction, and repression.

The hearings in England enjoyed considerable political support. Testimony was given by senior Labor MP Tony Benn. Labor MP Tam Dalyell submitted material on the complicity of Prime Minister Margaret Thatcher in the war planning. Eddy Newman, a Member of the European Parliament for Manchester, testified at the Manchester hearing about the resistance to the war within Parliament. Labor Party members who had opposed the Labor leadership's acquiescence in war were forced to resign from important party positions. Evidence from a union member in Manchester showed that similar retaliation occurred in the unions.

British media coverage of the hearings was similar to that in the United States. The sponsors had very good media connections, but were usually frustrated in their efforts to be heard. BBC World Service agreed to a 15-minute interview with me after the London hearing. I left the meeting early to make the BBC deadline, only to be kept waiting until the next segment, and finally having my interview cut to three minutes of hostile and uninformed questions.

Many of the hearings were subjected to intense government opposition. The hearing in Jordan, planned as a major source of testimony from refugee camps, Kuwait, and Iraq, was canceled by the government after months of preparation in a sweeping ban of political meetings in Amman. This city, with its very committed sponsoring group, had previously been home to the International Commission's regional organizing office that had organized to support and assist our fact-finding trip to Iraq and to refugee camps in April 1991.

Four Commission hearings were held in Turkey. All were subjected to government threats and harassment. The meeting hall in the Kurdish town of Cizre, near the border with Syria and Iraq, was machine-gunned two days before the event. Police closed off roads into the city, placed it under 24-hour curfew, and barricaded the streets during the day of the meeting to prevent people from attending. An armored car cruised the empty streets outside throughout the day. Sniper squads were on rooftops and stationed around street corners in the vicinity. Dozens of people stayed overnight in the hall to make sure they could attend. Another meeting was held in a small, crowded mosque.

There was sporadic shooting every day in the area. Civilian deaths from army gunfire were frequent. We visited the home of Hedaya Dilce, a 16-year-old Kurdish girl whom Turkish soldiers had killed 36 hours earlier during indiscriminate firing over the rooftops of her neighborhood to keep people inside. She was placing bedding on the roof for her family to sleep in the cooler open air and was hit with three bullets. She bled to death during the several hours it took to get an ambulance through the curfew.

The hearing in Istanbul, Turkey was originally scheduled for a stadium with a 6,000-person capacity, but the government forced its cancellation. The meeting was moved to the 500-seat Journalists' Association hall, and was packed despite the intense heat. Outrage at the U.S. assault was expressed by every speaker. It will take years of good relations to overcome such hostility.

Government opposition to Commission hearings arose more from Turkey's war against the Kurds than concern over the U.S. assault on Iraq. The Kurdish capital of Diyarbakir, where a major Commission hearing was held, had four weeks earlier been the site of the massacre by Turkish police of mourners at the funeral of Vezad Aydin, a Kurdish leader who had been assassinated by a right-wing death squad. Sixty-three Kurdish activists were murdered by death squads in southeast Turkey in June and July.

A movie theater jammed with nearly 1,000 people heard testimony and statements for nearly six hours in 100-degree temperature. Emotions were even hotter. The hall was in a near-constant uproar at the reports of the slaughter in Iraq and the analyses of the meaning for the Kurdish people. Two generations earlier, in the wake of World War I, it seemed that Woodrow Wilson's call for self-determination of peoples would certainly bring about the millennia-old dream of a Kurdish state. Now in the summer of 1991, the Kurds seemed more endangered than ever, and their sovereignty more remote.

The Commission's work involved tens of thousands of participants. Hundreds of organizations formally supported its work. The volume of data developed was enormous. In addition to the hearings and reports they generated, published materials from UN agencies, governments, scores of private organizations and institutions, press clips, TV and radio tapes, scores of books, and hundreds of articles were gathered. Summaries of the evidence, reports, and other materials were provided the Tribunal members over a period of several months before it commenced deliberations.

THE TRIBUNAL

Tribunal members first met together on February 27, 1992, in New York City. Most had attended one or more Commission hearings. All had reviewed the extensive summaries, reports, documents, and pictures provided by the Commission. Together they considered the evidence and attended proceedings for two days. On February 29, the anniversary of the official end of the war, the International War Crimes Tribunal members presided at the final hearing held in the auditorium of the Martin Luther King, Jr. High School. There were 22 judges present from 18 nations. They were from all races and many religions. Six were women. The oldest was 88; several were in their thirties. They included a former deputy prime minister, elected national legislators, sitting judges, a British Lord, numerous lawyers, the head of a human rights organization, an agronomist-ecologist, the president of a labor union, political party heads, an African-American Vietnam veteran, a peace council president, and several lawyers' association presidents. Several had endured lengthy prison terms for acts of conscience and political beliefs. Many are authors, one of more than 40 books.

When the Tribunal announced its unanimous decision of guilt against all defendants on all 19 charges after nearly six hours of testimony and reports, the 1,500 people filling the auditorium stood, and spontaneous, thunderous applause continued for many minutes.

Like Commission hearings in Jordan and Turkey, the Tribunal, though meeting in a country that espouses freedom of speech and expression, was subject to government attempts to disrupt it. The actions taken, while less severe than in Jordan and Turkey, were no less obvious. The morning before the event, with virtually all of the judges in town, one of the New York Commission's major Arab-American organizers, who had been under surveillance for weeks, was arrested. He was able to officiate at a Tribunal session hearing only after feverish legal activity secured his release on the eve of the hearing.

While receiving extensive coverage in the international press, the U.S. major media blackout of the Tribunal was almost complete. The first war crimes tribunal in history charging a victorious government leadership with war crimes on its own soil required some notice. Before the Tribunal meeting, I wrote to editors, news executives, and reporters about the work of the Commission, the Tribunal membership, and the final judgment to be rendered, urging them to be present to report the event. One internationally known and respected journalist, when asked by a Commission staffer in a

195

follow-up call to attend, replied, "What do you want me to do, lose my job?"

After the hearing, members of the media were sent copies of the final judgment and were again asked to inform the public about the Tribunal and its decision. The judges themselves, their history, position, and experience were significant stories. The voluminous evidence that had always been presented to the media as it was obtained had been ignored from the beginning. After five months of saturation propaganda for U.S. arms, demonization of an enemy, and celebration of violence, the U.S. media had never reported what happened to the people of Iraq, their cities, and their future. Like the scene in the Al-Rashid hotel lobby on the morning of January 15, 1991, where U.S. media personalities checked out on the slaughter of Iraq, the American media failed to report the Commission investigation of what happened and the Tribunal decision that war crimes were committed.

RECOMMENDATIONS FOR PEACE

During the hearings, recommendations on actions needed to prevent the recurrence of the tragic assault were received from many sources. The recommendations were addressed to the UN, international agencies, Congress, the President, other institutions of the United States, various international nongovernmental organizations, international and U.S. media, private groups, and the court of world opinion.

More than 50 proposals were set forth by the Commission for the Tribunal in a lengthy "Working Paper for Peace." They appear, somewhat modified, in the final chapter of this book. Their breadth covers most experience with war and ideas for its prevention. All are related in varying ways to evidence received by the Commission and experiences in or related to the Gulf crisis.

The first set are emergency proposals and address the immediate needs of Iraq. They propose the all-important lifting of sanctions, as well as providing adequate emergency food and needed supplies to the country and removal of the thousands of unexploded bombs that continue to claim lives. They call for the withdrawal of all foreign forces from the area. Justice demands that the needs of the Iraqi people be addressed.

The second set are general proposals, which fall into six areas. Many are ideas as old as history. Some have been carefully analyzed and set forth in great detail elsewhere. Many have been addressed

196

and partially developed by the UN and other institutions. Some are new. All are intended to stimulate a dynamic process of change.

The general recommendations call for measures designed to prevent further military assaults, oppression, and exploitation. Among other things, they are designed to end militarism and the arms race, and to reduce national armies; abolish nuclear weapons and technologies of destruction; promote peace through justice; reform the UN; establish a permanent War Crimes Tribunal; facilitate the conversion from militarism to economic justice; institute media reform; and establish internationally coordinated grassroots organizations and an International Peoples Assembly.

The whole undertaking was an effort to determine what happened in Iraq, how many people were killed, and who is responsible; to hold guilty parties accountable; and most important, to prevent such murderous acts from occurring again. The effort was premised on the faith that the truth can make us free, and that free we will act to establish lasting peace.

Without the truth, the U.S. public can be swayed into accepting and supporting further genocidal wars. Almost 500 years ago the Spanish people, with little access to information, supported the conquistadors who followed Columbus in the vast European intervention into the Western Hemisphere. They brought glory, empire, slaves, and the promise of wealth. But Columbus and others brutalized the "Indians," as he called them. He sought only their wealth and the way to Cathay.

But the Spanish people heard from powerful voices, including Bartolomé de las Casas, urging the humanity of the Indians and the immorality of their slaughter, and resisting their enslavement and the theft of their lands and properties. The Black Legend of Spain's crimes against the people of the Americas arose from the deaths of millions of Indians under the swords of Cortez and Pizarro and from the pestilences they spread from Mexico to Chile.

Millions died in Espanola and Cuba alone. Columbus described them as beautiful, healthy, gentle people without weapons, but saw them only as a source of gold and otherwise dispensible. The heroic struggle of Las Casas to save the Indians, persuading two Popes and Charles V of their equal humanity, made him, we are told by Eduardo Galeano, the most hated man in the Americas. But Las Casas showed that the essential moral issues could be seen by the participants in the great enterprise of empire and that people of courage and compassion could resist force, fear, and falsehood. Columbus was what the Spaniards were. Las Casas was what they could have been. Americans must choose what they want to be.

The choice will be important to the future of the world. A Simi Valley jury in Ventura County, California, hearing the case against police officers who were filmed brutally beating Rodney King, decided it is no crime for white police to assault poor blacks. The American public celebrating the slaughter in Iraq seems to have decided it is no crime for U.S. military forces to assault a whole nation of poor people of color. The Tribunal believed otherwise. Its judges and the thousands who worked with the Commission have struggled to show how we can avoid the human catastrophe that lies ahead.

More surely than the Spanish people in the decades after 1500 could see that their government's policies could take millions of innocent Indian lives, the American people today know that unless their government changes, militarism, hunger, and violence will cost hundreds of millions of innocent lives in the years ahead.

A billion more people will be on the planet by the year 2000. Nearly 80 percent will have beautiful, darker skin. The great majority of these will be desperately poor and will live in poor countries, though millions will live in poverty in rich America. They will be condemned to short lives of hunger, illness, ignorance, idleness, violence, pain, and misery unless humanity acts now to address the crisis caused by the use of force to exploit the planet and deepen the gulf between rich and poor.

CHAPTER 11

The Fire This Time

WAR was the only means by which the Bush administration could achieve its secret goals in the Middle East and establish unchallengeable control over the vast oil resources of the region. The destruction of Iraq—not its mere military power, but its political, social, and economic coherence—was the clear and consistent objective of President Bush's acts. The United States had started toward that goal long before the first day of the Bush presidency in January 1989, and continued its acts to further debilitate Iraq through the summer of 1992. This was a war of aggression to secure American domination of the Persian Gulf and, through its oil, the world beyond.

To see this clearly, it is necessary to observe what the United States did. We must follow the cynical advice of former Attorney General John Mitchell: Watch what the government does, not what it says. When the course of American conduct is identified, conditions in Iraq today can be seen as the natural, foreseeable, and intended consequence of those acts. Then, if we return to what was said contemporaneously, the words will be understood as designed to variously obscure, justify, and facilitate what was being done. Truth was as alien to the words as right was to the deeds.

PRELUDE TO THE FIRE

As evidence proves beyond a reasonable doubt, the United States planned its assault on Iraq for years, and provoked Iraq to invade Kuwait to justify a U.S. reaction. This was a crime against peace. It is very difficult for Americans, saturated with propaganda and wanting to love our country, to accept such a conclusion. However, a review of the ways of nations since the time of the Trojan horse makes this conclusion more than believable.

In World War I, the British easily misled Arab leaders into attacking their Ottoman rulers, who supported the Central Powers against the Allies, by promising them national independence. "False premises" is what T. E. Lawrence called these inducements in the *Seven Pillars of Wisdom*, after he learned England and France never intended to permit truly independent Arab states in the region after they dismembered the Ottoman Empire.

A generation later, Arabs and the world were deceived again, this time by British, French, and Israeli propaganda. Nasser had emerged in Egypt as the strongest Arab leader of the century. He called for Arab unity and took control of the Suez Canal. In 1956, England, France, and Israel concealed their joint plan in which Israel attacked Egypt claiming Egyptian provocation and France and England were to intervene to seize the Suez Canal and depose Nasser. In one stroke, the colonial powers would control the canal and rid Israel of its most dangerous Arab opposition. The plan and the brief war were only partially successful because President Eisenhower refused to approve it. Yet the American and European publics remained largely persuaded that Egypt was the aggressor.

From the mid-1950s through 1978, when the Shah of Iran served as its regional surrogate, the United States had a powerful presence in the region. The United States sold Iran more than $20 billion in military equipment between 1972 and 1977. Iraq was then a Soviet client, armed primarily with eastern bloc military equipment. With a population three times greater and a larger, better armed military, Iran easily overshadowed Iraq in the 1970s. Turkey, another neighbor and a NATO member, was even larger than Iran. Also allied with the United States, it had the largest standing army in NATO.

United States foreign policy depended on control of Iranian and Turkish military forces. It had strategic missile sites in both countries and key observation and monitoring locations for Soviet missile and nuclear testing. This was backed up with multibillion-dollar electronic surveillance facilities, NATO facilities, and strategic air bases in Saudi Arabia. Behind this commitment was the recognition of the importance of the Persian Gulf's oil resources to economic and geopolitical power throughout the world. The American policy toward the region was summed up in a December 1977 report issued by Senator Henry Jackson's Energy and Natural Resources committee just before the turbulent events of 1978 in Iran which led to the Shah's downfall in February 1979: "A U.S. commitment to the defense of oil resources of the Gulf and to political stability in the region must constitute one of the most vital and enduring interests of the U.S."

By mid-1980, mass desertions, assassinations, seizures of military equipment by local paramilitary groups, and fear of an angry Iranian public left the Shah's once-powerful military paralyzed and a fraction of its former size. After the fall of the Shah, the accession of the Ayatollah Khomeini, the seizure of U.S. Embassy personnel as hostages by students in Teheran, and the Soviet invasion of Afghanistan, Iraq attacked Iran in the fall of 1980 with U.S. encouragement. Henry Kissinger expressed U.S. policy when he said he hoped that the Iraqis and Iranians would kill each other. A war in which each country inflicted heavy casualties on the other was seen as the best way of protecting U.S. interests in the region. Major aid from Saudi Arabia, the Soviet Union, and Warsaw Pact countries enabled Iraq to sustain the war. And the U.S. approach of aiding both sides in the conflict prolonged a tragic war that cost the lives of a million young Iranians and Iraqis.

By 1988, the Soviet economy was nearing collapse. Its armed forces began to withdraw from Afghanistan. An exhausted Iran agreed to peace with an exhausted Iraq. The United States saw its first opportunity to move militarily in the Gulf without risking Soviet resistance or unified opposition from nations in the region.

Iraq, despite high casualties in the Iranian war and a staggering war debt, was still an emerging industrial country, building a comparatively strong national economy with its oil revenues. It was still underdeveloped, with a per capita income of only $2,500 for its 16 million people. It sought an international oil policy that would return greater revenues to petroleum-producing nations, at higher costs to developed nations. Because of its independent political position and its relatively large army, Iraq limited and threatened regional domination by the United States, Israel, and Europe. To secure domination, it was necessary for the United States to destroy any capacity for regional military action by Iraq, reduce its people to impoverishment, and control its oil resources and influence on world oil production and prices.

During 1988, the United States completed new military plans for direct intervention in the Persian Gulf against Iraq. The impotence of the USSR, the isolation and debilitation of Iran, and alliances with Saudi Arabia, Turkey, and Israel reduced the risk of regional government opposition to U.S. intervention. The United States proceeded with a strategy to further isolate, aggravate, and finally provoke Iraq into acts that would justify an assault.

A necessary ingredient in this strategy was the demonization of Saddam Hussein, only recently a U.S. ally. For the people of America and Europe, conditioned by generations of orientalism in literature, which treated Arab peoples as exotic, irrational, cruel, and cunning, this was an easy task. The American people and world opinion had also to be convinced that Iraq had a powerful military machine that intended to overrun the region. This was quickly accomplished because the sales of billions of dollars of arms in the region over several decades had created the assumption that huge Arab armies with advanced weapons systems were capable of waging high-technology war.

Suddenly, little Iraq was said to have the fourth-largest army in the world, capable of chemical warfare and nearing nuclear weapons production. The man whose forces the United States had recently supported against Iran became totally evil. Those who had criticized U.S. support for Iraq's aggression against Iran were called supporters of this newly discovered Hitler when they protested U.S. moves against Iraq.

If President Bush had wanted to prevent Iraq from invading Kuwait, would he have failed to inform Saddam Hussein? Instead, the Bush administration was sending other signals. Assistant Secretary of State Kelly and Ambassador Glaspie made it clear to the Iraqi leader that his dispute with Kuwait was a regional matter. Just four months before the invasion of Kuwait, Kelly had called Saddam Hussein a "force for moderation." The American public may not pay much attention to what Assistant Secretaries say, but foreign heads of state do. Knowing the critical importance of Persian Gulf oil resources to the European, Japanese, and U.S. economies, is it conceivable that the United States would have failed in the face of obvious military buildup by Iraq to act to prevent an invasion—if it wanted to prevent that invasion?

The stunning alacrity with which President Bush seized on Iraq's invasion to announce military support for Saudi Arabia, pressure the Saudis to accept it, rush forces to the scene, mobilize an all-out military and political assault, and prohibit useful negotiation is by itself convincing evidence of his intention to destroy Iraq. President Bush, though not interested in calling for the study of the spread of AIDS in Africa, though spending a pittance on AIDS in the United States, though neglecting homelessness in American cities, though unwilling to act when a democratically elected president is overthrown in nearby Haiti, never hesitated in his rush to cripple Iraq.

Beginning in August 1990, the world watched for nearly six months while the United States built its military machine in the Persian Gulf. Initially and for several months President Bush proclaimed the U.S. purpose was wholly defensive, when the forces being deployed were preparing for offensive military action. While many world leaders worked to the point of exhaustion to find a peaceful solution, President Bush insisted there would be no negotiation, no compromise, no facesaving, and no reward for aggression. This stance violated the heart of the UN Charter, which seeks peaceful resolution of disputes.

Iraq simply waited, much like a wild animal frozen in the headlights of an oncoming juggernaut. From August 12, 1990, Saddam Hussein repeatedly tried to communicate his desire to negotiate all issues, including withdrawal from Kuwait. The media ignored or distorted his offers, ridiculed them as false and diversionary, and trumpeted President Bush's characterization of Iraq's final effort to negotiate withdrawal as a "cruel hoax." In a November 1990 meeting with Saddam Hussein, I discussed with him the disastrous consequences of the Vietnam War, particularly for the Vietnamese. They lost more than one million people, and 15 years after the war were more impoverished by U.S. sanctions than they were by U.S. military action during the war. I spoke of the U.S. body counts which proudly overstated Vietnamese dead, and President Johnson's sad reference to a Vietnamese casualty as "another coonskin on the wall." During the meeting, Hussein observed that Islam defined a prophet as someone "who can love people who are far away." He was to learn that George Bush is no prophet.

The American public had a unique opportunity to mobilize opinion against aggression by its own government. For better than five months it saw all the familiar signals that Washington intended to take it to war. Yet most Americans only watched while their government continued its military buildup and increased its threats against Iraq.

Still, new coalitions of peace groups, comprised of African-American and Latino community groups, labor organizations, religious groups, environmentalists, and human rights groups, organized large protests. Tens of thousands of protesters marched against military action in cities all over the United States.

Some of the most courageous protests originated within the military itself. As the mobilization reached into every American community, hundreds of active duty and reserve sailors, soldiers, and marines refused to obey the callup. The media, presenting the confrontation as a struggle between good and evil, showed America's proud weaponry moving toward war, usually ignored the actions of the objectors and rarely suggested the lonely heroism of those who risked their freedom because they opposed the war. Only after the war, when the Pentagon moved harshly in nearly every conscientious objector case, did the press carry the story, telling the country celebrating the slaughter what a serious thing it is to disobey authority. However, the real story was the failure of American institutions in the rush to war.

The American political system failed the people. As President Bush pushed the country toward war, Congress was paralyzed and acted as if the prospect of a major military venture was not its concern. Although the Constitution delegates to Congress exclusive power to declare war, on January 9, 1991 President Bush proclaimed he had the "constitutional authority" to act without Congressional approval. By placing half a million U.S. troops in the Persian Gulf, and by using bribery and coercion to obtain approval from the UN Security Council to use all means necessary to expel Iraq from Kuwait, President Bush made it almost impossible for Congress to act against war.

President Bush's attitude toward Congress also reflected his confidence in the military outcome. After Vietnam it would have been utter recklessness to unilaterally lead the country into a military engagement that might be protracted or incur substantial casualties. But this time the President knew that the war would be short, that Iraq would be easily overwhelmed, and that the rewards would be great.

Executive control of the facts and its deceptive use of that power; the influence of military suppliers, oil companies, and transnational corporations; the powerful Israel lobby; the shrill *cri de guerre* of the media; and recognition that throughout U.S. history no political leader has prevailed by opposing war, joined to overwhelm the Congress. Congress failed its constitutional duty and acquiesced in the presidential use of force to destroy Iraq. Its utility in avoiding future presidential militarism will require a new assertion of constitutional power and political courage that only intense public insistence is likely to create.

The media also failed the public. It was more openly bellicose than the President. While he needed to avoid activating public opposition to his plans, and lied and misled the people to gain time and acceptance for his purpose, the press beat the drums for war. There can have been few more shameful violations of journalistic integrity on an important public issue than the frenetic special pleadings of A. M. Rosenthal, former executive editor of the *New York Times*, and columnist William Safire, urging President Bush to attack and destroy Iraq. For their part, the *New York Times* editors were so blinded by their desire to see Iraq crushed that they editorialized eight months after the slaughter — as thousands were dying from malnutrition, contaminated water, lack of medicine, and disease — that the Gulf War was just.

President Bush knew he could rely on the media to establish the various falsities needed to facilitate the U.S. attack on Iraq. The economic interests that own the media and profit from U.S. militarism had already demonstrated their near-total control of opinion-making power, having created overwhelming popular support for the massive assault on Grenada in 1983, the sneak attack on Libya in 1986, and the brutal invasion of Panama in 1989. The American people were reduced to accepting, even cheering, any absurdity said to justify using military force for what they were told was their benefit. The patent falsity, immorality, and illegality of the justifications for the war proclaimed by the press, and the clearly indiscriminate and wanton violence of the armed forces could be ignored only by a people blinded to the truth and conditioned to be unconcerned about the havoc wreaked on others by their forces.

The United Nations proved itself an even weaker hope for the world. Although created to end the scourge of war, in the fall of 1990 the UN was corrupted into an instrumentality of war by the United States. With Soviet influence disintegrating, most UN members experiencing economic hardship, and formerly nonaligned nations seeking favored status with the United States, the United States brazenly and publicly bribed and bullied nations for votes.

The U.S. used Resolution 678, for which it paid billions of dollars in cash and benefits to the Soviet Union, Egypt, and other nations, to destroy Iraq, though the resolution never mentioned the use of force and could not lawfully authorize attacks on civilians. Then, long after all Iraqi forces were destroyed or withdrawn from Kuwait, Resolution 678 was used as authority to blockade Iraq, killing tens of thousands of infants, children, the sick, and the elderly. There has been no effective effort at the UN to limit U.S. acts. Only radical reform can make the UN once again a hope for peace.

The appointed time for the assault on Samarra and its sister cities in Mesopotamia came as scheduled by President Bush. Scores of planes from remote places like Barksdale Air Force Base in Louisiana, Diego Garcia in the south Indian Ocean, England, Saudi Arabia, Turkey, and aircraft carriers in the Persian Gulf moved toward the cities of that ancient land.

THE FIRE COMES

On the night of January 16–17, 1991, the stars shone above, little changed since Hammurabi ruled from Babylon on the Euphrates 4,000 years earlier. The land remembered Ashurbanipal's great library with its collection of all existing writing from all known languages at Nineveh on the Tigris and its fabled Palace Without Rival of 3,000 years ago. The dreams of Alexander the Great died with him in Babylon as he strove to conquer the world over 2,000 years ago. Kublai Khan's brother Hulegu sacked Baghdad and executed the caliph in 1258; within two generations, the empire of the Khans was gone. And still the people tilled the earth, crowded into the cities, and absorbed the shards of the many cultures, races, energies, and imaginations that had populated the place.

The Tigris and Euphrates rivers flowed quietly toward the Gulf in the darkness of the early hours. The same stars silently witnessed another approach of human violence, unprecedented in its nature and intensity. The wind gently stirred the date palm fronds. In darkened cities, towns, and farms men, women, and children tried to sleep, not knowing what the night held for them. In Kuwait, the remaining population and Iraqi occupying forces backed up in southern Iraq by hundreds of thousands more waited for war. To the south, 540,000 U.S. troops and 150,000 from other countries were on alert, anxiously wondering what might happen to them, told they would engage a dangerous and powerful enemy in direct combat.

At 2:30 A.M. January 17, 1991 the bombs began to fall, and for 42 days U.S. aircraft attacked Iraq on an average of once every 30 seconds. U.S. technology smashed the cradle of civilization, leaving it crippled, and George Bush called it liberation.

The assault on Iraq was a war crime containing thousands of individual criminal acts virtually from beginning to end, as any violence against a defenseless adversary must.

President Bush voiced a different view. On July 1, 1992, the President appeared on CBS's national *This Morning* news, and angrily answered criticism of his policies and conduct toward Iraq. He described those who questioned what happened as "a bunch of people who want to redefine something that was noble and good — Desert Storm — and make it bad."

But look at what was done. Before 1991 was over, more than 250,000 Iraqis and thousands of other nationals were dead as a result of the attack. Most were civilian men, women, children, and infants.

U.S. war casualties, including those who died from U.S. "friendly fire," totaled 148, we are told. Out of an acknowledged 109,876 air sorties, total U.S. aircraft losses were 38, less than the accident rate during war games without live ammunition. The bombs dropped from those aircraft equaled the power of seven Hiroshima bombs. There was no war. There was only a premeditated, calculated slaughter of civilian life and defenseless soldiers.

Television networks turned the 42-day bombardment of Iraq into a running commercial for militarism and U.S. weapons systems. On television, the weapons' accuracy seemed miraculous and the U.S. omnipotent. However, on the ground, the immense air attack against Iraqi cities brought thousands of civilian casualties. Of the 88,500 tons of ordnance rained on Iraq, only 6,520 tons were precision-guided. Nearly 93 percent of the bombing was with dumb bombs, free falling from high altitudes, and no more accurate than the bombs dropped in World War II. The city of Basra was carpet-bombed by B-52s. The bombs killed indiscriminately, hitting Iraqis and others, Muslims and Christians, Kurds and Assyrians, young and old, men and women.

One of the great myths propagated by the Pentagon and the controlled media was that the surgical accuracy of U.S. weapons saved lives. This argument has been used before to justify U.S. violence against its enemies. When U.S. planes bombed the heart of crowded Tripoli in April 1986, Secretary of Defense Caspar Weinberger insisted that it was "impossible" that civilians were killed. In reality, nearly all of the hundreds of casualties were civilians.

What happened in the Gulf was an assault, not a war. There was no combat, no resistance, and few skirmishes. Iraq had no capacity to either attack or defend. It simply endured a pulverizing six-week assault. The U.S. did not lose a single B-52 in combat, as these planes dropped 27,500 tons of bombs. No Iraqi projectile penetrated a single Abrams tank, while the U.S. claimed to destroy 4,300 Iraqi tanks and 1,856 armored vehicles. There were over 1,500 verified kills of Iraqi tanks and armored vehicles by F-111s; the pilots came to call the sport "tank plinking." Finally, tanks and earth-moving equipment buried thousands of Iraqi soldiers — dead, wounded, and alive — while hundreds of tanks, armored vehicles, and artillery pieces and tons of ammunition were seized intact.

Bombs were dropped on civilians and civilian facilities all over Iraq. When I traveled through Iraq on the first anniversary of the bombing to revisit places I had seen during the bombing, I gathered statistics of civilian damage from Iraqi sources. The toll was devastating. Of all the assaults, those on the water and food supply were most deadly and revealing. The attack from the farm to the market was systematic and included every element essential to food production: irrigation, fertilizer, pesticides, tractors. Food importation, which provided 70 percent of the nation's requirements before the war, was vastly reduced by sanctions and other causes. Average daily caloric intake is less than half the prewar level. Malnutrition affects up to half the children in poorer urban areas. With the public debilitated from malnutrition, contaminated water, and disease, and with sanctions causing severe shortages of medical supplies, the Iraqi health care system is unable to care for the sick.

How many did the U.S. kill? General Colin Powell said it was not a figure he was terribly interested in. General William G. Pagonis, stating proudly that this was the first war in modern time where every screwdriver and every nail was accounted for, simultaneously defended General Schwarzkopf's policy against counting enemy dead. The generals knew but never mentioned that the Geneva Convention of 1949 required them not merely to count enemy dead, but to identify and honor them as well.

The U.S. government and members of the plutocracy are not as unconcerned with the number of Iraqi deaths as they portray. In the summer of 1991 in California's Bohemian Grove, where the rich, the powerful, and the political leadership gather for inspiration and information never shared with the people, former Navy Secretary John Lehman spoke on "smart" weapons. He told a gathering that the Pentagon estimated 200,000 Iraqis killed by the United States during the Gulf War. The public has never officially been told this — and would never have known at all if a *People* magazine journalist had not sneaked on to the Bohemian Grove compound.

Somehow, the number of Iraqi deaths has been a minuscule part of the debate over President Bush's handling of the Gulf War, perhaps because the slaughter of dark-skinned people by U.S. weaponry has become all too commonplace. On February 18, Brigadier General Richard Neal, while briefing reporters in Riyadh, observed that the United States wanted to be certain of speedy victory once they committed ground troops to "Indian Country." In two words, he revealed that the U.S. military honors its racist history and intended another slaughter of "savages."

Estimating the numbers of people killed by the U.S. assault is difficult and painful, yet critically important. Each life counts. To understate the casualties by counting only corpses actually found is to conceal the crime, diminish the lessons of history, and hide the truth. To overestimate casualties cheapens the horror of what actually happened by making the truth seem inadequate. Yet an accurate count is impossible under the circumstances, because powerful interests want to control this principal measure of the meaning of war.

Commission research, hearings, documentation, and analyses indicate between 125,000 and 150,000 Iraqi soldiers were killed. There is tragically an all-too-solid basis for believing the early reports of 100,000 military casualties, and in the European press, 200,000 killed. Did not the Pentagon state it would destroy the Iraqi military months before the assault? What could be expected from all that uncontested bombing?

As for civilians, organizations like Greenpeace and MEW, that were unable to send teams into Iraq during the bombing, have estimated less than 3,000 civilian deaths from bombing. The U.S. Census Bureau estimated 5,000 direct civilians deaths from the bombing, and tried to fire its researcher, Beth DaPonte, whose report set the figure at 13,000. But even the 13,000 figure requires a belief in the miraculous when the nationwide assault on civilian life is analyzed. How do you bomb and strafe throughout an entire country, make tens of thousands of sorties with missiles containing every kind of cluster bomb and antipersonnel weapon, destroy 8,400 homes, hundreds of vehicles on highways, thousands of shops, offices, stores, cafes, hotels, plants, bridges, train stations, bus depots, markets, schools, mosques, and bomb shelters, and not kill tens of thousands?

Experience, reason, and actual counts completed make the 150,000 minimum civilian deaths in Iraq since the beginning of the war until early 1992 a very conservative number. Although the American media saturated the U.S. with reports of Scud missile attacks on Israel, it showed little of the destruction in Iraq. Two Israelis died from two score Scud attacks. This was tragic. A quarter of a million Iraqis, military and civilian, died from 110,000 air attacks. This was genocidal.

How the Iraqis were killed was particularly cruel. Many thousands of civilians died from polluted water. Dehydrated from nausea and diarrhea, craving liquids, they had nothing to drink but more of the water that made them sick. Infants by the tens of thousands died from lack of milk formula and medication. The chronically ill, the sick, and the injured died from lack of medical care, medicine, clean water, and sanitation. Children, the weak, and the elderly died from diseases and malnutrition at several times the normal rate.

Soldiers died when bombs from planes they never saw rained down on them. Communications, supplies, water, food, and command were cut off. They risked death if they tried to move out. Deaths among the wounded ran very high because no evacuation was possible and little medical assistance was available. Thousands of wounded, sick, disoriented, and dead were buried when American tanks and earth-moving equipment bulldozed sand over their trenches. Thousands died from illegal fragmentation bombs, fuel-air explosives, and incineration along stretches of road with names like the seven-mile "Highway of Death." An even more horrific example was the destruction of a nameless 60-mile convoy reported 10 days after the ceasefire. Thousands of Iraqi soldiers died in assaults after the ceasefire. There was a continuing murderous intent to destroy units missed in the general slaughter.

An immediate result of the destruction of targets selected for aerial bombardment was the endangerment of the entire civilian population. Within days after the bombing began on January 17, there was no running water in any city, town, or village in Iraq. There was no electric power, and no communications. There was no air or rail transportation, and very limited bus, taxi, and private car transportation. The whole country was in constant jeopardy of a chance assault from the air.

The embargo imposed on Iraq since the war by the Sanctions Committee of the UN Security Council, at the insistence of the United States, is further evidence of the intention to destroy civilian life in Iraq. While the United States claims the embargo does not seriously affect the importation of food and medicine, the evidence to the contrary is indisputable. The sanctions constitute a continuing violation of humanitarian law.

By April 1991, doctors were finding among infants many cases of kwashiorkor, an extreme state of malnutrition in which the belly bloats and the arms, legs, and body wither. It had been virtually unknown to Iraqi doctors. By June, *Time* magazine reported that Qadisiyeh Hospital in Baghdad was admitting 10 new cases a day of infants suffering from marasmus, which it described as "an advanced case of malnutrition that causes a child's face and body to become as shriveled and haggard as those of a wizened old man." In October, the most extensive western medical survey of health conditions in Iraq, conducted by Harvard's International Study Team, found child mortality to be three times the prewar level. In February 1992, the director of Qadisiyeh Hospital showed me wards only 25 percent utilized because of the lack of medicine and equipment. He said that, even at this occupancy rate, there were 250 more deaths per month in the hospital than in 1990. Sadly, however, most deaths among the 800,000 population in the slums of Saddam City, which the hospital serves, went unreported.

Infant mortality doubled and in some areas tripled. About 750,000 infants were born in Iraq each year prior to the war. The infant mortality rate in 1989 was 69 per thousand live births. Doubling that rate for an entire year means an additional 51,750 infants would die as a direct result of U.S. bombing and sanctions. Mortality rates among children under five also rose drastically, threatening the majority and taking tens of thousands of young lives. Twenty-nine percent of all children were estimated to suffer severe malnutrition in the winter of 1991–1992. In the neighborhood of Qadisiyeh Hospital, the rate was a horrifying 50 percent. A large percentage of the survivors — a "stunted generation," according to one medical report — will live shorter lives with physical handicaps from malnutrition and disease caused by the destruction of water, sewage, health care, and medical facilities and the shortage of food and medical supplies caused by the embargo.

In late fall 1991, UNICEF predicted 170,000 Iraqi children under six years of age would suffer malnutrition by the end of the year unless drastic relief was provided, and that over half would die. OXFAM in late 1991 reported millions of Iraqis were suffering because of the strategic bombing of water, sewage, and health systems.

In the face of these facts, the UN Sanctions Committee acceded to U.S. insistence and maintained an embargo which limited food and medicine. A whole nation is being held hostage, tortured with threats, hunger, sickness, and violence, while scores of people die daily. The policy is genocidal and known to be so by the U.S. government and media, the informed public everywhere, the UN membership, and the Sanctions Committee.

President Bush repeatedly urged that aggression must not be rewarded. No one who wants peace will dispute that principle. But when it is remembered that the American assault on Panama eight months earlier was at least as lawless and considerably deadlier, his motives in Iraq must be reexamined. How does the United States explain Grenada, Libya, the Contras, and Panama? And what of the reward the Bush administration sought from the aggression against Iraq?

This is not to suggest that one case of aggression justifies another. It is to show the hypocrisy of the United States' argument and the political motives behind it. The United States wanted to crush Iraq, and it has. It wanted to dominate the region and its resources, and it does. The question now is whether this aggression will be rewarded, or whether the appropriate people will be held accountable.

U.S. EFFORTS TO JUSTIFY THE FIRE

Whether U.S. militarism continues to dominate U.S. foreign policy may depend in large measure on the ability of the government to persuade the American people that its attack on Iraq was justified and beneficial. It has used a wide range of arguments to make its case.

One such justification was destroying Iraq's purported nuclear arms program. During the fall of 1990, polls showed this was the one justification Americans approved for attacking Iraq. During the bombing of Iraq, the U.S. military announced the destruction of Iraq's chemical and nuclear production facilities, itself a war crime because of the risk to civilians of toxic emissions. And for a year after the assault on Iraq, claims of hidden nuclear and chemical warfare plants and equipment received more media coverage than did the catastrophe inflicted on the Iraqi people. However, in April 1992, experts of the International Atomic Energy Agency, after reviewing evidence brought back by UN inspection teams—who for months had seemed to validate the Bush administration's early hysteria over Iraq's nuclear capability—concluded that the Iraqi program was at least three years away from making one crude atomic weapon. As for Iraq's chemical weapons, it did not dare use those it possessed while the United States systematically destroyed the country.

The prevention of nuclear weapons proliferation must remain a high international priority. Yet the hypocrisy of the United States— the only country to have used the atomic bomb—claiming Iraq to be a nuclear threat is appalling. During the condemnation and destruction of Iraq, the huge U.S. inventories of nuclear, chemical, biological, and other weapons of mass destruction were ignored, as was the presence in the Gulf region of U.S. nuclear capability. Israel's stockpile of as many as 300 nuclear warheads and sophisticated rocketry in the heart of the volatile Middle East was rarely acknowledged. Still, the Security Council, its five permanent members the world's major nuclear powers and arms merchants, huddled over bleeding Iraq and threatened further attacks for its alleged hiding of nuclear materials. *Newsday* in February 1992 editorialized that if Iraq did not permit effective inspection, air attacks might be necessary to destroy suspected facilities.

Iraq's invasion of Kuwait and refusal to comply with UN resolutions requiring its withdrawal were presented as an aggression compelling worldwide action to liberate Kuwait by force. But for years, the United States had both committed and condoned far worse aggression and lawlessness. Israel's invasion of Lebanon, which took tens of thousands of lives; its continued occupation of southern Lebanon; its frequent military incursions into Lebanon which intensified during the long buildup against Iraq; and its renewed incursions in 1991 during the Madrid Middle East peace conference have all been supported and protected by the United States. Israel's failure over a period of decades to comply with UN resolutions requiring its withdrawal from occupied Palestine brought no serious U.S. action to achieve compliance.

The U.S. assault on Panama, less than eight months before Iraq invaded Kuwait, violated all the international laws applicable to the Persian Gulf, as well as Western Hemisphere laws and Panama Canal treaty rights. Whole neighborhoods were destroyed. Several thousand Panamanians were killed, while 300 Kuwaitis were killed during Iraq's invasion, according to the October 17, 1990 *New York Times*.

No nation introduced a resolution before the UN Security Council authorizing the removal of U.S. forces from Panama, though it was plain the invasion had nothing to with restoring "democracy." The United States took the Panama Canal Zone by force early in the century, maintained a constant major military presence there, and dominated the political and economic life of the country. After the invasion, the United States actively aided the corruption of democracy in Panama by spending millions to manipulate candidates and influence the election.

There was no justification for the brutal U.S. assault on Panama. U.S. soldiers have been assassinated since that invasion, as before. Drug traffic is greater than ever, politics more corrupt, social unrest and poverty more profound, and protests against the United States are at an historic high. The atrocities in Panama and the 40-year prison sentence imposed on Manuel Noriega have corrupted American justice instead of having brought freedom to Panama.

Neither the U.S. nor the Iraqi invasion was acceptable under international law, which seeks peaceful resolution of disputes. But Iraq had serious claims that it was victimized by British colonial acts in the late nineteenth century and after World War I, by Kuwaiti theft of its land and oil, and by U.S.-instigated economic warfare from 1988 through July 1990 through Kuwait.

Iraq, under its many names, was a coastal nation through the millennia. The ancient quinquereme of Nineveh left from there to sail the Persian Gulf and the Indian Ocean. But after World War I, Iraq was deprived of its coastal lands, now called Kuwait, by the British. Following World War II, Britain accelerated efforts to culturally separate Kuwait from Iraq. In 1945, the Iraqi school curriculum used in Kuwait was replaced with an Egyptian curriculum. Still, popular movements on both sides of the border sought integration. When Britain granted Kuwait independence in June 1961, Iraq's prime minister proclaimed that "Iraq considered Kuwait an integral part of its territory." Britain's response was to send military forces to Kuwait.

After the present Iraqi government came to power, it made continuous efforts to peacefully resolve its disputes over land and resources with Kuwait. The Iran–Iraq War interrupted this activity, but after the war ended, Iraq made new efforts to negotiate with Kuwait. However, a range of new disputes broke out: Kuwait wanted repayment on strict terms of the billions it had loaned Iraq during the war, although Iraq had defended Kuwait with the lives of its soldiers from threatened Iranian attacks. Iraq wanted Kuwait to stop draining oil from common pools that depleted Iraq's resources. And Kuwait's border checkpoints kept migrating north into Iraqi territory.

Most importantly, Kuwait constantly pressed for increased oil production quotas. This helped send the price of oil plummeting more than $10 per barrel, with disastrous effects on Iraq's economy. In May 1990, Saddam Hussein called Kuwait's actions "a kind of war against Iraq." In July, Iraqi foreign minister Tariq Aziz called them "tantamount to military aggression."

Whatever the merits of Iraq's claims against Kuwait, they were based on history and claims of right, not its colonial dominion over others.

Bush's cry for the liberation of Kuwait appealed to the love of freedom, as his objection to rewarding aggression appealed to the desire for justice. But the liberation of Kuwait was not the purpose for the U.S. assault on Iraq. Kuwait, created by England, had never been free. After crippling Iraq, the United States reinstated the Sabah family under its dominion and refurbished the Emir's palaces. The merits of Iraq's claims to sovereignty, land, and resources were ignored and then flouted by the UN's award to Kuwait of chunks of the long-disputed Rumailla oil field and part of Iraq's port Umm Qasr.

The cost to the Kuwaiti people and others living there of the U.S. "liberation" of the country was very great. On its return to power, the Kuwaiti government caused and condoned hundreds of summary executions, beatings, tortures, and arrests of people it found no longer desirable. Hundreds of thousands, including most Palestinians living in Kuwait, were forced to leave. People were prosecuted and threatened with execution for such lawful acts as working at a newspaper during the occupation. One man was condemned to death by a court for wearing a Saddam Hussein T-shirt and saved only when international protests caused the Emir to intervene.

Kuwait remains under the same arbitrary and authoritarian control of the handful of men who reigned before the invasion. One of the great problems of the poor nations of the Gulf region caused by the rich countries who use its oil is the control maintained over such vast wealth by a handful of irresponsible people relying on the continuing support of neocolonial powers. While hundreds of millions of Muslims live in unbearable poverty, powers like the United States place and protect resources that could alleviate suffering in the hands of a few who at a very high price serve their masters' interests. The arbitrary concentration of oil wealth in royal families in Saudi Arabia, Kuwait, the UAE, Brunei, and elsewhere is at war with human needs on the planet. U.S. war crimes committed in the name of liberty have restored an unacceptable condition in Kuwait. They will not bring peace, because they perpetuate injustice.

President Bush has claimed that Iraq refused to withdraw from Kuwait, and that force was required to make it do so. This claim ignores Bush's absolute refusal to negotiate. He frustrated all attempts to pursue a pacific settlement of the dispute, as required by the UN Charter. War was avoidable, but a negotiated settlement was vigorously opposed by those who wanted Iraq crippled. Columnists like William Safire urged an attack in the fall of 1990, fearing Iraq would withdraw from Kuwait and escape assault.

Saddam Hussein publicly stated repeatedly that every issue raised by UN resolutions was negotiable, including withdrawal from Kuwait. He told visiting leaders from the UN, heads of states, and people from public life that he wanted to negotiate, but the international media suffocated his appeals with silence and ridicule. He also told more than one visitor that he believed the United States intended to destroy him even if he withdrew. After I observed in a meeting with him in November 1990 that "Hiroshima happened," that disaster could also strike Iraq, and that he must act to save the Iraqi people, he expressed the belief that the United States would claim some provocation and attack if he began to withdraw. The history of U.S. fabrication of incidents — Tonkin Gulf, endangered medical students in Grenada, assaults on Americans in Panama — and the attacks on Iraqi troops far inside Iraq as they fled from Kuwait even after the ceasefire suggest he may have been right.

The U.S. claim that its important national security interests required Iraq to withdraw is a continuation of the colonial claim to Third World resources and dominion. This dominion has been realized by the establishment of a major military presence in the Persian Gulf. Bahrain alone is "de facto headquarters for the biggest U.S. naval armada assembled since World War II," as the *New York Times* noted on July 10, 1992. But Iraq is halfway around the world from us. The United States has no rights there. Rich countries have developed an unhealthy dependency on Persian Gulf oil that threatens both peace and the environment. It has also added to the impoverishment of the masses in Third World countries, placing power in brutal anti-democratic royal families and military dictators who at a price protect the interests of rich countries. If developed countries require oil from poor countries, they ought to pay for it, not take it by subterfuge or force. They ought to respect the people in those countries and their right to choose their own governments. They should not impose tyrannies that oppress these people.

The arguments advanced by the U.S. justifying war could be made only in an environment of intense prejudice and great ignorance. None can possibly justify the slaughter that occurred. Iraq's wrong — invading Kuwait — cannot justify the much greater wrongs of destroying Iraq, damaging Kuwait, disrupting the lives of millions of people in the Middle East and around the world, and signaling to the whole world that violence is master in the new world order as in the old.

THE FIRE GOES ON

Any rational people who want peace will demand that governments act diligently to resolve conflicts by peaceful means and renounce the resort to force. They will see the error of the advice of the anonymous Athenian Stranger in Plato's dialogue on *The Laws*, followed by nearly all governments with power, that sound leadership "orders war for the sake of peace." This advice has led to interminable war. Cleinas understood the purpose of such power when he replied to the Stranger, "I am greatly mistaken if war is not the entire aim and object of our institutions."

Beyond efforts to both deny and justify the destruction of Iraq, there is an enormous propaganda campaign to convince world opinion that great benefits have followed from it, that the ends justify the means. This argument ignores Martin Luther King, Jr.'s recognition that the means used must be harmonious with the end sought if they are to lead toward it. The means are inherent in the ends.

It is the means we experience. They are what happens. The ends are never clear, and never come. When Arabs, Muslims, and other dark-skinned people of the world see the violent means the United States used to slaughter Iraqis, how are they to assume their lives are valued? When military leaders, analysts, and scientists in Japan, Germany, and other nations more dependent on Persian Gulf oil than the United States see the technological capabilities of U.S. arms on CNN, what are they likely to demand of their policy makers?

The United States refused to permit the underlying problems of the region, which gave rise to human rights violations including hostage taking, to be directly addressed. It permitted Syria to expand its occupation of Lebanon as a price for its acquiescence to the assault on Iraq. Human rights violations by allies, including long standing police-state practices in Syria, Saudi Arabia, and Kuwait, were ignored, just as violations in Iraq itself, described in reports by Middle East Watch and Amnesty International in the year before August 2, 1990, had been ignored. The question of Palestine, Arab relationships with Israel, the vast military purchases burdening the region, the segregation of dire poverty and enormous oil wealth, the sovereignty of Lebanon, rising religious fundamentalism, the plight of minorities including Kurds and foreign workers — all of these problems were worsened by the Gulf war.

The deaths of thousands in Iraq after the ceasefire — primarily Shiites, Iraqi and Turkish Kurds, and Palestinians — all flowing from U.S. aggression and calls for uprisings, are too remote to arouse concern or anger unless Iraq can be blamed. The significant growth of religious fundamentalism, most prominent in Algeria, Tunisia, and Pakistan but also present in Egypt, Jordan, Saudi Arabia, Afghanistan, and former Soviet republics, fuels deep fears and prejudices. Yet, it is claimed to be unrelated to the destruction of a Muslim nation by foreign forces.

To argue that the war finally brought the Palestinians to the negotiating table with Israel is also incorrect. First, it assumes that the present negotiations have peace as their purpose. Second, it excuses the prior refusal of Israel to meet with Palestinian leaders and the failure of the United States and the UN to try to achieve that goal when the Palestinians had the ability to insist on their rights. After the war, Palestinians were in desperate straits. They had lost major financial support for Palestinian refugees in Lebanon and relief in the occupied territories that had been provided by Saudi Arabia, Kuwait, and the UAE. Income sent to the occupied territories from hundreds of thousands of Palestinians employed in Kuwait, Iraq, and Saudi Arabia was gone. Nearly 100,000 jobs in Israel to which Palestinians commuted daily from the West Bank were terminated. The long curfew in the occupied territories had prevented farmers from planting and tending fields and reduced economic productivity and commerce.

The Palestinians were thus forced to renounce their leadership and negotiate not in the interest of peace, but for their own subjugation. They were not allowed to choose their own negotiators. How can any peace conference be deemed fair if a major participant cannot

choose its own representation? They were forced to endure new seizures and settlements on their lands during the negotiations. How
can any peace conference succeed if one participant is so powerful
it can continue to seize land of another during the conference? Israel's repression in the occupied territories and military raids in Lebanon increased during the meetings. Is peace possible when parties
are coerced to accept conditions that deny justice, when they are
forced to submit to the conditions of power?

"War for the sake of peace" was another justification for the attack
on Iraq. Indeed, it has been a recurrent practice in the Middle East.
In the late 1970s, Israel initiated daily attacks against Lebanese villages that it claimed were bases for terrorist attacks. After more than
180 consecutive days of assaults, Israeli Chief of Staff General Rafael
Eitan was asked how the Israeli policy of "preemptive" strikes was
working. "Wonderfully," he replied, "in this entire time there has
not been a single terrorist attack in Israel." His answer ignored the
terror wreaked on the Lebanese, and his evaluation of the military
effect of the policy was incorrect. Palestinians continued to resist,
and Israel continued to attack. Two years later, Israel invaded Lebanon, killing tens of thousands and permanently occupying the southern part of the country.

The consequences of the Gulf War were disastrous beyond the immediate deaths and destruction inflicted.

Arms sales soared in the region after the Gulf War. While President Bush counseled restraint in weapons sales to the Middle East in
May 1991, in the following year, the United States alone sold $8.5
billion in arms in the region, excluding sales to Israel and Egypt. It
contracted with Saudi Arabia to deliver 72 advanced F-15s for an additional $5 billion. This compared to U.S. sales in the region of $15.4
billion during the five-year period 1985–1989, with $6.1 billion go-
ing to Israel, $5 billion to Saudi Arabia, and $2.9 billion to Egypt.
Saudi Arabia had received an unprecedented $14.8 billion in arms
from August 1990 through December 1991. In the year following the
war, the United States made two-thirds of all arms sales in the region. For many years the major arms purchaser in the world, the region seemed headed toward greater instability and more dangerous
conflicts after the United States destroyed Iraq.

Nor was direct violence by U.S. forces necessarily over. By the anniversary of the beginning of the bombing of Iraq, it was conventional wisdom in the United States that President Bush would act to
remove Saddam Hussein from power well before the presidential
election in November 1992. The war was seen as a triumph without
victory, marred by the survival of the demonized Saddam.

In fact, the United States was doing all it could to weaken Iraq. Sanctions were killing 300 children a day in April 1992, over a year after Iraq left Kuwait. That same month, the UN border demarcation committee awarded pieces of Iraq to Kuwait: part of its main port to the Gulf and parts of the oil-rich Rumailla oil field. Not long after that it was revealed that the United States was flooding the Iraqi economy with counterfeit currency, driving down the value of the dinar. As the United States used the UN to occupy northern Iraq to the 36th parallel, United States' planes fire-bombed Iraqi wheat and grain crops around the Kurdish city of Mosul in June 1992.

As the CIA worked to create the impression that the United States was threatened by Iraq's continuing efforts to build nuclear weapons, the Pentagon meanwhile was busy downgrading the number of casualties from the first assault. Its plans for supporting uprisings within Iraq, for renewed bombing, and even for a ground invasion became common media fare before the spring of 1992.

New interest in building armies in Europe independent of NATO and the nourishment of militarism in Japan may prove the most dangerous long-range results of the Gulf War. The exposure of the impotence of the Soviet Union and its submission to the will of the United States may have accelerated its disintegration. The spread of violence and instability among its former republics, the international access to its nuclear technology, and the loss of central control over its thousands of nuclear warheads are grave threats for the future.

The further strain on the U.S. economy and the appearance of Desert Storm veterans in the ranks of the homeless in American cities are tragic costs for the homefront. The failure of any public outcry at the cacophony of U.S. military threats against Iraq, Libya, North Korea, Cuba, and others suggests that if the American people are sensitive to such horror, they are unwilling or unable to act to prevent a recurrence.

One of the so-called benefits of the destruction of Iraq was proclaimed in front-page stories across the country some months after the bombing ceased. "Gulf War Gives Boost to U.S. Self Confidence," one story announced, "Americans Have New Faith in Themselves." A former State Department official now employed by the Rand Corporation was heard to say the war gave "a boost to the whole idea of competence."

The moral impoverishment of finding human benefit from such appalling human cost cannot be laid at the feet of leadership alone. The people, deprived of historical knowledge, contemporary fact, democratic power, and political wisdom, victimized by a culture that glorifies violence and worships Mammon, accepts the equation.

Therein lies the problem. Presidential popularity reached new heights in the polls after vicious assaults on Grenada, Libya, Panama, and Iraq. People wear "Just Cause" t-shirts with a racist pineapple-face portraying Noriega after the mindless bashing of a small neighbor. Orwell's doublespeak has become the official language of the Pentagon. The media was more adept and equally committed to the doublespeak and glorification of the war. It was largely responsible for the mauling of truth that enabled the American people to celebrate a slaughter and make heroes of those who ordered and committed it.

The apparent popular approval by the American people of the destruction of Iraq is the greatest threat to the future.

Can power be held accountable for war crimes? And if not, is peace possible? Victors' justice is essentially the continuation of war by judicial processes. The vanquished have already been defeated. Justice for victors alone merely enhances power over impotence, while justice for the vanquished victims of war crimes holds the possibility of deterring militarism. It can protect the weak from the powerful. It demonstrates a commitment to principle over power and to equality of accountability between victor and vanquished. And it has never happened.

THE MEANING OF THE FIRE

With the collapse of the Soviet economy and the end of the Cold War, logic suggests peace should be easy to establish and that social justice can be achieved with funds available from reduced military budgets. The reality is the opposite. Arms sales are rising in the Persian Gulf. Turkey is attacking Kurdish people in Turkey and Iraq, and Shiites in the south of Iraq are at risk. The strife in Yugoslavia threatens to spread chaos beyond its borders. Russia and the Ukraine dispute control of military and naval units, and the Caucasian republics are at war. West African nations are in revolt, and countries in Central America, East and South Africa, and Asia are plagued with violence.

Most dangerous of all, the United States in seeking a new world ordered at its command threatens Iraq, Libya, Cuba, Pakistan, North Korea, and others with military, economic, and psychological violence. U.S. naval vessels threaten a North Korean ship with a cargo for Iran and Syria, alleged to be missiles, while the United States prepares to sell 72 advanced F-15s to Saudi Arabia. Even those with short memories can see the cynicism of this new world order, achieved by overseas arms sales; the invasions of Grenada and Panama; the bombing of Libya; the brutalization of Iraq; the huge U.S. support for rebel forces in Afghanistan; and the Contra, UN-ITA, ULIMO, and other military campaigns trained, financed, and directed by the United States.

This has been a war against the Third World to limit power and to control resources. It is indifferent to life, financing insurgent forces or functioning through surrogate governments that the United States supports and protects. Overwhelmingly the enemies of U.S.-supported Third World governments are their own people. But this is hardly a new order.

It would be a fatal mistake to assume tensions among powerful nations are a thing of the past. While the United States seeks to dominate Third World countries and their resources, the most dangerous risks of conflict are with rich nations. The United States has steadily lost capital, markets, production, competitiveness, and economic power to Japan, Western Europe, and the Pacific Rim for nearly two decades. Its economy is burdened by a staggering debt. Much of its plant and infrastructure are obsolescent or decaying. It is plagued with unemployment and overconsumption. More profoundly affecting its future are the breakup of American families, the rise of crime, the growing permanent underclass and vast prison population, the widespread failure of its educational systems and its predominant values, wealth and violence.

Germany is burdened with unification, a leaderless Western Europe, and an uncertain Eastern Europe. Japan is isolated and has an economic policy with no apparent goal other than growth as an end in itself. Their problems only increase the risk of conflict with the United States.

The United States probably cannot effectively compete economically with a European common market, Japan, or even the Pacific Tigers. American values compel it to try to compete and to hate if it fails. Clearly the United States will try to coerce Europe, Japan, and other economic powers to maintain its dominance.

The fiftieth anniversary of Pearl Harbor revealed President Bush's attitude toward the use of U.S. military power, one shared by nearly all U.S. policy makers since World War II. While he felt Japan should apologize for Pearl Harbor, as it should, he could not conceive of apologizing for incinerating the people of Hiroshima and Nagasaki. It was the same value system that evoked his emotional cry after the destruction of Iraq: "By God, we've kicked the Vietnam syndrome once and for all!" This approach paints Vietnam as a military failure, when in fact, America was tormented more by what it did to Vietnam and itself by its militarism than by its failure to secure a military victory. The notion of apologizing to the Vietnamese, the Filipinos, the Mexicans, the descendants of African slaves or American Indians is alien to the conviction that America is right and chosen to rule.

The most chilling exposure of the fanatacism of this faith is the famous interview by Robert Sheer of the *Los Angeles Times* with George Bush during his unsuccessful presidential campaign in 1980. The aspiring Bush explained how to win a nuclear war: "You have a survivability of command in control, survivability of industrial potential, protection of a percentage of your citizens, and you have a capability that inflicts more damage on the opposition than it can inflict upon you. That's the way you can have a winner. . . . "

Can one holding such a philosophy care about the destruction of Iraq or the deaths of tens of thousands of infants as a consequence?

If the United States insists that Japan limit its markets and sales, what option does Japan really have? The United States can control oil from the Gulf and its navy can interdict oil from Brunei to Japan from Subic Bay Naval base in the Philippines or elsewhere in the region. If necessary, it can make direct military threats with U.S. forces in Korea and U.S. bases in Japan. Japan presently has no military capacity to resist. If the United States tries to coerce Japan, what alternative to rearmament will Japan have?

The arms race from the late 1940s to the late 1980s is one of the greatest crimes against humanity. Spreading arms around the world, it plagued poor countries with both war and famine. The cost of arms meant hunger, sickness, ignorance, and homelessness to tens of millions. Ultimately, it meant economic collapse for the Soviet Union and made the United States the world's largest debtor nation.

An arms race with Japan, Germany, and other technologically advanced countries would be much more dangerous and costly than anything yet experienced. After World War II, the Soviet Union was an underdeveloped country, with its industrial regions largely destroyed and 20 million of its people dead. Its scientific skills were limited and its domestic needs were vast. Germany's and Japan's commitment, skills, and economic development are far more advanced. This dynamic shows why the United States continues nuclear arms manufacture and testing, and why both France and the United Kingdom are increasing their nuclear production.

The Pentagon dream for U.S. world dominion has been presented to the public as if it were some unapproved, tentative contingency alternative for policy makers to consider. According to a *New York Times* story on March 8, 1992, the fantasy is set forth in a 46-page document asserting that "America's political and military mission in the post cold war era will be to insure that no rival superpower is allowed to emerge in Western Europe, Asia, or territory of the former Soviet Union."

It refers to the U.S. destruction of Iraq as a "defining event in U.S. global leadership," and says the "overall objective is to remain the predominant outside power in the region and preserve U.S. and Western access to the region's oil," concluding "we must continue to play a strong role through enhanced deterrence and improved cooperative security."

It states: "[W]e will retain the preeminent responsibility for addressing selectively those wrongs which threaten not only our interests, but those of our allies or friends, or which could seriously unsettle international relations." It continues: "Various types of interests may be involved in such instances: access to vital raw material, primarily Persian Gulf oil. . . . " The report goes on to threaten Russia, Cuba, Iraq, India, Pakistan, North Korea, and others. Regarding Japan, it warns that the United States will "buttress the vital political and economic relationships we have along the Pacific rim [to] maintain our status as a military power of the first magnitude in the area."

The overall purpose is summarized by the *Times* as "a world dominated by one superpower whose position can be perpetuated by constructive behavior and sufficient military might to deter any nation or group of nations from challenging American primacy." It requires a 1.6 million-member military at a cost of $1.5 trillion for the fiscal years 1994–1999. It is a vision of world empire worthy of Alexander, Caesar, or Genghis Khan.

It is not the vision of Pentagon planners alone. The American plutocracy wants nothing more. Its military technology makes the United States the new barbarian threatening the world with *Pox Americana*. How can other nations react? Must not Germany, Japan, Russia, and other countries capable of advanced technology develop their own military plans? Must not every regional power plan to frustrate and avoid such dominion? Hasn't history shown such visions are the road to war, disaster, and failure? Yet much more than the recent experience in Iraq makes clear that the United States intends to rule the world, and by force if necessary.

The United States has an enormous lead in weaponry. Its nuclear arms can threaten any country. The Trident II nuclear submarine, which is on no nuclear arms reduction list, is a weapon beyond imagination. It can launch 24 missiles while submerged. Each missile can contain up to 17 independently targeted, maneuverable nuclear warheads. Each warhead, 10 times more powerful than the bomb that destroyed Nagasaki, can travel up to 7,000 nautical miles and strike within 300 feet of the target. Four hundred and eight cities in Europe or Japan could be hit by nuclear warheads from a single launch. Twenty of these submarines were commissioned, and after the dissolution of the Soviet Union and the elimination of its major nuclear threat, the United States continues to complete the Trident II fleet.

It is against this background that the meaning of the slaughter of Iraq must be measured. Here was a small country whose troops were armed with equipment that was worse than useless against the United States, that actually endangered the troops because it enabled U.S. aircraft to target them. The United States was armed with the fruits of trillions of dollars of research, development, testing, and arms production with which it destroyed the Iraqi military forces and crippled the country. In the final moments of the slaughter, American soldiers shouted, "Say hello to Allah!" as they fired on defenseless Iraqis in what they called a "turkey shoot" and "shooting fish in a barrel."

The old slave song warned, "God gave Noah the rainbow sign, No more water, the fire next time." The Bush administration decided that for the people of Iraq it would be the fire this time.

THE FIRE AND THE AMERICAN DREAM

Since the beginning of recorded history, the powerful have done as they wanted with the weak. In the Peloponnesian War, Athens, needing timber to build ships, demanded the surrender of the island of Melos. Melos resisted, wanting to remain nonaligned. After negotiations failed, Athens withdrew from the peace conference, warning Melos that it failed to understand the nature of things. As the Athenian admiral told the Melians, this is a world in which the powerful do as they will and the weak suffer as they must. The Athenians, the people who produced Socrates, Aristophanes, Phidias, and Pericles, blockaded Melos, weakened it, and then overwhelmed it. They killed all the Melian men, sold the women and children into slavery, and recolonized the island. Some classical Greek scholars believe the destruction of Melos by Athens contributed to Athenian decline. In the nineteenth century, archaeologists found the damaged Venus de Milo in the ruins of Melos. A people who were destroyed were capable of creating rare grace and beauty.

More than 2,000 years later, at the Nuremberg trials after World

War II, Nazi defendants accused of war crimes shouted at their accusers, "What about Dresden? Hamburg? Hiroshima?" Their pleas went unanswered. Had the tribunal addressed the crimes of the victors, efforts to control the atomic bomb, other weapons of mass destruction, and military assaults on civilian life might have succeeded. Hermann Goering, the highest-ranking Nazi defendant, said in an interview during the trial, "Victors will always be judges, the vanquished the accused." While the chief U.S. prosecutor at Nuremberg, Robert H. Jackson, proclaimed that Nuremberg principles should apply equally to every nation, the powerful continue to do as they will, and the weak suffer as they must.

If crimes against peace, war crimes, and crimes against humanity are the most violent offenses a nation can commit, then the greatest love of country is to protest and seek to prevent one's own country from committing such violence. True patriotism requires citizens to insist that their nation be honest and just in all its acts. It ought to motivate the whole people to assure that their government is as good a neighbor in the community of nations as individual conscience motivates each citizen to be in the community where he lives. Such patriotism is essential to peace, freedom, and self-determined social justice, because it can motivate the people to a conscious, continuing commitment to compel government accountability for its role in both securing a just society and in peacefully supporting other peoples in the same pursuit. Too often has patriotism been the first refuge of scoundrels, as Ambrose Bierce defined it — glorifying war and the exploitation of others.

When patriotism proclaims a nationalist superiority over others, it is racist. When it compels absolute obedience to authority, it is fascist. When patriotism calls for the use of force to have its way, it becomes criminal. The greatest moral cowardice is obedience to an order to commit an immoral act. Might does not make right among nations any more than it does among individuals. When patriotism seduces a people to celebrate a military slaughter, the people have lost their vision.

Love of country carries the duty to know what your government does, to relentlessly seek the truth of its conduct, to evaluate its words skeptically, to analyze carefully what is learned, to make judgments, and to act on them. Sadly, the U.S. government, like nearly all others, takes an adversarial position against its own citizens regarding its acts. Officials lie to the people. The United States kept its bombing of Cambodia in the 1970s secret, not so Cambodians would be ignorant of it — they could hardly fail to notice. Rather, it was kept secret from the American people to avoid protest.

And when the people found out, their rage was so great and the government repression so violent that thousands were arrested on the streets of Washington, D.C., and students were shot dead on campuses at Kent State and Jackson State.

The government kept the press off the island of Grenada for a week during and after the U.S. invasion, not because it feared Grenadian forces might make some powerful counterattack, but to control the entire story given to the American people. To this day, Americans do not know why their government invaded Grenada, how many people it killed, how much it paid for the false trials of the surviving Grenadian leadership it captured, or what witnesses say actually happened. Of all the casualties in Grenada, and scores died, the death of the truth has had the most tragic effect. Since then the Pentagon has written heroic fiction to describe its violent acts. Democratic institutions cannot function in such a system.

But if the death of truth in Grenada has had the most tragic effect on the future, cannot the same be said for the failure of truth in American history and the American dream? Throughout the European experience in the new world, the idealized vision has been freedom, democracy, prosperity, friendship, giving. Overwhelmingly, practice has been just the opposite. The almost unbroken course of conduct toward native people has been violence, killing, stealing land and property, removing them from where they were to places where they could barely survive, afflicting them with European diseases, and destroying their cultures. The fear and hatred generated toward American Indians by false propaganda provided the seeds for racism that grew until Hollywood films could glorify the slaughter of Indians by cowboys. To kill Indians became a cultural virtue, while to befriend the rare maiden, child, or warrior estranged from a tribe showed cultural generosity and compassion.

The story of African slavery reveals an even deeper immorality. With the American Indians, Europeans took the land, and killed or drove the Indians from it. In Africa, Europeans invaded villages an ocean away, forced millions onto ships in which millions died, brought them thousands of miles to labor until exhaustion or age rendered them worthless. This was done so Europeans in America could accumulate great wealth from the sweat of slaves' brows and the pain of their bodies. After slavery, economic, social, and political conditions for most African Americans changed very little for half a century, very slowly for the next half century, burst forth briefly in search of equality during the Civil Rights movement of the 1960s, and receded into a growing permanent underclass, a Third World population in a rich country, by the 1990s. The enduring legacy has been a racism deeply ingrained in the character of the people and their institutions.

From the beginning, the Europeans in America often found their freedom from the barrel of a gun and the subversion of fact. Elements among them threatened every border and took what they wanted by force. The list of U.S. military interventions and annexations by force and its threat begins in the earliest years of the republic: Manifest Destiny from the Northwest Territory to the seizure of California, Arizona, and New Mexico; to "54–40 or fight," Liberia, Walker in Nicaragua, and invasions and seizures of Cuba, Puerto Rico, Panama, and the Philippines; to the scores of military interventions and funding of proxy troops in Central and South America, the Caribbean, Asia, and Africa.

U.S. Third World allies were almost always dictatorships that ruled by force: Chiang Kai-Shek, Somoza, the Shah of Iran, Diem, Pinochet, Marcos, Noriega, and others. While many have considered this to be ironic, it actually reflects U.S. interests. Dictators make for more reliable client states, for they will usually do as commanded for a price. In a democracy, however, the people will not permit foreign exploitation. Leaders like Mossadegh in Iran, Arbenz in Guatemala, and Allende in Chile were opposed by the United States for their independence and democratic commitment.

The U.S. has led in the arms race. It was the first to develop and use atomic weapons. It has outstripped the rest of humanity in advanced technology of violence, plunging on beyond all reason with omnicidal weapons like the Trident II.

In exploitation of other peoples, no empire ever matched America. After World War II and into the 1960s the United States, with 5 percent of the world's population, consumed more than half its product. Within the United States, the concentration of wealth and difference in conditions between rich and poor far exceeds that of any other developed country.

By 1992, the richest 1 percent of American families owned 37 percent of all assets, 62 percent of all business assets, 49 percent of all publicly held corporate stock, and 45 percent of all nonresidential real property. They owned the media and the advertisers that finance the media, assuring that a very limited range of ideas and information would be provided to the public. The United States' domestic and foreign policies reflected their interests, desires, and values. They are the ruling plutocracy.

In contrast, the numbers of homeless, unemployed, children living in poverty with neither natural parent, persons without any health care provision, and families living in poverty were growing steadily. A Third World labor market was developing in many regions of the nation where wages and working and safety conditions were dangerously low.

The American people outconsume any in history, seemingly as an end in itself and almost oblivious to the effect on their physical and moral health or on the planet and all its people. Other people throughout the poor countries could live handsomely on the cost of American packaging for its own consumption. Millions of people in other countries have been infected by the contagion of U.S. materialism and its glorification of violence shrouded in the cloak of freedom, democracy, good will, friendship, and multiethnic harmony peddled by American propaganda and cultural imperialism.

What then of the American Dream? The American dream was good. It spoke of freedom, equality, democracy, constitutional government, education, spiritual faith, family, work, human rights, peace. It offered a beautiful, bountiful land, open and available, promising prosperity for all. It protected the original inhabitants, freed the slaves, extinguished racism. It was a nation of immigrants attracting people of all languages, races, and national origins, the poor and oppressed, yearning to breathe free. It released human energies and imagination that enabled it to feed everyone and still export great quantities of food with less than 5 percent of its workforce in agriculture. It generously rebuilt Europe after World War II and aided developing poor nations. It outfaced totalitarians and supported human rights at home and abroad. It produced people, goods, literature, religion, movies, music that captured the hearts of the world.

But the dream is not the reality, though it could become much more nearly so. Yet it has been so pervasively presented as reality that few Americans can separate fact from fiction. As a result, for most the dream is all that is seen or is acceptable. When confronted with facts that are inconsistent with the freedom, equality, democracy, and justice of their dream, they are either angered or overcome with a profound disillusion. Over the years, everyone proclaimed for freedom and assumed it existed in America, but little was said about what American freedom meant. Now we see that, in America, freedom has become the largest prison population of any nation on earth in absolute and proportional numbers. It has become death rows with more than 2,600 persons waiting to be executed, an example of fear of death as a means of controlling conduct. It has become a pervasive fear of crime that imprisons people in their own homes and minds.

Freedom is good when understood as the negation of force, not its supremacy; as choice; as the chance for social justice and fulfillment for all; as sharing with others, not starving them; as the liberation of the imagination from the bonds of political, cultural, and social command; as applicable to Nat Turner and Mrs. Henry as it is for Patrick Henry; as love for others which is the essence of a free heart. Lincoln, anguishing over the slaughter of hundreds of black Union troops at Ft. Pillow, Tennessee, by Confederate cavalry led by General Nathan Bedford Forrest—later to found the Ku Klux Klan—said, "The world has never had a very good definition of the word *liberty* and right now the American people are badly in want of one." The American people must devote themselves to developing a concept of freedom that is more than a call to arms.

The challenge, for those who believe in the American dream, is to give context to its concepts, to struggle to live by them, and to insist that the truth be told about what Americans and their government do. America can become more nearly what it has always said it is. If it does, a new generation may be able to liberate this nation of Indians and immigrants that threatens the planet and establish democracy capable of seeking freedom, social justice, and peace. To do so we must speak truth and vow to fulfill the dream, as Langston Hughes did:

> *O, yes I say it plain*
> *America never was America to me*
> *and yet I swear this oath*
> *America will be!*

CHAPTER 12

A Vision of Peace

Where there is no vision, the people perish.
Proverbs

You see things; and you say "Why?" But I dream things
that never were; and I say "Why not?"
George Bernard Shaw

FOR all the horror, death, and inhumanity of the devastation of Iraq, the fact — or appearance — of popular American approval of what was done is a far greater threat to the future. It is doubtful if there has been a higher percentage of death, destruction, and long-term incapacitation inflicted on a whole country of Iraq's size or larger in a comparable period of time in the history of warfare. For a nation of 16 million to have 250,000–350,000 of its people killed or condemned to death, suffer a multiple of that figure injured and handicapped, and have water, sanitation, power, communication, transportation, and food production and distribution severely damaged in six weeks of violence is unprecedented. Most of the major participants in World War II — including China, England, France, Italy, and the United States — had a lower casualty rate among their total population during the long years of war than Iraq had in the few weeks it was bombed and the consequences that followed.

Despite inescapable awareness that a deadly blow of enormous magnitude had been deliberately inflicted on Iraq, the American public was easily led to celebrate the slaughter. Few public figures dared or cared to condemn it. Major media worked as hard to assure the public of the rightness and benefits of U.S. aggression as it had to glorify the violent assault itself. The *New York Times* editorialized in the late fall of 1991 that "if any war could be called 'just,' the gulf war qualified."[1] The Congress dared no dissent. President Bush began and ended his State of the Union Message in January 1992 with praise for Desert Storm. Going further later that month before the

230

National Religious Broadcasters annual convention, the President said, "we fought for good versus evil. . . . And today I want to thank you for helping America, as Christ ordained it to be a light unto the world."[2]

Before 1991 was out, the United States began to threaten Cuba, Haiti, Iraq, Libya, North Korea, Pakistan, Syria, and Vietnam with UN condemnation, greater sanctions, or violence if they failed to meet various U.S. demands. The U.S. media and political leadership spoke openly of new military actions as President Bush's postwar popularity sagged. The *New York Times* captured the arrogance and inhumanity of predictions of a new assault on Iraq in early February 1992 with front-page headlines about CIA Director Robert Gates's trip to Saudi Arabia and Israel: "Gates, in Mideast, Is Said to Discuss Ouster of Hussein; Next Turn of the Screw; Seeks Saudi and Egyptian Help in Scaring, Then Deposing the Recalcitrant Iraqi."

Presidential popularity soared after the invasion of Grenada, the bombing of Libya, the assault on Panama, and the destruction of Iraq. U.S. military violence of increasing magnitude was considered politically popular, and many expected a U.S. assault on some demonized country as a political ploy to help reelect President Bush. Millions foresaw more U.S. military actions as a principal means to achieve the "new world order."

The failure of the American educational system, media, democratic institutions, and national character makes this possible. The American people have been made to feel absolutely powerless over foreign affairs and most domestic issues. When they consider such questions at all, they generally act as if they were watching a spectator sport — rooting for the home team and believing that the visiting team doesn't play fair — with no more control over the outcome of U.S. interventions than over any televised basketball game. And there is widespread disbelief and cynicism about government and those who hold power in this country, revealed in a startling way by the movie *JFK*. Suddenly, almost three decades after the assassination, many moviegoers, perhaps hundreds of thousands, decided the U.S. government killed President Kennedy. A profound alienation among millions is necessary to allow a mere movie to make such a radical transformation among so many people.

Yet only the morally blind will fail to see that U.S. political and military leadership has proven itself totally untrustworthy to lead the world to a new order. Those who planned, ordered, and conducted the assault on Iraq are war criminals. Despite all the propaganda and one-sided media coverage, this violent assault was calculated and cold-blooded. How else to explain so many Iraqi deaths and so few U.S. casualties; a totally incapacitated Iraq and an American public that views the Gulf War as "ancient history"?

ENSURING PEACE IN THE FUTURE

Nothing can be clearer to people who want peace than the necessity for urgent, radical action to control militarism. During its hearings, the Commission of Inquiry developed many proposals to secure peace and social justice and avoid further U.S. aggressions. These proposals are outlined here. The first group is comprised of emergency acts that address immediate human needs resulting from the Gulf War. The second group includes far-reaching reforms that, if implemented, will help the world's people live in peace.

PROPOSALS TO MEET EMERGENCY NEEDS IN THE PERSIAN GULF

1. Immediate Shipments of Vital Supplies. Provide food, medical supplies, medical equipment, and potable water; seeds, seedlings and plants, and fertilizer; machine parts for water pumps and water purification processes, sanitation equipment, electric power generation, and transmission facilities; tractor, farm machinery, truck, and bus parts; and oil well, pipeline, pumping, and refinery equipment through UN and other international relief agencies to meet immediate needs throughout Iraq and in countries in the region that have been adversely affected or have needy Gulf War refugee populations.

2. Release the Stranglehold of Sanctions. End the embargo, sanctions, import-export controls, and travel restrictions imposed on Iraq, and release frozen bank deposits and assets.

3. Remove Unexploded Ordnance. Provide manpower and expert technical skills through the UN to help remove all unexploded bombs, shells, and other dangerous war materiel and nuclear debris from Iraq and Kuwait under the authority and supervision of those countries' governments.

4. Assess Legitimate Reparations. Create a UN arbitration commission to assess damages and reparations against responsible parties to be paid to all injured persons — including refugees — for deaths, injuries, property damage, and environmental damage in the Persian Gulf caused by war crimes and other illegal acts committed by the United States, Iraq, Kuwait, and other governments and their agents.

5. Stop Warlike Actions. Cease all threats and coercion of Iraq and resolve all disputes with it as an equal among nations in accordance with the requirements of international law for the pacific settlement of disputes.

6. Address Underlying Regional Issues. Create a UN arbitration commission to address ongoing regional disputes, and consider all peoples as equals in the proceedings and decisions. These disputes include remaining issues among Iraq, Kuwait, Iran, Israel, Jordan, Saudi Arabia, Syria, Turkey, and others in the region; the rights of the Kurds, Assyrians, and other peoples; the rights of Palestinians to an independent state in the West Bank, Gaza, and Jerusalem, to removal of all Israeli agencies and settlers who have unlawfully entered these territories and seized land or property, and to reparations from Israel; the withdrawal of Israeli, Syrian, and other foreign military forces from Lebanon; the rights to the Golan Heights; all border disputes in the region.

7. Remove Foreign Military Influence. Remove all United States and other foreign military forces from Saudi Arabia, Kuwait, the UAE, Turkey, and elsewhere in the Gulf region and close all foreign military bases.

PROPOSALS TO ENSURE FUTURE PEACE FOR THE WORLD

The sense of urgency throughout the Commission effort was second only to that of horror and shame at what had been done. The specter of militarism and exploitation is haunting our planet, and unless high human energy, bold imagination, diligent effort, and unremitting perseverance are devoted to changes essential to survival, a brutal and deadly future is inescapable. The threat of a new world order based on technological violence and designed to control the poor for the benefit of the rich has made organized and spontaneous worldwide effort absolutely essential for human fulfillment.

The evidence and opinion compiled by the Commission has demonstrated the ease with which government and law can be abused to kill, control, deceive, and impoverish humanity. The belief that governments will solve our problems may be the most dangerous opiate of the people. Whereas most of the proposals set forth in this section necessarily deal with government and law, the most important ones are those involving empowerment of the people and their capacity to ensure constant protection from, reform of, and accountability of government. Without this, none of the other devices can work for long.

In the several score hearings of the Commission, a stream of proposals addressing urgent human problems symbolized, caused, and revealed by the aggression against Iraq were presented by witnesses and participants. Many of these reflected preexisting concerns reinforced by events in the Gulf. Some dealt with reforms within specific nations that would inhibit or prevent future participation in war crimes and protect their governments and population from international bribery and coercion. Except for those regarding the United States, these have generally not been included here, and have been left to commissions within the other countries.

No proposal is considered to be an end in itself: each is intended to stimulate a dynamic process of change. All are presented in general terms for consideration, development, and implementation in the most effective form. The proposals fall into six general subject areas.

A. REFORMS TO PREVENT AND CONTROL WAR, WAR CRIMES, AND MILITARISM

Prohibit Weapons of War and Mass Destruction

1. Prohibit research, development, planning, manufacturing, transporting, or possession of any weapon of mass destruction: nuclear, atomic, neutron, biological, neurological, chemical, gas, antipersonnel, cluster, fuel air; and including the use of conventional explosives or other devices designed for or capable of killing or injuring groups of people or destroying property.

2. Prohibit research, development, planning, manufacturing, transporting, or possessing sophisticated equipment and weapons of warfare, including military aircraft, rockets, missiles, artillery, and automatic weapons; and laser, concussion, x-ray, or other devices designed to or capable of killing groups of people or destroying property.

Establish UN Oversight of Arms and Military Action

3. Create a UN Disarmament, Arms Limitation, and Military Control Agency governed by UN statutes with power to (a) inspect for compliance, police, and enforce laws prohibiting research, development, planning, manufacturing, transporting, possession, and international sales of weapons of mass destruction, equipment and weapons of warfare, and other arms; (b) prohibit, limit, register, license, and control international arms sales; (c) regulate, limit, register, and license all military arms and provide standards and super-

vision for the planned reduction of all national military forces and arms to achieve a size and arms limit no greater than that required for border control and internal public safety; (d) regulate, supervise, and conduct the dismantling and destruction of all existing prohibited and excess weapons.

4. Prohibit all international arms manufacture, sales, transportation, or possession not authorized, approved, and registered with the UN Disarmament, Arms Limitation, and Military Control Agency.

5. Create a UN Peacekeeping Force with exclusive authority to recruit, organize, and use military force, excepting only the right of each nation to exercise police power for border control and internal public safety. All personnel in the Peacekeeping Force shall owe allegiance to the UN and faithfully perform their duty to it. The force shall be equipped with conventional small arms sufficient to enforce resolutions, statutes, and decrees authorized by the UN or the international court system under an international command structure created and appointed by the UN. No single national origin and citizenship shall comprise more than 10 percent of any rank or unit of more than 10 persons in the Peacekeeping Force. In ranks or units with less than 10 persons, no two shall be of the same national origin and citizenship.

Create New Principles Controlling Military Force

6. Promulgate a Universal Convention Prohibiting Militarism, Crimes Against Peace, War Crimes, and Crimes Against Humanity that would do the following: (a) The Convention would make it an international war crime to create or use military force in violation of its terms and abolish all sovereign immunity for such offenses. (b) It would protect military personnel in the event of war by making it a war crime to use excessive force or illegal weapons, to attack defenseless troops or troops in retreat who do not have the capability of aggressive action, or to make a surprise attack or attack persons who have signaled the desire to surrender. (c) It would make it a war crime to attack cities, towns, villages, farms, or any civilian facilities including water, power, communication, health care, education, and transportation facilities; vehicles, housing, commercial properties, and offices; religious, historical, and archeological structures; and food production, storage, distribution, or sales facilities. It would also make damage to the environment by military or paramilitary action, or attacks on any civilians, war crimes.

The United States' erroneous claims that the Hague and Geneva Conventions, the Nuremberg Principles, the Laws of Armed Conflict, and the U.S. Rules of Engagement were not violated in the assault against Iraq make necessary the enactment of a comprehensive, detailed, modern set of principles protecting troops from excessive violence and civilians from all violence.

Prohibit Foreign Military and Political Influence in Other Countries

7. Prohibit foreign military bases anywhere in the world, as they are a vestige of colonialism and past wars, and pose a threat to peace. The United States should be required to withdraw its forces immediately, not only from the Persian Gulf, but from the many bases it used in its attack on Iraq. Bases in Saudi Arabia, Turkey, England, Diego Garcia, the Philippines, Spain, Japan, Germany, and elsewhere were used to commit war crimes against Iraq. Each caused strained relations and even hatred among nations. U.S. forces in NATO nations, South Korea, Japan, the Philippines, Singapore, Panama, and scores of other countries should be withdrawn and all bases closed.

8. Prohibit the intervention of military or police personnel from one country into another, the seizure of territory of another people, and attacks on another country under any circumstances. Authorize UN peacekeeping troops to enforce this prohibition, a violation of which is a crime against peace. No nation should recognize the claim of any nation to the land, resources, or property of another nation or people taken in violation of this provision, including all claims based on violations of these principles which occurred after 1945.

9. Prohibit all nations and private interests from providing bilateral economic aid, excepting humanitarian aid, political support, weapons, training, advisors, or police personnel to a government headed, controlled, maintained, or coerced by military or police authority as determined by the UN.

10. Prohibit governmental and private interference in governmental activity or electoral processes of another nation. Such operations as U.S. AID grants and National Endowment for Democracy programs funding political parties, candidates, and electoral processes and studies have been used to subvert democracy, self-determination, and independence, and should be prohibited. They are direct, unilateral forms of intervention.

Create UN Agencies to Deal with War and Its Results

11. Create within a new UN Agency for Human Resources a Division for War Refugees, War Casualties, and Emergency Wartime and Natural Disaster Relief that can provide water, food, shelter, physical protection, economic assistance, and other needs for war refu-

gees; investigate and report war crimes; account for all casualties from armed conflict, natural disasters, and their consequences; assure medical treatment for the wounded and injured in war and natural catastrophes; assure identification and decent burial for the dead; provide economic aid for surviving families and other victims of war and natural disasters.

12. Appoint an independent UN commission to investigate U.S. conduct in planning, conducting, and coercing others to participate in the destruction of Iraq; to require the United States to reveal all documents, reports, records, and data relevant to plans for and the conduct of the war; to require U.S. officials and others to produce documents and testify about U.S. plans and acts.

13. Create a permanent UN Agency for United Nations and International Law Reform charged with studying and recommending reforms needed to achieve the purposes of the UN as stated in its Charter. It should be independent of, but should coordinate activity with, the UN Law Committee and the UN Legal Counsel.

B. REFORM OF THE UNITED NATIONS TO PROVIDE FOR WORLD LAW, DEMOCRATIC POWER, INTEGRITY IN GOVERNMENT, AND WORLD PEACE

1. Create a federal system of international governance, delegating to the UN powers to secure peace, regulate international economic activity, and provide social justice for all, and reserving all other powers to the several nations and their people. Create legislative, executive, and judicial powers within the UN.

2. Replace the Security Council, with its permanent membership and veto power, with a World Council of representatives elected by the General Assembly from its membership. The General Assembly voting representatives should be divided into electoral units apportioned to provide the fairest attainable representation of all races, languages, cultural groups, religions, and geopolitical interests. Each World Council member should be elected from the full General Assembly by a General Assembly electoral unit representing approximately 100 million people, serve for four years unless the General Assembly calls an earlier Council election, and not be eligible for reelection within two years of any prior service which totals four years. One-fourth of the Council members should be elected each year. Persons of a single nation and national origin should not comprise more than 10 percent of the World Council or more than 20 percent of any General Assembly electoral unit. The World Coun-

cil should perform the duties delegated to the Security Council in the UN Charter. Council members should act and vote to benefit the general welfare of all peoples, not the special interests of their own nation or the electoral unit from which they are elected.

3. The General Assembly should be elected by a direct universal vote conducted in each nation for national representatives to the UN. Each nation should have one representative, plus an additional representative for each 10 million people resident within the nation up to 100 million. Nations with more than 100 million people should have one additional vote for each additional 50 million people. Nations with more than one vote should be divided into representative districts of equal population, fairly apportioned. Each representative should act and vote independently on all matters before the UN.

4. Require all disputes among nations to be addressed first by the means set forth in Chapter VI of the UN Charter. When those means are exhausted, any party to the dispute, the UN General Assembly, or the World Council can ask for resolution by the International Court of Justice. The decision of the Court shall be binding on the parties. If a state refuses to obey the Court's decision, the World Council and the General Assembly by a two-thirds vote of each body may direct the Peacekeeping Force to implement the decision if all pacific means of settlement have been affirmatively found by two-thirds of each body to have been exhausted.

5. The UN should have the power to tax nations, to charter international corporations, and to regulate and tax international commerce, trade, transportation, and wealth. However, no tax should be imposed that discriminates on the basis of race, citizenship, national origin, religious beliefs, political affiliation, or sex. Taxation on nations should be based on financial ability, keyed to per capita income, and should not exceed average national military expenditures for 1980–1990 as a proportion of gross national product (GNP), or 5 percent of GNP for nations with a per capita income up to $10,000 and 10 percent of the GNP in excess of $10,000 per capita. Taxes should not be imposed on nations with per capita incomes less than $2,000, but may be imposed on commerce and wealth of such nations.

6. The Secretary General, principle officials, agency and department heads, and commanding officers of the Peacekeeping Force should be elected by a majority of the General Assembly and serve at its pleasure. UN employees, including peacekeeping forces, should have the right to form unions, to bargain collectively, and to strike, and should be protected by civil service merit principles.

7. The United Nations shall create an International Court of

Criminal Justice with jurisdiction to hear and decide all formal charges of crimes against peace, war crimes, crimes against humanity and other crimes by and against nations; criminal violations of human rights by, or condoned by, a national government; crimes by and against international corporations or against commerce; crimes against the environment, labor, including the exploitation thereof, and natural resources; crimes involving transportation, including the destruction of aircraft, ships, vehicles, and facilities required for their performance and piracy; production, processing, and transportation of illicit drugs for international commerce; crimes against the UN, including bribery, corruption, coercion, or violence by or against its elected or appointed personnel. A criminal code should be enacted by vote of the General Assembly. Final decisions of the court should be subject to discretionary review by the International Court of Justice. The Legal Counsel of the UN should have an office of international crimes investigation and prosecution. It should receive complaints of criminal acts from individuals, organizations, or nations.

8. The Universal Declaration of Human Rights and other international covenants protecting civil, political, social, economic, and cultural rights should be embodied into positive and inalienable international law. An International Court for Human Rights and Habeas Corpus should have jurisdiction to prevent, enjoin, and assess damages for violations of such rights, with power to order protection from threatened violations, cessation of violations, restraint of violators, and release of victims. The court should have power to issue writs of prohibition, mandamus, and habeas corpus in accordance with statutes enacted by the General Assembly. Final decisions of the court should be subject to discretionary review by the International Court of Justice. If a nation, or any organization condoned by it, refuses to obey the court's decision, the World Council and General Assembly, by a two-thirds vote of each body, may direct the Peacekeeping Force to implement it after a finding that all pacific means of settlement have been exhausted. The court should receive and consider complaints from individuals, organizations, nations, and the UN Legal Counsel. The Legal Counsel should represent the UN in all proceedings before the court to which it is a party or in which it chooses to intervene. The UN Commission on Human Rights should be expanded and given greater resources for investigation, research, and reporting, and should be directed to refer criminal and enforcement matters to the appropriate international court.

9. The United Nations should create an International Boundary Commission with the power to negotiate and, where agreement can-

not be reached, arbitrate all boundary disputes and claims to the sea, seabed, airspace, and other common resources. The International Court of Justice should have the discretionary power to review any final decisions by the commission on the petition of a party to the dispute. A final decision by the commission or the court ought to be binding on the parties and enforceable by the Peacekeeping Force on approval by the World Council and General Assembly.

The purpose is to prevent border disputes from leading to violence while the greater goal of erasing borders is achieved. States in Africa, the Middle East, Asia, and elsewhere with artificial borders imposed by colonial powers should be aided by the UN in efforts to secure proper borders, and regions of the world should be encouraged to create new political and economic communities, units, and relationships. Nationalism should be discouraged, as it has historically been a major cause of war.

C. REFORMS TO ACHIEVE ECONOMIC AND SOCIAL JUSTICE AND ECOLOGICAL, NATURAL RESOURCE, AND ENVIRONMENTAL PROTECTION

The destruction of Iraq was a continuance of attempts by the United States and other rich nations to dominate and exploit the Third World. The assault on Iraq blasted an emerging country back into poverty and ensured foreign control of its oil and the resources of the region. It illustrated the actions of rich nations to further impoverish poor countries, and the poor within the rich countries, for the benefit of the rich. Through its power to tax, to cancel indebtedness, and to require reparations, the UN should address the following concerns.

1. *Health.* The World Health Organization ought to be financed to provide free inoculation programs worldwide; to educate, provide physical protection, and engage in research to prevent and care for persons with AIDS; to effectively address epidemics and health crises; and to assist poor countries to establish health care and maintenance and medical programs sufficient to meet the needs of all.

2. *Food.* UN agriculture agencies, including the Food and Agriculture Organization, ought to be combined, expanded, and financed to assist every region, subregion, and nation in the world to establish food production sufficient to feed their people and to secure sound trade relations that assure adequate food supplies. The International Fund for Agricultural Development should be expanded to achieve universal food independence and should be integrated into the new agency. Planning should include storing food to meet predictable fu-

ture needs as well as preparing for converting production to meet health needs, changes in climate, droughts, and other short- and long-range changes. A World Food Store ought to be financed and given the ability and duty to provide appropriate food for hungry people worldwide, supplementing food supplies to eliminate hunger and malnutrition. It must have the ability to provide emergency needs for food anywhere in the world whatever the cause at all times.

3. Water. Every poor nation should be provided with technical knowledge, skills, and funding to assure safe drinking water for its entire population. The UN should provide research and funding for this through health agencies.

4. Labor. A UN Agency for Human Resources should be created to prevent exploitation of labor markets in poor countries and of poor and alien workers in rich countries. Criminal sanctions should apply to serious violations, and the Court for Human Rights should have enforcement jurisdiction. The agency should have funding to register and protect alien workers and regulate multinational employer labor practices. The High Commission for Refugees office should be merged with this new agency and expanded to protect the rights of all political refugees, to prevent their forced repatriation, and to provide for the needs of all refugees including food, shelter, health care, education, and employment. The Office of Emergency Operations should be merged into this agency to coordinate the operation of Peacekeeping, Health, Food, Water, Housing, and other agencies in emergency situations. Such an agency would have gone far to protect the millions of Egyptians, Indians, Palestinians, Filipinos, Sri Lankans, Yemenis, Sudanese, and other workers and their families who were endangered, displaced, injured, and ignored during the Gulf War.

5. Education. The UN should finance and oversee a worldwide literacy program administered locally to end illiteracy. It should fund planning for local primary, secondary, college, and university curricula to be developed by local educators and representing the cultures, languages, and people in the area; it should financially assist public education systems in poor nations, including major universities devoted to regional history, culture, language, communications, and research in a world setting. Efforts should be made to provide multilingual, multicultural education at all levels. A common international language such as Esperanto should be developed, agreed upon, and taught universally.

6. Birth Control. The UN should finance a worldwide education program aimed at teenagers as well as adults to fully inform them of effective and safe methods of preventing conception. Males and females should be provided a choice among free, safe, effective contraceptive devices.

7. *Housing.* The UN should provide financing for national housing programs, including developing local building materials and facilities and mortgage capacity. Cities like Caïro, Rio de Janeiro, Manila, and Bombay have millions of homeless people, and inadequate resources to address the problem. Major UN and other international funding will be essential to meet these needs.

8. *Development, Employment, and Beneficial Use of Resources.* UN financial assistance should be provided for regional, subregional, and national planning under local direction to assist in the wise development and use of resources for the benefit of the region, to obtain full employment and training for greater skills, and to protect the environment. The UN Committee on Environment and Development should assist poor countries with environmentally wholesome development programs centered on eliminating poverty. Funding for resource development and employment programs should be prioritized on the basis of need and project feasibility. A UN Energy Agency should be created to research and develop inexhaustible supplies of energy using sound safety, health, conservation, and environmental standards.

Reliance on petroleum and other hydrocarbons, greatly increased by the Gulf War, should be sharply curtailed. The International Atomic Energy Agency should be merged into the new Energy Agency with the power of international inspection and control of all uses of nuclear energy in all nations. Research, waste disposal, authorization, construction, and safety measures for nuclear energy should be controlled by this agency. Investigation of environmental, genetic, and other effects should be vigorous. Development and use of nuclear energy should be subject to constant scientific evaluation for safety and health, carefully limited and conservatively authorized.

9. *Environmental and Ecological Protection.* UN financing for environmental protection should include air and water protection, rain forest and other resource preservation, and research and action for ozone protection and global warming effects. A UN Environmental Protection Agency should be created to investigate and enforce strict laws enacted by the General Assembly protecting all aspects of the planetary environment.

10. *Prevention of Economic Exploitation.* The UN should enact international laws criminalizing all forms of economic exploitation of poor countries, including seizure and all forms of theft and waste of

natural resources, strategic properties, and human labor and skills. The International Labor Organization should be strengthened and empowered to protect labor in all countries, to secure fair wages, and to ensure decent working conditions. The segregation of major petroleum reserves and other resources into artificial political jurisdictions such as Brunei, the UAE, Kuwait, and Saudi Arabia, and other jurisdictions where the result is unconscionable concentration of wealth, should be addressed by international conservation laws, taxation, and the imposition of participating interests in reserves, production, and sales for funding health, food, education, communications, housing development, and employment funds in poor countries.

11. Restriction of the Use of Embargos and Sanctions. International embargos and sanctions must not be used to impoverish nations, cause hunger and malnutrition, or deprive people of needed health care and medicine.

The United States has deliberately and severely damaged the Vietnamese economy and people through sanctions since the end of the Vietnam War, leaving that nation impoverished. Its embargo against Nicaragua caused extreme hardship to a people already burdened by a long, destructive war and natural calamities. The United States is trying to use its embargo on Cuba to destroy that country's economy and overthrow the government there. In 1992, the UN embargo of Iraq has caused the deaths of thousands of people and continues to kill thousands of infants, children, sick, and elderly each month.

Economic sanctions have been used in discriminatory ways. For instance, the Batista, Pahlavi, Duvalier, Pinochet, and other dictatorships were supported by the United States despite pervasive human rights violations, and these countries were never sanctioned.

Embargos must be directed only at economic activity that directly supports a government that is threatening peace, is engaged in war, or is violating human rights. The UN should prohibit their use for ideological reasons; because of religion, economic policy, political systems, or alliances; or to coerce submission to foreign domination and exploitation. All embargos must be carefully monitored to ensure they do not cause hunger, sickness, or impoverishment.

12. Redistribution of Wealth. The UN must act to redistribute wealth from rich countries to poor, for peace is not possible in the presence of widespread poverty. World population will increase by 1 billion during the 1990s. Eighty percent of these humans will have beautiful dark skins and be born in poor countries or in poverty in rich countries. The majority will live short lives of hunger, sickness, poverty, ignorance, idleness, pain, and violence unless radical programs are undertaken for their benefit.

Most debts of poor countries must be canceled and absorbed by rich countries and their financial institutions. New credit must be extended to poor nations whose debts have been canceled. Third World resources must be conserved and developed to benefit Third World people in ways that are economically and environmentally sound. Taxation of multinational corporations, international sales and trade, and contributions from rich nations must help finance poor peoples and nations. Bilateral national aid should be strictly controlled to avoid exploitation, coercion, corruption, and restraints on trade. UN aid should be provided by UN agencies wherever necessary and be carefully monitored to assure direct benefit to the people and to avoid corruption.

13. Prevention of Unfair International Trade Practices. International trade competition and trade disputes, particularly among the United States, Japan, and Europe, are a great threat to peace and are likely to become more so. All forms of threats and coercion by governments to obtain trade advantage, dominate markets, or exploit labor resources, or to monopolize, restrain trade, or secure unfair trade advantage should be prohibited. Compulsory binding arbitration of any trade dispute should be required on the request of any affected nation or the UN. The International Court of Justice should have power, in its discretion, to review any final arbitration decision on petition of a party to the decision. The General Assembly should provide for the enforcement of final decisions where any nation fails to comply.

D. REFORMS TO LIBERATE THE UNITED STATES

1. Liberation from Militarism. The United States has led the world in the arms race and created the most devastating weapons of mass destruction. It possesses the majority of all nuclear warheads. It has developed and maintains the most advanced weapons systems and most dangerous and excessive military power, which it deploys worldwide. It leads the world in arms sales. It has engaged most extensively in the use of violence against and within other nations in recent years.

The people of the United States must organize to force the abandonment of militarism, reduce military expenditures by 90 percent or more, and address domestic and international problems of health, hunger, homelessness, failing education systems, unemployment, and family disintegration.

2. *Liberation from Unconstitutional Government.* If there is to be integrity in constitutional government in the United States, charges against President Bush, Vice President Quayle, and other high officials of the United States responsible for the slaughter in Iraq must be processed for impeachment by the House of Representatives and trial by the Senate. If found guilty, these officials must be removed from office. Independent counsel should be appointed with authority to conduct criminal prosecution where investigations show individual criminal acts. All forms of immunity for such offenses must be abolished.

3. *Liberation from Plutocratic Control.* Democratic institutions, the economy, and the media must be liberated from the control of wealth for the Constitution to function. Universal automatic voter enrollment of residents 18 years of age or older should be established. Campaign financing by private wealth ought to be prohibited, as money dominates U.S. politics; and through politics, government itself. Public financing and free and fair access to the media for candidates and political parties must be afforded.

4. *Liberation from Concentration of Wealth.* Concentration of wealth in the United States exceeds that of any developed country. Laws to prevent economic coercion, bribery, corruption, and undue influence of government policy and public officials must be strengthened and strictly enforced. Antitrust laws to prevent monopoly, monopolization, restraints of trade, and anticompetitive practices, corporate raiding, conglomerate concentration, and economic discrimination based on race, sex, religion, or national origin should be strengthened. Tax reform should redistribute wealth and create tax equity, progressive rates of tax on wealth and income, and protection of the poor, handicapped, and disadvantaged. Labor laws should be strengthened to encourage free democratic unions of workers, to protect wages and working conditions, and to achieve economic justice. Eliminating poverty should be the highest national priority.

5. *Liberation from Punitive Social Control.* The United States has by far the largest prison population in the world. U.S. prisons are used as a means of social control for poor, young, disadvantaged minority males and others. This prison population should be reduced by 90 percent or more, and prisons should be replaced by programs for family support, special education, skills and job training, employment, special personalized health programs, community housing, and counseling. American police should transform their paramilitary approach, which is hostile to democracy and freedom, to a social service approach. Gun control should eliminate all handguns and concealable weapons, and prohibit all guns except registered rifles and shotguns available for licensed individuals on the basis of demonstrated need. The quantities of firearms should be reduced from the present 200 million to at most several million. The death penalty, the ultimate symbol and act of rule by government violence, must be abolished in the United States as it has been in most developed countries and democracies.

The United States has become the world's principal executioner of persons convicted of crime, with 2,600 people on death rows across the country. It discriminates against African Americans and other minorities, executing them with the retarded, incompetent, drug-addicted, aliens, unemployed, and minors, while protecting the rich and privileged.

6. *Liberation from the Consequences of Intervention in Foreign Countries.* U.S. military interventions, foreign military bases, and threats, economic coercion, and political domination of foreign states must be prohibited. Economic exploitation of foreign countries, their people, and resources must cease. The use of private wealth to buy valuable property in poor nations and former Communist countries at distress prices must be prohibited and equitable adjustments required where it has occurred. Interventions divert resources needed for domestic purposes, exploit U.S. citizens enlisted in foreign adventures, create divisions within the country, and cause hostility to Americans overseas.

E. REFORM OF INTERNATIONAL MEDIA AND INFORMATION

1. *Freedom of Information.* Fundamental human rights to knowledge, communication, and a robust, uninhibited, and diverse media free of political, ideological, and economic control should be assured. World opinion is deprived of information essential to meaningful choice and is often misinformed on issues of vital importance. Democratic institutions cannot fulfill their purposes when the public is uninformed, misinformed, or manipulated by news and other communications organizations. The 1979 Report of the International Commission for the Study of Communications Problems — the MacBride Report — should be updated and implemented to assure that its concerns are addressed, including stimulating a

greater flow of Third World information, greater access to the media by the poor and opposition groups, communications service for all languages, rights of rebuttal, greater truth in the media, and public identification of paid propaganda.

The UN should fund library and information centers in all nations to provide essential information about the world, the nation, and its communities. The centers should be democratically governed, and charged with reporting significant information from the nation that is not covered by the media or scholars who specialize in the region and subjects affecting it. Communications technology should be shared, newsprint subsidized, and equipment, training, and facilities financed by the UN for Third World communications.

UN efforts to assure freedom of information and adequate dissemination of vital facts and opinion have failed. In its first session in 1946, the UN General Assembly understood freedom of information as "the touchstone of all freedoms to which the United Nations is consecrated." The Economic and Social Council convened a UN conference on freedom of information in 1948. It drafted a convention on the gathering and international transmission of news, freedom of information, and the international right of correction. Only the Convention on Correction has been completed, and only a handful of nations have signed it. It provides that a government which believes it is a victim of false information by another government can transmit its view of the facts to that nation, which must make the communique available to the media within its territory. It failed, however, to require publication of the communique.

2. *Freedom from Media Monopolization.* Efforts to stimulate and broaden electronic and written communication from alternative media sources should be funded by the UN and private organizations interested in accuracy, full coverage, fairness in the media, and public access to information. This should include TV, cable, audio- and videocassette, radio, shortwave, newspapers, magazines, journals, pamphlets, and other means of mass communication. Efforts to reduce commercialization and advertising in electronic and print media are important to quality, diversity, and fairness in communications. The airwaves belong to the public and should be used to serve the public. Access by different voices, coverage of all important issues, rights of rebuttal, alternative news reports, public service announcements, multilanguage broadcasts, free time for political candidates, and minority and cooperative ownership and program time should be required of licensees.

Media monopolization is one of the worst forms of colonialism. More than any other single factor, it caused the people of the United

States to celebrate the slaughter in Iraq. Universities, colleges, community centers, labor unions, and others should form media councils and study groups to evaluate communications needs, develop communications resources and access, expand available information, and assure full diversity in viewpoints. Such organizations should undertake local, regional, national, and international media evaluations, and should demand access and criticize performances of TV, radio, newspapers, magazines, and books. Ratings of the media on their adequacy and fairness should be publicized. Priorities in media coverage, from nuclear arms control and world hunger to local police protection and garbage disposal, and strategies to fulfill them should be developed.

F. REFORMS TO MAKE INDIVIDUALS, PRIVATE GROUPS, AND NONGOVERNMENTAL ORGANIZATIONS RESPONSIBLE FOR PEACE AND SOCIAL JUSTICE

1. Create an International Center for Peace and Social Justice. A permanent International Center for Peace and Social Justice should be created to develop, perfect, provide alternatives to, propagate, and endeavor to implement the proposals outlined in this chapter. It should include private local, regional, national, and international organizations; seek to develop international political alliances to achieve its goals; emphasize multi-issue coalition building with existing networks; and engage in grassroots organizing and education for peace and social justice. It should monitor UN agencies and prohibited conduct as well as the military, arms sales, military research, military interventions, armed conflict, human rights violations, and others.

The major force for reform must come from the people. Just as war is carried out through human conduct, peace will be achieved by human conduct. It is a question of will, access to information, common sense, and perseverance. Proposals that are seemingly impossible to carry out when power is conceded to existing governments and supporting power structures are readily attainable if people assert their power.

Governments cannot be expected to reform themselves, or be trusted to implement reforms that are achieved. Methods for the constant exercise of power by the people over governments to monitor their actions, inform the public and concerned interests, force reform, police the faithful performance of reform, prevent the governments' misconduct, and ensure their accountability are essential to peace and social justice. Activity to these ends should be constantly stimulated through private organizations, including those concerned with peace, world government, human rights, hunger, health, redistribution of wealth, refugees, education, labor, children, women, military intervention, environment, racism, discrimination, and other issues. The International Center should provide research, library and information services, models, communications, coordination, and assistance for all individuals and private organizations working on such issues.

2. *The International Center's Role in the United States.* The International Center should directly address the proposals for the liberation of the United States because world peace and social justice depend on the success of this endeavor. In organizing within the United States to implement the proposals, the International Center should communicate through its worldwide contacts to inform world opinion and to encourage, enlist, and coordinate international support.

3. *The International Center's Global Role.* The International Center should develop strategies for economic and political cooperation and organization among poor nations and their peoples, developing supporting groups from poor communities and undocumented immigrants in rich nations to prevent economic exploitation of the poor. Unifying interests and issues of poor nations and peoples should be identified and united strategies developed to achieve their attainment. Means for protecting aboriginal peoples and dispersed peoples like the Kurds, exile populations, and overseas communities such as Indians in East Africa should be developed.

Independence, unification, and liberation movements are worldwide phenomena. There are scores of such situations, in which human rights are violated, violence is chronic, and war is possible. Meritorious movements should be supported, claims studied, and strategies for understanding and peaceful settlement pursued. Private action to support independence, sovereignty, self-determination, and healthy development for poor nations and peoples should be organized and supported.

4. *Affiliated Local Centers.* National, regional, and special Centers for Peace and Social Justice, affiliated with the International Center, should be established wherever feasible to develop private capacities to address issues and coordinate with, implement, and support International Center programs.

5. *Permanent People's Assembly.* A fully financed and independent Permanent People's Assembly representing all peoples and adversarial to government should be created to act as a shadow organization

to the UN and its agencies. It should be chosen democratically worldwide and patterned on the UN to make its actions most effective. UN nongovernment organizations and agencies should be free to coordinate their activities with the People's Assembly and its agencies. Policy positions, reports, proposals, and actions of the People's Assembly should be sent by the Assembly, by private groups active in such affairs, and by the media to all interested organizations and individuals as well as to the UN and other governments.

6. *Permanent People's Tribunal.* A fully financed and independent Permanent People's Tribunal should be created to review and report on the work of the International Court of Justice, the International Court of Criminal Justice, and the International Court for Human Rights and Habeas Corpus. The Tribunal should conduct hearings on matters adjudicated in UN courts when they are of major importance and when there is reason to believe these courts have erred. The Tribunal should hear cases of merit involving claims the international courts fail to hear, such as war crimes charges. The Tribunal should be comprised of jurists and other private international figures chosen by the People's Assembly. Its decisions should be widely disseminated, and interest groups should work to implement them.

No mere proposal can change things. Not even the provisions of a supposedly revered Constitution have force beyond the human will to obey them. Until people act, words, even incitations, are pieties. If we the people want peace, we will have to work for it without relent.

War reflects the character of a people. The preparation, planning, commitment to, and commission of war all occur through the conscious choice of some people and the acceptance or acquiescence of many others. War is chosen by people with power. Acts toward and in war are the willful conduct of those who commit them.

The victory of violence in the Persian Gulf presents a clear and present danger to the planet. No American intervention in Third World countries — there have been more than 200 in the Americas, Africa, Asia, and the Middle East — has accomplished any good. After generations of intimate association, Liberia and the Philippines, the U.S. colonies in Africa and Asia, are impoverished, largely illiterate, divided, sick in body, and wracked with violence. Yet American militarism and lust to exploit have never been greater.

The moral wrongness and practical failure of the arms race, the technology of death, bullying, lying, bribery, corruption, and killing are recognized by all, but have been accepted by the people. America has glorified the power of violence and ignored its pity. It has created the most materialistic society that ever existed. Yet for all its affluence, the U.S. infant mortality rate is higher than in most other developed nations and in a number of developing nations.

Americans seem to love things more than people. Millions of infants worldwide starve annually while American dairy farmers are paid $1,400 per milk cow each year to market dairy products. Thus, for a single milk cow, the taxpayers' cost is twice the per capita income of half the world's population. Overwhelmingly, American culture, TV, movies, literature, popular history, photography, and religion celebrates, embraces, and justifies violence, war, greed, wealth, exploitation, and power.

Most Americans have lost any sense of collective purpose and have resigned their obligation as social beings. Their government dominates poor nations, exploits their labor and resources, and abuses and neglects the poor at home while falsely proclaiming it acts in the name of democracy and freedom. Those it does not dominate it holds in thrall with the threat of war.

Human values, and action on them, will determine the future. A gentle people who love others and want to share will not war. A renunciation of all forms of violence, a clear and generous commitment to equality, respect for the rights of others, the love of children, and rejecting greed as the enemy of love and the corrupter of the spirit will be required to purge racism, hatred, fear, and force from human character.

War as a means of ordering affairs among nations and peoples has never achieved real or lasting peace, because that sort of peace is never acceptable to those without power. Those who have sought peace by waging war have always planted the seeds for the next war while corrupting their own character. While a conquering force may have its way for a while, it is an uneasy time that has usually ended disastrously for all.

The imperative need is a vision of peace that is real, desirable, and attainable. This is the major purpose to which people must devote their energies and imaginations. Nothing else will matter if we fail in this. No experience we have had suggests that national governments will find ways for permanent peace, for they know only a superior capacity for violence. Common sense compels the conclusion that modern technology for war will destroy everything unless abolished and controlled.

Thomas Aquinas observed what has always been known when he wrote that war is inevitable among sovereign nations not governed by positive law. World law is essential to peace. International institutions must have the power to prevent war, resolve disputes, enforce disarmament, address offenses by and against nations, protect human rights, provide food, health, education, and housing for the poor, assure independence and self-determination, and maintain economic freedom for all. Those institutions must be subservient to the will of the people.

Our capacity to achieve peace is clear. It is a matter of will. To forge an indomitable will, to pursue our vision of what the world can be, passion is essential; for passion is the vital spring of human action. Humanity's passion must be peace.

Letter to President Bush — February 12, 1991

Text of letter on the air assault's civilian impact to George Bush from Ramsey Clark after his trip to Iraq, February 2–8, 1991, during the U.S. bombing.

February 12, 1991

President George Bush
1600 Pennsylvania Ave NW
Washington, D.C.

Dear Mr. President:

During the period February 2 to February 8, 1991 I traveled in Iraq to assess the damage to civilian life there resulting from the bombing and the embargo, including civilian deaths, injuries, illness and destruction and damage to civilian property. I was accompanied by an experienced camera team that has filmed war and its destructiveness in many countries including Afghanistan, Angola, Cambodia, El Salvador, Nicaragua, the Philippines and Vietnam. Their film documents most of the damage I mention in this letter and some I do not. In our party was an Iraqi-American guide and translator who has family in Baghdad and Basra and is personally familiar with those cities and many other areas of Iraq. He had last visited Baghdad, Basra and Kuwait City in December 1990.

We traveled over 2,000 miles in seven days to view damage, learn of casualties, discuss the effects of the bombing with government officials, public health and safety agency staffs and private families and individuals. We had cooperation from the government of Iraq including Ministers, Governors, health and medical officials and civil defense personnel. The bombing in all parts of Iraq made travel difficult, requiring caution for bomb craters and damage to highways and roads and making night driving especially hazardous.

The damage to residential areas and civilian structures, facilities and utilities was extensive everywhere we went. Every city and town we visited or that was reported to us had no municipal water, electricity or telephone service. Parts of Baghdad had limited delivery of impure water for an hour a day.

The effect of damage to municipal water systems on health and safety is tremendous. The Minister of Health considered potable water for human consumption the single greatest health need in the country. Tens of thousands are known to suffer diarrhea and stomach disorders. There are believed to be hundreds of thousands of unreported cases. Several thousands are believed to have died.

There is no electric lighting in the cities, towns and countryside in daytime or the long winter nights, except for a few interior spaces like hospital emergency rooms where gasoline generators are available. The meaning of this is brought home most painfully in the hospitals at night.

In the hospitals, there is no heat, no clean water except limited quantities for drinking supplied in bottles, no electric light in wards and hospital rooms, and inadequate medicine, even for pain alleviation, in the face of a great increase in critically and severely injured persons. Doctors we talked with in four hospitals are deeply concerned over the absence or shortage of needed medicine and sanitary supplies. Surgeons and medics treating wounds cannot keep their hands clean or gloved, and work in the cold, in poor light with greatly increased numbers of patients in unrelieved pain. Seven hospitals are reported closed by bomb damage. Many if not most have had windows shattered.

Schools are closed. Homes are cold. Candles are the principal lighting. Telephone communication does not exist. Transportation is extremely limited. Gasoline is scarce. Roads and bridges are bombing targets. There is no television. Radio reception is limited to battery powered radios which can receive short-wave signals, a few transmissions from Iraq stations or nearby foreign stations. According to the Ministry of Health, hospital officials and the Red Crescent, there is a substantial increase in falls, home accidents, stress, nervous disorders, shock, heart attack, miscarriage and premature births and infant mortality. Nightly air raids, the sounds of sirens, anti-aircraft fire and the explosion of bombs have placed a great strain on the society as a whole, but particularly on children and individuals with nervous system or heart disorders.

Dr. Ibrahim Al-Nouri has been head of the Red Crescent and Red

Cross of Iraq for ten years. He is a pediatrician by training who interned at Children's Hospital in London, later headed Children's Hospital in Baghdad and served in the Ministry of Health for some years, rising to Deputy Minister. Dr. Noore estimates that there have been 3,000 infant deaths since November 1, 1990 in excess of the normal rate, attributable solely to the shortage of infant milk formula and medicines. Only 14 tons of baby formula have been received during that period. Prior monthly national consumption was approximately 2,500 tons.

One of the early targets of U.S. bombing was the infant and baby milk processing facility in Baghdad. No Iraqi with whom we talked assumed this was a coincidence. The U.S. claim that the plant manufactured chemical warfare material is false. A French company built it. The twenty or more people whom we interviewed, who operated it, who visited it before its destruction and who have examined it since without ill effect all say it was a plant processing infant and baby milk formula. In a lengthy and unrestricted examination of the plant, we saw no evidence to the contrary.

In all areas we visited and all other areas reported to us, municipal water processing plants, pumping stations and even reservoirs have been bombed. Electric generators have been destroyed. Refineries and oil and gasoline storage facilities and filling stations have been attacked. Telephone exchange buildings, TV and radio stations, and some radio telephone relay stations and towers have been damaged or destroyed. Many highways, roads, bridges, bus stations, schools, mosques and churches, cultural sites, and hospitals have been damaged. Government buildings including Executive Offices of the President, the Foreign Ministry, Defense Ministry, Ministry for Industry and Justice Ministry have been destroyed or damaged.

Ambassadors of member states should ask themselves if their capitals, major cities and towns were similarly destroyed and damaged by such bombing, would they consider the targets to be permissible under the International Laws of Armed Conflict. Imagine the reaction if water, electricity, telephones, gasoline, heating and air conditioning, TV and radio were denied to Lima and Arequipa, Lagos and Ibadan, Washington and Chicago, Paris and Marseilles, New Delhi and Calcutta, to Canberra and Sydney, while civilians were bombed in their homes, businesses, shops, markets, schools, churches, hospitals, public places, and roadways.

How can destruction of municipal electricity for Mosul, the telephone system for the people of Baghdad, the municipal water supplies for Basra, or shooting defenseless public buses and private cars on the road to Jordan and elsewhere possibly be justified as necessary to drive Iraq from Kuwait? If it can be so justified, then the United Nations has authorized the destruction of all civilian life of a whole nation.

The effect of the bombing, if continued, will be the destruction of much of the physical and economic basis for life in Iraq. The purpose of the bombing can only be explained rationally as the destruction of Iraq as a viable state for a generation or more. Must the United Nations be a party to this lawless violence?

I will briefly describe destruction to residential areas in some of the cities and towns we visited. In Basra Governor Abdullah Adjram described the bombing as of February 6 as worse than during the Iran-Iraq war. We carefully probed five residential areas that had been bombed.

1. A middle class residential area was heavily damaged at 9:30 P.M. on January 31. Twenty-eight persons were reported killed, 56 were injured, 20 homes and six shops were destroyed.

2. On January 22, an upper middle class residential neighborhood was shattered by three bombs destroying or extensively damaging more than 15 homes and reportedly injuring 40 persons, but without any deaths.

3. On January 24, an upper middle class neighborhood was bombed, killing eight, injuring 26 and destroying three homes and damaging many others.

4. On February 4, described by officials as the heaviest bombing of Basra to February 6, at 2:35 A.M., 14 persons were killed, 46 injured and 128 apartments and homes destroyed or damaged together with an adjacent Pepsi-Cola bottling plant and offices across a wide avenue. The area devastated was three blocks deep on both sides of streets. At least fifteen cars were visible, crushed in garages. Small anti-personnel bombs were alleged to have fallen here and we saw what appeared to be one that did not explode embedded in rubble. We were shown the shell of a "mother" bomb which carries the small fragmentation bombs.

5. On January 28, about eighteen units in a very large low cost public housing project were destroyed or severely damaged, killing 46 and injuring 70. The nearby high school was damaged by a direct hit on a corner. The elementary school across the street was damaged.

On the evening of February 5 at 8:30 P.M. while our small group was dining alone by candlelight in the Sheraton Basra, three large bomb blasts broke glass in the room. We went upstairs to the roof.

From there I saw one bomb fall into the Shatt-Al-Arab beyond the Teaching Hospital to the south throwing a column of water high into the air; another bomb hit near the Shaat. As agreed upon earlier, civil defense officials came to take us to the blast sites. They were 1.2 km down the street near the Shatt Al Arab. I had walked by the area about 6:30 P.M.

We found two buildings destroyed. It is an apartment and residential home area. One was a family club, the other a night club. If either had been open scores of people would have been killed. Palm trees were sheared off and shrapnel, rocks, dirt and glass covered the street for several hundred feet. We were unable to enter the buildings that night.

We returned the next morning and were told both buildings were empty at the time by the owners who were looking at the damage. The teaching hospital, about 150 yards distant, which had been closed for a week following earlier bombing, was without windows. It apparently received no new damage. As with all the other civilian damage we saw we could find no evidence of any military presence in the area. Here, there was no utility or facility that were frequent, if illegal, targets either. There were only homes, apartments and a few shops, grocery stores and other businesses found in residential areas, plus two small bridges connecting the hospital to the mainland.

We were informed by a variety of sources including visual observation during extensive driving in Basra, that many other residential properties had been hit and that the five areas we filmed were a minor fraction of the civilian damage that had occurred.

At the central market where more than 1,000 shops and vendors sell fruits, vegetables, fish, meat, foodstuffs and other items, a bomb leaving a huge crater had demolished a building with a grocery store and other shops and damaged an entry area to the market at about 4:00 P.M. It reportedly killed eight persons and injured 40.

We examined the rubble of a Sunni Moslem Mosque, Al Makal, where a family of 12 had taken sanctuary. The minaret remained standing. Ten bodies were found under the rubble and identified by a family member who had returned from his military post when informed of the tragedy. The dead included his wife and four young children.

In Diwaniya, a smaller town, we examined the same types of civilian damage we witnessed elsewhere and that was reported everywhere. In the town center, apparently seeking to destroy the radio telephone relay equipment in the post office, bombing had damaged the tower and the office. We saw many similar or identical relay towers in the region that had not been attacked. Adjacent to the Post Office on the central circle of the city, three small hotels of 30 to 50 rooms were destroyed together with a host of shops, cafes, and offices including those of doctors and lawyers. We were told 12 people were killed and 35 injured. More damage could be seen across the circle among business and apartment buildings from one or more bombs that fell there.

Near the outskirts of town, four more-or-less contiguous residential areas had been bombed. Twenty-three persons were reported killed and 75 injured. Two schools were badly damaged. There was no water, electricity or telephone service. A water irrigation station was destroyed. Other damage was witnessed while driving around the town. On the outskirts an oil tank was on fire, one of more than a dozen we saw burning during our travels.

Baghdad has been more accessible to foreign observation than Basra and other places in Iraq. It will only be highlighted. We examined extensive damage on a main street in the blocks next to and across the street from the Ministry of Justice which had all its windows on one side blasted out. I know that area as a busy poor commercial residential area from walking through it on the way to the National Museum and visiting the Justice Ministry. A large supermarket, eight other stores and six or eight houses were destroyed or badly damaged. Across the street, one bomb hit on the sidewalk and another was a direct hit on housing behind the street front properties. Six shops, a restaurant and several other stores plus 9 or 10 homes were destroyed, or badly damaged. We could not get an agreed account of casualties from the 40 or 50 people standing around the damage. Some said as many as 30 died and many more were injured.

We visited a residential area where several homes were destroyed on February 7. Six persons in one family were killed in an expensive home and several others in adjacent properties. One 500 lb. bomb had failed to explode and the tail was seen above the thick concrete roof when a member of our team first drove by. When we returned, the bomb had been removed. Our camera team visited the hospital where the injured were taken later that afternoon. The critically injured father from the home where the bomb failed to explode was there. This was one of four hospitals treating persons injured in bombings that we visited.

A bus station was hit by a bomb and the stained glass in a nearby mosque shattered. We were unable to learn if anyone was killed though 40–50 people were at the station near midnight when we drove by on our arrival.

We saw five different damaged telephone exchanges while driving around Baghdad and many destroyed and damaged government and private buildings. Bridges in Baghdad were a frequent target though damage to them was minimal when we left. The bridges are not a legitimate military target. Even Defense Ministry buildings are occupied by non-combatants. The telephone exchanges run by civilians are overwhelmingly processing non-military calls. The military has the most extensive independent communications capacity in the country. These are not legitimate targets and the effort to bomb them necessarily takes civilian lives.

Damage in Basra appeared to be considerably more extensive than in Baghdad and the actual bombing there was much more intensive than at any time we were in Baghdad. There were civilian deaths every night we were in Baghdad.

Visits to the towns of Hilla, Najaf, and Nasiriyah by press corps representatives and our crew found civilian casualties in residential areas of each, damages to a medical clinic, 12 deaths in one family, and 46 deaths in one night of bombing in one town. A small town was bombed a few minutes before we passed through on our drive back from Basra. We saw no military presence there. Smoke could be seen from three fires.

Over the 2,000 miles of highways, roads and streets we traveled, we saw scores, probably several hundred, destroyed vehicles. There were oil tank trucks, tractor trailers, lorries, pickup trucks, a public bus, a mini-bus, a taxicab and many private cars destroyed by aerial bombardment and strafing. Some were damaged when they ran into bomb craters in the highways or road damage caused by bombs and strafing. We found no evidence of military equipment or supplies in the vehicles. Along the roads we saw several oil refinery fires and numerous gasoline stations destroyed. One road repair camp had been bombed on the road to Amman.

As with the city streets in residential, industrial and commercial areas where we witnessed damage, we did not see a single damaged or destroyed military vehicle, tank, armored car, personnel carrier or other military equipment, or evidence of any having been removed. We saw scores of oil tank cars driving between Iraq and Jordan and parked in Jordan, as well as five or six that were destroyed by planes on the highway. We saw no evidence of any arms or military materiel on or around the destroyed and burned out tank trucks, or those not hit.

No one in the press corps or among the civilians we encountered reported to us that they had seen any evidence of the presence of military vehicles having been hit on the highways or having been in the vicinity of civilian property, or private vehicles hit before, during or after an aerial strike. We saw no evidence of any military presence in the areas of damage described in this letter.

It is preposterous to claim military equipment is being placed in residential areas to escape attack. Residential areas are regularly attacked. The claim reveals a policy of striking residential areas, because it purports to establish a justification for doing so. If there had been military vehicles in the civilian areas we examined, or on the roads and highways we traveled when bombing occurred, it is inconceivable that among all that debris we would not find some fragments of military vehicles, material, equipment or clothing. Not only did pinpoint precision fail to hit military targets in civilian areas, they were not collaterally damaged in the attacks on civilian life. Had they been present they would have been hit.

The government of Iraq has vastly understated civilian casualties in Iraq. This is not an uncommon phenomenon for governments in wartime.

The inescapable and tragic fact is thousands of civilians have been killed in the bombings. The bombings are conducted with this knowledge.

Dr. Nouri, with more than four decades in medical service and ten years as head of Red Crescent, estimates 6,000 to 7,000 civilian deaths, and many thousands of injuries from bombings. Red Crescent vehicles transport medicine and medical supplies into Iraq from Jordan and Iran. They make deliveries as often as two to three times a week to some cities and hospitals but regularly to hospitals throughout the country. These contacts and hospital requests for medicines and supplies along with the relationships established over the years provide a solid base for his opinion.

He adds to the toll thousands of deaths from failure to obtain adequate supplies of infant formula and medicine, from contaminated water and from increased death rates from stress, heart attacks and similar causes.

While I applaud the UN initiative in designating a mission to Baghdad to carry medical supplies and ascertain the health needs of the Iraqi people, I urge you to seek major funding now or release of Iraqi funds for supplying 2,500 tons of infant and baby milk formula, greatly needed medicines and sanitation supplies, municipal water system restoration and water purification.

The bombing constitutes the most grievous violation of international law. It is intended to destroy the civilian life and economy of Iraq. It is not necessary, meaningful or permissible as a means of driving Iraq from Kuwait.

No UN resolution authorizes any military assault on Iraq, except as is necessary to drive Iraqi forces from Kuwait. The bombing that has occurred throughout Iraq is the clearest violation of international law and norms for armed conflict, including the Hague and Geneva Conventions and the Nuremberg Charter. It is uncivilized, brutal and racist by any moral standard. With few if any exceptions we witnessed, the destruction is not conceivably within the language or contemplation of Security Council Resolution 678/44.

I urge you to immediately notify the Member States of the General Assembly and the Security Council of the information herein provided. I urge you to ask for the creation of an investigative body to examine the effect of U.S. bombing of Iraq on the civilian life of the country. Most urgent, I ask you to do everything within your power to stop the bombing of cities, civilian population, public utilities, public highways, bridges and all other civilian areas and facilities in Iraq, and elsewhere. If there is no ceasefire, bombing must be limited to military targets in Kuwait, concentrations of military forces in Iraq near the border of Kuwait, operational military air fields or identified Scud launching sites or mobile missile launchers in Iraq. If a cease fire is not achieved, the immediate cessation of this lawless bombing of civilian and noncombatants is essential.

The use of highly sophisticated military technology with mass destructive capacity by rich nations against an essentially defenseless civilian population of a poor nation is one of the great tragedies of our time. United States annual military expenditures alone are four times the gross national product of Iraq.

We have 6–7 hours of videotape of much of the damage to civilian life and property described above. It includes painful hospital interviews with children, women and men injured in these assaults. The tape was not reviewed or in any way examined by anyone in Iraq before we left, and the actual filming was largely unobserved by any Iraqi official. This footage is being edited. I will send you a copy as soon as it is ready within the next few days. If you wish to have the entire tapes reviewed, let me know and I will arrange a screening.

Copies of this letter are being sent to Secretary Perez de Cuellar, President Hussein, and the United Nations Ambassadors for the United States and Iraq.

Sincerely,
Ramsey Clark

Letter to Senate Committee on Foreign Relations

April 13, 1991

Sen. Claiborne Pell
Committee on Foreign Relations
U.S. Senate
Suite SD-419
Dirksen Building
Washington, DC

Dear Senator Pell:

In its consideration of legislation concerning war crimes committed in the Persian Gulf conflict, the Committee on Foreign Relations must address the conduct of all the parties. Two important principles dictate this.

The first duty of every nation is accountability for its own conduct. Each nation and its citizens as well have the duty of insuring their own compliance with international law. Before you can credibly judge others, you must judge yourself by the same standard. Otherwise your foreign relations are based on power, not principle.

Second, nothing is more fundamental to the idea of government embodied in our Constitution than equal justice under law. Nothing is more corrupting of law than "victor's justice," an oxymoron. No nation, no person, is above the law.

The United States is primarily responsible for the systematic destruction of civilian water systems, power generation plants, telephone communications equipment, fuel oil pumping, refining, storage and distribution facilities, irrigation works, food production, storage and distribution centers, foodstuffs and residential, commercial and business structures. At least 25,000 civilians died from the bombings and many thousands more from its consequences including deaths from polluted drinking water, lack of health care capacity and shortages of medicines. Commission staff members presently in Iraq have sent an alarming report of medical opinion that typhus, hepatitis, cholera and other illnesses that are a consequence of the destruction will rise sharply with the summer months. Of course, these casualties involve all the people of Iraq, Shiite and Sunni Moslems, Kurds, Chaldeans and others.

U.S. aircraft made civilians the object of attack, bombed indiscriminately, deliberately destroyed facilities and objects indispensable to the survival of the civilian population, failed to take precautions to spare the civilian population, used prohibited weapons and caused excessive and unnecessary suffering. The very ratio of more than 100,000 Iraqi military deaths to fewer than 200 U.S. military deaths evidences the excessive use of force by the U.S. against Iraq's army.

Among others, the conduct described violates provisions of the Hague Conventions of 1907, the Geneva Conventions of 1949 and Articles 51–57 of Protocol I, Additional to the Geneva Conventions of 1977, the Nuremberg Charter of 1945, and the several U.S. military service manuals addressing the laws of armed conflict.

Your Committee will fail in its duty to the American people if it does not hear independent evidence on issues of crimes against peace and war crimes committed by the United States and require executive branch witnesses to testify about U.S. military actions, including bombing targets.

The Commission of Inquiry for the International War Crimes Tribunal which is conducting its independent investigation requests the opportunity to present evidence in public hearings. I am available for discussion, testimony or other assistance.

I am enclosing a copy of a letter I sent to President Bush, dated February 12, 1991, after my visit to Iraq during the bombing and an announcement of the formation of a Commission of Inquiry for the International War Crimes Tribunal.

Sincerely,
Ramsey Clark

Complaint Charging President Bush with War Crimes

Initial Complaint Charging George Bush, Dan Quayle, James Baker, Dick Cheney, William Webster, Colin Powell, Norman Schwarzkopf, and others to be named with crimes against peace, war crimes, crimes against humanity, and other criminal acts and high crimes in violation of the Charter of the United Nations, international law, the Constitution of the United States, and laws made in pursuance thereof. Dated May 6, 1991.

The Nineteen Charges Against Bush, Cheney, et al.

1. The United States engaged in a pattern of conduct beginning in or before 1989 intended to lead Iraq into provocations justifying U.S. military action against Iraq and permanent U.S. military domination of the Gulf.

2. President Bush from August 2, 1990, intended and acted to prevent any interference with his plan to destroy Iraq economically and militarily.

3. President Bush ordered the destruction of facilities essential to civilian life and economic productivity throughout Iraq.

4. The United States intentionally bombed and destroyed civilian life, commercial and business districts, schools, hospitals, mosques, churches, shelters, residential areas, historical sites, private vehicles and civilian government offices.

5. The United States intentionally bombed indiscriminately throughout Iraq.

6. The United States intentionally bombed and destroyed Iraqi millitary personnel, used excessive force, killed soldiers seeking to surrender and in disorganized individual flight, often unarmed and far from any combat zones and randomly and wantonly killed Iraqi soldiers and destroyed materiel after the cease fire.

7. The United States used prohibited weapons capable of mass de-

struction and inflicting indiscriminate death and unnecessary suffering against both military and civilian targets.

8. The United States intentionally attacked installations in Iraq containing dangerous substances and forces.

9. President Bush ordered U.S. forces to invade Panama, resulting in the deaths of 1,000 to 4,000 Panamanians and the destruction of thousands of private dwellings, public buildings and commercial structures.

10. President Bush obstructed justice and corrupted United Nations functions as a means of securing power to commit crimes against peace and war crimes.

11. President Bush usurped the Constitutional power of Congress as a means of securing power to commit crimes against peace, war crimes, and other high crimes.

12. The United States waged war on the environment.

13. President Bush encouraged and aided Shiite Muslims and Kurds to rebel against the government of Iraq causing fratricidal violence, emigration, exposure, hunger and sickness and thousands of deaths. After the rebellion failed, the U.S. invaded and occupied parts of Iraq without authority in order to increase division and hostility within Iraq.

14. President Bush intentionally deprived the Iraqi people of essential medicines, potable water, food and other necessities.

15. The United States continued its assault on Iraq after the cease fire, invading and occupying areas at will.

16. The United States has violated and condoned violations of human rights, civil liberties and the U.S. Bill of Rights in the United States, in Kuwait, Saudi Arabia and elsewhere to achieve its purpose of military domination.

17. The United States, having destroyed Iraq's economic base, demands reparations which will permanently impoverish Iraq and threaten its people with famine and epidemic.

18. President Bush systematically manipulated, controlled, directed, misinformed and restricted press and media coverage to obtain constant support in the media for his military and political goals.

19. The United States has by force secured a permanent military presence in the Gulf, the control of its oil resources and geopolitical domination of the Arabian Peninsula and Gulf region.

List of Commission of Inquiry Hearings and Meetings

INTERNATIONAL AND U.S. COMMISSION OF INQUIRY HEARINGS AND MEETINGS HELD IN 1991 FOR THE INTERNATIONAL WAR CRIMES TRIBUNAL

AUSTRALIA
Sydney

DENMARK
Copenhagen

ITALY
Rome

PHILIPPINES
Manila

BELGIUM
Brussels

EGYPT
Cairo

JAPAN
Tokyo

SPAIN
Madrid

BRITAIN
London
Birmingham
Manchester
Bradford

FRANCE
Strasberg

GERMANY
Stuttgart
Berlin

JORDAN
Amman

MALAYSIA
Kuala Lumpur

SWEDEN
Stockholm

TURKEY
Ankara
Cizre
Diyarbakir
Istanbul

NORWAY
Oslo

CANADA
Montreal
Toronto
Hamilton

HONG KONG

INDIA
Delhi

PAKISTAN
Lahore

NEW ENGLAND
New Haven, CT
Amherst, MA
Boston, MA

MID-ATLANTIC
Washington, DC
Long Island, NY
New Paltz, NY
New York, NY
Syracuse, NY

MIDWEST
Ames, IA
Des Moines, IA
Indianapolis, IN
Cleveland, OH

SOUTH
Atlanta, GA
New Orleans, LA
Raleigh, NC
Nashville, TN
Charlottesville, VA

SOUTHWEST
Houston, TX

WEST COAST
Los Angeles, CA
Petaluma, CA
San Francisco, CA
San Luis Obispo, CA
Portland, OR
Seattle, WA
Santa Rosa, CA

Final Judgment of International War Crimes Tribunal

For the International War Crimes Tribunal

Final Judgment

The Members of the International War Crimes Tribunal, meeting in New York, having carefully considered the Initial Complaint of the Commission of Inquiry dated May 6, 1991 against President George W. Bush, Vice President Dan Quayle, Secretary of Defense Richard Cheney, Chairman of the Joint Chiefs of Staff Colin Powell and Gen. Norman Schwarzkopf, Commander of the Allied Forces in the Persian Gulf charging them with nineteen separate crimes against peace, war crimes and crimes against humanity in violation of the Charter of the United Nations, the 1949 Geneva Conventions, the First Protocol thereto, other international agreements and customary international law;

having the right and obligation as citizens of the world to sit in judgment regarding violations of international humanitarian law;

having heard the testimony from various Commissions of Inquiry hearings held within their own countries and/or elsewhere during the past year and having received reports from numerous other Commission hearings which recite the evidence there gathered;

having been provided with documentary evidence, eyewitness statements, photos, videotapes, special reports, expert analyses and summaries of evidence available to the Commission;

having access to all evidence, knowledge, and expert opinion in the Commission files or available to Commission staff;

having been provided by the commission, or otherwise obtained, various books, articles, and other written materials on various aspects of events and conditions in the Persian Gulf and military and arms establishments;

having considered newspaper coverage, magazine and periodical reports, special publications, TV, radio and other media coverage and public statements by the accused, other public officials and other public materials;

having heard the presentations of the Commission of Inquiry in public hearing on February 29, 1992 and the testimony and evidence there presented;

and having met, considered and deliberated with each other and with Commission staff and having considered all the evidence that is relevant to the nineteen charges of criminal conduct alleged in the Initial Complaint make the following findings:

Findings

The Members of the International War Crimes Tribunal finds each of the named accused Guilty on the basis of the evidence against them and that each of the nineteen separate crimes alleged in the Initial Complaint, attached hereto, has been established to have been committed beyond a reasonable doubt.

The Members believe that it is imperative if there is ever to be peace that power be accountable for its criminal acts and we condemn in the strongest possible terms those found guilty of the charges herein. We urge the Commission of Inquiry and all people to act on recommendations developed by the Commission to hold power accountable and to secure social justice on which lasting peace must be based.

Recommendations

The Members urge the immediate revocation of all embargoes, sanctions and penalties against Iraq because they constitute a continuing crime against humanity.

The Members urge public action to prevent new aggressions by the United States threatened against Iraq, Libya, Cuba, Haiti, North Korea, Pakistan, other countries, and the Palestinian people, fullest condemnation of any threat or use of military technology against life, both civilian and military, as was used by the United States against the people of Iraq.

The Members urge that the power of the United Nations Security Council, which was blatantly manipulated by the U.S. to authorize illegal military action and sanctions, be vested in the General Assembly; that all permanent members be removed and that the right of veto be eliminated as undemocratic and contrary to the basic principles of the UN Charter.

The Members urge the Commission to provide for the permanent preservation of the reports, evidence and materials gathered to make them available to others, and to seek ways to provide the widest possible distribution of the truth about the U.S. assault on Iraq.

Charges of Other Countries

In accordance with the last paragraph of the Initial Complaint designated Scope of Inquiry, the Commission has gathered substantial evidence of criminal acts by governments and individual officials in addition to those formally presented here. Formal charges have been drafted by some Commissions of Inquiry against other governments in addition to the United States. Those charges have not been acted on here. The Commission of Inquiry or any of its national components may choose to pursue such other charges at some future time. The Members urge all involved to exert their utmost effort to prevent recurrences of violations by other governments that were not considered here.

Done in New York this 29th day of February 1992.

Judges of the International War Crimes Tribunal

JUDGES ON THE INTERNATIONAL WAR CRIMES TRIBU-
NAL, NEW YORK, FEBRUARY 28–29, 1992

Aisha Nyerere, TANZANIA. Resident Magistrate of the High Court in Arusha, Tanzania.

Olga Mejia, PANAMA. President of the National Human Rights Commission in Panama, a non-governmental delegated body representing peasants' organizations, urban trade unions, women's groups' and others.

Bassam Haddadin, JORDAN. Member of Parliament, Second Secretary for the Jordanian Democratic Peoples Party.

Sheik Mohamed Rashid, PAKISTAN. Former deputy prime minister and agriculture minister. Political prisoner in battle against British colonialism.

Laura Albizu Campos Meneses, PUERTO RICO. Past President of the Puerto Rican Nationalist Party and current Secretary for Foreign Relations.

Dr. Sherif Hetata, EGYPT. Medical doctor, author. Member of the Central Committee of the Arab Progressive Unionist Party. Political prisoner 14 years in 1950s and 1960s.

Dr. Haluk Gerger, TURKEY. Founding member of Turkish Human Rights Association and professor of political science. Dismissed from Ankara University in 1982 by military government.

Abderrazak Kilani, TUNISIA. Representing the Tunisian Bar Association. Former President of the Tunisian Association of Young Lawyers. Founding member of the National Committee to Remove the Embargo from Iraq.

John Jones, USA. Community leader in the state of New Jersey. Vietnam veteran who became leader of movement against U.S. attack on Iraq.

Susumu Ozaki, JAPAN. Former justice, imprisoned 1934–1938 for violating Security Law under militarist government for opposing Japan's invasion of China. Labor lawyer after World War II ended.

Opato Matamah, of the MENOMINEE NATION of North America. Involved in defense of human rights of indigenous peoples since 1981.

Peter Leibovitch, CANADA. President of United Steel Workers of America, USWA, Local 8782, and of the Executive Council of the Ontario Federation of Labor.

John Philpot, QUEBEC. Attorney, member of Board of Directors of Quebec Movement for Sovereignty. Organizing Secretary for the American Association of Jurists in Canada.

Rene Dumont, FRANCE. Agronomist, ecologist, specialist in developing countries, author.

Lord Tony Gifford, BRITAIN. Human rights lawyer practicing in England and Jamaica.

Dr. Alfred Mechtersheimer, GERMANY. Former member of the Bundestag from the Green Party. Former Lieutenant Colonel in the Bundeswehr, current peace researcher.

Deborah Jackson, USA. First vice president of the American Association of Jurists, a body of attorneys, judges, and legal scholars from South and North America and the Caribbean.

Gloria La Riva, USA. Founding member of the Farmworkers Emergency Relief Committee and Emergency Committee to Stop the U.S. War in the Middle East. Community and labor activist.

Key Martin, USA. Arrested frequently for anti-war organizing during Vietnam War. Current chapter chairperson of Local 3 of the Newspaper Guild.

Michael Ratner, USA. Currently attorney and former director of the Center for Constitutional Rights, past president of the National Lawyers Guild.

Serving in absentia:

Tan Sri Noordin bin Zakaria, MALAYSIA. Former Auditor General of Malaysia. Known throughout his country for battling corruption in government.

P. S. Poti, INDIA, former Chief Justice of the Gujarat High Court. In 1989 elected president of the All-India Lawyers Union.

Letter to President Bush — February 1992

March 4, 1992

President George Bush
1600 Pennsylvania Ave NW
Washington, D.C.

Dear Mr. Bush:

In May, 1991, you were sent an initial complaint by the International Commission of Inquiry containing the 19 charges against you and others of crimes against peace, war crimes and crimes against humanity. You were asked to submit any evidence you wished in your own defense and invited personally or by representative to attend any hearings and examine all evidence against you. The Commission has since conducted hearings in more than 20 countries with over 30 hearings in the United States alone.

On Saturday, February 29, 1992, in New York, the International War Crimes Tribunal, having considered the evidence gathered by the Commission, held the final hearing. At the conclusion of the hearing, you were found guilty of all 19 charges. The other defendants — Vice President Dan Quayle, Secretary of Defense Richard Cheney, Joint Chiefs of Staff Chair Colin Powell, former CIA director William Webster, and General H. Norman Schwarzkopf — were also found guilty of the charges against them. Enclosed is a copy of the Final Judgment of the Tribunal, a copy of the charges and a printed list of the Tribunal Judges.

The consequences of your criminal acts include the deaths of more than 250,000 children, women and men, mostly civilians, and the crippling of an entire country. You are held accountable by hundreds of millions of people around the world, as you will be by history. You have placed another bloody stain on the honor of your country and its people.

273

You must not engage in further violence, murder and militarism. You must not let your arrogance, falsity and hostility for the poor and the weak — all of which were aided by the silence of the media — lead you to commit further crimes.

If you have anything to say for yourself, the Commission and the Tribunal will hear you or your representative.

Sincerely,
Ramsey Clark

Letter to UN Secretary General Ghali — March 1992

His Excellency Boutros Boutros-Ghali
Secretary General
Room 3800
United Nations
New York, NY 10017

Dear Secretary General Ghali,

I am writing to inform you of the decision rendered by the International War Crimes Tribunal regarding U.S. conduct in the Persian Gulf War.

The Tribunal considered evidence gathered by hearings of the Commission of Inquiry, held in 20 countries and more than 30 cities in the United States.

On Saturday, February 29, 1992, in New York, the Tribunal's international panel of judges, having considered the evidence gathered by the Commission, held the final hearing. At the conclusion, U.S. President George Bush was found guilty of all nineteen charges brought against him by the Commission. The other U.S. government defendants — Vice President Dan Quayle, Secretary of State James Baker, Secretary of Defense Richard Cheney, former CIA director William Webster, Joint Chiefs of Staff Colin Powell, General H. Norman Schwarzkopf — were also found guilty of the charges against them.

Enclosed is a copy of the Final Judgment of the Tribunal, a copy of the charges and a printed list of the Tribunal judges.

I call your particular attention to charge 10, which reads: President Bush obstructed justice and corrupted United Nations functions as a means of securing power to commit crimes against peace and war crimes.

The evidence supporting this charge is overwhelming, as I am sure you know. It includes bribes and threats employed by the U.S. to use the UN for purposes of war. I am sure you are familiar with the statement made in the Security Council by the U.S. representative to the Yemeni representative: "That was the most expensive 'no' vote you ever cast." Three days later, the U.S. canceled its $70 million aid package to impoverished Yemen.

I wish also to highlight a number of the judges' recommendations, which read:

The Members urge the immediate revocation of all embargoes, sanctions and penalties against Iraq, because they constitute a continuing crime against humanity.

The Members urge public action to prevent new aggressions by the United States threatened against Iraq, Libya, Cuba, Haiti, North Korea, Pakistan, other countries and the Palestinian people, as well as fullest condemnation of any threat or use of military technology against life, both civilian and military, as was used by the United States against the people of Iraq.

The Members urge that the power of the United Nations Security Council, which was blatantly manipulated by the U.S. to authorize illegal military action and sanctions, be vested in the General Assembly; that all permanent members be removed and that the right of veto be eliminated as undemocratic and contrary to the basic principles of the UN Charter.

The UN, founded to "save succeeding generations from the scourge of war," was used by the U.S. as a tool to wage war against the people of Iraq, killing 250,000 children, women and men, mostly civilians, and to cripple an entire country. I urge you to do everything in your power to make sure it never happens again. I ask also that you consider the charges enclosed and to call our office for any clarification, evidence or relevant proof.

Sincerely,
Ramsey Clark

Letter to the Media — March 1992

To the Press,

I urge you to search your conscience to see if you believe your publication's failure to cover the decision of the International War Crimes Tribunal constitutes a breach of your professional responsibility to the public. It was held last Saturday and was covered extensively by the foreign media. Some 80 correspondents from outside this country felt that the trial of United States government officials for the devastation they had wrought on Iraq was an important news story. The foreign media was present as an international panel of 22 judges gave the pronouncement of guilt to a spontaneous, thunderous and lengthy standing ovation by an audience of 1,500.

The Tribunal was a historic event, culminating a year of Commission hearings held in more than twenty countries, with over thirty hearings in the United States alone.

Enclosed is a copy of the Final Judgement of the Tribunal, a copy of the charges and a printed list of the Members of the Tribunal.

I call your particular attention to charge 18 of the Commission's Initial Complaint which reads: President Bush systematically manipulated, controlled, directed, misinformed and restricted press and media coverage to obtain constant support in the media for his military and political goals.

The evidence supporting this charge is overwhelming, as I believe you know. It includes what can only be described as a five-month running commercial for militarism preceding the actual assault.

For those who believe the truth can make us free, the saddest illustration of media corruption is the cashier's desk at the Al-Rashid hotel in Baghdad on the morning of January 15, 1991. There waiting in line to check out and leave Iraq on the eve of what was to be one of the major news events of recent years were some the most famous and highly paid personalities in the American media.

If, as we are told, the reason the U.S. media fled Baghdad was for personal safety, does this not prove they believe that the millions of civilians in Iraq were also endangered?

The consequences of Bush's criminal acts include the deaths of more than 250,000 children, women and men, mostly civilians, and the crippling of an entire country. The Bush administration is held accountable by the hundreds of millions of people around the world as he will be by history. He has placed another bloody stain in the honor of our country and its people.

Feel free to call if you have any questions; if you care to examine any evidence gathered by the Commission; to interview staff or any Member of the Tribunal; to quote from our transcripts, affidavits, hearings, or reports, or use any photos or videotapes in our possession.

Sincerely,
Ramsey Clark

Letter to UN Security Council — March 1992

Sent to the members of the UN Security Council concerning threats of renewed military intervention and continued sanctions against Iraq.

March 12, 1992

Dear Mr. Ambassador,

I am transmitting herewith a copy of the charges, list of judges and final judgment of the International War Crimes Tribunal. These documents were sent to the Secretary General when the judgment was printed, but you may not have seen it.

I call your particular attention to the finding of the Tribunal that the 5–6,000 deaths monthly caused by the combination of bomb damage and UN sanctions are a continuing crime against humanity. President Bush for purposes of his domestic presidential campaign may require the elimination of Saddam Hussein, but your sanctions are killing infants, children, the sick and the elderly and you know it.

The war crimes of which U.S. officials have been convicted have resulted in the deaths of at least 250,000 human beings to date and the crippling of Iraq's civilian society. The U.S. claims 148 U.S. combat deaths, many from its own weapons. There was no war, only a simple, merciless slaughter of tens of thousands by 110,000 aerial sorties dropping 88,000 tons of explosives, 93% free falling on a defenseless country.

The arrogance of the United States and its Ambassador Thomas Pickering, speaking of the "lamentable performance" of Iraq's Foreign Minister in the wake of its murderous performance, is equalled only by the threats of further military violence against Iraq by nuclear powers like the U.S., the United Kingdom and France.

Before further punitive measures are taken against Iraq, the Security Council should ask:

• What has the Security Council done to prevent further arms sales to the Middle East, most by permanent members of the Security Council including the proposed sale by the U.S. of 72 advanced F-16s to Saudi Arabia?

• What has the Security Council done to cause Israel to obey UN resolutions over a biblical generation whose violations have been the principal reason for political unrest in the Middle East, or to account for its 300 nuclear warheads and to dismantle them?

• What has the Security Council done to eliminate weapons of mass destruction by its own members and compliance with the Non-Proliferation Treaty? The U.S. possesses most nuclear warheads on the planet, produces most technology for destruction and could obliterate any Member, including Iraq, or even the People's Republic of China with a single launch of nuclear missiles from a Trident II submarine.

• What security can the Security Council offer any Third World country from U.S. aggression, considering its assaults on Grenada, Libya, Panama, Iraq and funding of insurrections against Afghanistan, Angola, Nicaragua and support of military dictators in just the last decade, if it authorizes further sanctions or violence against Iraq?

• What conceivable threat can a rational mind find from a crippled and bleeding Iraq that fully armed couldn't defend itself against U.S. technology? Did it dare use gas and chemical weapons it clearly possessed when it was under murderous attack? Did the U.S. use such illegal weapons as fuel-air explosives, super bombs, anti-personnel fragmentation bombs, napalm and make civilians and civilian facilities the direct object of attack? You know it did. Will it again? You know it will. Ask Panamanians about the Stealth bomber. Remember that on January 9, 1991, President Bush reiterated his opinion that he needed neither UN, nor U.S. Congressional authority to attack Iraq.

Of course, the United Nations should seek to eliminate weapons of mass destruction. It should not use war or hunger and sickness as means, however, and must address the real problems, the nuclear powers, the diffusion of nuclear arms and knowledge from the Soviet Union, and the arms merchants.

Also enclosed is a preliminary copy of a book on U.S. War Crimes prepared by the Commission. The final report which is in preparation will document all the crimes, as found by the Tribunal, beyond a reasonable doubt. History will confirm this judgment, as it will judge your acts in this moment of moral crisis.

Sincerely,
Ramsey Clark

Selections on International Law

PROTOCOL 1 ADDITIONAL TO THE GENEVA CONVENTIONS – 1977

Part IV
Civilian Population
Section 1. General Protection Against Effects of Hostilities
Chapter I. Basic Rule and Field of Application

Article 48. Basic Rule

In order to ensure respect for and protection of the civilian population and civilian objects, the Parties to the conflict shall at all times distinguish between the civilian population and combatants and between civilian objects and military objectives and accordingly shall direct their operations only against military objectives.

Article 49. Definition of Attacks and Scope of Application

1. "Attacks" means acts of violence against the adversary, whether in offense or in defense.

2. The provisions of this Protocol with respect to attacks apply to all attacks in whatever territory conducted, including the national territory belonging to a Party to the conflict but under the control of an adverse Party.

3. The provisions of this Section apply to any land, air, or sea warfare which may affect the civilian population, individual civilians, or civilian objects on land. They further apply to all attacks from the sea or from the air against objectives on land but do not otherwise affect the rules of international law applicable in armed conflict at sea or in the air.

4. The provisions of this Section are additional to the rules concerning humanitarian protection contained in the Fourth Convention, particularly in Part II thereof, and in other international agreements binding upon the High Contracting Parties, as well as to

other rules of international law relating to the protection of civilians and civilian objects on land, at sea, or in the air against the effects of hostilities.

Chapter II. Civilians and Civilian Population

Article 50. Definition of Civilians and Civilian Population

1. A civilian is any person who does not belong to one of the categories of persons referred to in Article 4A (1), (I), (3), and (6) of the Third Convention and in Article 43 of this Protocol. In case of doubt whether a person is a civilian, that person shall be considered to be a civilian.

2. The civilian population comprises all persons who are civilians.

3. The presence within the civilian population of individuals who do not come within the definition of civilians does not deprive the population of its civilian character.

Article 51. Protection of the Civilian Population

1. The civilian population and individual civilians shall enjoy general protection against dangers arising from military operations. To give effect to this protection, the following rules, which are additional to other applicable rules of international law, shall be observed in all circumstances.

2. The civilian population as such, as well as individual civilians, shall not be the object of attack. Acts or threats of violence the primary purpose of which is to spread terror among the civilian population are prohibited.

3. Civilians shall enjoy the protection afforded by this Section, unless and for such time as they take a direct part in hostilities.

4. Indiscriminate attacks are prohibited. Indiscriminate attacks are:

a. those which are not directed at a specific military objective;

b. those which employ a method or means of combat which cannot be directed at a specific military objective; or

c. those which employ a method or means of combat the effects of which cannot be limited as required by this Protocol; and consequently, in each such case, are of a nature to strike military objectives and civilians or civilian objects without distinction.

5. Among others, the following types of attacks are to be considered as indiscriminate:

a. an attack by bombardment by any methods or means which treats as a single military objective a number of clearly separated and distinct military objectives located in a city, town, village, or other area containing a similar concentration of civilians or civilian objects; and

b. an attack which may be expected to cause incidental loss of civilian life, injury to civilians, damage to civilian objects, or a combination thereof, which would be excessive in relation to the concrete and direct military advantage anticipated.

6. Attacks against the civilian population or civilians by way of reprisals are prohibited.

7. The presence or movements of the civilian population or individual civilians shall not be used to render certain points or areas immune from military operations, in particular in attempts to shield military objectives from attacks or to shield, favor, or impede military operations.

The Parties to the conflict shall not direct the movement of the civilian population or individual civilians in order to attempt to shield military objectives from attacks or to shield military operations.

8. Any violation of these prohibitions shall not release the Parties to the conflict from their legal obligations with respect to the civilian population and civilians, including the obligation to take the precautionary measures provided for in Article 57.

Chapter III. Civilian Objects

Article 52. General Protection of Civilian Objects

1. Civilian objects shall not be the object of attack or of reprisals. Civilian objects are all objects which are not military objectives as defined in paragraph 2.

2. Attacks shall be limited strictly to military objectives. In so far as objects are concerned, military objectives are limited to those objects which by their nature, location, purpose or use make an effective contribution to military action and whose total or partial destruction, capture or neutralization, in the circumstances ruling at the time, offers a definite military advantage.

3. In case of doubt whether an object which is normally dedicated to civilian purposes, such as a place of worship, a house or other dwelling or a school, is being used to make an effective contribution to military action, it shall be presumed not to be so used.

Article 53. Protection of Cultural Objects and Places of Worship

Without prejudice to the provisions of the Hague Convention for the Protection of Cultural Property in the Event of Armed Conflict of 14

May 1954, and of other relevant international instruments, it is prohibited:

    a. to commit any acts of hostility directed against the historic monuments, works of art or places of worship which constitute the cultural or spiritual heritage of peoples;

    b. to use such objects in support of the military effort;

    c. to make such objects the object of reprisals.

Article 54. Protection of Objects Indispensable to the Survival of the Civilian Population

1. Starvation of civilians as a method of warfare is prohibited.

2. It is prohibited to attack, destroy, remove, or render useless objects indispensable to the survival of the civilian population, such as foodstuffs, agricultural areas for the production of foodstuffs, crops, livestock, drinking water installations and supplies, and irrigation works, for the specific purpose of denying them for their sustenance value to the civilian population or to the adverse Party, whatever the motive, whether in order to starve out civilians, to cause them to move away, or for any other motive.

3. The prohibitions in paragraph 2 shall not apply to such of the objects covered by it as are used by an adverse Party:

    a. as sustenance solely for the members of its armed forces; or

    b. if not as sustenance, then in direct support of military action, provided, however, that in no event shall actions against these objects be taken which may be expected to leave the civilian population with such inadequate food or water as to cause its starvation or force its movement.

4. These objects shall not be made the object of reprisals.

5. In recognition of the vital requirements of any Party to the conflict in the defense of its national territory against invasion, derogation from the prohibitions contained in paragraph 2 may be made by a Party to the conflict within such territory under its own control where required by imperative military necessity.

Article 55. Protection of the Natural Environment

1. Care shall be taken in warfare to protect the natural environment against widespread, long-term, and severe damage. This protection includes a prohibition of the use of methods or means of warfare which are intended or may be expected to cause such damage to the natural environment and thereby to prejudice the health or survival of the population.

2. Attacks against the natural environment by way of reprisals are prohibited.

Article 56. Protection of Works and Installations Containing Dangerous Forces

1. Works or installations containing dangerous forces, namely dams, dikes, and nuclear electrical generating stations, shall not be made the object of attack, even where these objects are military objectives, if such attack may cause the release of dangerous forces and consequent severe losses among the civilian population. Other military objectives located at or in the vicinity of these works or installations shall not be made the object of attack if such attack may cause the release of dangerous forces from the works or installations and consequent severe losses among the civilian population.

2. The special protection against attack provided by paragraph 1 shall cease:

a. for a dam or a dike only if it is used for other than its normal function and in regular, significant, and direct support of military operations and if such attack is the only feasible way to terminate such support;

b. for a nuclear electrical generating station only if it provides electric power in regular, significant, and direct support of military operations and if such attack is the only feasible way to terminate such support;

c. for other military objectives located at or in the vicinity of these works or installations only if they are used in regular, significant, and direct support of military operations and if such attack is the only feasible way to terminate such support.

3. In all cases, the civilian population and individual civilians shall remain entitled to all the protection accorded them by international law, including the protection of the precautionary measures provided for in Article 57. If the protection ceases and any of the works, installations, or military objectives mentioned in paragraph 1 is attacked, all practical precautions shall be taken to avoid the release of the dangerous forces.

4. It is prohibited to make any of the works, installations, or military objectives mentioned in paragraph 1 the object of reprisals.

5. The Parties to the conflict shall endeavor to avoid locating any military objectives in the vicinity of the works or installations mentioned in paragraph 1. Nevertheless, installations erected for the sole purpose of defending the protected works or installations from attack are permissible and shall not themselves be made the object of attack, provided that they are not used in hostilities except for defensive actions necessary to respond to attacks against the protected

works or installations and that their armament is limited to weapons capable only of repelling hostile action against the protected works or installations.

6. The High Contracting Parties and the Parties to the conflict are urged to conclude further agreements among themselves to provide additional protection for objects containing dangerous forces.

7. In order to facilitate the identification of the objects protected by this article, the Parties to the conflict may mark them with a special sign consisting of a group of three bright orange circles placed on the same axis, as specified in Article 16 of Annex I to this Protocol. The absence of such marking in no way relieves any Party to the conflict of its obligations under this Article.

Chapter IV. Precautionary Measures

Article 57. Precautions in Attack

1. In the conduct of military operations, constant care shall be taken to spare the civilian population, civilians, and civilian objects.

2. With respect to attacks, the following precautions shall be taken:

a. those who plan or decide upon an attack shall:

i. do everything feasible to verify that the objectives to be attacked are neither civilians nor civilian objects and are not subject to special protection but are military objectives within the meaning of paragraph 2 of Article 52 and that it is not prohibited by the provisions of this Protocol to attack them;

ii. take all feasible precautions in the choice of means and methods of attack with a view to avoiding, and in any event to minimizing, incidental loss of civilian life, injury to civilians, and damage to civilian objects;

iii. refrain from deciding to launch any attack which may be expected to cause incidental loss of civilian life, injury to civilians, damage to civilian objects, or a combination thereof, which would be excessive in relation to the concrete and direct military advantage anticipated;

b. an attack shall be canceled or suspended if it becomes apparent that the objective is not a military one or is subject to special protection or that the attack may be expected to cause incidental loss of civilian life, injury to civilians, damage to civilian objects, or a combination thereof, which would be excessive in relation to the concrete and direct military advantage anticipated;

c. effective advance warning shall be given of attacks which may affect the civilian population, unless circumstances do not permit.

3. When a choice is possible between several military objectives for obtaining a similar military advantage, the objective to be selected shall be that on which the attack may be expected to cause the least danger to civilian lives and to civilian objects.

4. In the conduct of military operations at sea or in the air, each Party to the conflict shall, in conformity with its rights and duties under the rules of international law applicable in armed conflict, take all reasonable precautions to avoid losses of civilian lives and damage to civilian objects.

5. No provision of this article may be construed as authorizing any attacks against the civilian population, civilians, or civilian objects.

PRINCIPLES OF THE NUREMBERG TRIBUNAL — 1950

Principles of International Law Recognized in the Charter of the Nuremberg Tribunal and in the Judgment of the Tribunal

Adopted by the International Law Commission of the United Nations, 1950.

Introductory Note. Under General Assembly Resolution 177 (II), paragraph (a), the International Law Commission was directed to "formulate the principles of international law recognized in the Charter of the Nuremberg Tribunal and in the judgment of the Tribunal." In the course of the consideration of this subject the question arose as to whether or not the Commission should ascertain to what extent the principles contained in the Charter and judgment constituted principles of international law. The conclusion was that since the Nuremberg principles had been affirmed by the General Assembly, the task entrusted to the Commission was not to express any appreciation of these principles as principles of international law but merely to formulate them. The text below was adopted by the Commission at its second session. The Report of the Commission also contains commentaries on the principles (see *Yearbook of the International Law Commission* [1950], Vol. I, pp. 374–378).

Principle I

Any person who commits an act which constitutes a crime under international law is responsible therefore and liable to punishment.

Principle II

The fact that internal law does not impose a penalty for an act which constitutes a crime under international law does not relieve the person who committed the act from responsibility under international law.

Principle III

The fact that a person who committed an act which constitutes a crime under international law acted as Head of State or responsible Government official does not relieve him from responsibility under international law.

Principle IV

The fact that a person acted pursuant to order of his Government or of a superior does not relieve him from responsibility under international law, provided a moral choice was in fact possible to him.

Principle V

Any person charged with a crime under international law has the right to a fair trial on the facts and law.

Principle VI

The crimes hereinafter set out are punishable as crimes under international law:

    a. Crimes against peace:

       i. Planning, preparation, initiation or waging of a war of aggression or a war in violation of international treaties, agreements or assurances;

       ii. Participation in a common plan or conspiracy for the accomplishment of any of the acts mentioned under (i).

    b. War crimes:

Violations of the laws or customs of war which include, but are not limited to, murder, ill-treatment, or deportation to slave-labor or for any other purpose of civilian population of or in occupied territory, murder or ill-treatment of prisoners of war, of persons on the seas, killing of hostages, plunder of public or private property, wanton destruction of cities, towns, or villages, or devastation not justified by military necessity.

    c. Crimes against humanity:

Murder, extermination, enslavement, deportation, and other inhuman acts done against any civilian population, or persecutions on political, racial, or religious grounds, when such acts are done or such persecutions are carried on in execution of or in connection with any crime against peace or any war crime.

Principle VII

Complicity in the commission of a crime against peace, a war crime, or a crime against humanity as set forth in Principle VI is a crime under international law.

CHARTER OF THE UNITED NATIONS

Preamble

We the people of the United Nations determined to save succeeding generations from the scourge of war, which twice in our lifetime has brought untold sorrow to mankind, and to reaffirm faith in fundamental human rights, in the dignity and worth of the human person, in the equal rights of men and women, and of nations large and small, and to establish conditions under which justice and respect for the obligations arising from treaties and other sources of international law can be maintained, and to promote social progress and better standards of life in larger freedom. . . .

Article 2

The Organization and its Members, in pursuit of the Purposes stated in Article 1, shall act in accordance with the following Principles.

1. The Organization is based on the principle of the sovereign equality of all its members. . . .

3. All Members shall settle their international disputes by peaceful means in such a manner that international peace and security, and justice, are not endangered.

4. All Members shall refrain in their international relations from the threat or use of force against the territorial integrity or political independence of any state, or in any other manner inconsistent with the Purposes of the United Nations.

Article 33

1. The parties to any dispute, the continuance of which is likely to endanger the maintenance of international peace and security, shall, first of all, seek a solution by negotiation, enquiry, mediation, conciliation, arbitration, judicial settlement, resort to regional agen-

cies or arrangements, or other peaceful means of their own choice.

2. The Security Council shall, when it deems necessary, call upon the parties to settle their disputes by such means.

Notes

CHAPTER 1

1. "Letter from His Majesty King Hussein to H.E. President Saddam Hussein of Iraq: Excerpts," in *White Paper: Jordan and the Gulf Crisis, August 1990–March 1991*, The Government of the Hashemite Kingdom of Jordan, Document VII.

2. Patrick Tyler, "U.S. Strategy Plan Calls for Insuring No Rivals Develop," *New York Times*, March 8, 1992, A1.

3. *Middle East Economic Survey*, May 12, 1961.

4. *New Statesman*, July 15, 1983.

5. David Wise, "A People Betrayed," *Los Angeles Times*, April 14, 1991, M1.

6. Kermit Roosevelt, *Countercoup: The Struggle for Control of Iran* (New York: McGraw-Hill, 1979).

7. Gerard Chaliand and Ismet Seriff Vanly, *People Without A Country: The Kurds and Kurdistan* (London: Zed Press, 1980), 184. See also Daniel Schorr, "1975: Background to Betrayal," *Washington Post*, April 7, 1991, D3; and Christopher Hitchens, "Minority Report," *The Nation*, May 6, 1991, 582.

8. William Safire, *New York Times*, February 12, 1976.

9. See Chaliand and Vanly.

10. See Chaliand and Vanly.

11. Christopher Hitchens, "Why We Are Stuck in the Sand— Realpolitik in the Gulf: A Game Gone Tilt," *Harper's Magazine*, January 1991, 70.

12. Dilip Hiro, *The Longest War* (New York: 1991).

13. Seymour Hersh, "U.S. Secretly Gave Aid to Iraq Early in Its War Against Iran," *New York Times*, January 26, 1992, 1.

14. Shahram Chubinl and Charles Trip, *Iran and Iraq at War* (Boulder, CO: Westview Press, 1988), 207.

15. See Hersh.

16. The Christic Institute, "Covert Operations, the Persian Gulf War and the New World Order" (Washington, DC: The Christic Institute).

17. *Foreign Report* (London: *The Economist*, May 6, 1982).

18. Francis A. Boyle, "International Crisis and Neutrality: U.S. Foreign Policy Toward the Iraq–Iran War," in *Neutrality: Changing Concepts and Practices* (New Orleans: Institute for Comparative Study of Public Policy, University of New Orleans, 1986).

19. See The Christic Institute.

20. See Boyle.

21. U.S. Energy Information Administration, Annual Reports, 1984, 1985. See also Stephen C. Pelletiere et al., *Iraqi Power and U.S. Security in the Middle East* (Carlisle, PA: Strategic Studies Institute, U.S. Army War College).

22. Leslie Gelb, "Bush's Iraqi Blunder," *New York Times*, May 4, 1992, Op-Ed page.

23. Douglas Frantz and Murray Waas. "Secret Effort by Bush Helped Iraq's War Machine," *Los Angeles Times*, February 24, 1992.

24. "'Nightline' on the Bush-Iraq Connection," in *Israel and Palestine Political Report*, June 1991 (No. 164), 5.

25. *Toward 2000* (Istanbul: March 16, 1991).

26. *Far Eastern Economic Review*, December 19, 1991.

27. Report of the Congressional Committees Investigating the Iran–Contra Affair, Appendix A: Vol. 1, Source Documents, Frankfurt Meeting, Tape 12, 1500.

28. Fred Halliday, *Arabia Without Sultans: A Political Survey of Instability in the Arab World* (New York: Vintage Books), 1975.

29. Ibid.

30. Ibid.

31. Ibid.

32. See Roosevelt.

33. See Blackwell.

34. William Webster, "Threat Assessment; Military Strategy; and Operational Requirements," Testimony to Senate Committee on Armed Services, January 23, 1990, 60.

35. H. Norman Schwarzkopf, "Threat Assessment; Military Strategy; and Operational Requirements," Testimony to Senate Committee on Armed Services, , February 8, 1990, 577–579.

36. United States Army, "A Strategic Force for the 19902 and Beyond," January 1990, by Gen. Carl E. Vuono, U.S. Army Chief of Staff, 1–17

37. Patrick Tyler, "While Fear of Big War Fades, Military Plans for Little Ones," *New York Times*, February 3, 1992, A1.

38. See Schwarzkopf.

39. See Blackwell.

40. U.S News & World Report, *Triumph Without Victory: The Unreported History of the Persian Gulf War* (New York: Time Books, 1991), 28–30, and Chapter 2.

41. Tom Mathews, et al., "The Road to War," *Newsweek*, January 28, 1991, 54, 57, 58, 60, 61.

42. See Blackwell.

43. See Pelletiere et al.

44. "News of the Week in Review," *New York Times*, August 5, 1990.

45. Glenn Frankel, "Imperialist Legacy; Lines in the Sand," *Washington Post*, August 31, 1990, A1.

46. Thomas Hayes, "Big Oilfield Is at the Heart of Iraq–Kuwait Dispute," *New York Times*, September 3, 1990, A7. See also G. Henry Schuler, "Congress Must Take a Hard Look at Iraq's Charges Against Kuwait," *Los Angeles Times*, December 2, 1990.

47. Pierre Salinger and Eric Laurent, *Secret Dossier: The Hidden Agenda Behind the Gulf War*, translated by Howard Curtis (New York: Penguin Books, 1991), 2, 46–63, 94–117, 112, 114.

48. See Hayes.

49. See Schuler.

50. See Salinger.

51. See Pelletiere et al.

52. Knut Royce, "A Trail of Distortion Against Iraq," *Newsday*, January 21, 1991.

53. Michael Emery, "Jordan's King Hussein on the Gulf War," *San Francisco Chronicle*, March 13, 1991, Z-3.

54. Milton Viorst, "A Reporter at Large: After the Liberation," *The New Yorker*, September 30, 1991, 37–72.

55. Ibid.

56. Ibid.

57. Ibid.

58. Kuwaiti intelligence memorandum, labeled top secret, from Brigadier General Fahd Ahmad Al-Fahd, Director-General of the State Security Department, to Shiekh Salem Al-Sabah Al-Salem Al-Sabah, Minister of the Interior; allegedly recovered from Kuwait's

Internal Security Bureau by Iraqi forces. (Translation from Arabic supplied by Iraqi embassy.)

59. George Lardner, Jr., "Iraqi Charges Alleged Kuwaiti Memo Proves a CIA Plot Against Baghdad," *Washington Post*, November 1, 1990, A30.

60. Saddam Hussein, "Saddam Husayn on the Post-Cold War Middle East," *Orbis*, Winter 1991, 117–119.

61. John K. Cooley, *Payback: America's Long War in the Middle East* (London: Brassey's, 1991), 185.

62. Khalidi Walid, "Iraq vs. Kuwait: Claims and Counterclaims," in *The Gulf War Reader*, Micah Sifry and Christopher Cerf, eds. (New York: Times Books, 1991).

63. Ibrahim Youssef, "Iraq Threatens Emirates and Kuwait on Oil Glut," *New York Times*, July 18, 1990.

64. Dr. Michael Emery, "How Mr. Bush Got His War: Deceptions, Double-Standards & Disinformation," Open Magazine Pamphlet Series No. 9, April 1991 (Westfield, NJ: Open Magazine). 7. See also "How the U.S. Avoided Peace" and "In the Middle of the Middle East; After 38 Years of Diplomatic Dexterity, King Hussein Keeps His Balance," *Village Voice*, March 5, 1991.

65. Dr. Michael Emery, invitation from Saudi Arabia's King Fahd to the Kuwaiti Emir to the July 31, 1990 summit in Jidda, Saudi Arabia.

66. Ibid.

67. See Emery, Open Magazine Pamphlet Series No. 9, 8.

68. George D. Moffet III, "PLO Chief Says US Thwarted Efforts to Resolve Gulf Conflict," *Christian Science Monitor*, February 5, 1990.

69. Foreign Broadcast Information Service, "Columnist Urges Kuwait to Reject U.S. Support," Jordan, FBIS-NES-90-140, 20 July 1990, 27; Mu'nis al-Razzaz, Amman AL-DUSTUR (in Arabic), "Last Station: The Real Dispute: Between the Near and the Far," JN2007102590.

70. Ellen Ray and William Schaap, "Disinformation and Covert Operations," *Covert Action Information Bulletin*, 9.

71. *American Foreign Policy: Current Documents*, Document 260 (Washington DC: Department of State), 458.

72. John Gittings, "Introduction," in *Beyond the Gulf War* (London: Catholic Institute for International Relations), 8.

73. See Hedges.

74. *Keesing's Record of World Events, 1990*, Ref. 37390 for Tunisia statement and Britain's interception of "supergun" parts.

75. Murray Waas, "Who Lost Kuwait?" *Village Voice*, January 22, 1991.

76. UN Security Council, Document S/PV.2933, Statement on Resolution 661 Authorizing Sanctions Against Iraq by Ricardo Alarcon, Cuba Ambassador to the UN, 41.

77. See Schwarzkopf, Armed Services Committee Testimony.

78. See Cooley, 184.

79. See Waas.

80. See Gelb, May 4, 1992.

81. John Pilger, "Sins of Omission," *The British New Statesman*, February 8, 1991, 8.

82. James Tanner, "Iraq–Kuwait Strains May Disrupt OPEC Bid for Pact to Prop Up World Oil Prices," *Wall Street Journal*, July 25, 1990, A2.

83. "The Glaspie Transcript: Saddam Meets the U.S. Ambassador," in *The Gulf War Reader*, Micah Sifry and Christopher Cerf, eds., (New York: Times Books, 1991), 130.

84. Leslie H. Gelb, "Mr. Bush's Fateful Blunder," *New York Times*, July 17, 1991, A21.

85. Thomas Friedman, "Envoy to Iraq, Faulted in Crisis, Says She Warned Hussein Sternly," *New York Times*, March 21, 1991.

86. "U.S. Messages on the July Meeting of Saddam Hussein and American Envoy," *New York Times*, July 13, 1991. See also Sydney Blumenthal, "April's Bluff: The Secrets of Ms. Glaspie's Cable," *The New Republic*, August 5, 1991.

87. Stewart M. Powell, "Critics Ask if U.S. Sent Iraq Wrong Signals," *San Francisco Examiner*, September 24, 1990, A12.

88. Developments in the Middle East, July 1990. Report of the Subcommittee on Europe and the Middle East of the Committee on Foreign Affairs, House of Representatives (Washington, DC: U.S. Government Printing Office, 1990), 14.

89. See Salinger.

90. James Ridgeway, *The March to War* (New York: Four Walls Eight Windows Press, 1991), 60.

91. See Emery, Open Magazine Pamphlet Series No. 9.

92. See Salinger, 112.

93. Ibid.

94. See UN Security Council.

95. Ibid.

96. Michael Emery, interview, January 14, 1992.

97. See Cooley, 201.

98. See Woodward.

99. See Mathews, 59.

100. See Woodward, 258–259.

101. See Woodward, 276.

102. Andrew Rosenthal, "Bush Sends U.S. Forces to Saudi Arabia as Kingdom Agrees to Confront Iraq," *New York Times*, August 8, 1990, A8.

103. See Sifry and Cerf, 197.

104. "Transcript of President's Address to Joint Session of Congress," *New York Times*, September 12, 1990, A20.

105. See U.S. News & World Report, *Triumph Without Victory*, 97–98.

106. Jean Heller, "Public Doesn't Get the Picture with Gulf Satellite Photos," *St. Petersburg Times*, January 6, 1991. Reprinted in *In These Times*, February 27–March 19, 1991, 7.

107. Ibid.

108. "Where Are the Troops?" *Newsweek*, December 3, 1990.

109. *In These Times*, February 27–March 19, 1991, 7.

110. See Ridgeway, 84.

111. Thomas Friedman, "U.S. Jobs at Stake in Gulf, Baker Says," *New York Times*, November 14, 1990.

112. Ibid.

113. See Ridgeway, 84.

114. Seymour Hersh, *The Samson Option: Israel's Nuclear Arsenal and American Foreign Policy* (New York: Random House, 1991).

115. See Pelletiere, et al., 14–15.

116. John Broder and Douglas Jehl, "Experts Say Iraq's Military Is Formidable, But Flawed," *Philadelphia Inquirer*, August 19, 1990, A13 (reprinted from the *Los Angeles Times*).

117. Middle East Watch, "Kuwait's 'Stolen' Incubators: The Widespread Repercussions of a Murky Incident," *White Paper*, Vol. 4, Issue 1 (February 6, 1992), 5.

118. Ibid.

119. John R. MacArthur, "Remember Nayirah, Witness for Kuwait?" *New York Times*, January 6, 1992, A17.

120. See Middle East Watch.

121. *Newsweek*, September 10, 1990, 17.

122. Robert Parry, "The Peace Feeler That Was," *The Nation*, 480–482.

123. Youssef M. Ibrahim, "Saudi Prince Hints at Deal with Iraq for Kuwaiti Port," *New York Times*, October 23, 1990, 1.

124. Ibid.

125. Philip Shenon, "Hussein Offers to Talk with U.S.," *New York Times*, November 16, 1990, A14.

126. See Ridgeway, 63.

127. See Ridgeway, 135.

128. Fred Bruning, "Hussein Accused of Running a 'Hostage Bazaar,' " *New York Newsday*, October 25, 1990, 13.

129. See Ridgeway, 172.

130. George Bush, "The Letter to Saddam — January 9, 1991," in *The Gulf War Reader*, Micah Sifry and Christopher Cerf, eds. (New York: Times Books, 1991).

131. Bill Moyers, *PBS Special Report: After the War*, Spring 1991.

132. See Bush, "The Letter to Saddam," in Sifry and Cerf.

133. See Mathews.

134. See Emery, Open Magazine Pamphlet Series No. 9, 15.

135. Scott Armstrong, "Eye of the Storm," *Mother Jones*, November/December 1991, 75.

136. Editorial, *Los Angeles Times*, August 11, 1990.

137. Rick Atkinson, "U.S. to Rely on Air Strikes if War Erupts," *Washington Post*, September 16, 1990, A1 .

138. Editorial — "Lunging for War?" *New York Times*, May 5, 1991, E16.

139. See Woodward, 353.

CHAPTER 2

1. Michael Kinsely, "TRB from Washington: Dead Iraqis," *New Republic*, March 18, 1991, 6.

2. Scott Armstrong, "Eye of the Storm," *Mother Jones*, November/December 1991.

3. Matti Peled, "United States' Irresponsibility," *Third World War*, Summer 1991 (published by Spokesman for the Bertrand Russell Peace Foundation, Nottingham, U.K.).

4. Rick Atkinson, "U.S. to Rely on Air Strikes if War Erupts," *Washington Post*, September 16, 1990, A1.

5. Craig Whitney, "B-52 Crews in England Tell of High-Altitude Strikes on Iraqi Targets," *New York Times*, March 8, 1991.

6. Anthony Cordesman, "The Persian Gulf War: An Analysis," in *The World Almanac and Book of Facts: 1992* (New York: Pharos Books, 1991), 35.

7. William Branigin, "Iraqi Losses 'Horrendous,' Official Says," *Washington Post*, Februay 20, 1991, A7.

8. John Balzar, "Marines Feel Pity as B-52s Pound Iraqis," *Los Angeles Times*, February 5, 1991, A1.

9. R. W. Apple, Jr., "Commander Claims Gains in Breaking Iraqi Army's Will," *New York Times*, February 5, 1991, A1.

10. John Cushman, Jr., "Military Experts See a Death Toll of 25,000 to 50,000 Iraqi Troops," *New York Times*, March 1, 1991, A1.

11. Melissa Healy and John Broder, "Number of Iraqis Killed in War May Never Be Known," *Los Angeles Times*, March 8, 1991, A7; see also Simon Tisdall, "No Haven from the Horror," *Manchester Guardian/Le Monde* (Weekly English Edition), March 31, 1991.

12. See Branigin, "Iraqi Losses 'Horrendous.' "

13. This information was gathered during my February 1992 trip to Iraq.

14. Patrick Tyler, *New York Times*, March 23, 1991, A1.

15. Youssef M. Ibrahim, "General's Star Feat: Desert Armies Come, and Go," *New York Times*, November 8, 1991, A4.

16. James Gerstenzang, "Tens of Thousands of Iraqi Soldiers' Bodies Left Behind," *Los Angeles Times*, March 1, 1991, 8.

17. Walter Mossberg and David Rogers, "Iraqi Troop Deaths Totaled at Least 100,000, U.S. Says," *Wall Street Journal*, March 20, 1991.

18. James Adams, "Iraqi Toll Could Be 200,000 Dead," *London Times*, March 3, 1991.

19. Interview with Ted Saunders, Director, Illinois Veterans Task Force, Chicago; see also *Heroes Today, Homeless Tomorrow?: Homelessness Among Veterans in the United States* (Washington, DC: National Coalition for the Homeless, November 1991), vi.

20. Patrick Sloyan, "Officials: U.S. Faced Fewer Iraqis," *Newsday*, January 24, 1992, 17.

21. See Gerstenzang.

22. See Healey and Broder.

23. Paul Rogers, "The Myth of the Clean War," *Covert Action Information Bulletin*, Summer 1991, 29.

24. David Noble, "Professors of Terror," *Third World Resurgence* (Penang, Malaysia) 18/19 (February–March 1992), 34.

25. *Los Angeles Times*, October 5, 1990.

26. Michael Kinsley, "No Mathew Brady for Iraq," *Washington Post*, February 28, 1991.

27. Jeffrey Smith, "U.S. Ground Plan Aims at Quick Strikes, Mass Surrender," *Washington Post*, February 23, 1991, A11.

28. "Allies Drop Napalm on Iraqi Lines," *International Herald Tribune*, February 25, 1991.

29. Ann DeVroy, "Bush Gives Iraq Until Noon Today to Begin Withdrawal from Kuwait," *Washington Post*, February 23, 1991, A1.

30. Stephen Sackur, *On the Basra Road* (London: London Review of Books, Ltd., 1991), 23.

31. Jeffrey Lenorovitz, "Air National Guard Unit's F-16 Pilots Say Small Arms Fire Is Primary Threat," *Aviation Week and Space Technology*, February 25, 1991, 42.

32. See Balzar, "Marines Feel Pity."

33. See Rogers.

34. Mark Crispin Miller, "Operation Desert Sham," *New York Times*, June 24, 1992, A21.

35. "Hussein to Be Target in War, Says Pentagon," *Minneapolis Star-Tribune*, January 11, 1991, 7. Reprinted from *Newsday*.

36. "The Last-Gasp Effort to Get Saddam," *U.S. News & World Report*, January 20, 1992, 42.

37. Patrick Tyler, "Cheney Cancels News Briefings on Gulf Assault," *New York Times*, February 24, 1991, A1.

38. Mike Erlich, Testimony, European Parliament Hearings, March–April 1991.

39. John MacArthur, *Second Front: Censorship and Propaganda in the Gulf War* (New York: Hill and Wang, 1992), 202.

40. Jim Hoagland, *Washington Post*, March 3, 1991.

41. Rick Atkinson, "Outflanking Iraq: Go West, 'Go Deep'; After Months of Preparation, Army Swept Quickly Around and Through Opposition," *Washington Post*, March 18, 1991, A1.

42. Reuters News Agency, "Getting Blown to Bits in the Dark," *Toronto Globe and Mail*, February 25, 1991.

43. William Branigin, "Gruesome Examples of Horrors of War Abound in Iraqi Desert," *Washington Post*, March 3, 1991, A34.

44. Michael Gordon, "G.I.'s Recall Destruction of Powerful Iraqi Force," *New York Times*, April 8, 1991.

45. Knute Royce and Timothy Phelps, "Pullback a Bloody Mismatch," *Newsday*, March 31, 1991, 7.

46. Patrick Sloyan, "Massive Battle After the Ceasefire," *Newsday*, May 8, 1991, 4.

47. Patrick Sloyan, "Buried Alive," *Newsday*, September 12, 1991, A1.

48. See Royce and Phelps.

49. Bill Moyers, *PBS Special Report: After the War*, Spring 1991.

50. See Royce and Phelps.

51. Steve Coll and William Branigin, "U.S. Scrambled to Shape View of Highway of Death," *Washington Post*, March 11, 1991, A1.

52. Bob Drogin, "On Forgotten Kuwait Road, 60 Miles of Wounds of War," *Los Angeles Times*, March 10, 1991, A1.

53. See Moyers.

54. Frank Smyth, "Who Are Those Guys? How Intelligence Agents Are Trying to Remake the Iraqi Opposition," *Village Voice*, March 26, 1991.

55. *PBS: Frontline:* "The War We Left Behind," October 29, 1991.

56. Michael Wines, "Kurd Gives Account of Broadcasts Tied to CIA Urging Iraqi Revolt," *New York Times*, April 6, 1991, 1.

57. See Moyers.

58. Barton Gellman, " 'Voice of Free Iraq' at Heart of Debate over U.S. Backing of Rebels," *Washington Post*, April 9, 1991, A17.

59. Elaine Sciolino, "Radio Linked to CIA Urges Iraqis to Overthrow Hussein," *New York Times*, April 16, 1991, A9.

60. Michael Wines, "CIA Joins Military Move to Sap Iraqi Confidence," *New York Times*, January 19, 1991; see also Gellman, " 'Voice of Free Iraq.' "

61. Associated Press, "CIA Reportedly Got OK to Help Rebels," *San Francisco Chronicle*, April 5, 1991.

62. See Tisdall, "No Haven from the Horror"; see also Edward Gargan, "Stoic, Iraqis Surrender to a Journalist," *New York Times*, April 16, 1991, A9.

63. "One Million Kurds Reported Fleeing Iraq," *Facts on File*, April 11, 1991, 254.

64. David Hearst, "Refugees Face Death by Aid," *Manchester Guardian Weekly*, April 21, 1991.

65. "Allied Troops Begin to Leave Iraq Safe Zone; Few Refugees Remain in Camps," *Facts on File*, June 27, 1991, 473.

66. Reuters, "Turkey Attacks Kurdish Rebels Inside Iraq," *New York Times*, August 9, 1991, A6.

CHAPTER 3

1. Barton Gellman, "U.S. Bombs Missed 70% of the Time," *Washington Post*, March 16, 1991, A1.

2. Adeeb Abed and Gavrielle Gemma, "Impact of the War on Iraqi Society"—Report on Commission Trip to Iraq from April 3, 1991 to April 14, 1991.

3. Barton Gellman, "Allied Air War Struck Broadly in Iraq," *Washington Post*, June 23, 1991, A1.

4. Rudy Abramson and Melissa Healy, "Wide Range of Military Paths Open to Bush," *Los Angeles Times*, August 5, 1990, A1.

5. Rick Atkinson, "U.S. to Rely on Air Strikes if War Erupts," *Washington Post*, September 16, 1990, A1.

6. "Allied Strategy Follows Disgraced Dugan's Predictions," *London Times*, January 29, 1991, 2.

7. See Gellman, "Allied War Struck Broadly in Iraq."

8. Ibid.

9. Ibid.

10. See Gellman, "U.S. Bombs Missed 70% of the Time."

11. Michael Gordon, "Desert Missions by Commandos Aided in Victory," *New York Times*, March 1, 1991, A1.

12. Michael Evans, "How the SAS Took Out the Scuds . . . by Major," *London Times*, May 15, 1991, 1.

13. Paul McEnroe, "Commandos in Iraq Guide Allied Bombers," *The Minneapolis Star-Tribune*, February 21, 1991, 1A; Joshua Hammer, "'Special Ops': The Top-Secret War," *Newsweek*, March 18, 1991, 32.

14. Patrick Tyler, "U.S. Officials Believe Iraq Will Take Years to Rebuild," *New York Times*, June 3, 1991, A1.

15. See Gellman, "Allied War Struck Broadly in Iraq."

16. Michael Gordon, "Pentagon Study Cites Problems with Gulf Effort," *New York Times*, February 23, 1992, A1.

17. See Abed and Gemma.

18. Dennis Bernstein and Larry Everest, "Health Catastrophe in Iraq," *Z Magazine*, June 1991, 27.

19. Testimony of Dr. David Levinson, M.D., at the Commission of Inquiry hearing in San Francisco, September 14, 1991, and Los Angeles, September 15, 1991.

20. "Summary of International Telecommunications Union (ITU) Mission Findings on Telecommunications in Iraq," from Report to the Secretary General on Humanitarian Needs in Iraq by a Mission Led by Sadruddin Aga Khan, Executive Delegate of the Secretary-General, dated 15 July 1991, Annex 10.

21. See Bernstein and Everest.

22. Testimony of Paul Walker, Director of the Institute for Peace and International Security at the Massachusetts Institute of Technology, at Commission of Inquiry hearing in Boston, June 27, 1991, and New York, May 11, 1991.

23. Mark Fineman, "Refugees from Iraq Describe Hellish Scenes," *Los Angeles Times*, February 5, 1991, A1.

24. Rick Atkinson and Ann DeVroy, "Allies Step Up Gulf Air

Offensive; Strikes Focus on Iraqis in Kuwait," *New York Times*, Febraury 12, 1991.

25. Rick Atkinson, "Allied Bombs Hit Two Iraqi Ministries," *Washington Post*, February 13, 1991, A1.

26. Alfonso Rojo, "Bombs Rock Capital as Allies Deliver Terrible Warning," *The Guardian*, February 20, 1991.

27. Rick Atkinson and William Claiborne, "Baghdad Announces Retreat; Allies Encircling Iraqi Forces," *Washington Post*, February 26, 1991.

28. Ed Vulliamy, "Limbs and Lives Blasted Away by Allied Bombs," *The Guardian*, May 3, 1991.

29. Middle East Watch, "Needless Deaths in the Gulf War: Civilian Casualties During the Air Campaign and Violations of the Laws of War" (New York: Human Rights Watch, 1991), 99.

30. Laurie Garrett, "The Dead," *Columbia Journalism Review*, May/June 1991.

31. European Parliament hearings on U.S. War Crimes in the Gulf, March–April 1991, Brussels.

32. Miriam Martin, Gulf Peace Team, Interviews with Residents in the Al-Amariyah Neighborhood, submitted to the Commission of Inquiry, Copyright 1992 Sati-Castek-Martin.

33. Ibid.

34. Testimony of Professor Mohammed Khader at the International War Crimes Tribunal, February 29, 1992, New York City.

35. Ibid.

36. Security Council Document S/22205, February 7, 1991, from Permanent Representative of Jordan to the Secretary General.

37. Alan Cowell, "More Air Attacks on Road to Jordan," *New York Times*, February 1, 1991.

38. See Middle East Watch, 205.

39. Chronicle Wire Services, "New Reports That Allied Bombs Have Hit Civilians on Highway," *San Francisco Chronicle*, February 1, 1991, 25.

40. See Walker.

41. Testimony of Paul William Roberts at Commission of Inquiry meeting in Montreal, November 16, 1991, 54–58.

42. Stated to members of the Muhammad Ali Peace Delegation to Iraq on November 30, 1990 by Iraqi Deputy Prime Minister Ramadam.

43. David Lauter and Kim Murphy, "Trade Embargo Already Putting Squeeze on Iraq," *Los Angeles Times*, August 9, 1990, A1.

44. Security Council Document S/2236, Report to the Secretary-General on humanitarian needs in Kuwait and Iraq in the immedi-

ate post-crisis environment by a mission to the area led by Mr. Martti Ahtisaari, Under-Secretary-General for Administration and Management, March 20, 1991, 6.

45. James Rupert, "At the Vortex of Crisis, Baghdad Residents Focus on Carrying on as Usual," *Washington Post*, October 7, 1990, A31.

46. E. Faye Williams, *The Peace Terrorists: A Personal Story on the Middle East Crisis* (Washington, DC: EFW Publishers, 1991).

47. James Fine, "Exceptions to the UN Trade Embargo Against Iraq: Security Council Resolutions 661 and 665 and Humanitarian Law," Office of the International Programs, University of Pennsylvania, September 15, 1990.

48. See Williams.

49. International Physicians for the Prevention of Nuclear War, "Middle East Trip Report," December 14–22, 1990 (Cambridge, MA: IPPNW, 1990).

50. Testimony of Ann Montgomery, International Gulf Peace Team, at New York Commission of Inquiry hearing, May 11, 1991

51. See Ahtisaari, 13.

52. Ibid., 5.

53. Larry Everest, "Child Mortality Rate Soars in Postwar Iraq," *San Francisco Chronicle*, August 7, 1991.

54. Ibid.

55. Ibid.

56. See Ahtisaari, 5.

57. Bernd Debusmann, "Iraqi Crisis Said to Kill Close to 100,000," Reuters News Agency, February 4, 1992.

58. Anne McIlroy, "Plan to Save Iraqi Children Stalled by Federal Inaction," *Ottawa Citizen*, May 14, 1992.

59. See Aga Khan, 33.

60. "Iraq Can't Afford Food," *The Washington Report on Middle East Affairs*, July 1991, 44.

CHAPTER 4

1. Patrick Tyler, "Saudis Press U.S. for Help in Ouster of Iraq's Leader," *New York Times*, January 19, 1992.

2. William Safire, "The April Surprise," *New York Times*, January 13, 1992, Op-Ed.

3. See Tyler.

4. Paul Lewis, "U.N. Survey Calls Iraq's War Damage Near-Apocalyptic," *New York Times*, March 22, 1991, 1.

5. See Tyler.

6. Ibid.

7. Tom Furlong, "Reconstructing Iraq a Risky Business," *Los Angeles Times*, March 8, 1991, D1.

8. John Goshko, "UN Sets Curbed Sale of Iraqi Oil," *Washington Post*, August 16, 1991, A1.

9. Sadruddin Aga Khan, "Help Iraq Help Its People," *New York Times*, September 14, 1991, Op-Ed.

10. Trevor Rowe, "U.N. Approves Sale of Iraqi Oil," *Washington Post*, September 20, 1991.

11. *San Francisco Bay Guardian*, May 15, 1991.

12. Patrick Tyler, *New York Times*, June 3, 1991.

13. John M. Goshko, "U.S. Seeks Fast Payment from Iraq," *Washington Post*, June 4, 1991, 10.

14. See Tyler, June 3, 1991.

15. See Furlong.

16. *New York Times*, February 7, 1992, A1.

17. Mike McNamee, "Iraq's Creditors Form Long, Unruly Line," *Business Week*, March 18, 1991.

18. Larry Everest, "The Times Aren't a-Changing," *San Jose Mercury News*, 7P.

19. H. Norman Schwarzkopf, "Threat Assessment; Military Strategy; and Operational Requirements," Testimony to Senate Committee on Armed Services, February 8, 1990, 577–579.

20. Ibid.

21. Ibid.

22. Scott Armstrong, "Eye of the Storm," *Mother Jones*, November–December 1991, 76.

23. Michael R. Gordon, "Cheney, in Riyadh, Appeals for the Right to Store Arms," *New York Times*, May 7, 1991.

24. Ibid.

25. Commission interview with investigative journalist Scott Armstrong, February 1992.

26. See Armstrong.

27. *New York Newsday*, May 29, 1992, 30.

CHAPTER 5

1. Keith Schneider, "Environmental Rule Is Waived for Pentagon," *New York Times*, January 30, 1992.

2. Ibid.

3. Randall Palmer, "World Can't Wait for More Global Warm-

ing Research, Leaders Say," Reuters News Agency, November 7, 1990.

4. "Carbon Releases in the Persian Gulf," *Earth Island Journal*, Summer 1991, 45.

5. Penny Kemp, "For Generations to Come: The Environmental Catastrophe," from *Beyond the Storm: A Gulf Crisis Reader*, Phyllis Bennis and Michel Moushabeck, eds., (New York: Olive Branch Press, 1991), 326.

6. Brian Tokar, "Disaster in the Gulf and Poison at Home," Z *Magazine*, December 1991, 57.

7. See Kemp, 332.

8. Randy Thomas, Gulf Environmental Emergency Response Team, Vancouver, Canada.

9. Quoted in "Violations of the Geneva Protocols on the Environment by the U.S." (San Francisco: Arms Control Research Center).

10. Ibid.

11. Neil MacFarquhar, "Firefighters Say Six-Month Delay in Equipment Hampering Efforts," *Associated Press*, June 8, 1991.

12. "Excerpts from Briefing at Pentagon by Cheney and Powell," *New York Times*, January 24, 1991, A11.

13. *New York Times*, January 31, 1991.

14. *Financial Times* (London), February 4, 1991; see also "Counting the Human Costs of the Gulf War," *MET Report Background Papers* (London: Medical Educational Trust, July 1991), 15.

15. *Earth Island Journal*, Spring 1991, 44.

16. Testimony by Ross Mirkarimi, Persian Gulf Project Coordinator of the Arms Control Research Center in San Francisco, at Los Angeles Commission of Inquiry hearing, September 15, 1991.

17. Nick Cohen, "Radioactive Waste Left in Gulf by Allies," *London Independent*, November 10, 1991.

18. James Ridgeway, "Using Nuclear Bullets (Moving Target Column)," *Village Voice*, February 15, 1991.

19. Patrick Sloyan, "Disaster in the Desert," *New York Newsday*, November 10, 1991.

20. See Cohen.

21. John M. Miller, *Hidden Casualties, Volume II: Environmental and Human Impacts of the Gulf War* (Brooklyn, NY: Arms Control Research Center).

22. See Sloyan.

23. See Miller, *Hidden Casualties*.

24. Gerald Seib, "U.S. Takes Kuwaiti Island; Saudis Down Two Iraqi Jets," *Wall Street Journal*, January 25, 1991, A3.

25. Alan Cowell, "Iraq Closes Border with Jordan, Cutting Off Escape for Foreigners," *New York Times*, January 25, 1991, A1.

26. John M. Miller, "Environmental Fallout from the Gulf War," *Fellowship*, April/May 1991; see also Laura Glassman and Jacquelyn Walsh, "Oil Spills and Oil Fires," *Earth Island Journal*, Spring 1991, 43, 48.

27. Working Group on the Environmental Implications of the Gulf War, *Collateral Damage: Environmental and Other Considerations of the War in the Gulf* (Toronto: Institute for Environmental Studies, University of Toronto), 40.

28. Philip Shenon, "Another Oil Spill Imperils the Gulf," *New York Times*, January 31, 1991, A11.

29. R. W. Apple, "U.S. Says Iraq Pumped Kuwaiti Oil into Gulf; Vast Damage Is Feared from Growing Slick," *New York Times*, A1.

30. Malcom Spaven, "Gulf Oil Slick: Whose Pollution?" *Earth Island Journal*, Summer 1991, 48.

31. Andrew Rosenthal, "Bush Calls Gulf Oil Spill a 'Sick Act' by Hussein," *New York Times*, January 25, 1991, 5.

32. See Spaven.

33. Louis Peck, "The Spoils of War," *The Amicus Journal*, Spring 1991.

34. See Glassman and Walsh.

35. Friends of the Earth, Washington, DC.

36. Randy Thomas, "Nations Paralyzed as Oil Pours from a Wounded Earth," *Earth Island Journal*, Summer 1991, 48.

37. Harvard International Study Team, "Environmental and Agricultural Survey: The Impact of the Gulf Crisis on the Environment and Agriculture in Iraq," Appendix B, A.3.2 of *Health and Welfare After the Gulf Crisis: An In-Depth Assessment*, October 1991.

38. John Horgan, "Science and the Citizen: Burning Questions" and "Why Are Data from Kuwait Being Withheld?" *Scientific American*, July 1991, 20.

39. Joni Seager, "Poison Gulf," *Village Voice*, March 5, 1991.

40. Tom Fiedler, "Up to 50 Oil Fires Smother Kuwait in Pall of Smoke," *San Jose Mercury News*, February 13, 1991.

41. "Statement by Iraqi Revolutionary Council," *New York Times*, February 23, 1991, 6.

42. John Horgan, "Science and the Citizen: Up in Flames" and "U.S. Gags Discussion of War's Environmental Effects," *Scientific American*, May 1991, 17–24.

43. Ibid.

44. See Horgan, "Burning Questions."

45. See Horgan, "Burning Questions" and "Up in Flames."

46. See Horgan, "Burning Questions."

47. O. J. Vialls, "Another Middle East Oil Disaster?" *Australian Guardian*, March 25, 1992.

48. Charles Hirshberg, "Hell on Earth," *Life*, July 1991, 45.

49. O. J. Vialls, Letter to Commission of Inquiry, October 29, 1991.

50. O. J. Vialls, "Possible Strategic Disinformation: The Ignition of 500 + Oil Wells in Kuwait and Iraq," Memo to Senator Jo Vallentine, West Australia, April 17, 1991.

51. See Horgan, "Burning Problems."

52. See Tokar.

53. Randy Thomas (GEERT), quoted in Angela Blackburn, "Deadly Ecological War Rages On in the Persian Gulf," *Oakville Beaver*, September 20, 1991, 3.

54. William Booth, " 'You Can Taste the Oil,' " *Washington Post*, April 12, 1991, A29.

55. See Randy Thomas in Blackburn, "Deadly Ecological War."

56. See Booth.

57. Matthew Wald, "Experts Say Kuwait Fires May Shorten Lives," *New York Times*, August 14, 1991, A29.

58. Anne McIlroy, "Ecological Legacy of the Gulf War Still Unknown Factor in Iraq, Kuwait," *The Vancouver Sun*, November 22, 1991, A13.

59. Fred Pearce and Stephanie Pain, "Oil from Kuwaiti Wells Still Pouring into the Desert," *New Scientists*, November 9, 1991.

60. Ibid; see also Tokar.

61. Matthew Wald, "Burning Oil Pool Kills 5 in Kuwait," *New York Times*, April 26, 1991, A5.

62. Glennda Chui, "Desert Wounds: Burning Oil, Tanks, Troops Take Their Toll," *San Jose Mercury News*, January 15, 1991.

63. Arms Control Research Center, San Francisco.

64. Michael Hiltzik, "Sifting Through the Wreckage of a Shattered Ecosystem," *Los Angeles Times*, March 5, 1991.

65. Reto Pieth, "Toxic Military," *The Nation*, June 8, 1992, 773.

66. See Pieth.

CHAPTER 6

1. Joe Stork and Ann Lesch, "Why War?" *Middle East Report*, November/December 1990.

2. See George Abed, "The Palestinians and the Gulf Crisis," *Journal of Palestine Studies*, Winter 1991, 29.

3. Kate Muir, "Besieged on All Sides in a Kuwait Ghetto," *London Times*, March 26, 1991, 1.

4. Middle East Watch, "A Victory Turned Sour: Human Rights in Kuwait Since Liberation," September 1991, 3–4.

5. *New York Times*, June 30, 1991.

6. See Middle East Watch, "A Victory Turned Sour."

7. Associated Press, "Kuwaiti Royalty: Killers?" *New York Newsday*, March 29, 1991.

8. Amnesty International, London.

9. John Kifner, "Kuwaitis Urged to Halt Attacks on Palestinians," *New York Times*, April 3, 1991.

10. Andrew Rosenthal, "Bush Not Pressing Kuwait on Reform," *New York Times*, April 3, 1991.

11. Jonathan Broder, "Kuwait Will Expel Most Palestinians, Ambassador Says," *Orange County Register*, June 17, 1991.

12. See Middle East Watch, 57.

13. Ibid.

14. Unclassified 200-page Pentagon white paper on the reconstruction of Kuwait by U.S. forces.

15. Sandy Close and Dennis Bernstein, "Pentagon Planners Outline Key U.S. Military Role in Kuwait Recovery," *Pacific News Service*, February 25, 1991.

16. Robert Fisk, "Palestinians Face Gunmen's Revenge," *The Independent* (London), March 4, 1991.

17. Testimony of Dr. M. A. Samad-Matias, Professor of African and Caribbean Studies at City College of New York, at the New York Commission of Inquiry hearing, May 11, 1991.

18. Ibid.

19. Ibid.

20. Ibid.

21. Chris Hedges, "Foreign Women Lured into Bondage in Kuwait," *New York Times*, January 3, 1992.

22. Judith Miller, "Ousted Yemenis a New Burden to Their Nation," *New York Times*, October 30, 1990, A1.

23. Ibid.

24. Ibid.

25. See Hedges.

26. Ibid.

27. Ibid.

28. Ibid.

29. Ibid.

30. Ibid.; see also Middle East Watch, 21–23.

31. KUSP Community Radio (Santa Cruz, CA) News Release, January 17, 1992; see also letter from Edward Gnehm, Jr., United States Ambassador to Kuwait, to Naim Ismail Farhat, January 15, 1992; letter from Naim Ismail Farhat to Edward Gnehm, January 19, 1992, copies sent to U.S. Representative Leon Panetta, Jesse Jackson, Ramsey Clark, the Lebanese Ambassador to the United States, and others.

32. Gregory Nojeim, American-Arab Anti-Discrimination Committee, Washington, DC.

33. Jinsoo Kim and Beth Stephens, Letter from Center for Constitutional Rights, New York, January 31, 1991.

34. Tod Ensign, "Resistance Grows," *On Guard* 11, 1991 (published by Citizen Soldier, New York).

35. Robert S. Rivkin, "Kuwaiti-Style Military Justice at Camp LeJeune," *The National Lawyers Guild Practitioner*, Spring 1991, 51–53.

36. Vince Bielski, "A Marine No More," *San Francisco Bay Guardian*, January 9, 1991.

CHAPTER 7

1. Zechariah Chafee, *Free Speech in the United States* (Cambridge: Cambridge University Press, 1948), 21.

2. Quoted in Thomas I. Emerson, *The System of Free Expression* (New York: Random House, 1970), 51.

3. Leonard W. Levy, *Freedom of Speech and Press in Early American History* (Cambridge, MA: Harvard University Press, 1960), 87.

4. Paul Leicester Ford, ed., *The Writings of Thomas Jefferson*, Volume 9 (New York, 1892–1899), 452.

5. Jim Naureckas, "Gulf War Coverage: The Worst Censorship Was at Home," *EXTRA!* (Fairness and Accuracy in Reporting), May 1991.

6. Ibid.

7. *New York Times*, March 4, 1991.

8. Robert Fisk, "War Journalism: Media Surrender," *San Francisco Examiner*, February 6, 1991 (reprinted from the *London Independent*).

9. See Naureckas.

10. Marjorie Williams, "Saddam Hussein: Monster in the Making," *Washington Post*, August 9, 1990, D1.

11. Jack Anderson and Dale Van Atta, "The Demonization of Saddam Hussein," *Washington Post*, October 25, 1990, C13.

12. *The New Republic*, September 3, 1990.

13. *Time*, August 13, 1990.

14. George Will, "Wolf Out of Babylon," *Washington Post*, August 3, 1990.

15. Norman Solomon, "Media Denies, Anesthetizes, Inverts War," *The Guardian*, February 13, 1991.

16. See Naureckas.

17. Carl Nolte, "Searching for the Real War," *San Francisco Chronicle*, January 23, 1991, A1.

18. John Carman, "All the News That Fits the Pentagon," *San Francisco Chronicle* "Datebook," January 25, 1991.

19. Richard Berke, "Pentagon Defends Coverage Rules, While Admitting to Some Delays," *New York Times*, February 21, 1991.

20. Dennis Wharton, "Cronkite Blasts War Pool," *Variety*, February 25, 1991.

21. Peter Ford, "Pool System Inadequate, Western Journalists Say," *Christian Science Monitor*, February 12, 1991, 3.

22. William Boot, "The Pool," *Columbia Journalism Review*, May/June 1991, 24.

23. Ibid.

24. Incidents in this paragraph, unless otherwise noted, are taken from "STOP PRESS: The Gulf War and Censorship," *Article XIX*, February/March 1991 (London: International Centre Against Censorship).

25. See Naureckas.

26. Alexander Cockburn, "When the U.S. Press Fled Baghdad," *The Nation*, January 27, 1992, 78.

27. Max Robins, "NBC's Unaired Iraq Tapes Not a Black and White Case," *Variety*, March 4, 1991.

28. John Chancellor, "War Stories," *New York Times*, April 1, 1991, A17.

29. All incidents in this paragraph are taken from "Casualties at Home: Muzzled Journalists," *EXTRA!* (Fairness and Accuracy in Reporting), May 1991, 15.

30. See "STOP PRESS: The Gulf War and Censorship."

31. Ibid.

32. Reuters-Associated Press, "Even Troops Blanch at Death Video," *Toronto Star*, February 24, 1991.

33. Ibid.

34. "The Daily Grind" column, *San Jose Mercury News*, April 11, 1991.

35. Michael Gordon, "Six Iraqi Pilots Defect and U.S. Claims a Psychological War Gain," *New York Times*, January 8, 1991, A11.

36. "Pentagon Retracts Report of Iraqi Defections," *New York Times*, January 9, 1991, A9.

37. Barton Gellman, "U.S. Denies Iraqi Copter Defections," *Washington Post*, January 11, 1991, A13.

38. Michael Wines, "CIA Joins Military Move to Sap Iraqi Confidence," *Washington Post*, January 19, 1991, 9; Jim Hoagland, "Those Phantom Helicopters," *Washington Post*, March 3, 1991, C4.

39. Ellen Ray and William Schaap, "Disinformation and Covert Operations," *Covert Action Information Bulletin*, Summer 1991, 11–12; John Cooley, *Payback: America's Long War in the Middle East* (New York: Brassey's, 1991), 223.

40. "Where Are the Troops?" *Newsweek*, December 3, 1990.

41. Molly Moore, "Bombing Damage Hard to Assess," *Washington Post*, February 7, 1991, A1.

42. Pentagon press release, July 1991.

43. Rick Applebombe, "Year After Gulf War, Joy Is a Ghost," *New York Times*, January 16, 1992, A1.

44. Michael Burton, "US Media Look Back at Desert Storm: The Iraqis That 'Got Away,' " *EXTRA!*, April/May 1992, 27.

45. "Desert Storm Plus 1: Vigilance Is the Price for Leaving Saddam Hussein in Power" (editorial), *Houston Post*, January 16, 1992, A34.

46. See Burton, "U.S. Media Look Back at Desert Storm."

47. William Safire, "Comeback Coming," *New York Times*, February 27, 1992, A25.

48. A. M. Rosenthal, "After Saddam, What?" *New York Times*, February 28, 1992, A31.

49. Patrick Tyler, "U.S. Strategy Plan Calls for Insuring No Rivals Develop," *New York Times*, March 8, 1992, A1.

50. Leslie Gelb, "Foreign Affairs: $1.5 Trillion 'Defense,' " *New York Times*, April 17, 1992, A17.

51. Sean MacBride, *Many Voices/One World: The MacBride Report* (Paris: UNESCO, 1980).

52. Philip S. Foner, ed., *The Complete Writings of Thomas Paine*, 1945, Volume 1, 604.

CHAPTER 8

1. *U.S. News & World Report, Triumph Without Victory: The Unreported History of the Persian Gulf War* (New York: Times Books, 1991), 97.

2. Stephen C. Pelletiere et al., *Iraqi Power and U.S. Security in the Middle East* (Carlisle Barracks, PA: U.S. Army War College Strategic Studies Institute), 51–52; Michael Wines, "Years Later, No Clear Culprit in Gassing of Kurds," *New York Times*, April 28, 1991, 13, and *Washington Post*, May 3, 1990.

3. Phyllis Bennis, "U.S. Bribes, Threats Win U.N. War Support," *The Guardian*, December 12, 1990.

4. Phyllis Bennis, "Bush's Tool and Victim," *Covert Action Information Bulletin*, Summer 1991, 4.

5. Rick Atkinson and Barton Gellman, "Iraq Trying to Shelter Jets in Iran, U.S. Says; Saddam Says Much Blood Will Be Shed," *Washington Post*, January 29, 1991, A1.

6. *United States v. Wunderlich*, 342 U.S. 98, 101 (1951), dissenting opinion.

7. James Madison, *Letters and Other Writings of James Madison, Fourth President of the United States*, Volume II (New York: R. Worthington, 1884), 131.

8. Bob Woodward, *The Commanders* (New York: Simon & Schuster, 1991), 318–320.

9. "Day 3: Remarks in Congress During the Last Hours of the Debate," *New York Times*, January 13, 1991, 10.

10. Henry Gonzales, "Terms of Impeachment," *The Texas Observer*, January 25, 1991.

11. James D. Richardson, ed., *Messages and Papers of the Presidents*, Volume 1 (Bureau of National Literature and Art, 1903), 326–327.

12. *Youngstown Sheet & Tube Co. v. Sawyer*, 343 U.S. 579 at 642–43 (1952), concurring opinion.

13. Maureen Dowd, "Immersing Himself in Nitty-Gritty, Bush Barnstorms New Hampshire," *New York Times*, January 16, 1992, A1.

CHAPTER 9

1. Steven Keeva, "Lawyers in the War Room," *ABA Journal*, December 1991, 52.

2. Ibid.

3. Ibid.

4. Ibid.

CHAPTER 12

1. "For Veterans, A Prouder Time (editorial), *New York Times,* November 11, 1991.

2. "Remarks by President George Bush to the Religious Broadcasters, Sheraton Washington Hotel, January 27, 1992," Federal News Service/Cox Newspapers, January 30, 1992.

Index